THE
......

Preschool
Years

......

THE
Preschool
Years

Family Strategies That Work from Experts and Parents

ELLEN GALINSKY

& JUDY DAVID

Ballantine Books   **New York**

All photographs courtesy of Ellen Galinsky.

Grateful acknowledgment is made to the following for permission to reprint previously published material.

Bantam Books: Excerpt from *Toilet Training* by Vicky Lansky. Copyright © 1984 by Vicky Lansky. Reprinted by permission of Bantam Books, a division of Bantam, Doubleday, Dell Publishing Group, Inc.

Exchange Press, Inc.: Excerpts from "What Really Constitutes Quality Care?" and "How Do Child Care and Maternal Employment Affect Children?" by Ellen Galinsky from *Child Care Information Exchange*. Reprinted by permission of Exchange Press, Inc.

National Association for the Education of Young Children: "Staff-Child Ratios Within Group Size," excerpted from *Accreditation Criteria and Procedures of the National Academy of Early Childhood Programs*. Copyright © 1984 by the National Association for the Education of Young Children. Used with permission.

National Committee for Prevention of Child Abuse: Excerpt from "Talking About Child Sexual Abuse" by Cornelia Spelman. Copyright © 1985. Reprinted by permission of the publisher, the National Committee for Prevention of Child Abuse, Chicago, Illinois.

Whittle Communications L.P.: Excerpt from "How to Find Child Care" by Ellen Galinsky. Reprinted with permission from the 1986–87 issue of *New Parent Adviser*. Copyright © 1986 by Whittle Communications L.P.

Library of Congress Catalog Card Number: 90-93217

ISBN: 0-345-36597-6

This edition published by arrangement with Times Books, a division of Random House, Inc.

Cover photo by Luis Castañeda

Manufactured in the United States of America

First Ballantine Books Edition: January 1991

10 9 8 7 6 5

To the late Betty Boegehold—for her poetic and joyous appreciation of the everyday moments of being a preschool child and a preschooler's parent

To Bernice Weissbourd for shaping the policies and practices of the family support movement and thus changing the course of life for so many families in the United States

ACKNOWLEDGMENTS

To   Carol Shookhoff for reading the manuscript, and preparing the bibliographies and footnotes. Carol's vast insight and wisdom added immeasurably to *The Preschool Years*.

To   Betsy Grob for helping with so many details of the book and sharing her invaluable perspective as a parent and early childhood educator.

To   Leah Lipton for combing through hundreds of transcripts of parent interviews and seminars toward compiling the solutions in this book.

To   Marilyn Roll and Susan Maycock for conducting many, many insightful interviews with parents.

AND TO   Noreen Winkler and Robin Greenwood for interviewing parents.

To   Judith Baumrin; Andrea Bolz; Bernice Callahan; Karen Diamond; Ruthanne Griffin, the Mothers of Preschoolers (MOPS) in Abidjan; Jeannette Lofas; Janet Kalatat; Olivia McQueen; Susan Schmidt, Mothers' Center of Central N.J.; Claire A. Scott Miller; Lynda Nichols; Gail Solit; Nancy Stickel; Sharon Stine; Patsy Terry; Nancy Travis; Bernice Weissbourd; Suky Werman; Jan Yocum for helping to arrange parent interviews.

To   Irene Mordkowitz for her good humor and great advice while typing the manuscript.

To   Alan Lewan for typing and for his flexibility, warmth, and perfectionism.

AND TO　Gary Beaner, Wendy Shotwell Ruopp and Tom Ruopp Shotwell, Kathy Ruopp, Evanne Weinrich, Debra Schecter, Peggy McGinley and Amy Greenberg for typing interviews and parts of the manuscript.

To　　　John Leach and Beth Puffer of the Bank Street Bookstore for their knowledge and patience in answering all of our questions.

To　　　Berry Brazelton, Jim Garbarino, Judy Gardner, Joan Levine, Pat Libbey, Nancy Samalin, Edna Shapiro, and Ed Zigler for reading and commenting on the manuscript.

To　　　Gloria Norris for instigating this book based on expertise from parents and professionals. And to Jo Ann Miller for her good advice in designing the book.

To　　　Ginger Barber, our agent, for her steadfastness and support in seeing this book through from beginning to end.

To　　　Jonathan Segal and Elisabeth Scharlatt, our editors, for having the highest standards for what this book could be.

To　　　Doug Leavens for sharing the joys of parenthood.

To　　　Norman, Philip, and Lara Galinsky for being wonderful and loving.

CONTENTS

INTRODUCTION

....

This book has two purposes:

1. To bring the impressive wealth of knowledge that researchers in child and adult development have been accumulating to bear on the everyday questions that parents of young children (from two through five years old) have, from "What are the most effective ways to discipline?" to "Why do preschool children have trouble sharing?" to "How can I manage time to get everything done?"

2. To present a range of practical suggestions—from both parents and professional experts—on how to solve these everyday problems.

As a researcher on work and family life, I* felt that the knowledge that I and other professionals were learning would be tremendously helpful to parents; it could help untangle the mysteries of "Why is my child acting this way?", "Is it normal or not?", and "Why am I as a parent responding as I do?" Although the shelves of bookstores and libraries are bursting with books for parents, there was virtually no book (other than those for academics) that presented these data.

As a parent myself, I know that I rarely pick up a book for parents unless I have a burning question: "Why are my children picking on each other?" "How do you put a child to bed and get her to stay there?"

* The "I" in this book refers to Ellen Galinsky.

As an educator, I was dissatisfied with the solutions that most books give: the expert presented *the* answer; there was only one way to do things. It is quite clear that what works for one child does not necessarily work for another. Furthermore, I believe that the purpose of parent education is not to foster reliance on an expert but to develop the ability of every parent to solve problems.

Since the first edition of my book *The Six Stages of Parenthood* was published in 1981, I have conducted well over fifty seminars for parents each year. They have been in corporations such as Exxon, AT&T, and American Express, and in family resource programs. They have been held in churches and synagogues, corporate and civic auditoriums, and in union halls. I began to experiment with an approach that I felt met the needs of today's parents. At each session, I asked those attending to take an index card and write down the question or questions that led them to the seminar. I then discussed the questions in light of current research knowledge, and the parents and I generated solutions together.

When parents and other educators urged me to put this approach in book form, I began with the index cards (which by then numbered in the thousands). After identifying the questions most frequently asked by parents of young children, I set out to compile a more complete profile of the research data on each of these questions with my colleague from Bank Street College, Judy David.

At the same time, with the help of a team of parent educators, I began to interview parents about their successful strategies. In all, over three hundred parents were interviewed for this book.*

We focused on the preschool years because it's a time when parents are eager to learn. The relationship between parent and child has changed; parents feel jolted from the harmony established during infancy into dissonance. The baby they held, comforted and cared for stands on his or her own two feet and says no or "I won't go" or "I won't do it." During these moments children's physical stature seems to grow and they can become threatening opponents, almost an equal whom parents must overcome. At these times it's easy to forget how different young children are from adults. Yet afterward parents wish they knew more: "What propels my child to act that way?"

Several principles have emerged in the five years that Judy David and I spent researching and writing this book:

• *Parents do not simply mold their children as if from a shapeless piece of matter.* Children are born with characteristic ways of behaving and reacting (temperaments). Some children are active, others more quiet; some are slow to warm up, others quite sociable. Parents, too, have styles of

---

* For the sake of privacy, the names of the parents in this book have been changed.

responding, the result of their own inborn temperaments and their experiences. The match between the style of the parent and that of the child significantly affects how the child develops. This is not to say that parents don't have a formative influence on their children—they do, but they do within the context of their child's and their own temperaments.

• *Parents do not raise children in a vacuum.* The circumstances of their immediate world affect them, from their friends and neighbors to the choice of preschools that exist in their communities as well as to the pressures from their jobs that are carried home. The larger world has an impact too —rapid technological change, the plague of AIDS, and stranger danger. In the words of Urie Bronfenbrenner, the developmental psychologist from Cornell University, children grow up in micro- and macro-environments, and both affect and are affected by these settings.

• *Expectations are a powerful force in development.* Children begin to develop images of how the world is—for example, how mothers and fathers act or what toys are "boy" toys versus "girl" toys. Such expectations guide their behavior and form the basis of their concepts. Many times their expectations are different from adults'. As children encounter new information and experiences, they revise their ideas and gain new understanding about how the world works and what people are like, including themselves.

Adults, too, have expectations about the events they encounter. When their experiences clash with these expectations, they feel pain—guilt, upset, anger, disappointment. But it is in the process of realigning their expectations and experiences (either by changing to live up to their images or adapting these images to be more realistic) that they grow. Thus, progress for us as parents comes from an ever-deepening understanding of our children and ourselves.

• *The process of learning is one of problem-solving.* In the research from many different fields—from the studies of stress and coping to investigations of the effectiveness of different parental discipline techniques—comes the finding that knowing how to solve problems is fundamental to resilience in the face of adversity as well as to good mental health. Thus, again and again in this book we suggest ways that parents can teach children how to resolve some of the problems that confront them in the normal course of growing up. Listening to and respecting preschoolers' ideas and signals may take time, but in the long term, the listening and respect help children become independent, self-confident, curious, and creative.

• *Children are resilient.* Although we may feel our children can be irrevocably injured by a particular experience or event, that is very seldom the case. Negative patterns can become positive ones; change is possible.

• *Help from others is essential in parenting.* Although our culture stresses independence, throughout life we are inextricably linked to others. To the degree that we can turn to others, to express our feelings and to seek practical help, we are strengthened. At best, those we rely on should enable rather than belittle us, should enlarge rather than shrink our perspective, so that we emerge from these supportive relationships more able to appreciate ourselves and our children.

It is our hope that this book offers such support, albeit in written form. It has been modeled on the tenets that have guided the growth of the parent support movement. The giants of this field, Bernice Weissbourd, Ed Zigler and others have often stated that parent support builds upon the strengths of each family. The aim of this book is to help parents through the predictably rough spots of parenthood by elucidating child and adult development and offering practical solutions.

Although this book is problem-focused, problems constitute only one aspect of our daily lives. Much of the time, things go smoothly. It is very important to stop and take note of the many exhilarating moments in being a parent of a preschooler. Enjoy their hand in yours, the way they stop to observe a bug crawling on the sidewalk or an airplane leaving a vapor trail across the sky. Enjoy the pleasure they take in a new taste, the way they sing a favorite song over and over, or their ability to create miniature worlds in their play. These are magic moments in the preschool years.

ONE
....

Discipline

Developmental Issues for Children and Their Parents in the Preschool Years

What is it like to be the parent of preschool children?

   ■ ■ ■ *Some days it's one adventure after another. There was the time my four-year-old and three-year-old took all the drawers out of the dresser and turned it against the wall. A little while later they turned the rocking chair upside down and jammed it against the door so they could use it as a slide. Later still, they locked themselves in the closet. After that, they yanked the window blinds so hard that they came down.*

Like many parents of preschoolers, this mother imagines that her children are more rambunctious than most—perhaps because they are so close in age.

The mother of a three-year-old tells of a different kind of adventure:

   ■ ■ ■ *I took my daughter, Gabrielle, and her friend shopping the other day. They both wanted to look at themselves in the store mirror but there wasn't enough room for the two of them. Gabrielle pushed her friend out of the way. Then her friend pushed back. Gabrielle started screaming: "I want the mirror! It's mine!"*

This mother wonders whether her daughter is more demanding than other children because she is an only child.

As parents of preschoolers, each of us imagines that while in everyone else's house parents and children are sitting cozily side by side talking and looking at books, only our child is jumping on the dining room table. While other people's children are playing catch, only our child is throwing the ball at our face. While other people's children are going cheerfully to bed at night, only our child is standing at the top of the stairs saying that there are monsters in the room. We imagine that our child is being difficult because we are older parents or younger parents, because we work too hard at our jobs or we've devoted ourselves to our children too much, because we're rich or poor, because. . . . Yet in all of our homes, no matter the circumstances, similar scenes are taking place:

> SCENE ONE: *You need hiking boots to trudge through the pile of toys beside your three-year-old's bed. Dozens of pieces from the puzzles and stacking toys have been jumbled together. It's time to clean up. But how to begin?*

> SCENE TWO: *Your three-year-old disappears into your bedroom. You follow immediately but enough time (one minute maybe) has elapsed for him to pull all of your shirts out of the drawer and leave them in a wrinkled heap on the floor.*

> SCENE THREE: *Your four-year-old insists on wearing new slippery patent leather shoes and a pink ruffled party dress to nursery school. At school the children dig in the dirt, climb on jungle gyms, swing on swings, play ball, and paint with poster paints. "I need to wear this," she insists. "I promise I'll just sit in a chair and not do anything all day."*

> SCENE FOUR: *Your two-year-old marches up to a plant and starts to scatter the dirt all over the floor. You say no and he runs away, then rushes back and picks up another handful of dirt. When you repeat no, walking toward him, that becomes his cue to take the dirt and throw it.*

> SCENE FIVE: *Your five-year-old son and three-year-old daughter are playing peacefully together. Suddenly the boy marches to the refrigerator, looks his sister straight in the eye, takes the cookie she's been saving, and eats it down to the last crumb. Within seconds they are rolling around the floor, pounding each other.*

These scenes can stir up strong feelings that we may not have felt since we were children ourselves, being confronted by the teasing or bullying of another child or the demands of a parent. We feel that, somehow, it's not fair. These scenes challenge the deal we made with ourselves before becoming parents: "I'm going to be a different kind of parent." It is the "if/then" deal:

If I love my children enough, *then* they will love me back all or at least most of the time.

If I say and do the right things, *then* they will cooperate.

If I am a reasonable and considerate adult, *then* my child will also be reasonable and considerate.

If I handle problems well, *then* all will be perfect.

The desire for perfection is a normal part of being a parent of an infant. The wish to do the best possible job gives us the energy to face the sleepless nights or long bouts of fussiness. We are rewarded by the knowledge that the infant needs us; we feel virtuous providing comfort and sustenance. But, as the child becomes a toddler, this feeling begins to shift. Now there are times when even as we do our best, our efforts are met with resistance and rebellion from our child: "I won't" or "You can't make me." We don't feel as virtuous saying no to a preschooler as we did feeding, soothing, and playing with our infant. Whether it's a vague or vivid memory, we can recall how it felt to be disciplined long ago.

The dissonance between the way we want our child to be and the way he or she is, between what we expect of ourselves and the way we actually behave, between the world as we wish it to be and the way it is, makes us question our earlier expectations of perfection, the if/then deal that we hoped for. It makes us reevaluate our ideas and come to terms with being simply "good enough."

The developmental task for preschool children is establishing a sense of control over their bodies and their lives. In the process, they vacillate from being independent and strong (the child who runs ahead without looking back) to being dependent and needy (the child who clings to your legs, pleading "carry me").

As the father of a two-year-old put it:

. . . *Sam runs the gamut from unadulterated joy to abject despair in a one-minute period of time. He's looking for some constraints, but at the same time he resents them intensely. But it's a wonderful time, too, because Sam is full of all this spontaneous affection. He's learning new things every day. When Sam is difficult he's very, very difficult, and when he's in a good mood, there's nobody better. It's an age of incredible extremes.*

Children in the preschool years live in the here and now, thus the complex drama of their needs and wants has a constant immediacy: they want what they want "now" and the parental response of "soon" or "later" may seem like forever or never.

To children, parents seem solid and strong, all powerful. Despite their testing and pushing us, they also imbue us with magical powers—able to read their thoughts, cause a power blackout, even make a flower grow faster so "I can pick it."

A mother of a preschooler says:

■ ■ ■ *When my daughter, Maggie, was two and a half, we were walking down a windy street, near the river. She turned to me and said, "Mommy, stop the wind."*

Another parent says:

■ ■ ■ *I was in the park with my five-year-old son, who was practicing riding his bicycle. When he fell off, he came over and kicked me. At this point in his life, all authority and thus all fault lies with the parents.*

Just as children are passing through a stage in their development, so are parents. The issue for parents in the preschool years parallels that of the children—establishing control, figuring out when to say yes or no, and how to enforce it. I call this the Authority Stage because the major task is determining the kind of authority you want to be.

This chapter addresses disciplinary questions raised by parents. I have been dissatisfied with most of the books on discipline because they give pat answers with the assumption that if you follow the prescribed formulas, your problems will disappear immediately. They neglect the parents' feelings of disappointment, resentment, anger, amusement, appreciation, and love. As we all know, our attitudes make a crucial difference. Many of these books neglect the everyday realities of being "on the front line."

My approach is different. It is based on the findings from research on children's compliance and cooperation combined with the wisdom of thousands of parents I have worked with over the years, as well as my own experience as a parent. This approach deals with the needs of parents as well as of children, understanding that while it may take both of us a long time, changes are always possible.

Q *How can I discipline effectively?*

When I am asked this, I ask parents to describe the purpose of discipline:

■ ■ ■ *I want my child to listen to me, especially in a dangerous situation like touching the stove or running out into the street.*

■ ■ ■ *I want to teach my child how to express feelings in a constructive way rather than to yell, to negotiate rather than to demand, to be able to wait rather than to insist on something now, and ultimately to balance what she wants with the needs of others.*

As these parents note, discipline has two purposes: The first goal is to stop children from doing something dangerous, hurtful or annoying to themselves and to others; that is, *to control children.* The second goal is to impart values—that is, *to teach children.* For both these goals, there are short-term and long-term implications. The control we provide now will develop into self-control. The values we teach, we hope are lasting. As the parent of a young child, we function as teacher, police, coach, protector, and defender. But as time passes, we will not always be there between our child and other children in the neighborhood, or between our child and a teacher; our child will eventually become a teenager who drives a car and leaves home. In considering how to discipline today, we must consider what we hope for tomorrow.

Alice Honig, a psychologist and educator from Syracuse University, uses the terms "compliance" and "self-control." Compliance is the short-term goal of discipline: "an immediate and appropriate response of the child to an adult's request." Self-control is the future goal when compliance has been internalized.

Lawrence Balter in *Dr. Balter's Child Sense* notes the paradox in these goals:

> *We want our children, in the long run, to be leaders, critical in their thinking, to have good judgment and a strong character. But in the short term, in our day-to-day life, we want that children will not talk back to us. . . .*

Balter asks the critical question: "How do we get children to obey us today, and yet still become independent individuals?"

In a number of studies, researchers have observed preschool children and their parents in order to investigate the effectiveness of various discipline techniques. In homes and experimental laboratories, using videotape or coding lists, these researchers have monitored what parents did or said and how often each technique led to compliance or noncompliance by the child.

One of the consistent findings that emerges from these studies is that all preschool children are noncompliant at least some of the time. As Haswell, Hock, and Wenar conclude, oppositional behavior is the norm for children between eighteen months and six years and, in fact, represents a positive milestone in development:

> *The struggle for autonomy is at the heart of oppositional behavior as the preschool child grows in mastery and ex-*

*plores her/his growing need for independence. Thus, whereas
oppositional or negativistic behavior is frustrating for parents, educators, and all those involved in the care of preschool
children, it is a normal and crucial aspect of early childhood
development.*

When researchers have calculated the overall percentage of children's
compliance, it falls in the 40 to 60 percent range; that is, children do what
adults tell them to do from two- to three-fifths of the time. As Martin L.
Hoffman states, "in the two- to four-year-old range, children experience
pressure . . . to change their behavior on the average of every six to eight
minutes throughout their waking hours, and in the main end up complying."

Another finding from many studies is that the kind of discipline approach
used by parents makes a difference. Diana Baumrind from the University
of California at Berkeley has identified three disciplinary styles: authoritarian (the "do it because I'm the parent, that's why" approach), authoritative
("do it because there is a reason" approach) and permissive (the "do whatever you want" approach).*

According to Baumrind's observational studies of preschool children:

- Parents who were authoritarian (controlling but detached and not very
  warm) had children who were more likely than the other children to be
  discontent, withdrawn, and distrustful.
- Parents who were permissive (noncontrolling, nondemanding but warm)
  had children who were the least self-reliant, explorative, and self-controlled of all the children studied.
- Parents who were authoritative (controlling but encouraging, firm, warm,
  rational, and receptive) were more likely to have children who were self-
  reliant, self-controlled, explorative, and content.

TECHNIQUES OF DISCIPLINE

The following thirteen discipline techniques can be grouped under the ru-
bric of an authoritative approach. The underlying principle is that discipline
is both the suppression of unacceptable behavior (i.e., the don'ts) and the
teaching of values and skills (the dos). Authoritative techniques that respect
the child as a human being will teach children to:

* The effects of these disciplinary styles last at least through adolescence. According
to Sanford Dornbusch, professor of sociology at Stanford, authoritative parenting
was correlated with better academic grades in high school, whereas authoritarian
and permissive parenting styles were generally related to lower grades.

- control their impulses
- consider the feelings of others
- solve problems by generating alternate solutions
- negotiate with others
- achieve their objectives in socially acceptable ways

There is little doubt that using these thirteen techniques to deal with the more difficult moments of parenthood will ultimately produce more harmony in your family and promote self-discipline in your child.

Overall, parents regularly face two kinds of discipline situations: getting their child to *do* something and getting their child to *stop* doing something. Before considering specific techniques to deal with these two situations, I will describe two general techniques: teaching by example and anticipating problems.

Technique 1: Teaching by Example

Numerous studies indicate that the way parents act toward their children profoundly influences the way children behave. This is one of the assumptions that parents frequently question during the preschool years (*If* I am considerate, *then* my child will be considerate, or *if* I am loving, *then* my child will be loving). Because this proposition does not seem to hold (at least not absolutely), some parents begin to feel it does not really matter what they do. Yet, as we have discussed, you must consider the children's developmental stage. All children push toward autonomy during the preschool years, and while it may take a long time to learn how to strive for independence in constructive ways, this new capacity is a positive force in growth and can become the forerunner of later behaviors such as standing up for oneself, having the courage to try new things, and taking initiative. Thus, we have to eliminate the idea that if children don't model our behavior all the time, then they aren't learning much from us.

Stayton, Hogan, and Ainsworth found that mothers—mothers have been studied much more frequently than fathers—who are sensitive (attuned to the children's needs), who accept the responsibilities of being a parent, and cooperate (do not unilaterally impose their will on their babies), had nine- to twelve-month-olds who were more cooperative, and who responded more positively to what their mothers asked.

Lytton and Zwirner have shown that "power assertion techniques"— hitting, criticizing, and threatening (the "I'm bigger than you are, that's why" approach) tend to accomplish the opposite of what parents want. In home-based observations of 136 male two-and-a-half-year-old children, they found that these techniques were much more likely to lead to noncompliance than compliance.

But, you protest, is this a cause or an effect? Was the parent harsher because the child was more disobedient, or was the child less cooperative because the parent was more willing to use physical punishment?

It is clear to me that the argument that parents are harsher because the child is more difficult has only limited validity. A child who is by temperament more irritable, harder to calm down, more active, and more demanding can create a cycle in which the parent feels less and less confident and thus more likely to slip into coercive or permissive patterns (see section on temperament, pages 170–181. Nevertheless, the adult is able to anticipate in a way that a child cannot, know the consequences of an action, and control his or her own behavior. The adult can change the course of events, preventing a self-defeating battle of wills because he or she suspects or knows that in such a battle, everyone ultimately loses—the child and the adult.

Furthermore, the research on mother-child attachment counters the argument that the child has the dominant influence on the relationship. Given supportive circumstances for the parent (primarily other people to turn to for help), parents can establish a cooperative relationship with hard-to-manage children.

In sum, many studies relate a more accepting, loving, yet firm parental style with more cooperative children. The harsher the parents, the angrier and more aggressive the children.

It is not only what you do when you discipline that matters; it is how you do it. An in-depth longitudinal study of the development of children's ability to cope from birth through adolescence conducted in Topeka, Kansas, under the direction of Lois Barclay Murphy found that warmth in parenting made a difference. The mothers who enjoyed their children, beginning in infancy, had children in later years who were more trusting and could cope and resolve the problems they faced more effectively.

Gerald Patterson from the Oregon Social Learning Center is directing research on five hundred families and has found that parents who were customarily irritable (frowning, snapping at the children, being sarcastic) had school-age children who were more likely to be disruptive in the classroom. In fact, children who stole, fought with other children, and had temper tantrums at school were three times more likely to have parents who related to their children with irritability.

Children learn from their parents in two ways. When they are younger, they imitate their parents. As they grow they begin to identify with the parents and to internalize their voices, their behavior, and their standards. Thus, parents have a profound influence. Those who control their children's impulses in a respectful way will eventually engender cooperation as well as teach their children what to do.

Technique 2: Anticipating Problems

An important aspect of discipline is prevention. When parents can anticipate problems, they can short-circuit the process. If your child always grabs
at the knobs on your record player, you can place it out of reach.

One study has documented the efficacy of avoiding conflict. George
Holden from the University of North Carolina at Chapel Hill observed
twenty-four two-and-a-half-year-old children and their mothers during two
trips to the supermarket, an event which he describes as a triple threat to
the mother: "There is food shopping to be done, a child to be managed
who is afforded a diverse array of enticing objects, and all the while both
mother and child are in the public eye." Not surprisingly, the supermarket
provided a rich opportunity to observe discipline techniques—children interrupted their mothers almost constantly to ask for something. The least
demanding and difficult children had mothers who practiced preventive
measures; that is, they directed the child's attention to acceptable behavior,
giving the child either something to eat or a toy to play with, or steered the
shopping cart down the middle of aisles so that the child was unable to
reach the shelves. In effect, these mothers were teaching the child acceptable
behavior and avoiding a build-up to conflict.

Three types of preventive techniques are particularly useful.

Child-Proofing the Child's Environment.   Make sure that the places
where the child spends the most time are set up for as few nos as possible.
Obviously these places have to meet the adult's needs too; however, the
more tempting "no-touch" objects are around, the greater the opportunity
for conflict.

Channeling Behavior in Acceptable Ways.   If you know that errands in
the car lead to fussiness and arguing, you and your child can pack a bag of
car toys or snacks. You can also play car games. Tell your child how you
expect him or her to behave beforehand.

Planning Schedules.   Parents know the worst and best times in their
children's day, the times when they can cope well versus the times when
any demand sets them off. Plan events to fit your children's rhythms as
much as possible. For example, Holden found that the mothers who managed the supermarket with the fewest problems were cognizant of the
child's rhythms and arranged to shop when the child was at his or her best.

GETTING YOUR CHILD TO DO SOMETHING

> SCENE: *You need hiking boots to trudge through the pile of
> toys beside your three-year-old's bed. Dozens of pieces from
> the puzzles and stacking toys have been jumbled together. It's
> time to clean up. But how to begin?*

Technique 3: Focusing the Child's Attention on the Task

One of the most effective ways to elicit cooperation in getting something accomplished is to use a sequential strategy that begins by focusing the child's attention on the job.

Observational research confirms the usefulness of this technique. Typically, the researcher instructs the parent to ask the child to do something (play with toys, put away toys, follow directions in performing a task, etc.) and the methods the parent uses are compared to the frequency with which the child cooperates.

In one study, for example, Schaffer and Crook observed twenty-four mothers with fifteen-month and twenty-four-month-old children in a directed play situation. Mothers were told to make sure their child used all of the toys present. Children were more cooperative when their mothers used a verbal or nonverbal means to direct the child's attention to the next task: They pointed or they said, "Look at this," or "When you finish that, let's play with this." Timing was important. Asking for something out of the blue or interrupting an involved child led to greater resistance.

For the child with the messy room, the parent who directs the child's attention to the job, forewarning him, will probably have greater success: "In a few minutes it will be time to clean up the toys." However, children differ in their capacity to respond to warnings. Some need a substantial amount of time to complete what they are doing before switching into a new activity. Lengthy and perhaps repeated warnings may be effective with them while for others, warnings that are far in advance can be anxiety provoking. Thus, it is important to adapt any technique to your child's style.

Technique 4: Using Neutral, Positive, and Reflective Language

Several studies have found that how parents phrase requests makes a difference. In the Lytton research, suggestions elicited more cooperation than commands ("Do this!"). However, the response to commands improved if they were preceded by positive action: the parent smiling, praising, or helping the child.

Numerous how-to-discipline techniques have been built on the subtle importance of language. They counsel against putting the child down with such comments as "You keep your room like a pigpen." The PET method, for example, suggests giving "I" messages rather than "you" messages: "I don't like it when your room has toys all over the floor" rather than "You are a sloppy child." The method developed by Haim Ginott further suggests using neutral language so that an ego battle (me against you) is not precipitated: "Your room needs cleaning."

The language we use can imply that we no longer love the child because he or she is not doing what we want. According to the research of Martin L. Hoffman, threatening to withdraw love is very punitive because it raises "the ultimate threat of abandonment or separation" and can thus produce powerful fears. When parents say, "I won't speak to you until you say you are sorry" or "I don't like *you* when you do that," children can become afraid. Hoffman says, "The notion that your parent does not love you is terrifying to a child. It can leave him so anxious and inhibited that he is afraid to do most anything." Instead, parents can say, "I don't like it (not you) when your room gets so messy" and not imply, directly or indirectly, that they do not love the child.

The way parents praise children also makes a difference. Global, undifferentiated praise ("You're the best child in the world") can lead the child to feel inadequate ("How can I be the best child in the world? They must be making that up.") Praise that is specific to the task is more effective: "You picked up your room so well—look, all the books are back on the shelves."

It is equally important to listen to your children's point of view. The best way to do this is to reflect back their words: "You are upset at me because I won't let you eat ice cream before dinner." This technique tends to steer the conflict away from parent versus child and instead give the child the feeling that he or she is being heard and understood.

Technique 5: Using Reasoning

When children are told *why* they should or should not do something, it becomes a learning situation. The parental request is not arbitrary but has a reason behind it. Hoffman calls this the inductive approach. For example, the parent facing the jumble of toys can say, "We need to pick up all the pieces of these puzzles together so neither of us has so much to do," or "so they'll be in one place and we can use them again." Using this kind of approach teaches children to develop standards of what's right and wrong based on their own independent thinking rather than on fear of punishment.

Technique 6: Giving a Limited Task

Asking or telling the child to "clean up your room" may seem overwhelming and impossible to the child. It is more effective to assign limited tasks such as, "Pick up your stuffed animals."

Technique 7: Giving Valid Limited Choices

Because the quest for autonomy is at the core of the child's testing and refusals, many parents give their children certain kinds of choices: "Would you like to put the napkins or the forks on the table?" The wording of the choice is important. For example, do not say "Would you like to set the table?" unless you are willing to take no for an answer. Saying, "What would you like to do to help?" can also overwhelm the child because of the myriad possibilities. Choices should be limited; for example, "would you like to pick up the dolls or the books?" Sometimes choice is not possible: "There is no choice. We're all going to the store. But you can pick out one thing to buy there."

Techniques for Getting Your Child to Do Something

Focusing the Child's Attention on the Task:
> *not*
> Get dressed right this second.
> *but*
> I'll set the timer so you can finish your drawing. When it goes off, it will be time to get dressed.

Using Neutral, Positive, and Reflective Language:
> *not*
> You eat like a slob. If anyone saw your table manners, I'd be embarrassed to death.
> *but*
> Try putting just a few Cheerios on your spoon so they don't all spill off.

Using Reasoning:
> *not*
> Hurry up, slowpoke.
> *but*
> We need to walk fast so we can get to the store before it closes.

Giving a Limited Task:
> *not*
> Clean the living room.
> *but*
> Pick up the magazines that are all over the floor and put them in a pile on the table.

Giving Limited Choices:
> *not*
> Would you like to get ready for bed?
> *but*
> Would you like to wash your face or brush your teeth first?

GETTING YOUR CHILD TO STOP DOING SOMETHING

Besides enlisting children's help, parents must also find ways to stop their children.

SCENE: *Your three-year-old disappears into your bedroom. You follow immediately, but enough time (one minute maybe) has elapsed for him to pull all of your shirts out of your drawer and leave them in a wrinkled heap on the floor.*

Technique 8: Using "Other-Oriented Discipline"

Martin L. Hoffman coined the above term to refer to a discipline technique in which the child is made aware of the effect of his behavior on another person. This may mean pointing out the direct consequences for someone else ("When you throw my shirts on the floor, I have to spend time ironing them") or explaining another's feelings ("I hate to iron so I'm very upset when I find my shirts on the floor").

Hoffman tested his hypothesis that children would be more considerate when parents used an other-oriented approach. This was true unless the parent also used power assertion techniques (physical force, harsh orders, threats, etc.). Apparently the use of physical force blocks the child's ability to assimilate what the parent is trying to teach. The message of consideration for others delivered with physical force is a message that cannot be heard.

Technique 9: Providing Alternatives

When discipline is seen as eliminating "bad" behavior, then "stopping the child" becomes the end goal. When discipline is seen as an opportunity to teach, part of that process includes a permissible substitute for the unacceptable behavior: "I don't want you to throw my shirts on the floor, but if you want to throw, let's take a ball and go outside."

Providing alternatives has the advantage of not chipping away at the child's self-esteem: the child's impulse (to throw, to run, to jump) is healthy, but some expressions of this desire are more permissible than others ("Jump over pillows rather than jumping on the couch").

Some behaviors, such as playing with matches, have no substitutes. Even so, other activities can be suggested: "Matches are dangerous, but you can play with this flashlight."

Technique 10: Providing Consequences and Following Through

The importance of providing consequences is twofold: First, children are afraid of the free rein of their impulses. They find it frightening to be out of control as well as to risk the loss of parents' love and approval. Thus, they need their parents to exercise control. Second, it is necessary to make children aware of the impact of their behavior. If rules are broken, there should be consequences.

In *Children: The Challenge,* Dreikurs and Soltz present a theory of discipline based on logical consequences. If a child deliberately spills a glass of milk, the consequence of being deprived of a favorite TV show does not make sense. It does not teach the child why this action bothers his or her parents, whereas helping to clean up the milk does.

Clearly, the child who has pulled out the father's shirts is too young to iron them, but he could help by putting the shirts back in the drawer. When a child empties her toy box on the floor she can help put the toys back. The logical consequence of a child's hitting, however, is not to hit back (that teaches that hitting is acceptable). Use other-oriented discipline: "I don't like to be hit; it hurts," and provide alternatives: "Hit the pillow when you're mad," "Use words."

Michael Meyerhoff and Burton White have studied effective parenting for the past twenty years. They found out children fared better if parents "reacted by letting the children know in no uncertain terms that other people had rights. Sooner or later, all parents would admonish their children for certain undesirable activities. But the effective parents always made sure to follow through." Pat Libbey, a parent educator from Minneapolis, outlines a three-step process—"The Three Cs"—commitment: figuring out how important is this rule to you; communication: making sure the children understand the rule as well as the consequence for breaking it; and consistency: following through if the rule is broken.

Technique 11: Setting Up a Time-Out

There are moments when no matter what language or technique you use, the child will refuse to cooperate. You ask for help putting the toys back and she begins to toss her books on the floor. You ask for help putting the shirts in the drawer and he runs around the room. These are the occasions to use time-out, both for your sanity and the child's.

In time-out, the assumption is that the child has learned to get attention in negative ways; rather than reinforce this pattern by responding to the misdeed, you isolate the child, remove him or her from all attention for a short period of time until the child feels "I can manage." Parents generally designate a certain space as the time-out place: a chair in the center of a room for a toddler, or the child's own room for an older child.

Getting Your Child to Stop Doing Something

Picking the Issue and Setting Limits:
   not
   Everything you do is wrong.
   but
   One of the important rules we have in this house is no hitting.

Using Other-Oriented Discipline:
>   *not*
>   Don't take Johnny's truck. You're cruel and nasty.
>   *but*
>   Johnny feels very upset when you take his truck.

Providing Alternatives:
>   *not*
>   Stop it right this instant.
>   *but*
>   You can't hammer on the table. Go hammer at your woodworking bench.

Providing Consequences and Following Through:
>   *not*
>   If you don't stop drawing on the wall you won't play with any friends for a week.
>   *but*
>   I don't want crayon marks on the wall so you'll have to get a sponge and cleaner to wash them off.

I have grouped the above techniques on the basis of controlling or stopping the child and teaching or enlisting the child's help. There is obviously much overlap. For example, while I classified other-oriented techniques as a control measure, they are equally effective in enlisting the child's cooperation: "I'm tired and I need help in fixing dinner."

Technique 12: Teaching Problem-Solving Skills

In my view this technique is the most important one no matter what the disciplinary situation. The other techniques do not fully address the cause of conflict: the child's need for greater autonomy. Even offering choices does not enable the child to avoid or resolve problems in the future, because the parent is doing the thinking for the child.

Some of you may be saying to yourself, "This sounds good on paper, but day in and day out it's hard to do those things," or "If I said I don't like my shirts all over the floor, my child would look at me and say, 'So what?' "

I have one of those children so I understand your doubts and misgivings. He was the kind of two-year-old who would get up at five A.M. and push buttons on the telephone until he awoke someone in California. One afternoon while I thought he was napping, he took his screen window apart and was getting ready to dangle outside the second-story window. Then there was the time he pushed the latch on the bathroom door in a motel and locked himself in. The manager had to come and remove the door in order to get him out. There are more stories—and now that he is a teenager, they seem funny, but at the time, life with him was a three-ring circus and it was not always fun.

I developed one technique that was particularly effective: engaging him in problem-solving. When he was almost four, I said I wanted to have a meeting with him. I explained that there were times I needed him to cooperate quickly but the things I was saying were not working very well. "What ideas do you have? What words could I say that would work better?"

I was *not* giving him control over limits—he had to stop when I said stop—but I was giving him the opportunity to tell me how to do it more effectively.

He said that I should say "warning."

I said I needed a word that would work fast. He said the word "warning" would.

He did cooperate. If he was climbing out of his seat belt, the word "warning" would stop him. The next step was to encourage him to think about what he wanted and to consider the consequences of getting it one way instead of another.

"If you get out of your seat belt, how do you think I'm going to react?"

"You're going to get upset."

"Why?"

"Because it isn't safe."

"Why did you want to get out?"

"I was bored."

"What else could you do?"

"We could sing, 'Michael Row the Boat Ashore.' "

Two researchers from the Hahnemann Community Mental Health Center in Philadelphia, Myrna Shure and George Spivack, have studied the problem-solving approach. They say: "We believe that even very young children can, or can learn to, think for themselves and solve everyday interpersonal problems. Those who can do this are more likely to be better adjusted than those who cannot."

Several skills are involved in this kind of approach.

Generating a Range of Solutions to a Problem. At this point in the process, judgment is suspended and the child is encouraged to think of as many solutions as possible: "How could you get Ben to give you the toy besides hitting?" It is essential that the parent listen to all possible solutions without criticizing.

Considering the Impact of These Solutions on Oneself and Others. As a second step, the child is asked to think about what might happen if she or he followed through on each of the suggested solutions. Thus, the child learns to evaluate the efficacy of the solution: "How will Ben react if you grab the toy? How will he act if you ask him?"

Figuring Out How to Carry Out the Selected Solution.   Finally, the child is asked to anticipate what problems might arise in carrying out the selected solution and how to overcome them: "You've decided to use a timer to say when it's your turn. What if Ben says 'I'm not finished yet'?" Eventually, the child might need to select another solution.

Shure and Spivack conducted training programs to teach these skills to preschool children. The results showed that in one year's time, the children had learned these techniques well. The researchers also found that the children, even those who had been impulsive or inhibited, were better adjusted in school than those who had not been taught these skills.

The strategy that emerged as most crucial was the ability to generate alternative solutions to a problem:

> *These thinking skills helped impulsive children learn to wait, to become less overemotional when frustrated, less nagging and demanding, and less aggressive. Inhibited children became more socially outgoing, more able to stand up for their rights when attacked, and more expressive of their feelings.*

The setting for teaching problem-solving skills can vary—the parent and child alone or a family meeting. The child must not be so upset or angry that he or she cannot listen. If there is an important family issue to resolve, the child does not have a choice about participating.

In family meetings, it is best to have understood and agreed upon routines. Here are mine:

1. The adult states the problem to be solved: "Dinner time is too hectic and there is too much fighting going on."

2. The adult asks for others' feelings about the subject. No accusations are allowed. Each person says what "I" feel, and no one may interrupt.

3. A range of solutions is generated without criticism or comment. Even when my children could not read, they liked to see their ideas written down. It also reinforced the message that the problem was not "his fault" or "her fault" but existed apart from all of our personalities.

4. The pros and cons about each solution are discussed and written down.

5. A solution is mutually agreed upon.

6. Generally, a trial period of a few days is determined and plans are made to talk at a future date about how the solution is working and to revise it, if necessary.

Q *You say that it's important to be firm, but sometimes I'm not sure I know how I feel.*

SCENE: *Your four-year-old insists on wearing new slippery patent leather shoes and a pink ruffled party dress to nursery school. At school the children dig in the dirt, climb on jungle gyms, swing on swings, play ball, and paint with poster paint. "I need to wear this," she insists. "I promise I'll just sit in a chair and not do anything all day."*

Most books and articles about discipline say that parents are more effective when they take a stand. Experience confirms this wisdom. We know that when we are wishy-washy, our children sense it. They push, wheedle, cajole, demand until something in us snaps. We are no longer waffling and say so in no uncertain terms. We have reached what I call "the final no." And almost magically, the rebellious child takes off the party clothes and puts on sneakers or stops banging a spoon on the kitchen table or demanding to buy a television toy.

Why is it, then, if we know that clarity and consistency work, do we not follow our own instincts? There are several reasons.

The Fumbling Stage. In the beginning of the preschool years, we are not always sure what we think or know. We are not sure whether our child should learn that party clothes at school are a hindrance by wearing them once or by our intervening. We are not sure whether eating before a meal really spoils one's appetite. Would it really be so awful if the child had a snack or even dessert before dinner? Is it worth a struggle? We don't know because we've never lived through some of these situations and we're not sure if it matters, if we care, and if one way of doing things is more effective than another way.

I call this the "fumbling period" and I think that it is a normal part of the task of becoming an authority.

As the Chicago mother of a two-year-old says:

• • • *Some things are very clear. It's not okay to run into the street, touch the stove, stick your finger in an electric socket. These are black and white. But there are a million things throughout the day that are gray. That's where I have a harder time.*

A Los Angeles mother of two young children says:

• • • *I remember the nursery school teacher always saying, "Make the battlegrounds important things." It's just that it's hard to know what's important.*

It is comforting to realize that a fumbling period is normal. It is a time in which you figure out the consequences of taking different courses of action, when you determine what you do and do not care about. Perhaps you're a person who doesn't care if your child gets a party dress dirty; perhaps you do. You don't usually know that until you have experienced it.

When I was at this stage of parenthood, I eventually made a list of the overall principles that were most important to me. My list was:

No hurting others physically

No hurting others emotionally (name-calling, etc.)

Knowing that these aspects of discipline mattered most to me, the smaller rules followed more easily.

Wanting Our Children's Friendship. Another cause of indecisiveness may be the hidden wish not to have to take a stand or to become the authority. The mother of two children says:

• • • *When my daughter was two, she would demand to wear what she wanted to wear, have her hair done the way she wanted to have it done, and just throw temper tantrums until she got her way. I kept placating her and placating her. I think that initially I wanted to be her pal rather than her parent.*

Many parents have this wish. We want to keep our children happy and the easiest way seems to be going along with their demands. When our children were babies, we needed to be responsive to their needs and to satisfy them. Then as children begin to assert themselves, we are caught off guard. Saying no instead of yes is less satisfying. We want to maintain the earlier closeness and not become the police. And so, initially, we try to please, try to go along with children. But the more we give in, the harder they seem to push against us, pushing to find where the limit is as if being stopped is a safety net that protects them against their more primitive urges. MELD, a national parent education program, uses the adult analogy of driving across a bridge with no guard rails to make parents aware that children need limits to make them feel safe and secure. As the mother of two concluded, "It seemed that when I placated my children nobody was getting what they really wanted out of the situation."

When you feel things are unclear and unsure, ask what's behind the indecision: Are you are in the fumbling period and not sure what you think? Do you want to please your child?

Just as young children are learning when and how to assert themselves, so are parents. Figuring out when and how to become an authority is the task that parents face during these preschool years.

Technique 13: Picking the Issues and Setting Limits

In the process of becoming an authority, parents have to decide which issues to confront, otherwise they could be at war with their children all day long. They have to learn when to say yes, when to say no, and how to mean it. If you think it's really important that your child learn to take good care of her possessions, then when she dumps her toys on the floor or wants to wear a party dress to school, you will take a stand. But, another family may decide these same issues are not critical.

Identify the issues you care about most and follow through on them, but do not assume that every conflict is a matter of life and death. Educator Shana Lowitz, from Family Focus, a parent center in Chicago, wisely concluded a session with parents of preschoolers by saying:

. . . *When I think back, I made so many mistakes with my first child, and probably two-thirds as many with the second one. They both grew up to be really lovely human beings and I'm not the only one who thinks so. We have this idea that when we're faced with a two-year-old every day that we have to do the right thing all the time or they'll be scarred. That's ridiculous.*

We are all learning—children and parents. We can learn from our mistakes and use them as an impetus to change.

Q *There are days that regardless of what I do or say, my child resists. He's looking for a fight. What do I do?*

I call these the "no-win" situations because the way you handle the situation *seems* to make very little difference.

SCENE: *Your two-year-old marches up to a plant and starts to scatter the dirt all over the floor. You say no and he runs away, then rushes back and picks up another handful of dirt. When you repeat no, walking toward him, that becomes his cue to take the dirt and throw it.*

A father of a two-year-old says:

. . . *When Ben is playing with his ball, he sometimes throws it in my face: I try to be calm and take it but he'll pick up whatever else is handy and look right at you like "What are you going to do now?" And that's when I don't know what to do. We're at a standoff. Then I usually become exasperated, throw up my hands, and I end up giving in or yelling.*

Other children express resistance by whining or crying. According to the mother of a three-year-old:

... *My biggest problem is the crybaby business. Everything that doesn't go right, Samantha cries. Sometimes it's just whining, sometimes it's throwing herself on the floor or running to her room and slamming the door.*

Whenever parents describe no-win situations, I ask them to recall what happened just before one of these battles of wills takes place. Samantha's mother feels the trigger is her child's desire to control things. During these early years, children are trying to gain mastery over their world and yet this mastery can seem far from their grasp. To gain some control is a positive desire, but when it doesn't happen, Samantha loses even the semblance of control she has and cries, whines, and fusses out of frustration.

The child's need to control is poignantly illustrated by a scene between a mother and her three-year-old. When this mother saw her daughter's runny nose, she reached over with a handkerchief and said, "Blow." The daughter complied and then began to scream: "Give me back my sneeze." For twenty minutes she railed at her mother. She finally whimpered that she wanted to take the sneezed-in handkerchief to school.

The trigger for the two-year-old who liked to throw things was experimentation. Certain actions (such as throwing the ball at his father) created commotion and he found that attractive. Again he threw the ball, again his father responded. It became a testing game, one with high energy that could lead to intriguing, but frightening possibilities—his father falling apart.

Some children, by nature of their inborn temperament, are more easily aroused to a fight or are less tolerant of things not going their way:

... *From the moment he was born, my son was very highstrung, nervous, anxious. He was born screaming with clenched fists. He didn't sleep through the night until he was two.*

The trigger for a no-win battle can also be circumstantial—the child is hungry or bored. In probing the antecedents of these problems, parents can also find that at certain times of the day, children are more prone to problems:

> ∎ ∎ ∎ *I realized that one of the roughest times was coming home from playgroup because my son was hungry, tired, and wanted to be carried. But I was tired and hungry too and didn't have the energy to carry him.*

This mother notes that her own mood and energy level play an important part in how she reacts to her child's "bids for a war":

> ∎ ∎ ∎ *When I'm not pressed for time, I have enough patience to head off a problem. Other times I'm really harassed and lose my mind. I feel like a split personality. If I'm in a good mood, I can explain things. If I'm not, I can't.*

Parents' own style, the way they have learned to cope with conflict, also determines their reaction:

> ∎ ∎ ∎ *I'm a screamer. I don't know why I have a voice left some days because I just feel like I spend my whole day yelling at my daughter. I know I'm not by nature a calm person, so keeping myself cool would take more energy than I think I have at the moment.*

SOLUTIONS

While it may seem that how you deal with no-win situations does not matter, in fact, your strategies do make an important difference.

Using Prevention

If there is a characteristic time of day when the child instigates fights, try to think of a time when it didn't happen. What was different then?

The mother with the cranky two-year-old said her daughter's first words in the mornings were "Go wake Daddy." Usually, her father was gone by the time she got up. When told "Daddy's gone," her tears would start. One morning she woke up before her father had left and it was a pleasant morning; so from then on, the mother awoke her daughter earlier.

The parent with the child who was exhausted after playgroup says, "We come home a little earlier now, before we're both pressing the limit."

Reflecting Back Their Words

When a child attacks us verbally, it is easy to counterattack: "It's not my fault. You started this." But this method brings further resistance, setting up the no-win situation. Instead, for the moment, accept the fact that the child has something valid to say, and reflect back his or her words: "You feel it is my fault." The child will usually open up, the tone of the encounter will change, and you can begin to solve the problem together.

Speaking in a Quiet Voice

To the mother who said she was a screamer, another mother suggested that she try whispering:

▪ ▪ ▪ *I have learned that my tone of voice matters. I sometimes whisper very calmly when I tell Jennifer she can't do something. She has to quiet down and listen hard if I speak softly.*

Giving Alternatives

The father whose son throws things at people felt that talking quietly would not work for his child. "He'd just pick up the ball and throw it again. He looks at us, kind of smiles, and does it again."

This father could say "I don't like being hit with the ball" and then provide another, acceptable action: "Can you throw the ball into the wastebasket . . . as far away as the bush?"

Some behaviors you can control—you can take the ball away, for example—but some you cannot. As a parent, you cannot make a child eat, sleep, go to the bathroom, or stop screaming. As another parent noted:

▪ ▪ ▪ *Whenever Mark gets very excited about seeing his friends, he screams. One of his friends came over a couple of days ago and he started screaming and his screaming startled his friend and drove me absolutely crazy. So I said, "Look, you're not supposed to scream." And he just looked at me and screamed even louder. I said, "If you scream you're going to go outside and you can go scream there."*

It finally occurred to me: You can strap them into their car seats, you can shove them into their coats, but you can't make them stop screaming. So now I realize I have to provide a substitute. He can scream outdoors.

Final Nos

Once you see that you are heading into a no-win situation, you can say no in such a way that the child responds. As a father says: "Josh tends to sense when we mean business." A mother adds, "I have learned when you take a stand, when you're saying that something's really important and when you are totally unambivalent about it, the child responds to that."

In our family, we call this the "final no." When either my husband or I said "Final no," the children knew that whatever they were doing had to stop and they almost never resisted because they knew we would not change our minds once we said "Final no." I believe the success of the final no derives from a parent's utter, unshakable conviction that this no is irrevocable and admits no appeal. Children recognize this state of mind.

Trying to Keep Your Sense of Humor

Whenever my children launched into a no-win situation about whether I was going to drop everything to take them to a movie or buy an expensive TV toy, I could often forestall a battle by using humor. I would say, "You're going to say 'I need to go to the movies,' and I'm going to say 'I can't now —what about Saturday?' and you're going to say 'Now' and I'm going to say 'No,' and you're going to yell and I'm going to say 'Final no.' Let's prevent all this from happening and I'll say 'Final no' now and ask you to think of another way to solve the problem."

Because I would smile and dramatize the dialogue, my children would usually laugh. Humor served to move them away from a dead-center conflict in order to generate other solutions to the problem. Of course, the humor must be directed at the situation, never at the child.

Using Time-Out

Another important technique to use before the no-win situation escalates is time-out for you and the child. The use of time-out is well illustrated by the following conversation among preschool parents at a parenting center in the Midwest. One woman begins:

• • • *What I really found helpful is to set up some steps that we go through when Joey (age two and a half) is doing something I don't want him to do. I start out with saying "No, you can't do that." and if he keeps doing it, I go over, look him in the face and say, "I told you you can't do that." If he keeps going, I warn him: "Look, if you can't stop, you're going to sit in the time-out chair." I use one of our living room chairs.*
   The first ten times he was in the time-out chair, he hated it. He would just sit there and call "Mommy, get down, get down!" And I'd say, "No, you can't get down until you're quiet and you tell me you're not going to do it anymore."

"And he actually stays in the chair?" asked one of the parents in the group.

• • • *Well, you have to do it with a look on your face and the tone of your voice so that he knows that you mean business. That's the ultimate thing that can happen to him and he knows it.*

"When he gets off, what's it like?" asked another participant.

■ ■ ■ *I go over and give a hug and kiss to let him know that I'm not angry anymore, because otherwise he gets upset. I try to make a point of taking him over to the toys and saying, "Let's get a puzzle," or something. It's important to let him know it's over. Otherwise he goes around with hurt feelings.*

"Are there certain times when you use the chair?"

■ ■ ■ *It depends on my mood. If I'm in a bad mood and I say, "Joey, Mommy's really tired—please stop banging on that drum," and if he won't—he's just looking at me with that look in his eyes like "I'm going to bang on this drum forever," that's usually when I put him on the chair.*

"When you lock horns?"

■ ■ ■ *Yeah. It's important not to overuse the time-out chair or it loses its power. If I get upset and am ready to fight him, that's when I use it. Then I can go and try to calm myself down. It's a time-out for me, too.*

The no-win situations constitute the most trying moments in parenthood. If you lock horns and turn the no-win situation into a power struggle, then truly everyone loses. If you can cope well, then the no-win situations have the possibility of everybody winning.

Q *My child has temper tantrums. That's worse than the no-win struggles. I can't see how anyone can emerge from temper tantrums unscathed.*

"The biggest problem I think I ever dealt with was Courtney's temper," says the mother of a child now four:

■ ■ ■ *When she got to be independent, around eighteen months to two years, she had temper tantrums. She'd get uncontrollable. Her eyes would just get buggy and she'd scream and she'd be on the floor and there was nothing you could do to calm her down.*

Any parent who has ever had to deal with tantrums would find "uncontrollable" an apt description. It is as if the child passes a critical point and falls apart, screaming, yelling, kicking, and shouting until the charge is spent and the child tries to remuster self-control.

The first step in resolving tantrums is to attempt to understand them. Often a tantrum is the end result of an escalating situation. Ask yourself whether certain circumstances inevitably lead up to tantrums (dinner is too late, it's been an exhausting day, etc.) and see if you can step in earlier to prevent the explosion.

Certain children, by nature of their inborn temperaments, cannot help having tantrums. Like the colicky crying of an infant, the tantrum represents a build-up of tension which is released in the only way a child knows how. If your child is hypersensitive to noises, sights, or sounds, is persistent and stubborn, is more serious and cranky, tantrums are more common. As parents, we tend to interpret the child's behavior as designed to "get" us, but that is not necessarily the case, especially for these children who cannot help themselves.

The best remedy resides in helping the child learn self-management techniques. Use problem-solving with an older preschooler. During a calm moment, ask the child to come up with a plan he or she can use to quiet down:

- One child picked a "mantra" of sorts to say to himself: "Cut, stop, that is all of that." When upset, he repeated these words over and over.
- Another child decided to go off to her own room and pound her pillow.

When children come up with ideas for managing, they are more likely to try them out. Furthermore, a situation which all too often results in eroding the child's self-esteem can result in strengthening the child's competence and confidence.

If your child cannot think of any plans to try, here are some.

Stanley Turecki, author of *The Difficult Child*, asks children to think of a color that they feel when they have a tantrum, for example, purple. Then he suggests thinking of a color that reminds them of feeling calm, such as blue. The next time they feel they are about to fall apart, he suggests they try to think hard about the calm color.

The mother of a four-year-old got a plain notebook which she labeled "The Angry Book." When this child was about to go into a rage, she directed him to the book, in which he would draw pictures of witches and monsters. This redirected his anger and kept him from lashing out at the rest of the family.

The one common element in all these methods is that the child goes off alone when having a tantrum, does something to expend the anger, and then regains self-control.

Younger children, however, cannot be sent off to be alone:

■ ■ ■ *When my daughter was two and old enough to try to reason with, I started to put her in her room and hope that she would eventually calm down. That didn't work. She'd kick and bang on the door and put dents in it. She tore her clothes off the hangers and threw them on the floor. I felt frustrated and angry. So I went into her room with her, let her pound her pillow until she calmed down.*

While many books and articles on discipline advise parents to ignore the tantrum, that is possible for some parents but not for others. The mother of a three-year-old describes her success at ignoring:

■ ■ ■ *A magazine I read said ignore tantrum behavior. At first, that was very difficult, especially in public. I told myself that I'd never see these people again and they'd never see me. I realized I had to do what was best for me and my child. And it worked.*

On the other hand, the mother of a two-year-old found this approach was not effective:

■ ■ ■ *I couldn't ignore the tantrums because my daughter wouldn't let me—she'd be coming and beating on me. I had to deal with it, but when I was able to keep my cool I could deal with it better.*

This mother held her daughter on the bed. If she tried to kick or hit her, she held her arms and talked softly to her.

Because children experience tantrums as a frightening loss of control, they may attribute responsibility to others, not themselves:

■ ■ ■ *My daughter will say, "I was crying because you were mad at me." But it doesn't start out that way. She'll start crying over something unimportant and I'll say, "Stop crying," and she'll say, "Don't start fighting with me, Mommy." I'll say, "I'm not fighting, I just want you to calm down." And then she'll start falling apart and blame her mood on me. So it's usually my fault when she has a tantrum now.*

When the mother says, "Stop crying," the child feels blamed; then the two progress into the "it's my fault—it's your fault" routine. This mother

could circumvent some of the tension by helping the child regain control
through problem-solving: "How can I help you feel better?" Later the
parent might say, "What do you think would help you control yourself the
next time you feel like you're about to have a tantrum?"

With this statement, the parent is saying that a tantrum is not acceptable
behavior. She has set a limit but is also asking the child to figure out a way
to comply.

The child may come up with some bizarre ideas:

"I'd like a Kleenex to hold."

"Are you sure that would help you?"

"I want a Kleenex to hold."

"Okay, we'll try it."

If you don't undermine it ("A Kleenex—that's a stupid idea. I know that
won't work"), it just may be successful. If it is, keep using it until it loses
its potency and then go through the problem-solving again:

> *The Kleenex doesn't work anymore. We really need to find
> something that works because you don't like having tantrums
> and I don't like seeing you that upset. What other ideas do
> you have that will work?*

The art of parenthood is the ability to face problems and work at solving
them.

Q *All of these discipline procedures sound feasible if you have one
child but what if you have two? Then it can be a real zoo.*

> SCENE: *Your five-year-old son and three-year-old daughter
> are playing peacefully together. Suddenly the boy marches to
> the refrigerator, looks his sister straight in the eye, takes the
> cookie she's been saving, and eats it down to the last crumb.
> Within seconds they are rolling around the floor, pounding
> each other.*

Several disciplinary procedures are applicable to handling discipline issues with siblings.

Enlarging the Concept of Family

This may sound like a strange idea, especially when your children are
pounding each other. But it is a precursor to effective discipline.

In thinking about what family means, most people have idyllic visions
of peace and tranquility. My view is slightly different. I think that a family
must learn to fight well together as well as love well. Far too many adults

have troubled marriages because they never learned to fight fairly and instead use such tactics as blaming, accusing, attacking, or defending. There is no better opportunity than sibling fights to teach positive negotiation skills.

Another assumption I have is: Different children should be treated differently. What you do with one child is not necessarily what you do with another (because that child is older, younger, more aggressive, less aggressive, etc.).

I have found it useful to share these ground rules with my children:

> *I'm not interested in who started the fight or whose fault it is*
> *—I'm more interested in who can resolve it.*
>
> *Fair does not mean the same for both of you.*

(See section on siblings, pages 279–288, for an elaboration of these ideas.)

Promoting Other-Oriented Thinking

The mother whose children are fighting over the cookie could say: "Annie, you were so angry when Howard took your cookie. Howard, do you see how angry she is? But Annie, when you hit, it's hard for Howard to understand what you're feeling—when people get hit, all they want to do is protect themselves. Tell Howard how you feel in words."

Promoting Problem-Solving

Problem-solving is very effective in dealing with discipline issues and siblings. I often used this method with such issues as fighting in the car. Pulling over to the side of the road didn't help much (and was not always possible), lecturing didn't help, and getting upset certainly didn't help.

What did work was problem-solving. Before we got in the car, I would announce the rule: "No fighting in the car—it's too dangerous when I'm driving." Then I'd say, "Do you have any thoughts about how you could manage that?"

My son suggested a "car kit": a lot of activities so he would not be bored. My daughter agreed that this was a good plan, and they each collected toys in a small shopping bag for their car kits before getting into the car.

It is reassuring to fantasize that once the children have come up with an idea, then the problem has been eradicated once and for all. Unfortunately —or fortunately perhaps—problem-solving is a process, not a product. I say fortunately because both adults and children grow and change by confronting and dealing with (rather than avoiding) difficulties. Any solution you have forged will last for a while and then begin to wane, and you have to begin the process again: "The car kits are not keeping you from fighting in the car anymore. There can be no fighting while I'm driving. Who has another plan?" As research indicates, the ability to solve problems promotes cooperation.

Q *When you let the children help in problem-solving, it sounds as if you are handing parental authority over to them. They are too young to be in charge—they need adults to tell them what to do.*

When discussing children's participating in problem-solving, it can appear that the adult is shedding responsibility, turning over the difficult task of discipline to the children themselves. Going back to the example of the children fighting in the car, remember, however, that the adult set the rule: "No fighting in the car." The children's role was not to determine *what* would happen—but rather to figure out *how* this rule might be enforced.

This question raises an important point, however. Every strategy of discipline can be used so that it contradicts its original intention. Following are pitfalls to some of the approaches and how to avoid them.

Preventing Problems

It is normal for parents to want to control things, to avoid hardships, to anticipate and prevent problems. As a discipline strategy, it can save us from many difficult moments. Yet, like every other disciplinary technique, it can be carried to excess. As one parent explains:

• • • *When parents don't give their children any freedom at all, they don't allow them to experience risk or failure. I know a kid whose parents have her on such a tight leash that when her parents are out of the picture, that kid is off the wall.*

Prevention is a useful concept, but it must be tempered with the knowledge that not every problem can be avoided.

Setting Limits

Limits make children feel safe. Parental limits are the basis of the child's future self-control, but a balance must be struck between making rules about everything and giving children some freedom to exercise autonomy.

How limits are expressed makes a critical difference. One mother tells how saying no became a rejection:

• • • *My three-year-old would rather play with me than other kids. I felt that it couldn't go on this way, but when I said so she took it as a rejection. She went through this thing of "you don't love me—you don't want to play with me."*

Possibly because this mother felt ambivalent, her daughter read the message as a rejection. As this mother became more certain that what she was doing was right, she could set the limit more supportively, saying, "Mommy can't play now because Mommy is doing something else."

Giving Explanations

This mother explained why she could not play. Providing a reason for behavior gives children an important tool; they learn to conform not just because an authority gives an order but because there is a logical purpose for doing so. They are thus given a technique that in the future will help them make decisions for themselves rather than depend on others to tell them what to do.

Using reasoning can be overdone, however, if it includes lengthy details or is formulated beyond the child's understanding. As many young children have been heard to say, "I don't want to know that much." Keep your explanations brief and to the point. For example, when a child has left his clothes all over the floor, just saying "clothes!" can be sufficient.

Using Other-Oriented Discipline

Sensitizing children to other people's feelings and reactions helps them begin to understand how their own behavior affects others, especially us. There is, however, a fine line not to be crossed. The child should not be made to feel responsible for the parent's well-being. This phenonemon has been termed "the parentalization of the child" and means that the adult confides in the child in such a way that the child begins to feel in charge of the parent's moods and emotions.

When children push parents too far, many of us at one time or another feel so sad or angry that we fall apart. When that happens, an amazing transformation can occur: the children shift from being demanding or bullying to being solicitous. Sometimes they look frightened as they try to soothe and comfort. Because this approach works, i.e., the children become cooperative, it can be tempting to use as a regular strategy. But its success would be very short-lived. Children truly need us to remain adults, to be in charge, to weather their growing pains.

Giving Choices

Providing children with choices works exceedingly well in the preschool years because it feeds into the child's need for increasing independence. Giving choices can backfire, however, when it is overused. Having choices about every situation (from what to wear in the morning to when to go to bed) can be overwhelming—it's as if the parents do not care or have no expectations for the child.

Unlimited choice has a similar effect. One father asked his two-and-a-half-year old to select from eight different breakfast cereals. The child, of course, insisted on a ninth brand which the father did not have. Parents are more likely to avert this sort of situation, by offering a limited choice: "Would you like Special K or Rice Krispies?"

Children can manipulate the use of choices. One child who was a sweets fancier used to announce to his parents that they could give him pie and cake for dessert or ice cream and cookies. A skilled adjudicator, he would say, "You have a choice." The parents, impressed with his cleverness, went along initially, but then concluded:

■ ■ ■ *Certainly Richard has the right to tell us what's on his mind, but we have the final say. Like, there are not going to be two desserts every night.*

Using Logical Consequences

Logical consequences can be self-evident to the parent. For example, if a child scatters food on the kitchen floor, the reasonable response is to ask her to clean it up, not to deprive her of a play date on Saturday. If a child is unruly at a friend's birthday party, then taking the child aside and asking if he or she can manage may be helpful; if the child can't manage, then leaving the party is a logical course of action. Sometimes, however, there are no apparent consequences to a certain act and then you, the adult, must use your own judgment on how to handle the situation.

Parents also wonder how far to go with logical consequences. If their child is slow moving and always late for the nursery school car pool, do they let the car pool leave him behind? Some parents have, some have not. One parent learned, however, that when she left her child at home, her daughter had a wonderful time and then began to stall on purpose. This mother subsequently arranged for a day off for activities together, but when her daughter missed her car pool again, she refused to entertain her.

In addition, the use of logical consequences can be taken to extreme. For example, in the name of logical consequences, one parent poured a glass of milk over her son's head when he spilled milk on her. Also in the name of logical consequences, a father slapped his child when his child hit him. These actions are revenge and retaliation, not logical consequences. Furthermore, physical attack is likely to be imitated. It is more effective to express displeasure—"I don't like to be hit"—and to remove the child rather than strike back.

Using Time-Out

Time-out can be effective with fighting. However, if time-out triggers a power struggle, it does not serve its purpose of helping the child gain control. This is what happened in a family with a five-year-old:

■ ■ ■ *Alex would have a temper tantrum, so I would say, "Okay, Alex, just to help you control yourself, go to your bedroom and calm down." He refused.*

These parents ended up carrying Alex to his room. They would hold the door closed and engage in a shouting match. It would have been more effective to stay with Alex in his room rather than yelling back and forth, which only escalated the tension.

Time-out is also misused if it becomes rejection. If the time-out is lengthy, if the parents refuse to speak to the child, withholding their love, then the child's ensuing fear of loss can blind him or her to the purpose of the disciplinary action. Time-out is intended to remove the child from the so-called scene of the crime and from the attention (usually negative) of the parent in order for both to regain self-control.

A parent in a seminar I conducted called discipline strategies "tricks of the trade." These are methods that we can learn to manage parenthood more effectively. Tricks of the trade always involve the human element. Any act depends on our underlying intention, our mood, and the circumstances. The same words said in two different ways can yield widely different results. Yet it is in this give and take, this trial-and-error process, that the greatest learning can take place for children and parents. Children learn how to navigate complicated emotions; they learn about others and themselves—and so do we as parents. We see ourselves in all our strength and weakness, and we have the opportunity to become the kind of parents we want to be.

Q *I know all the strategies that work best, but sometimes I'm so angry that I don't want to use them. I feel like getting back at my child. How can parents handle their anger at their children?*

This is one of the most important questions of parenthood. Many books and articles I've read on discipline make no mention of the parent's emotions, yet in the over three hundred interviews conducted for this book, the specter of the parent's own anger and how to deal with it was omnipresent.

Before we had children, we observed parents insulting a child at the supermarket, hauling a child across a street, and we were appalled: we pledged never to treat our children that way. Yet one of the more humbling experiences of parenthood is to experience, as our children grow, feelings that led "*those* parents" to act that way. Now we understand.

I once asked parents at a seminar to write down what made them angriest. When I read their answers aloud, the parents laughed in embarrassment because, at a distance, the reasons seemed so trivial:

"She says 'doody.' "

"He dribbles mashed potatoes outside his mouth when he eats."

Yet these experiences trigger something deep in us. In the course of growing up, our children do or say something that strikes at our Achilles heel. The power of reducing an adult to shambles is both frightening and exciting for children. And so they repeat the same behavior again and again, perhaps to test their prowess and to learn how to deal with their parent's collapse. In this process, a family pattern begins to take shape.

Despite our different histories and our different thresholds of anger, certain things that children do upset most adults.

Calling Names

With all of the time and effort we devote to parenthood, many parents have an unspoken expectation that if children don't show gratitude, they at least will not show disdain. But this is not what happens. Despite the endless times we have gotten up in the night with them or soothed their hurt feelings or bodies, they turn around and call us names: "dummy," or "poopy," or "stupid." Even saying "You're not nice" can seem like a slap in the face.

Damaging Our Property

Our property becomes a stand-in for us. Finding our drawers in disarray, a magazine we care about with pages missing, or a wall in our home decorated with magic markers can seem like a direct affront.

Hurting Us

If hurting our possessions becomes symbolic for hurting us, the actual act of hitting, pinching, or slapping can feel like a violation.

Reminding Us of Our Parents

Our child annoys us and out of our mouth comes "I hope your face freezes that way," or "I hope your child gives you one-tenth the trouble you've given me." Moments later, we feel upset: How could I have said that when I so disliked my own parents saying it to me?

Reminding Us of Other Family Members

Our children's behavior can trigger anger by reminding us of others. A rambunctious two-year-old can have mannerisms similar to those of a ne'er-do-well uncle. We feel we must eradicate this behavior once and for all, even though in reality the child is behaving like a normal toddler. A demanding daughter seems like a replica of your ex-wife and that must be stopped, even though the child's behavior may be a response to stress and not a permanent personality trait.

Reminding Us of Ourselves

Perhaps the most painful (and thus aggravating) behaviors in our children are those that remind us of ourselves in ways we dislike. A shy child can resurrect our own memories of the pain of being fearful long ago. If our child snaps at another child the way we snap at our husband, it can enrage us. A child's rudeness may resemble the way other adults once put us down. Our angriest moments are linked to our inner selves.

Envy

Sometimes anger is born of jealousy. Although it's hard to admit, these comments by a parent reveal the understandable envy we can feel:

▪ ▪ ▪ *One of my frustrations is that my son lives in his own fantasy world. I'll say, "Pick up your shoes," or "Go brush your teeth," but he doesn't hear me because he is so engaged in his toys. Part of me says: "How marvelous. He doesn't even hear what I am saying."*

It really brings up a deep ambivalence in myself. I would love to be lolly-dolling all the time and so deeply engaged. I'd love to be relieved of all that responsibility of organizing and managing of my family.

The Loss of Expectations

Anger is usually the result of a loss of an expectation. As parents, we have many images of the way things are supposed to be. When one of these expectations is confounded, we feel the pain of loss, anger, disappointment, or distress.

A common expectation is that love will conquer anger. As the mother of two preschool boys says:

▪ ▪ ▪ *There's a myth that parents aren't supposed to get angry at their kids. When you feel that anger, you say, "This is not supposed to be." You imagine that it's only you—that everyone else in their peaceful home is feeling loving all the time.*

Another common expectation is of reciprocity. Many parents unconsciously make a bargain: if I take care of your needs, you will either take care of me or will at least let me take care of myself. Yet it takes a long time for children to learn to reciprocate. The mother of a young child says:

• • • *Nowadays we have problems shopping. Becky and I will spend ages shopping for her and on the way out, I'll say that I want to stop by one counter for me and she begins to wail "No-o-o-o." I become livid.*

Feeling Judged

Many parent/child confrontations take place in public. At this point in parenthood, because we feel so connected to our children, their name-calling or resistance seems like an indictment of our ability as parents. It is as if a judge flashed a card on the screen: C+ father or C+ mother.

As if on cue, others appear to watch us with disapproval. One mother remarked:

• • • *Have you ever noticed that when your kid is putting you down in public, other people gather like rubberneckers on the highway? They can't wait to see what you are going to do and you wonder: "Am I going to let this kid make a fool out of me in front of other kids and other parents?" And you really begin to feel out of control then.*

External Realities

External realities play an important role in anger. A single-parent mother who must leave the house at seven-fifteen or lose her job regularly becomes angry at her slow-moving child. This particular mother realized that becoming upset with her child was setting up a no-win situation, so she turned her anger to the situation, saying, "I wish my job didn't begin so early."

Losing Control

In my conversations with parents, the words used to express anger describe a loss of control: "losing it," "falling apart," "going crazy," "becoming apoplectic." Ironically, the fear of losing control is what pushes us to lose control.

Why Do Children Push Us?

The paradox of preschoolers' development is that they yearn for independence, to "do it myself," to test their own prowess, yet are aware of their
dependence, their need to be cared for. And so they resist and cling to us.
During every period when increased independence is being negotiated—the
preschool years, the adolescent years—turmoil ensues. No one breaks away
without strife. Children need us, want to need us, and don't want to need
us all at the same time. According to several parents:

■ ■ ■ *Their pushing us has to do with separation: "I want to be*
different but I want to be close."

■ ■ ■ *Sometimes when they start pushing, they don't have the control*
to stop.

■ ■ ■ *They have to plumb the depths of our relationship.*

■ ■ ■ *If parents and children never got angry with each other, it*
would be like an artificially imposed moratorium on living. You
would not expect to live with another adult and never be angry.
The same is true with children. But there is a definite line that
is not to be crossed.

Q *How should I express anger to children?*

If there is a line that must not be crossed, what is that line? Many parents
today want to be more honest with their children than their parents were
with them. They don't want to be remote and unreal. They want to be open
—but how open?

It is important to think about what children stand to gain or lose in the
process before we begin to draw our own demarcations. In such encounters
children can learn about how people function—they learn that their behavior has consequences. And they begin the life-long process of fathoming the
fact that we, their parents, are human.

The mother of two small sons says:

■ ■ ■ *The positive consequence of expressing anger is that you share*
with your kids that you are vulnerable and imperfect, and
that's an important lesson. At some point, they begin to under-
stand that they too can have imperfections. But if your anger
is expressed with such frequency and intensity that the kids
start feeling that they're not just vulnerable, they're fragile,
then you're creating problems.

SOLUTIONS

Trying to Understand the Source of Your Anger

Since anger usually results from a dissonance between what you expect (what "should" happen) and what actually happens, think through what you are expecting. Is it realistic? If so, what can you change to make it happen? If not, can you change your expectation to be more realistic?

Trying to Change the Perception that Your Children Are "Out to Get You"

It's amazing how powerful a different outlook can be. Recently, my teenage daughter asked me to bring some clothes to a friend's house where she was dressing for a party. When I brought the wrong white dress, she marshaled her attack. I was ready to retaliate with a lecture about how ungrateful she was (didn't she know I had gone out of my way to drive the clothes to her?), but I stopped and focused on her disappointment. "I'm sorry. I made a mistake," I said. She smiled and the almost-war was averted. I had realized that she was not trying to make my life miserable but merely expressing her own upset feelings.

A mother of two preschoolers came to a similar conclusion:

. . . *My children did something outrageous and a friend said, "They're just being children." I realized that was true. They were dealing with their feelings in the only way they knew how. My job was to teach them more socially acceptable ways of expressing themselves.*

Using "I" Messages

Before yelling all the vituperative things you feel, put your statement in the "I" rather than the "you" form: "I can't stand it when you pound on the piano. It hurts my ears," rather than, "You are a selfish, spoiled child for making so much noise."

Reflecting the Child's Words

It also helps to curb our anger if we reflect our children's words. It gives us a moment to cool off while they feel understood: "You're saying that because you're too tired to pick up your toys."

Using a Code Word

If you want to say something nasty, think of a made-up word that you can say. Ours was "phumfer."

In another family, the mother says "dammit." According to her, the kids always repeat it: "Dammit, dammit, dammit. If we can manage to laugh at that point, we've made it."

Keeping a Sense of Humor

Try to see the humor in what's happening. In the midst of finding my son finger-painting on the new carpet, I tried to think of it as a funny family story (and so it has become) and thus was able to handle the event with much more equanimity.

Another technique is to imagine writing up the event for a TV sitcom or a humorous magazine article.

Keeping Your Emotional Distance

A mother of two describes how she learned not to overreact:

■ ■ ■ *I walked into the supermarket and saw a friend's child lying in the middle of an aisle screeching at the top of his lungs. His mother Suzie was shopping very calmly. I said, "Hi, Suzie." She said, "Hi," and turned the corner into another aisle. Aaron picked himself up, followed her into the next aisle, threw himself on the floor and started again. Suzie was amazing: she just kept shopping.*

Aaron's mother served as a role model for her friend. She became an internal reminder not to get down to the children's level when they are upset. The child's anger does not have to become the parent's anger.

Taking Time for Yourself

If scenes like that make you too angry, don't keep just an emotional distance—keep a physical distance. A New York City mother with two sons, ages five and three, says:

■ ■ ■ *Occasionally, I get so angry that I say, "I'm going off duty. I'm warning you, I'm going off duty." I go into the bathroom and close the door. I do this very rarely, perhaps once every two months—but otherwise I would hit them.*

Channeling Your Anger

If you are feeling angry in general, try to find a productive outlet such as exercise or sports.

Taking Good Care of Yourself

Parents are much more susceptible to anger if they are overworked, tired, or hassled. To the extent that you can, make sure your own needs are being met.

How to Tell if Your Anger Is Inappropriate

Ask yourself:

- Are you using anger at your children as a way of gratifying yourself, of expressing your own frustrations?
- Are you using anger to control behavior, as a method of discipline?
- Does the anger linger past the immediate event so that people do not make up and resolve the problem?
- Is the anger replacing other feelings such as love and affection?

If you answer yes to these questions, you are probably expressing anger inappropriately. Look closely at the circumstances of your anger and try to sort out the instances that involve your children.

Seeking Help

If you can't handle situations without exploding, for your sake and your children's, seek help. Call in your spouse. If that does not work, call your best friend on the telephone. Find other friends to talk about the joys and satisfaction of being a parent. Join a parents' group. Seek professional counseling. If you think you are potentially psychologically or physically abusive, call the National Hotline maintained by Childhelp USA, (800) 422-4453, or Parents Anonymous: (800) 421-0353 except in California; in California, call (800) 352-0386. Help really helps.

PARENTS SPEAK: CONTROLLING ANGER

Don't Give Mixed Messages

Charlotte Powell, a substitute teacher from North Carolina, has two daughters, seven and five:

• • • *My daughter often hollers. Sometimes I holler back at her to quit yelling. Then I say to myself, "This is dumb. Why am I asking her not to do what I'm doing?" She probably is learning to yell just from watching me. I guess I've been giving her mixed messages.*

Don't Make Idle Threats

Karen Rosen lives in California with her three children, six, three and one:

. . . *One day I made a mistake and I realized it. I don't even remember what my three-year-old pulled, but I used school as punishment. I told her she was not going to school the next day just because I didn't know how else to get her goat. After I calmed down, I realized I didn't want her to see school as a punishment or as a reward, so I wound up taking her to school the next day.*

Don't Insult or Humiliate

Marsha Stiles lives in Texas with her four-year-old:

. . . *When you insult and humiliate children, they will fight with every ounce of strength they have for their honor and their pride. They look so defiant and strong, but if you really look in their eyes, you can see fear. They are afraid because they are really fighting for their lives.*

Don't Chase

Tempie Crunk is from Hendersonville, Tennessee. She has a five-year-old:

. . . *Have you ever played "Let's Run from Mommy," when a child knows he did something wrong?*

The chase is on and the winner is . . . the child. I have a suggestion that worked for me—refuse to play—do not chase. Sit down and read a magazine, be collected. The children will edge their way back to you, usually having thought about their deed and maybe a little confused because of your reaction. Now is your chance for good, calm communication. Remember, it takes time.

Don't Get into a Power Struggle

Edward Grant is the father of two in upstate New York:

. . . *My daughter often wants something in the supermarket that I don't think is healthy for her. You could go around and around forever, if you choose to: "I want" . . . "You can't" . . . "I will" . . . "You won't."*

I've learned to avoid power struggles by giving her some

acceptable but real control: "You pick the dessert—but we have to look at the ingredients together to make sure it doesn't have chemicals in it."

More important than the actual words you use is how you use those words—with a clarity within yourself and an understanding for what the child is feeling.

Don't Give Negative Attention

Nina Joseph lives in New York City with her two children, a son, five, and a daughter, three:

• • • *My son was born with extreme nervous energy. He'd go into the bathroom and empty every shelf in the room. It was driving me crazy because I really didn't know how to cope.*

Children have a radar that hones in on whatever makes the parent anxious, and for the longest time he was doing all this negative acting out and I would respond in a very negative way: negative to negative—two negatives.

In the last couple of years, I've come to understand that he's a child who needs positive, loving, warm attention and I've worked and worked on that and have begun to make a dent.

We now don't say anything negative about our son to anyone. We only talk positively about him—in front of him and to other people. The more positively we think about him and talk about him, the more positively we act toward him. And it's paid off. His image of himself has improved enormously.

Q *What about spanking?*

Several months ago I was invited to speak about positive approaches to discipline during a town's "No Hitters Day." The children of the town had designed buttons for a contest and the winning button said "Hugging— Not Hitting."

The experience was full of contradictions. Although several hundred parents sat in the audience sporting the "Hugging—Not Hitting" buttons, most of them believed in the necessity of physical punishment. The moderator began the meeting by saying that teachers should be allowed to hit children in school. The high school football coach said that he needed to hit the players every once in a while "to shape them up." Most of the parents agreed that at times children need spankings. "Why?" I asked the parents.

. . . *I've hit my child since he was little. He listens to me. He does what I say. When I'm not home, he gets away with murder from my wife. But when I come home, I just have to look at him with a stern face and he knows if he doesn't snap to, he'll be spanked.*

This father argues that spanking works. His son (age five) is obedient with him. But not with his wife. And not with his teachers.

. . . *He's been getting into trouble at school lately. He's disruptive and picks fights. I've told him if I ever hear from a teacher that he's caused another fight, he's really going to get it.*

It's not surprising that this child is disruptive with others. He has been taught that you obey only because someone is more forceful than you. If that person is absent, there is no reason to obey. This is the "do it because I'm going to make you" approach.

Using spanking to stop fighting says that if an adult can be aggressive with someone smaller and less powerful, then it is permissible for the child to do the same. One parent at No Hitters Day said:

. . . *I was hit as a child. I was wild and crazy, and if my parents hadn't spanked me, there's no betting on how I would have turned out. I'm okay now, so I don't see how spanking could hurt my child.*

Alice Miller, a Swiss psychoanalyst, has found that adults tend to idealize their childhoods and so may repress their anger and resentment at spankings. It is not at all uncharacteristic for a parent to use a method of discipline that he or she disliked, but use it for reasons very different than for the child's "own good." She writes:

> *In beating their children [parents] are struggling to retain the power they once lost to their own parents . . . only now when someone weaker than they is involved, do they finally fight back, often quite fiercely.*

Some parents at the meeting felt that the kind of spanking made a difference:

. . . *You're talking about a cruel spanking, one in which the parents lose control and really hurt their children. I don't approve of that because the parents are using the spanking to satisfy their own needs, not to discipline the children. But I don't see any-thing wrong with a few whacks on the behind to teach the child a lesson.*

But do parents really spank in this detached way? When I asked the parents, the majority said they spanked primarily in a flush of anger. What, then, is the child really learning? One child I know threw something at his mother. She spanked him; he stopped immediately and was quite contrite. Several days later when he became frustrated, he threw something again. After several repetitions of this pattern, the mother decided that the child was using the spanking as a way to control his behavior rather than learning how to express frustration in an acceptable way.

"How do you feel after you have spanked a child?" I asked the partici-pants at the No Hitters Day. While one or two in the group felt all right after spanking, the majority felt an immediate sense of unease, guilt, or remorse.

▪ ▪ ▪ *My hand burns for a long time. I guess that's where the statement that "this hurts me more than you" comes from.*

I think that the uneasiness after spanking a child is most telling. While most of us at one time or another resort to spanking, subconsciously we know that it is wrong, that it is not effective.

Spanking does not accomplish the purpose for which it is intended. It teaches children to operate from fear rather than reason, and it breeds anger. The research evidence is also clear that physical force creates more resistance and much less cooperation.

Psychological Maltreatment

Physical force, however, is just a form of what at its worst can be maltreat-ment. There is also psychological maltreatment. James Garbarino and his colleagues have identified five types of psychological maltreatment:

- *Rejecting:* The adult denies the legitimacy of the child's worth.
- *Isolating:* The adult cuts the child off, leading the child to believe that he or she is all alone.
- *Ignoring:* Although physically present, the adult remains emotionally un-available.
- *Terrorizing:* The adult uses scare tactics or bullies.
- *Corrupting:* The adult reinforces antisocial or other deviant misbehavior.

In his research, Garbarino finds that children can rarely overcome the effects of being rejected, isolated, ignored, terrorized, or corrupted.

Ways to deal effectively with children's misbehavior have been detailed in this chapter. Underlying these methods is respect for the child, valuing what the child needs and wants balanced with respect for the parent. We should listen to what the children in that school district said: hugging—not hitting.

Q *Should I apologize to my child?*

As parents, we all make mistakes—as do our children. These mistakes can lead to guilt and remorse or be the impetus for change.

For me, the issue is not *whether* to apologize but *how* to apologize. We serve as an important model to our children in demonstrating how to deal with mistakes.

Don't use apologies as an excuse to clear your conscience so you can do the same thing over again. Many adults say they're sorry and immediately repeat what they have done. The apology erases their own discomfort and goes no deeper than that.

Don't let your children use your apology to flagellate you. In situations where we feel we should apologize, our children are generally angry with us. The opportunity for them to express their anger is healthy. As Alice Miller says:

> *Those who were permitted to react appropriately throughout their childhood—i.e., with anger—to the pain, wrongs, and denial inflicted upon them . . . will retain this ability to react appropriately later in life. When someone wounds them as adults, they will be able to recognize and express this verbally.*

When permitting children to express their anger, we must remember we are the parents, they are the children. They have no right to punish us. We can say: "I know you're upset and I'm sorry, but use words to tell me how you feel."

Apologize in appropriate ways. We are teaching ourselves and our children how to recover from difficult encounters. In the process, we can help children understand their own feelings:

I'm sorry I yelled at you. I must be hungry.

I'm sorry that I said something that wasn't nice—I guess I was worried.

Long explanations force the child to take care of us. Giving presents to atone for mistakes is not necessary. Concern for the child's well-being is gift enough.

Q *With all of this concern for the children, won't we be spoiling them?*

> SCENE: *You permit your child to express his anger and he is sounding off: "I don't like you. You're so mean." You can't help but think: this is a spoiled child.*

> SCENE: *You go to the supermarket at the best time for your daughter. You prepare her for what she can buy and give her a snack before entering. The thought crosses your mind: this child is running the family, I'm really spoiling her.*

> SCENE: *You have been away and return with a present for your son. Before you say anything, he demands his present. When he opens it, he says, "That's not what I wanted." "This is a spoiled child," you say to yourself.*

What is the line between meeting the needs of young children and spoiling them? How much of children's demandingness and insensitivity is "just a stage" and how much is a part of their personality?

In the preschool years, children are wrapped up in themselves. They see the world through their own needs and desires and are only beginning to learn to take into account the perspective of others, to understand and empathize with what others are feeling (see pages 135–149 on moral development). Is this an excuse for what seems to us like spoiled behavior?

In considering this issue, we must differentiate between needs and desires. Young children have specific needs: to be fed, to be clothed, to be sheltered, to be protected, to be respected, to be listened to, to be loved, to learn and play, to be given limits.

Wanting a particular present is a desire, while wanting to express disappointment is a need: it is the need to be listened to and respected. Yet the parent also has needs—parents need respect, too. So while we are listening to the child, we can also state our needs.

For example, consider the child who refuses to go to sleep. You read a story, sing songs, get your child a drink of water, say good night, and leave. Five minutes later, your child yells that there are monsters in the room. So you go back in, reassure, and leave again. Three more minutes pass, and this time your child hears a funny, scary noise. So you go back again, but this time you don't feel as patient. You were planning on this time for yourself. This is the point where you start to suspect you are spoiling your child.

Let's differentiate again between the child's needs and desires. The child needs to feel protected but desires your presence for protection. The need is legitimate. Most of us can recall the terrifying thoughts we conjured up in our own dark rooms as children—spiders dangling from the ceiling, snakes in the closet, a robber outside the window.

These memories arouse our empathy, yet the child's desire—to have us return every few minutes—may not be a satisfactory solution. There are other ways to meet the child's need. You can ask, "What could you do to make yourself feel less afraid?" If your child has no ideas, you could suggest some: "I know a boy who was afraid of the shadows in his room so he left the light on. And I know a girl who kept a flashlight in her room."

Remember that the child also needs limits, and you are setting one: "It is time to be in your room and to go to bed."

Children are never spoiled when you meet their needs. In fact, the opposite occurs: they are strengthened.

There is an almost-guaranteed way to differentiate between when you are spoiling your child and not. Ask yourself if you are doing something for your child because you really want to and/or because you believe it is the right thing to do. Then you are not spoiling your child. If, however, you are doing something against your better judgment because you feel guilty, then you may be setting up a problematic pattern.

Children let us know when we are spoiling them. They become insatiable; what we've given is never enough. When that balance of power has tipped to their side, they feel frightened and try to tip the scales back again by pushing and pushing us. Children do need limits.

Q *What about a child who doesn't push you, who doesn't express anger?*

Research on temperament suggests that inhibition is an inborn characteristic. Children who are inhibited are not as likely to express frustration and anger:

. . . *Dick is such a quiet child—he always goes along with what I say. He's never bossy or demanding. I'm tempted to sit back, relax, and thank my lucky stars I have a child like this, but I can't help wondering what will happen when he is a teenager. Will he go along with whatever his friends want, too?*

As this mother notes, it is important to teach children who are not as vocal in expressing no, when and how to say it.

SOLUTIONS

Modeling Ways to Express Anger

Parents can demonstrate how to express negative feelings by their actions and words. If a parent explodes, it may send the inhibited child more into his shell, but a quieter expression will demonstrate how to express oneself: "I really felt upset when I lost my car keys."

Teaching How to Say No

Some inhibited children say no to everything, including new ventures such as play dates or outings. It is important to differentiate between children's standing up for themselves (in which case they should at times be allowed to say, "No, I won't go") and their resistance to something new.

Try to find out the reason behind the refusal. If there is a minor problem ("I don't want to go to Jennifer's house because she takes my toys away"), explore ways to resolve it. Research conducted by Jerome Kagan on inhibited children shows that parents can successfully encourage them to be more outgoing.

Teaching Problem-Solving

Shure and Spivack found that teaching inhibited children to generate a number of solutions to problems ("What could you do when Jennifer takes your toys?") increases their social competence. When such children were taught to solve problems in school (using puppets or pictures to address hypothetical as well as real-life problems), they were more likely to try more than one way to solve a problem and not give up too quickly.

Q *How can we deal with the fact that my spouse and I have different ways of disciplining?*

A mother of a four-year-old says:

■ ■ ■ *All day long I teach my daughter Lucy to eat healthy food and then my husband comes home and hands her candy kisses. It makes me furious because he's undermining what I'm telling her.*

A father of a five-year-old says:

■ ■ ■ *Ryan will ask me to buy a toy and I'll say no. So he'll go to my wife and she'll say sure. What do we do then?*

These can be among the most difficult moments in being the parent of a young child. We are not only establishing a disciplinary relationship with our child but also dealing with triangular relationships:

child
↗   ↖
mother ↔ father

First, there is our own relationship with our spouse. This relationship changes immeasurably after children are born. There is certainly less time and attention to devote to each other. (See the section on parent/parent/child relationships, pages 267–270.) Another change occurs in the couple relationship. Both fathers and mothers tend to feel possessive about their new child: "My child is safe only with me." This possessiveness can engender competition. New parents, often to their own surprise, can resent the attention their spouse gives the child. They feel displaced and jealous. When their spouse handles situations differently than they do, it can become an affront. Because the new parent's skills in parenting may seem so tenuous, differences often become very threatening.

Additionally, parenthood reveals vulnerabilities in ourselves and our spouse that we did not know existed:

▪ ▪ ▪ *My husband gets really irritated when the children eat sloppily. They're just little children and if he doesn't make too big a deal of it, I'm sure this will go away. But it bothers him intensely.*

Against this backdrop, books and magazine articles advise mothers and fathers to be consistent. New parents often take this to mean that they should be monolithic: they should agree about everything.

My view is different. I have rarely known parents, try as they might, who could be totally in unison. Thus, my approach centers on figuring out when and how to agree and to disagree.

SOLUTIONS

Determining the Negotiable and the Non-Negotiable Nos

The process of becoming an authority involves figuring out your disciplinary priorities. What is most important to you to enforce? What is less important? This process is not usually discussed. By trial and error, we arrive at the values we care most about (no hurting, for example) and those that are less central. I advocate making this process conscious and then sharing your conclusions with your spouse.

The strictures that are most important to you I call the "non-negotiable nos." One husband who was irritated by his wife's criticism of their children remembered that his own parents had criticized him similarly. It took him many years to feel more positive about making mistakes, and he did not want his own children to suffer this kind of pain. So he asked his wife to try to stop using critical language. His wife was upset when he let the children climb up on the kitchen counters (where food was prepared) to reach things in the high cabinets. So in return she asked him to support her on that, and he agreed.

Other differences were less important. For instance, he gave the children chewing gum and she disliked hearing them chew it. They decided that he would give them gum in moderation but she never would. This became a "negotiable no"—the children had different rules from each parent and would be told so.

In effect, this couple agreed when to agree as well as agreed when to disagree. This approach recognizes that parents do have different styles. As I've said, children certainly can and do learn to live with differences as long as they are clearly presented.

Avoiding Behavior That Undermines Your Spouse

The real problem occurs when parents use differences to undermine each other. For example, the father who gave his daughter candy was using this gift to buy her alliance. He told her, "Your mother is silly for not letting you have candy. Candy won't hurt you." This put Lucy in the middle of a conflict between her parents—she was the pawn with which they waged their own dispute.

If you find yourselves engaging in this kind of power struggle, try to discuss it and arrive at an agreement. If that is not possible, seek a counselor, therapist, or mediator to help you resolve these conflicts.

CONCLUSION

We want our children to be perfect and we blame ourselves when they aren't. We have children who wake up cranky, who throw things, who reject dishes we have cooked especially for them. We want perfection for ourselves, yet we, too, are at times impatient, irritable and angry.

One of the most critical aspects of this period of parenthood is coming to terms with the differences between our fantasies of ourselves and our children, and the realities. It is moving from a crippling desire for perfection to a desire to be good enough that enables us to profit from our experience.

We begin to see the big picture.

▪ ▪ ▪ *I try to give myself the benefit of the doubt and figure Russell is not going to grow up to be a criminal if I get upset at times.*

Part of the big picture is understanding the child's development and perspective. A parent who had participated in a parent education group for several weeks concluded:

■ ■ ■ *What impressed me most last week was the discussion about how normal it is for children to test us. I notice that when I stick to my guns, she's calmer. The same things that make her go "Ooh, Mommy—plane!" or "Ooh, Mommy—duck!"— the awe and the excitement over the littlest things—are the same things, I think, that cause frustration in her. It's a really big world, and I've sort of shrunk down to her size this week. Seeing her at eye level has really changed my attitude, and I have a lot more patience. I think she senses this change in me, and so things are better between us.*

TWO

The Learning, Growing Child

Introduction:
Portrait of the Preschooler

The child from two to six exhibits tremendous growth, from the toddler's initial forays away from his or her parent's side to the kindergartener's bold declaration, "I can cross the street all by myself." Erik Erikson, the well-known child psychoanalyst and theorist, rightly characterizes the psychosocial milestones in this period as developing a sense of autonomy and initiative. Two-year-olds' struggle for independence is heralded by loud, clear assertions of "No" or "Me do it" or "Mine." Much of the day is spent defining their separateness from parents, caregivers, and other children. But the declarations of independence are often fleeting—a few minutes later, they may want to be carried, rocked, or may resist feeding themselves, or may ask to stay in diapers. As the sense of autonomy becomes more firmly established, the assertions die down and older preschoolers, now more sure of themselves, work at establishing a sense of initiative as if to say: "I can make things happen and use my newly developed skills." They take great pleasure in their capacity to forge friendships, to create in play, to solve problems, to exercise self-discipline in the face of temptation. (See the section on dependence and independence, pages 94–103.)

The preschool years bring quantum leaps in language and play. As the child becomes able to think in representational or symbolic ways, where one thing stands for another—a word for an object, a doll for a person—whole new worlds of communication and fantasy open up. Toddlers describe the here and now and play with language: "biggie piggie." They offer a bottle to a crying doll or make car sounds as they push a block across the floor. Older preschoolers can speak eloquently across a sweep of time, of future plans and of their past as a "teeny" baby. They propose complex ideas in play: "Let's pretend we're going on a camping trip; I'll be the forest ranger." They listen to and discuss stories and mimic reading by turning the pages. They take pride in remembering information taught by their parents: "These are hexagons on the sidewalk." They can recognize their names, labels of products, and maybe write some familiar words. Their ability to think—to hypothesize, to generate ideas, to understand cause and effect, to solve problems—has matured, though there still can be a blurring of fantasy and reality.

Between two and six years, young children's sense of self expands into an increasingly complex, differentiated concept. Two-year-olds can label themselves boys or girls, but older preschoolers have firm convictions about what this means in terms of appearance, friendships, and activities. The beginnings of a moral sense emerge. Whereas toddlers take little responsibility for their actions, five-year-olds are proud of knowing the difference between right and wrong and like to assert the rules. Still, their conscience is fragile and guilt is fleeting. Preschoolers begin to identify themselves as members of family, racial, ethnic, or religious groups. A three-year-old proudly states, "I'm half-Chinese, half-Jewish, and all-American." The elaboration of self-identity is gradual, as children learn about themselves from other people, books, the media. But, importantly, the sense of self also derives from their own activities. As preschoolers explore and experiment, play and problem-solve, they develop confidence in themselves as learners and as worthy people.

As children's sense of self expands, so does their awareness of the outside world. Toddlers' existence is centered primarily around their family and other adults who love and care for them. The rhythms of their lives are grounded in daily routines—eating, sleeping, bathing, going to child care. As preschoolers venture forth, they meet other children and learn firsthand about sharing and aggression. Three-year-olds enjoy playing with friends, but by five years, friendships are solid and enduring based on mutual interests. Preschoolers learn from books and stories told them. Television opens up new worlds, and that's both favorable and unfavorable. They can learn about earthworms and see puppets enact fairy tales, but they can also be exposed to superheroes and ads for war toys and sugared cereals. Older preschoolers see pictures of people dying in the newspapers and wonder what war means. Preschoolers' play reflects their learning about the world —from the scenes of domestic life common among twos and threes to the older preschoolers' enactment of brides and grooms, restaurants and fish markets.

The Preschool Child's Thinking

Much of what we know about children's intellectual (cognitive) development we owe to Jean Piaget, the eminent Swiss psychologist. He describes four broad stages:

1. Sensory-motor period (about birth to two years). The infant understands the world in terms of his or her overt physical actions.

2. Preoperational period (about two to seven years). Action has now become internalized as symbols. The child can manipulate mental symbols (images, words, gestures) that stand for objects and events.

3. Concrete operational period (about seven to eleven years). The child acquires logical thought structures but can apply them only to concrete, knowable situations.

4. Formal operational period (about eleven on). The adolescent can apply logic to hypothetical, purely verbal, contrary-to-fact problems.

Each stage is marked by different ways of thinking about cause and effect, space, time, number, and relationships between people, including friendship and morality.

Piaget characterized preoperational children's thinking as egocentric. This term doesn't mean selfish, but cognitively self-centered. Each child looks out on the world from his or her perspective and fails to realize that there are other, different perspectives. This egocentrism reveals itself in how preschoolers act, think, and feel. For example, they may attribute human feelings to inanimate things, worrying that pulling the button on a sweater will cause the button pain, or believing that the wind is alive because it moves. They think that natural events serve their own needs: "it's dark because I want to go to sleep"; "it's snowing so I can go outside and build a snowman." Judgments about number and amount are based on how things look: if a row of ten raisins is spread out, it has "more" raisins than ten raisins squished together. Children's thinking is literal; they are amazed at such idioms as "I have a frog in my throat." Egocentrism and limited objectivity are also apparent in the mix of reality and fantasy in young children's thinking. Dreams may be regarded as real events, taking place in real space; TV figures seem like real people located inside the set; wishing someone harm is equivalent to causing harm. Knowing some of the typical features of young children's thinking helps us as adults understand how children see and interpret the world differently than we do.

Yet recent research suggests that the child's egocentrism is not as all-pervasive as once thought. Psychologist Margaret Donaldson found that preschoolers can take the perspective of others if the problems presented to them are meaningful and understandable. Studies of children's emotional development also reveal that many toddlers display empathy and awareness of how other people feel. It seems fair to conclude that young children have the capacity to be nonegocentric depending upon the demands of the situation.

Development in the Preschool Years

Many strands come together. Biological maturation is one factor. As muscles develop, the crawling infant is propelled into an upright position, the tottering toddler becomes the sure-footed preschooler who climbs and kicks a ball. Small muscles mature, making it possible for the five-year-old to control a pencil and deftly hammer a nail. Maturation of the brain underlies many advances in language and thinking during the preschool years.

However, genetic potential needs environmental support to be realized. No child will walk or run unless given an opportunity; children who are not spoken to with meaningful, responsive language will be language-impaired. Although research suggests that children are born with the capacity to play, they still need adults to elicit gleeful, playful interaction.

The innate temperament of the child also influences development. Some children are born with a heightened sensitivity to change and are slow to warm up to a new food or a new school. Other children take change in stride, adjusting easily and rapidly.

Socialization efforts by parents become intense during the preschool years and underlie many aspects of development. Basic impulses are expected to come under control, as toilet training gets under way and sharing is stressed. Children are told to use words—"I'm angry"—instead of fists; to say, "I want a turn" instead of whining. Boys and girls are taught, both consciously and unconsciously, what is acceptable sex-role behavior. Parents are important models, as children imitate the way they brush their teeth or find comforting words to soothe a crying baby. At a deeper psychological level, children identify with their parents, wanting to be like them and adopting their values and beliefs.

Although parents are the child's primary socializers, other care givers and playmates have a role, too. In our culture, TV is also a socializer. Some programs reinforce parental efforts; others undermine them.

One of the child's best teachers is his or her own activity. Younger children spend much of their time exploring, seeing what will happen if they throw a ball to a friend, touch the paint, climb on a box and leap into their father's arms. Older preschoolers actively impose themselves on their environment, shaping it to their fancy. They design with clay, turn themselves into a baker or Dorothy in *The Wizard of Oz,* and build castles.

Child development experts emphasize that in order to grow and learn, children need problems to solve. Many challenges arise in play: "How can I make this hiding place big enough for me?" "Janie and I both want to be mommy. Can we have two mommies?" They puzzle out why water passes through a sieve and rocks don't. They wonder about many things, including death, God, and where babies come from. When problem-solving, children may discover that the present doesn't mesh with prior experience and knowledge, and they are forced to generate new insights. It is through this process of adapting old information to new circumstances that mental growth proceeds.

Developmental processes do not always move along a straightforward path. There are fluctuations—even temporary regressions—as children muster their energy and resources for a leap forward. A toddler who's beginning to assert his autonomy may also insist on being carried; a preschooler who leads other children in play reveals her vulnerability when she cuddles with her stuffed animals at bedtime.

For some children, development is more pronounced in one area than another. One four-year-old is gifted physically but is still learning how to play with others, while his contemporary is socially mature but not ready to write his name.

Our goal in this chapter is to look at many facets of preschoolers—their play, struggle for independence, social and moral life, sexual and sex-role development, and view of death. We hope to illuminate the preschool years in all of their complexity and richness, with an understanding of the ways in which children are like us and yet very different from us.

Play and Learning

Q *What do children get out of play?*

Given its all-consuming and pervasive nature, it is not surprising that play makes major contributions to growth and development during the preschool years.

1. *Play fosters a positive self-concept.* For young children, there is no greater satisfaction and pleasure than that achieved through play. Play is the great confidence builder; the players are free to do things their way according to their wishes and views. There are no rules to follow, no right or wrong, no pressure to succeed. Where else can children take risks without fear of failure, and in so doing, stretch their capacities?

Examples are everywhere: a baby bats at her crib mobile and makes it move, or a toddler holds a block out so his mother will drop it in the bucket and hence begins a game. A preschooler constructs a barn for farm animals and coordinates this with her best friend, who is building the house for the family. In play, children derive a sense of "I can do" and "I can make things happen" and end up feeling good about themselves and their competence.

There is evidence that play contributes directly to children's emotional well-being. Studies show that children who enjoy playing more seem to be happier, even when not playing, than those who don't play much. Furthermore, children who are good players usually are liked and have friends, which also contributes to a positive sense of self.

2. *Play promotes language development.* From studying mother-infant pairs playing peek-a-boo, psychologist Jerome Bruner and his colleagues have identified a complex rule structure underlying the game. The hider goes through a certain sequence of actions, and at appropriate moments, the seeker responds. In this simple game, the foundation is being laid for conversational exchanges: "You say this; then it's my turn to say that." Children are learning turn-taking and cooperation, essential for communication.

In pretend play with their young children, parents teach them how to use language to connect actions. For instance, a two-year-old who puts a blanket on the doll might say, "Blanket on," but then the adult is likely to say, "The baby's tired." The parent is enriching the theme of the play and providing an explanation for the child's actions.

Language itself becomes a wonderful tool in play. Infants spend hours repeating the sounds they hear around them. Toddlers love to practice grammatical structures: "big bear, big door, big man . . ." Older children like to play with the meanings of words: a three-year-old points to her head and says, "Belly;" her playmate giggles and points to his foot, "Arm." One British researcher reports that during play, children talk in more complex ways than during other conversations. Their utterances are longer; they use more adjectives and adverbs. Why does this happen during play? Probably because play gives children the freedom to test the limits of their skills, thereby gradually extending the boundaries.

3. *Play stimulates thinking and problem-solving.*

> *A toddler pushes an empty cardboard box across the floor. When he gets to the wall, he turns around and begins to pull it behind him.*

> *Two children stand in the wading pool, dropping rocks, pieces of wood, and paper in the water.*

> *Bailey announces, "We're selling juice." He asks Bobby if he wants to buy some. Bobby wants three bottles and Bailey picks up three blocks, counting, "One, two, three." Bobby takes the blocks over to other children and tells them it will cost $20. They pretend to pay. When Bobby returns to Bailey and Philip with the good news that he has sold the juice, Philip explains, "We're not selling things. Get the juice back. We're only letting people borrow things."*

In the space of a few minutes, a lot happens in play. All of these children are figuring out concepts, trying to understand relationships and how things work. The toddler is learning about cause and effect—what happens when I push and pull this object? He's also learning about himself and the strength of his body. The children in the wading pool are having an elementary science lesson—experimenting with sinking and floating. Bailey and Philip are thinking about money and counting, buying and borrowing. Play involves mental activity as young children work out their ideas, hypotheses, and questions.

Pretend play has a unique role in children's intellectual development. It is thinking at a symbolic level: the child uses one thing to represent another and re-creates experience. A two-year-old pretends to drink hot chocolate out of a seashell; a three-year-old pushes a block along the floor and makes car sounds. A four-year-old transforms a spoon into a telephone and becomes a telephone repairman. The pinnacle of pretend play is when children coordinate their symbols into what the psychologist Greta Fein calls "collective symbolization": For example, one class of four- and five-year-olds agreed to build a restaurant out of blocks, discussed where the kitchen and tables went, assigned roles of chef, waiters, and cashier. With their teacher's help, they cooked a meal, wrote up a menu, and printed paper money.

In pretend play, children acquire an understanding of how symbols work and a facility for manipulating them. This activity is preparation for other kinds of symbol use. In school, the child will be required to use the symbol systems of our culture—the words and numbers—necessary for our lives. So pretend play is an important transition toward more abstract thought and academic tasks.

Play promotes positive attitudes toward problem-solving. A group of researchers presented preschoolers with the materials to solve a problem: retrieving a piece of chalk from a box that was out of reach. The children who played with the materials in advance were no better at solving the task than the nonplayers, but they were more goal-directed, more persistent, and used more effective strategies in the situation. In the words of one of the researchers, "They were happier problem-solvers."

4. *Play enables children to understand the world.* It is by playing that children assimilate and make sense of their experience. After a trip to the aquarium, a four-year-old, taking on the role of a deep-sea diver, fashions an oxygen tank out of cardboard tubes and a rubber hose. The father of a five-year-old describes how his son invents his own world as a way of understanding the real one.

■ ■ ■ *Todd has made up a place called Fix-It-Shop Land with a Fix-It-Shop language (which he is teaching us) and fully detailed customs, laws, schools, houses, factories, and even a fish store.*

In the Fix-It Shop, he creates world-saving inventions, such as an electronic monitor that halts all traffic whenever someone steps into the street.

These play episodes exemplify what educator Barbara Biber calls "learning about the world by playing about it." By building houses, pizza parlors, and roads and by becoming zookeepers and farmers, children bring the real world closer and make it comprehensible.

5. *Play is a forum for children to express and resolve their feelings.* In play, children express their wishes, concerns, and fears. From the Freudian perspective, this is the primary purpose of play. Within the safe realm of make-believe, children gain control and mastery over scary and powerful feelings that they cannot put into words.

Sometimes, children "play out" their feelings around traumatic events like a death in the family, but more often they enact ordinary concerns. Claire's mother describes how her three-year-old uses play to cope with her fear of having her hair washed:

- - - *Claire pretends to wash her doll's hair. When the baby gets soap in her eyes, Claire not so gently wipes it away and scolds, "Now that's not so bad. It's just baby shampoo." Then she consoles, "Now baby, don't cry. Just one more rinse." At the end, she rewards the good baby: "Here's a little candy, crunch, crunch."*

In this scene, Claire reverses roles and becomes the mother. She is a kind mother who comforts her unhappy baby, even rewards her. This is rehearsal for the hair-washing ritual Claire herself faces later that night.

Yet play is more than a catharsis for frustrations and negative feelings. Pleasant experiences and positive emotions are reenacted. A three-year-old pretends to read stories to her doll, and a five-year-old re-creates an excursion with her stuffed animals: "I'll take you to the zoo so you can see the elephant and give him peanuts."

In play, children express the psychological conflicts characteristic of their developmental period. Two- and three-year-olds typically enact family scenes in which they act out their feelings about separation and their ambivalence about staying a baby and growing up. At four and five, children enact scenes from the wider world of the community. Sometimes their heroes are real-life people—firemen, brides and grooms—and sometimes they are fantastic creatures with superpowers. Among the predominant themes at this stage in development are the control of aggression, Oedipal fantasies, and the acquisition of sex roles. It is not surprising that child development experts consider play vital to a child's emotional development.

6. *Play enhances creativity.* Most adults are enthralled by the unencumbered imagination of young children's play, and the association between play and creativity has been of great interest to researchers. Professor Brian Sutton-Smith, a noted authority on play, describes play as "variation-seeking," that is, looking for the novel in the familiar. Research shows that if children are allowed to play with objects, they will come up with a variety of new uses for them. Thus, one way play contributes to creativity is by establishing a playful, flexible orientation. But play does more than foster creativity in the individual; it helps society evolve. As Sutton-Smith says, it is in the context of "toying" with new ideas and thinking of "what ifs" that cultural change becomes possible.

Not surprisingly, the child-rearing environment influences the play and creativity of young children. One study found that mothers who had more flexible attitudes and were more supportive of their children's play provided more toys in the home and raised more creative children.

What happens to the rich, imaginative play of the preschool period? Most observers note that it seems to disappear as the children get older and become involved in structured games and sports. It is more likely, however, that instead of disappearing, children's fantasy becomes internalized. What the young child acts out, the older child and adult play out in their mind. For example, most of us find it useful, even necessary, to rehearse a job interview, a first date, a financial deal.

7. *Play develops social skills and social thinking.* Fantasy play allows children to begin to identify and try on the varied and sometimes confusing roles in our society. For the youngest child, the first roles are those of child and adult. There are certain behaviors, styles of talking and dressing that typify "mommies, daddies, and kids." There are other adult roles that the child tries to understand: the doctor, sales clerk, and child-care provider. From stories and TV come make-believe roles of supernatural heroes, kings and queens, and adventurers.

Together, children try out role relationships:

> *Greg says to Robbie, "Let's pretend this is a house for a superlion." Robbie pretends to be a lion and Greg walks him. He gives Robbie food and water and tells him, "Don't growl because the hunters are after us." When Robbie begins to move off in a different direction, Greg pretends to yank his chain—hard.*

Greg and Robbie are learning through play what it is like for one to be dominant and the other submissive. This is an easier, more enjoyable way to learn than if they confront one another outside of play. Because it is play, it is nonthreatening ("it's only pretend") and either player can call it off when he has had enough.

As children begin to engage in pretend play with others, a range of social behaviors emerge. Sharing, helping, and cooperating are necessary for children to coordinate their roles and agree on the theme: "Let's pretend this is the train and we're going on a trip to Disneyland. You drive the train and I'll collect the tickets."

Sometimes there are conflicts when children do not want to play their assigned roles or disagree about how the play should proceed, as one researcher observed in this episode between two young children:

> *Father:* So long, I'll see ya later. It's time to go to work.
> *Mother:* Hey, wait for me. I gotta go to work, too!
> *Father:* Hey, my mom don't work . . . you stay here.
> *Mother:* Well, my mom works . . . lotsa women work you
> know. My mom is a perfessor at the unibersity.
> *Father:* Okay then, just hurry, so we won't be late. Are you
> sure you wanna work?

The child playing father ends up accommodating to the notion that some mothers have jobs and has broadened his knowledge of the social world. Likewise, the child playing mother has learned that not all mothers are like her own; some stay home. In Piaget's terms, this is an example of how play breaks down the child's egocentric perspective. Research shows that after being tutored in fantasy play, preschoolers were more able to take the perspective of others.

Play is essential to every aspect of a child's well-being—emotional, intellectual, physical, and social. In fact, play is so characteristic of children that when children do not play, it is cause for concern. The absence of play may result from temporary distress brought on by fatigue, illness, or a change in circumstances such as moving to a new home or school. But sometimes a child's inability to play signals a more serious long-term disturbance in development. Then professional intervention is usually necessary.

Play seems to come naturally to young children, as if they were born knowing how to play. In fact, the capacity to play seems inherent in the human species, but it takes a supportive environment to bring out its potential. There are many ways that parents can support a young child's impulse to play.

SOLUTIONS

Creating the Atmosphere for Play

Set a relaxed, pleasant tone so that children can play to their fullest. If children worry about getting their clothes dirty, making too much noise, or breaking something, their play will be inhibited and less creative. Some limits are necessary, but choose those that really matter to you.

Providing the Space and Props

Set aside a play area—a portion of a room is sufficient—where a child is free to play with toys and act out fantasies. If an area is crowded with "don't touch" items, play will be stifled or ultimately disruptive. One parent who lives in a small apartment let her daughter convert the bottom shelf of a closet into a doll hospital; she also takes her daughter into a quiet corridor of the building to play a bowling game.

Sometimes play requires privacy. Creativity and imagination seem to flourish where children (and adults) are free to arrange their playthings, to move about, to experiment without being interrupted by others or watched and made to feel self-conscious. A tent can be made under a table or behind a sofa. A packing box can become an office. Have toys and materials around that children can use creatively and symbolically. If you are not sure what is appropriate, *Mister Rogers' Playbook* is a rich source of excellent ideas.

Valuing Play in Your Children's Lives

Recognize the contributions that play makes to your child's development. Take time to step back and observe your child's activity. You may be amazed at the ideas and imagination expressed in play. You may also be amazed at the energy and persistence of your child when involved in play. A mother of a four-year-old says:

• • • *I always thought he had a short attention span until I watched him one day as he was building a zoo. It went on for over thirty minutes. The difference is that he was doing something he wanted to be doing, not something I wanted him to be doing.*

Think twice before you say things like "Stop playing with your food." Instead say: "It's time to eat your food. The peas belong on the plate." Try to think of play in positive terms.

Valuing Play in Your Own Life

If you can tap your own playfulness, imaginative capacities, and childhood pleasures, you will be a better partner in play with your children. Dorothy and Jerome Singer, well-known authorities on play as well as television, suggest the following for parents:

- Reminisce: recall your childhood. Memories of favorite books, records, playmates, activities, hiding places will begin to come back. This will increase your sensitivity to a child's way of thinking and experiencing and may give you some ideas for playing with your own children.
- Keep a dream log: write down as much as you can remember of your dreams when you awaken. You will become more aware of emotions or motives in your own life, and in turn, be more sensitive to the kinds of material your children enjoy in stories and fantasy play. In addition, you will see that it is sometimes difficult to separate reality and fantasy, appreciating how hard it may be for a young child to make that distinction.
- Use your daydreams: they carry us far afield, suggesting some of our wishes and hopes. Share them with your children—on a rainy day, think of a summer beach vacation and your children can pretend to pack the picnic basket, find seashells, etc. Let your fantasies help you find creative solutions to problems and open up new ways of seeing things.

Providing Real-World Experiences

Your children's play, especially fantasy play, will be enriched by a variety of real-life experiences. Events that seem ordinary to us—going to the gas station, preparing a meal, detouring around street repairs—hold endless fascination for young children. Include them and talk about what is happening: "The water pipe is broken and the machine is pumping out the extra water." Develop their observational skills: "Why do you think that repairman has a flashlight on his helmet?"

By the time most children are five, they like to represent their experiences with words and numbers. If your child wants to write a story about going to the laundromat, encourage him. At first he may dictate the story to you, but if he wants to try writing it himself, let him.

What's My Role in My Child's Play?

How can you best promote your child's play? *Participate!*

- Model good play. Young children learn to play, in part by watching others play. You can pretend to set the table or roll out a piece of play dough in the shape of a snake or pancake.
- Join in. This is where your own imagination and playfulness can be expressed. But remember that play is the child's creation. So don't take over or dominate the child's imaginative ventures.

- Supervise. Sometimes it is more appropriate for you to just observe or provide props.

Exactly how to participate depends on several factors:

Your Child's Individual Style.   Some children like to be actors and take on various roles; others get more involved in creating a mini-scene and manipulating toys and figures; still others prefer to make designs with materials. With the child who likes to act you will probably be expected to take on a role; with the child who likes to construct scenes or build designs, you will do more of that.

Your Own Style.   Some parents simply follow the child's lead and use their joint play as a time for relaxed, low-keyed interaction. Others take on more of a teaching role, posing questions or introducing new ideas.

Studies have found that there are often differences in the way fathers and mothers play. Fathers are more likely to engage in rough and tumble play than mothers. One parent describes this as "a lot of yelling, giggling, and running around screaming." Some studies of animal and human behavior suggest that rough and tumble play teaches the difference between physical contact that is playful and that meant to hurt. During this kind of play, children learn how to control their aggression when in intimate contact with others.

If you and your spouse play differently with your children (whether or not you fit the above stereotypes), that's fine. Diversity stretches children's capacities. Remember, though, it is important to remain the adult and not let the rough and tumble play turn into a contest between you and your child.

If your child asks you to join in and you don't particularly like the kind of play that's going on, it's all right to say you don't want to play now, but then try to participate another time when the play is more suited to your style.

The Child's Age.   Infants often need adults to initiate and maintain their social play, such as in peek-a-boo. Toddlers can start on their own, but may need your participation to keep the play challenging. With pre-schoolers, the adult is often less of an active participant, but can interject comments or suggestions that stimulate richer play.

Pretending with Toddlers

Twos and threes love to imitate burping a baby, talking on the phone, driving a car, and other everyday activities. We are usually delighted when they imitate us, putting on our shoes and clomping around or reading the comics (upside down). This kind of imitation needs little encouragement; just doing what you usually do is inspiration enough.

How can you actively encourage your toddler's pretend play? A good way is to do it yourself—pick up a doll, start feeding it, and say, "Oh, she loves this spaghetti." Your activity will capture the child's attention much more than questions such as "What do you want to play with now?" or "What shall we do now?"

Pretending with Older Preschoolers

Fours and fives are interested in the worlds of real and imaginary heroes. Play experts Marilyn Segal and Don Adcock describe how Terry's father extends his son's thinking as they play firemen:

> *Driving to an imaginary fire, they strapped pillows on their backs for oxygen tanks and began to crawl around the living room on their stomachs . . .*
>
> Father: I think I'm trapped in the fire.
> Terry: No, you're not trapped in the fire. The people are
>   trapped in the fire.
> Father: Should we try to rescue them?
> Terry: I'm crawling in the fire.
> Father: What are you going to do?
> Terry: Put them in the ambulance. I'm taking them to the
>   hospital.
> Father: What will we do next?
> Terry: Well, we have to get the dog out and the mommy
>   and the daddy . . .
> Father: We have the fire out.
> Terry: Now we have to put the ladder back.

By making statements or asking questions about the play, Terry's father guided the conversation through various aspects of putting out a fire. Sometimes a question encouraged Terry to describe what he was doing; sometimes it opened up a new direction for the play. The comments of Terry's father followed naturally from his son's actions and allowed Terry to determine the course of the play.

Some adults end up controlling children's play. They offer too many directives: "Build the block tower this way," "No, that's not the right way to draw a person." Remember that in order for children to learn from play, *they* must be in charge and experience a sense of competence and efficacy. Playing with young children should never be a contest of wills or a competition to see who can build the best building. The best strategy is to play *with* your child, enjoy being together, marvel at his or her abilities and imagination, and engage your own playfulness.

Don't Take Pretend Play Literally

Remember that children's fantasy is just that—it is not an exact replication of reality. It provides an opportunity for children to represent reality the way they want, to express inner feelings, to be in charge. Don't impose adult logic on pretense; rather, go along with the fantasy. Children usually know that it is only pretend. Instead of saying, "Oh, no, horses don't eat Egg McMuffins for breakfast. They eat hay and grass," try joining in: "Your horse is really hungry. Does it like ketchup on its food?"

Maintaining the Reality-Fantasy Distinction

Sometimes when parents take on pretend roles, children lose sight of what's reality and what's fantasy. Is their mother, now the storekeeper, still their mother? Reassure your two- or three-year-old that you are still the mother and that you are only pretending. And if your child still looks confused, save the role playing until your child is older.

When adults take on scary roles in play, children often become frightened and the play ends. If your child suggests scary play, it's better to let him or her be the monster and you be the victim. As the adult, stick to more benign roles and let your child's playmates, who are his equals in size and power, have the scary roles.

Q *What kinds of toys stimulate play?*

Playthings are an important part of the environment. As a parent you will want to make wise selections. Ask these questions when choosing toys:

- Is it safe? Obviously, you will avoid toys that your infant might swallow or whose sharp edges might cut your preschooler. Look for hidden hazards—lead paint, wires, etc. The Consumer Product Safety Commission publishes safety guidelines.
- Does the toy suit the child's interests? Would a set of construction blocks or a stuffed animal be appreciated? Some parents remember their own favorite dollhouse or electric train and conclude that their child would automatically love one, too. Ask yourself, "Is this what my child would really like or am I really wanting it for myself?" Remember that manufacturers' suggested age ranges are simply that.
- Does the toy challenge without frustrating? A toddler with chubby fingers will not be able to do a puzzle with many tiny pieces. Of course, children like novelty, so toys that can be played with in new ways are appealing.

- Does the toy have more than one use? Unstructured materials, like paints, blocks, and dolls, can be used in many different ways. But the latest electronic gimmicks have limited play potential and often end up in the closet.
- Is the toy well made? Will it last and not break? Since toys are among the first objects children claim as their own, toys should feel, look, and sound good.
- Will the toy have long-term interest? The most valued playthings grow with the child. A set of blocks will be used one way by a two-year-old, and other ways at ages four and six.
- Does the toy perpetuate sexist or ethnic stereotypes?
- Does the toy stimulate aggression and violence? Interactive war toys can lead to very hostile play.
- Does the toy allow the child to participate? The best toys elicit active participation. Toys that a child can only watch passively are quickly forgotten. Responsive toys teach children that their behavior can influence their environment.

Parents wonder what kinds of toys really stimulate a child's imagination. The answer depends on your child's interests; if she likes dramatic role-playing, then cast-off clothes might be just the thing; if he prefers music, then a small guitar is better. Unstructured materials such as clay, paints, and blocks allow children to do with them as they will. On the other hand, a coloring book limits their responses.

How realistic should toys be to encourage imaginative play? Research indicates that young children under the age of three or so need concrete reminders of the real thing. A toy bus that looks like a real bus helps the young child recognize that this is a bus and can be used in a buslike way. As children get older, their imagination will be stimulated by unstructured and less realistic-looking playthings. Fours and fives can impose their imagination on an object and turn a roasting pan into a bus, a cradle, or a shovel.

It helps to have toys and materials arranged so they are accessible and easy to clean up. Toy chests can be problematic if they have heavy lids that children cannot open. They also promote clutter if things are piled inside helter-skelter. Shelves and open boxes, plastic bins, or stacking trays are preferable. Organize the materials logically—for example, place the blocks and their accessories (the farm animals, the trucks) together. Having some order or system to the toys will help the child take responsibility for picking them up. It will also teach the child to categorize—these are "drawing"-type things.

If you spend a lot of time in one room, keep some toys there. For instance, one mother put a toy telephone in the kitchen so that when she was on the phone, her son would be able to play nearby. She also reserved a bottom shelf for his "cooking" utensils—wooden spoons, plastic bowls, empty milk cartons. This way he was having fun but not underfoot when she was preparing meals.

It's a good idea to put some toys away periodically when the space gets too cluttered. In fact, young children get overwhelmed with too many toys and play better when fewer are available. Always keep out the favorites, but then you can surprise your child with some items he or she hasn't seen in a while.

How do you keep the preschooler's toys out of reach of a younger sibling? One way is to let older preschoolers keep a few of their favorite things on a high shelf or in an airline tote bag or a small suitcase that they can keep closed or carry into another room.

Parents and teachers have long noted children's interest in war toys. The impulse to be associated with symbols of power and strength is strong in preschoolers. If children are very attracted to commercial war toys, set limits on what you will buy. Encourage them to use their imagination and make their own toys and props instead. However, even if commercial toys are banned from the home or classroom, children still use their fingers or sticks as weapons. One four-year-old liked to bite his graham cracker into the shape of a gun. It is virtually impossible to prohibit all expressions of war play, but peace educators Nancy Carlsson-Paige and Diane Levin suggest it is important to help children move beyond a violent focus. You can ask, "How does this warship work?" "What would happen if this gun shot glue instead of bullets?" This way you are respecting their interests but redirecting them. Of course, limits on play that guarantee children's safety and security are sometimes necessary: "No shooting at other people."

Q *Would it be better if my child played less and learned letters and numbers?*

... *I read in magazines about these superbabies who can read at age three. I get ads in the mail for some of these teaching materials. Is that what little children should be doing?*

... *The family down the street has enrolled their son in a prekindergarten program that promises to prepare the children for school. He comes home with ditto sheets. My daughter, who goes to nursery school, just brings home paintings. Should I switch her to the other program?*

... *My husband says that our three-year-old has already had time to play. He wants us to begin "teaching" her.*

Many parents feel pressured to groom their children for academic success. All parents want their children to do well later on, but what is the best way to go about it?

For preschoolers, time spent in play is the best answer. During early childhood, play in the home and school is the fastest, surest route to learning, self-confidence, and mastery of skills. As children play with cups and spoons in the sandbox, they are forming concepts of full and empty, more and less, essential to an understanding of numbers. Arguing over who has built the longest road, two preschoolers puzzle over how they can find the answer—ask the teacher or a friend, measure? A class of five-year-olds visits the neighborhood grocery store and they have many questions: How do the meat and fruit get to the store? How do you know how much to pay? Does the cashier keep the money? Back in the classroom, the children create their own store and take on the roles of shopkeepers, suppliers, and customers. Their play teaches them about systems of transportation, money, and ownership.

Playing Is Preparation for Academics

Many preschoolers do learn numbers or letters; what's important is how they learn. Consider these different ways of learning about the number 4.

In one preschool, children trace the number 4 on ditto sheets. They cut out and paste numbers in order on a large sheet: 1, 2, 3, 4. They color in four pumpkins, four fish, four shoes. If they have free time, a few can play with a number puzzle. Next week the school will use the same approach for the number 5.

In another preschool, children count how many steps out to the playground, how many buttons on their shirts. They talk about the number 4: "I'm four years old"; "we get Channel 4 on TV"; "I have two red and two blue trucks . . . hey, that makes four!" Some children build a tower four blocks high; others set places for four dolls in the housekeeping corner.

In the first setting, the children learn about "fourness" by using paper and pencil, by being told by the teacher what four is. In the second situation, children learn the concept of four through a variety of hands-on activities. The teacher's goal is to provide many experiences with numbers as the foundation to reading and writing them later on. Eventually, children begin to make a transition from experience-based learning to more abstract tasks in the elementary school years.

Research supports the second approach to learning. The consensus is that early childhood programs that address all the needs of the child—social, emotional, intellectual, and physical—promote development best (see the section on early childhood programs, pages 410–422). In particular, programs which allow children to play facilitate growth. In a study by Dina Feitelson of Haifa University, Israeli preschoolers were either tutored to use the reading worksheets recommended by the Department of Early Education or given puzzles, mosaics, and blocks to play with. The children who were allowed to play made fewer mistakes on a prereading task than those given the formal exercises. Furthermore, the children in the worksheet group were more dissatisfied with their work and agreed to persevere only if they could play with the toys later on. The researcher concludes "that certain types of play may well be more effective in developing prereading skills than the paper and pencil tasks so often used for this purpose."

When a preschooler comes home with worksheets, how does he or she feel if the answers are incorrect? Is he learning that others know the answer and he doesn't? Does she doubt her ability to learn and do well? Such concerns do not plague the child who is free to paint, build, or dictate stories.

Play Is Learning

The father who felt his child had had enough oportunity to play and now should be learning was making a conceptually misleading distinction between play and learning.

Children are constantly learning, and in myriad ways. Fascinated by the world around them, they observe and listen, they touch and smell things, they absorb ideas and knowledge wherever they go. Adults are important teachers, passing on information and values. For preschoolers, the world is new and enticing; they want to understand how the world works and how they are to interact with it. For them, learning means more than skill with letters and numbers or the intake of facts.

Play—which is what children choose to do, not what they are asked to do—is a realm in which anything is possible, in which a box can be a box and a boat at the same time. In play, children are in control and are free to synthesize, test, and express experience, the same repertoire of skills that we as adults use when we are truly engaged in our work.

Play also provides children with the skills they need as future learners. In play, children learn how to learn. Bruno Bettelheim, noted child psychologist, explains:

> [Play] teaches [the child] without his being aware of it the habits most needed for [intellectual] growth, such as stick-to-itiveness, which is so important in all learning . . . It is through play that a child begins to realize that he need not give up in despair if a block doesn't balance neatly on another block the first time around. Fascinated by the challenge of building a tower, he gradually learns that even if he doesn't succeed immediately, success can be his if he perseveres.

What Is Reading Readiness?

The best reading readiness consists of giving children experiences in the real world, materials to play out those experiences, and discussions that help them understand these experiences. What is essential is providing a language-rich environment through conversation and reading aloud. For parents who wonder about teaching phonics to their three-year-olds, a far more effective approach is to continue exposing children to books and storytelling and discussing the stories. Twos and threes often enjoy "telling stories" as they turn the pages of a book. As they recall the plot and recount the details, they are learning about the basic format of a story. Parents can help by asking, "What happened next?" All this will provide the basis for understanding that the squiggles (words) on the page convey meaning, a prerequisite for learning to read.

Children will let you know when they are interested in letters and sounds. Most fours and fives are eager to recognize certain words—their own names, the name of their school or their favorite cereal. They express curiosity—"What letter is that?" "What does that word say?" Informal teaching—"That's an A. Can you find an A in your name?"—is better than rote memorization of the alphabet. Two studies of children who could read prior to school entry report that drilling by parents did not promote reading skill. More important was the parents' responsiveness to their children's requests for help with or information about reading.

The Dangers of Pushing Your Child

David Elkind, author of *The Hurried Child* and *Miseducation,* worries about the child who has not experienced the richness of childhood. Children who are denied play and taught academics before they are ready fall into this group. They can often count and recite the alphabet but lack the conceptual understanding of what numbers and letters signify. Some children who have been forced to read at an early age may show an initial advantage, but those who've had a rich, varied language experience not only catch up but generally become better readers. If children start off as eager, spontaneous readers, reading is more likely to remain a lifelong pursuit.

When children are not allowed to play and learn in a way suited to their level of development, they risk becoming turned off to school. They see school as a place where they don't belong and can end up feeling like school failures.

What Kinds of Home Environment Make a Difference?

Early childhood educators recognize that parents are the most influential teachers their children will ever have. Parents teach by listening, responding, and elaborating on what their children already know. This style of parent-child interaction promotes curiosity, problem-solving, concept building, and positive self-esteem.

After studying the development of talent in famous artists, scientists, and athletes, Benjamin Bloom from the University of Chicago concludes that the origins of talent were more in the child-rearing practices and the strong interest the parents took in their child than in the child's precocity. For example, parents, older siblings, and relatives gave "informal lessons" whenever the child showed an interest or when the family was involved in an activity.

Good early childhood programs and parent education programs reinforce this role for the parent. One such project is Parents as First Teachers, initiated in 1981 by the state of Missouri in four school districts and now spread throughout the state. The goal is not to create superbabies, but to help parents be effective and responsive by providing informal lessons during the child's first three years. The participating parents and schools are enthusiastic about this method. The children in the program have scored higher on measures of language and intellectual functioning than the control group.

What Is Intelligence?

Intelligence has many manifestations. Howard Gardner from Harvard, who has done extensive research on intellectual development, dismisses the notion of a single, unifying intelligence that we each possess in a greater or lesser amount (as exemplified in an IQ score). He suggests that we are all born with the potential to develop multiple intelligences: verbal, mathematical, kinesthetic, spatial, musical, interpersonal, and self-reflective. Starting in early childhood, we need to find ways to support the development of all these capacities. Preschool programs that offer a variety of activities and play opportunities are most likely to stimulate children's multiple intelligences.

Are Educational Toys a Must?

The only reason educational toys are called educational is that the manufacturer has labeled them as such. Any object that is fun and challenging is educational, including a flashlight, a doll, or paints. So-called educational toys are useful as long as the child is not expected to learn only what they are designed to teach but can play with them as he or she chooses.

In their eloquent book *The Gift of Play,* Maria Piers and Genevieve Landau remind us of the lifelong learning we owe to play:

> *Later lessons acquired in school are often forgotten, but the things we learn at play—hard but playfully won—we never*

forget. All of us recognize that one never really forgets how to ride a bike, say, or throw a ball or any other self-taught, practiced-and-practiced skill, even though the skill may go unused for years. So, too, we never forget the delicious softness of our favorite pillow or the painful bump on the head we got when we crawled under the table. Not that we recall such things consciously, but we have learned for all time about hard tables and soft pillows, and we take their nature for granted on the basis of that early learning.

Q *My child starts something and says, "I can't do it. You do it." What should I do?*

Your four-year-old has just picked up a puzzle, but after trying to fit in a few pieces, has given up. He wants you to finish it. It's important to ask yourself: "What's behind his giving up?"

- If he's too tired and needs a less demanding activity, acknowledge his fatigue, tell him he can come back to the puzzle another time, and suggest an alternate activity.
- If he's trying to engage you when you're doing something else, decide just how busy you are. If you can't join him right away, suggest, "You do half the puzzle—fill in the top part of the tree and then I'll do the rest."
- If this is a new puzzle and he really doesn't know how to do it, use this as a teaching opportunity.

When your goal is to teach problem-solving skills, here are some approaches:

> *This puzzle is new and a little hard. Let's look at the picture. Here's the giraffe's head, his body, and legs. The head is at the top; let's start there.*

You can point out how the shapes provide clues:

> *This piece has a jagged edge. Feel where it sticks out? It fits with another jagged piece on the board. Rub your finger there. Try the puzzle piece in that spot. See how the two edges go together?*

Direct your efforts toward helping him learn to do it for himself. He will feel a sense of mastery only when *he* does it, not when *you* do it. Sometimes it's fun to do a puzzle or game together: "You put in one piece, then I'll do the next." This teaches the skill of cooperation.

Of course, you'll need to assess whether a puzzle or game is appropriate for your child's level of development. Materials that are too simple will be boring, those that are too challenging will be frustrating. But if your three-year-old wants to play with a hundred-piece puzzle that's suited for a five-year-old, let her use it her way—maybe to sort the pieces by color. If she completes part of the puzzle and then loses interest, that's fine.

Sometimes children want you to do something because they're dissatisfied with their own ability and think you can do it better. The mother of Laney, age five, encounters this dilemma frequently:

■ ■ ■ *My daughter begins to draw a picture, then drops her crayon and implores me or my husband, "Will you draw a house . . . a person . . . a dog? I like the way you do it."*

Laney is at the age where she wants her drawing to look like the real thing —a picture of a dog should be doglike. Younger children don't care: they draw to express themselves and their version of reality and to experiment with the medium. But Laney wants to demonstrate her accurate grasp of reality and is frustrated because her skills aren't there yet.

Laney's parents do what many parents in this situation do. They encourage her to draw any way she wants. They suggest she look at their dog or a picture and ask, "What do you see?" "Does he have a long nose or a short nose?" They praise her efforts.

This gentle encouragement sometimes works and sometimes doesn't. When Laney refuses to try and insists that her parents draw for her, they refuse. Her mother says:

■ ■ ■ *It's okay with me if she doesn't draw at this moment. I'm not going to do it for her. I suggest she find something else to do.*

Laney's parents are right not to do it for her. The danger of taking over is that your child will become even more dissatisfied with her own efforts. Then, you will be setting up a cycle where you, not your child, are responsible for solving problems. Children need to learn that they can take risks and make mistakes if they are going to face all the new learning that lies ahead.

The father of a three-year-old finds that his child also wants him to draw, but the motivation is different than Laney's:

> ... *I've discovered that what he really wants is companionship. It's enough that I just sit next to him and hold a paintbrush in my hand. I'll make a few absentminded dabs on my own paper and that's it.*

Coloring books and prepackaged materials often suggest to children that there is a right way to draw and that neatness is paramount. Most preschoolers lack the muscular coordination to stay within the lines; furthermore, they have no motivation to make a picture "pretty" or even to finish it. As parents you need to reassure your child that however he or she draws, builds, or molds clay is fine. The task is to find a way of encouraging—even helping—without taking over.

Q *How can we make the most of TV viewing?*

Almost all preschoolers grow up with a television; indeed, many have several sets in their home. On average, preschoolers watch over three hours a day—slightly more than either elementary school children or adolescents. As has been said for years, the TV has replaced the hearth at the center of the family.

The Gains   What is the scorecard on TV? According to parents and research, here are some of the positive aspects:

TV Promotes Prosocial Behavior

> ... *I overheard my son and his friend saying, "Cooperate. That's what we're supposed to do." They got that right from Sesame Street.*

> ... *My children are safety conscious from watching some of the action shows. In the car, Barbara will tell me, "Daddy, you're going too fast. Are you going the speed limit?" Or the younger one will remind me that my door is unlocked.*

The educational programs that emphasize prosocial themes, such as affection, consideration, sharing, expressing feelings, and control of aggression, seem to get their messages across. Researchers have shown a 10- to 15-minute prosocial film from *Mister Rogers' Neighborhood* to a group of young children. Afterward, the children improved in task persistence, self-control, and tolerance of delay in comparison to children who viewed either anti-social or neutral films. After watching educational TV, children in another study increased their social contacts with playmates and adults in nursery school and their giving of positive reinforcement.

TV Stimulates the Imagination

What parent or teacher hasn't seen a child pretending and wondered where she got that idea? Often, it comes from TV:

> ▪ ▪ ▪ *Betsy was pretending to be a dolphin. I was amazed. My husband and I had a science special on TV several Sundays ago. I didn't think Betsy was paying much attention, but obviously she was.*

Many TV characters and events appear in children's play: superheroes, Oscar the Grouch, even the weatherman. TV characters are especially attractive because the medium can capture their action in vivid, concrete terms. Psychologists Dorothy and Jerome Singer, co-directors of the Yale University Family Television Research and Consultation Center, have found that situation comedies stimulate more imaginative play than action-adventure shows, which elicit more aggression. The imaginative potential of educational TV is also more effective with children who are initially low in imagination.

The Singers have also found that when an adult discusses the fantasy parts of an educational show, the children's play becomes more imaginative than if they watch it alone.

TV Teaches Letters and Numbers

> ▪ ▪ ▪ *As Marie takes her bath, she loves to sing the ABC song. Although we speak Spanish at home, she's learned it in English from Sesame Street.*

In one study, children of both sexes and all socioeconomic levels gained in letter and number recognition by watching *Sesame Street*. Remember, however, that even when children can count or recognize numbers from one to twenty, they still may not understand what the numbers actually mean. Learning by direct experience is still the most effective method.

TV Expands Concepts and Prereading Skills

> ▪ ▪ ▪ *My children love animal shows. The other night they saw a special on chimps and how they raise their young. Now they like to be chimps and pretend to "fish" for termites with sticks.*

They also have a lot of questions about how animals learn to do things.

TV (particularly the science and nature shows) introduces preschoolers to new ideas. Children quickly learn to recognize the titles of shows and the words in familiar labels from commercials. They may not recognize these words out of context (i.e., off the TV screen), nevertheless, they are beginning to sight read. Some psychologists assert that children learn to sit still and increase their attention span in front of the TV. However, excessive watching may also limit opportunities to learn from real experience and play.

The Minuses On the other side, there are major criticisms.

TV Promotes Aggression

Children's programs are far more violent than adult fare. According to George Gerbner of the Annenberg School of Communications, prime-time shows over the past twenty years have averaged 6 to 8 violent acts per hour, whereas children's daytime weekend programs (primarily cartoons), averaged 20 to 25 violent acts per hour. Some parents believe that viewing aggression breeds aggression, and they cite examples of how their children enact scenes from superhero shows or police shows. Other parents think that TV provides a catharsis, allowing children to express their aggression vicariously and get it out of their system.

The evidence favors the first interpretation. Many laboratory studies indicate that even after viewing a brief episode of TV violence, children act in more aggressive or hurtful ways. Several studies find a direct connection between children's viewing habits at home and aggressive behavior. In one of the most ambitious studies of preschoolers' viewing habits, the Singers asked 150 families to keep TV logs over a one-year period. The children's spontaneous play and aggression in nursery school were observed regularly. The heavy viewers, especially those who watched action adventures or cartoons, were more aggressive and less cooperative with their playmates. The researchers speculate that these children imitated the violence they saw on TV.

In a longitudinal study of boys from eight to eighteen years, Leonard Eron and his colleagues reported that heavy doses of violent TV in childhood was causally related to aggression at the older age. They suggest that there might be a sensitive period beginning in early childhood when children are susceptible to the effects of viewing violent TV. The National Institute of Mental Health's 1982 update of the Surgeon General's Report on Television and Social Behavior, which reviewed 2,500 studies, also concluded that watching televised violence led to increased aggression in children.

But TV violence has other effects. Many young TV viewers report having nightmares or being frightened. Sometimes children repeatedly play out scary TV scenes in an effort to understand them. A mother of a four-year-old says:

. . . *After he saw a show in which people died in a fire, he would pretend there was a five-alarm fire. He put the bodies on a stretcher and buried them. He was very graphic and hyper, which made me think he was anxious.*

TV violence does not affect all children in the same way. Children who are more aggressive to begin with seem to be more susceptible to the aggression they see on TV. Perhaps a cycle is established in which these children learn to act more aggressively, lose friends, and therefore turn back to the TV. Also, children who are less achievement-oriented are more likely to believe that aggressive content on TV is real, and are therefore even more likely to be influenced by what they see.

The family environment can either exacerbate or reduce the effects of TV violence. Even when children are disposed toward aggression, if they seldom watch TV unsupervised, have opportunities to play and read, and are not punitively disciplined, seeing aggression on TV will have less impact on their behavior. Not surprisingly, parents' own viewing habits make a difference, too. In a study of six- to fourteen-year-olds in Canada, parents who watched little TV violence themselves *and* actively discouraged their children from doing so had children who were less aggressive at home. Of course, many factors contribute to violent behavior and TV alone cannot be blamed, but the medium can be a potent factor for some children.

TV Interferes with Educational Achievement

Parents ask: Does TV promote school achievement by increasing children's knowledge and information? Or does it interfere by taking time away from reading and active play, and by encouraging a shorter attention span?

For the most part, TV hampers children's academic performance. Heavy viewers do worse in school, on average, than light viewers. An English researcher, Hilda Himmelweit, studied over 4,000 children in the 1950s before and after TV came to their communities; the brighter children tended to watch less TV. Other data from Canada indicates that TV viewing interferes with reading. Children from a town without TV scored higher on reading tests than children who had TV. Once TV was introduced into the first community, the reading scores dropped. Singer and Singer report that the best predictors of good reading comprehension in primary school children are minimal TV viewing during the preschool period, nonphysical discipline, a curious, resourceful mother, and an orderly household routine. The Singers and others report that some children of low-income families or lower IQ are helped in school by watching more TV. In this case, TV may be more stimulating than the home environment.

In *The Plug-in Drug,* Marie Winn argues that heavy viewing favors the right hemisphere of the brain, associated with spatial-visual processing, to the detriment of the left hemisphere, responsible for verbal-analytic processing. Although Winn's claim is somewhat controversial, schooling traditionally requires verbal skills and heavy TV viewers may be at a disadvantage.

TV Fosters Passive Learning

TV affects educational achievement in yet another way. We know that young children learn through interaction with objects and people. By experimenting and exploring, they try out their ideas and gather information. But TV is like no other experience for the young child. In the words of the late Dorothy Cohen, a Bank Street educator,

> *The active child learns to be unnaturally passive. The talking child learns to listen and expects not to have someone to whom to respond.*

Older children admit that "It's easier to watch TV than it is to read a book."

Even if TV elicits a response from a child—e.g., counting along—it is still not interactive. In other words, the child's response, whether right or wrong, completed or not, makes no difference to what follows on the screen.

Other Problems with TV

- It perpetuates stereotypes. According to the updated 1982 Surgeon General's Report, males outnumber females three to one on TV; women tend to be portrayed in more deferential roles.
- TV's fast pace promotes impulsiveness and an inability to persist with tasks. Some researchers conclude that heavy TV viewers do not develop the more reflective style of thought necessary for learning in school settings. Teachers complain that children expect to be entertained in the classroom.
- Commercials foster materialism and create appetites for expensive items that have little real value and in the process create parent-child conflict. After watching a program interspersed with an ad for cereal, preschoolers in one study attempted to influence their mothers to buy the advertised

product, as well as to buy other things. The mothers, in turn, reacted with more efforts to control the child.

- Although children may want to relax in front of the TV set, after an hour or two of viewing many children are cranky and irritable.
- Heavy TV viewing inhibits the imaginative play of preschoolers and older children; children who watch a lot of TV indiscriminately are also less likely to create imaginary companions.
- Watching frightening scenes and scary movies can stimulate fears and night terrors in young children.

TV and the Preschooler's Level of Development

A well-known educator tells the following story about her four-year-old grandson. She appeared on a television panel, and of course her grandson was allowed to watch Grandma on television. But when he next saw her in the flesh, he went into a stream of accusation. "You didn't answer me when I talked to you, Grandma. Why didn't you answer me? You looked at me but you didn't answer me. Why didn't you answer me?"

Because TV is so lifelike and vivid, young children have difficulty separating the TV image from the real thing. For four-year-olds the TV message seems real: if they're told the cereal makes them strong, they are likely to believe it; if the toy fills up the entire screen, then it must be that size. Some cannot distinguish between the purpose of a commercial and that of a program. Furthermore, preschoolers' lack of experience makes them more vulnerable to stereotyped portrayals of sex roles and ethnic groups.

Preschoolers show some TV literacy—that is, they learn how to understand some of the symbolic conventions used. They can make sense of a series of shots, like fades and dissolves, and follow the story line for a childen's program. But they are less able to comprehend the technology when the subject matter is advanced. Thus, one of the dangers of exposing young children to adult shows is that they do not understand what they see.

Print vs. TV

In her informative book *Mind and Media,* Patricia Greenfield, professor of psychology at UCLA, compares the media of print and TV. She asks: what are their unique features and what is each best at teaching? Greenfield makes a number of important points:

- The language used by TV and print differ. On TV, language is terse, action-oriented, and the meaning is often conveyed by gestures and visual images. Since print relies only on words, it requires a greater degree of explicitness. The language is vivid, emotional, reflective, factual, given to abstract generalizations. TV presents simpler vocabulary and grammatical structure than books do.

- TV is an excellent teacher of action and dynamic processes. Understanding the growth process of a plant is easier when seeing it than when reading about it. But print is better suited to teach facts and details and to convey people's internal feelings and thoughts.
- TV is rapidly paced and always in motion. Print allows for repetition, for the child to keep his or her own pace. It promotes a more reflective, articulate style than TV.
- Whereas TV makes characters and their behaviors, places and scenes visually explicit, the verbal medium stimulates the imagination. The reader has to imagine just how a character moves or talks.
- Print invites young children and their parents to read together. When most families watch TV, there is minimal verbal exchange.

Children have control over their books in a way that they cannot with TV shows. They can look at favorite books over and over, moving ahead, skipping backward, staying on the same page and repeating favorite refrains.

In a word: TV and books are different experiences. TV should not replace the primacy of books in children's early years.

SOLUTIONS

There is consensus that if the best is to be gotten from TV and the worst avoided, you must actively guide your children's viewing. As Patricia Greenfield suggests, think of your role not as a censor but as a socializer conveying values and knowledge to your children.

Deciding What's Worth Watching

Programs geared to young children (other than most cartoons) are among the most appropriate. They make an effort to present positive role models, to solve problems by thinking and talking rather than by physical force, and to teach concepts.

When young children are first exposed to TV, the best choices feature live, parental characters and a slow pace such as in *Mister Rogers' Neighborhood*. Older preschoolers might watch a greater variety of programs: animal shows and familiar stories, nonviolent fairy tales or certain cartoons. In general, shows that stimulate play and that clearly distinguish fantasy and reality are advisable. Avoid programs that show animals or humans in great danger, that are especially scary, or that are far beyond children's comprehension (such as a graphic depiction of illness).

News programs should probably be avoided, given their penchant for gory and tragic stories. A mother of a preschooler says:

■ ■ ■ *After seeing an auto accident on the news, my son was afraid to drive in traffic. He would ask, "Are we going to get in an accident?" He was getting too upset, so now my husband and I watch the late night news after he's in bed.*

Once you have decided what shows you are willing to have your child watch, make your reasons clear: "We're watching a special on whales because you like them and because we all want to learn more about them." Also make it clear why you are not watching other shows: "There is too much violence and fighting."

Turning the TV On ... and Off

Keep the TV on only when you or your child are actively watching it. If you use the TV as background noise while doing something else, your children may be watching. Although you may be able to tune out the negative messages or blatant distortions, young children cannot. They are coming away with impressions. You can't make them turn away from violence and watch only the happy moments.

It's also very convenient to use TV to occupy a child and to give yourself some time off. If you use TV as a babysitter, be selective about what your children watch. Ask yourself if there are any other activities your child might enjoy that would serve the same purpose.

Another frequent use of TV is for adult relaxation. A parent of a two-year-old says that at the end of a working day, she sometimes just flips on the TV to wind down.

■ ■ ■ *Billy likes to climb up on the bed with me. He usually lies down and sucks on his bottle. I wonder if he understands these action shows with police and fighting that I like.*

Billy is using the TV as a way of being close to his mother after a day apart. This is important for both of them, but violent programs need not be the backdrop for snuggling and being intimate.

It's important not only to limit the content of what preschoolers watch but also the time they spend in front of the TV. How much TV is appropriate? If the Singers had their way, no child would watch TV until good reading habits were well established. But they realize this vision is unrealistic for most American families. Ultimately, you'll have to make your own decision about what's best for your child. We tend to agree with the American Academy of Pediatrics that from one to two hours of quality programming per day is long enough for a preschooler.

What can you do if your child is a TV addict? To cut back viewing time:

- Set limits and make them clear. If you decide that one hour a day is enough, explain in a way that your child can understand: "You can watch two short shows." You will probably also want to set limits on the kinds of programs (e.g., cartoons) your child watches.
- Use a timer to signal when it's time to turn the TV off. This helps objectify and depersonalize the situation.
- Plan other activities. "After the show is over, we'll go for a walk."

Involve your child in finding a solution to the dilemma. Explain: "We think you're watching too much TV. Any ideas of other things you'd like to do?"

Modifying Your Own Viewing Habits

Much research indicates that if parents watch a lot of violence, their children do too. Furthermore, their children are more likely to act aggressively at home and at school. Ask yourself whether you are a good model of a TV viewer to your children.

Giving Children Choices

Teach your children to make thoughtful choices about what they watch. Usually this means that you set the ground rules (for example, no more than an hour of TV on weekdays, two hours on weekends; no violent shows), then together, you discuss their selections. The point is to encourage children to think about their options and make informed decisions.

Viewing and Discussing Together

This is one of the most important steps parents can take. Talk about what happens on the shows. Counter the negative messages by presenting your version of reality.

- Discuss the motives that underly the actions. One reason young children are often confused about what they see on TV is that they don't understand intentionality and misinterpret what characters are doing. First try to elicit the child's ideas, "Why do you think the mother said that?" Then you are in a position to clarify misconceptions.
- Help your child distinguish fantasy and reality: "Could this really happen?"
- Define difficult words and ideas.

- Combat stereotypes of minorities and other groups with personal experience, books, and other means.
- Engage the child's critical faculties: "Whom did you like most—least?" "What do you think will happen next week?" "Why?"

Describe how shows are created by writers, producers, actors, and clarify what seems like magic to naive viewers. For example:

- Explain commercials. "The reason they're telling you the candy is good is so you'll buy it." "The people who make the cereal want you to learn their song so you'll remember the name in the store. But just because you know the name is not a good enough reason to buy this cereal."
- Explain special effects, like lighting and camera angles. Demonstrate sound effects: crinkling a piece of cellophane sounds like a blazing fire; rubbing a balloon sounds like a creaky door.

One of the major strategies promoted by Peggy Charen from ACT, an organization that has been both a watchdog and an advocate for improving children's programming, is to help your child become a critical viewer.

Counteracting Violence on TV

If your child has seen a violent episode on TV, discuss it. The mother of a five-year-old says:

▪ ▪ ▪ *Becca saw someone killed on a show and then saw the same actor a week later. She told me, "Mommy, he got undead." I said it was just a story, that he really wasn't shot. But I had to explain this a number of times. You have to keep on your toes when you consider what you're exposing them to.*

Certain cartoons perpetrate violence. A parent who had decided to forbid cartoon watching altogether gives this rationale:

▪ ▪ ▪ *When my six- and four-year-olds used to watch cartoons, I was appalled at how the fragility of life was ignored. A character can be mowed down and then get up and run away. I told them a human being or an animal couldn't do that. The children had a very hard time making this distinction. So I said, "No more cartoons until you're older."*

Expanding the Positive Messages

Build on the concepts that TV presents. When you see examples of cooperation and consideration, point them out. Science and animal shows can open up new worlds that are not a part of children's everyday experience. If your child wants to learn more, follow up with a trip to the library.

Making TV Time Family Time

Make a special TV program an occasion for the entire family. A mother remembers:

. . . When we were growing up, if there was a ballet or children's show like Peter Pan on TV my parents would put down a blanket in front of the TV and we'd all have a picnic. Although we looked forward to the program, we were even more excited about the picnic and the fun time we had together.

Using TV to Stimulate the Imagination

Let TV enrich your children's capacity for make-believe. Suggest they play out stories, for example, *Peter Pan,* and help them find props. Take advantage of the explicitness of the visual medium and encourage them to imitate a character's voice or walk.

Becoming a Children's Advocate

Let your local stations know what you think of their programming. Call or write them. Encourage your children to do the same. Most stations are quite responsive to the concerns of parents. Join national organizations that advocate improved children's programming and reduced violence on TV.

TV is a powerful influence and one that is here to stay. Its use can be positive, however, if it is a supplement—but never a substitute—for the play and direct experiences that young children need to learn and grow.

Q *Should my preschooler learn to use a computer?*

Parents wonder if preschoolers belong in the computer revolution. They ask the following questions:

- Are they too young to become computer literate or is this the right age to begin?
- If they don't begin now, will they be handicapped later?

At this point, the answers are still coming in; experiments are being conducted and parents and teachers are observing children using computers. According to the late Betty Boegehold, Bank Street reading specialist, young children do like computers. They love to push buttons, manipulate levers and make images appear on the screen. They like to play and experiment randomly with the computer and try out computer games and word processing programs.

Arguments for Computers in the Early Years

The mother of a four-year-old and an eight-year-old says:

> ■ ■ ■ *When we got the computer, it was like getting a new child in the family. Corey, my younger child, was mainly interested in typing something and then pressing down a key which changes all the letters into symbols of various kinds and then back again. My eight-year-old liked to fill the screen with her name. Neither one was intimidated. They just saw it as something they had a natural right to use. It's been a great addition to the family.*
>
> *It's helped with letter and number recognition. If Corey makes a mistake, he can easily erase. Yesterday he was singing the alphabet song. Then he wanted to put the alphabet on the computer. As he sang, he pecked out the letters, and got them pretty much in order. He was delighted with himself and called me over to read it.*

Many parents and educators feel that computers provide valuable learning experiences for preschoolers. They say that computers develop eye-hand coordination and fine motor skills, longer attention spans, high levels of motivation, and a sense of control. Although these claims are not always backed up by research, these are certainly desirable outcomes.

Computers are said to teach young children how to think and foster prereading and math skills. Are these claims valid? Two early childhood educators, Anselmo and Zinck, placed computers and developmentally appropriate software in nursery school classrooms that also had a variety of other materials, such as blocks and paints. The children were shown how to operate the computers and then allowed to use them freely. They were shown how to use software only if they were interested or had questions. The researchers found that the computers promoted skill development in comprehension, memory, evaluation, problem solving, and creativity. Furthermore, cooperation was fostered as the children helped one another and worked together. The researchers concluded that if used in developmentally appropriate ways, computers could stimulate thinking skills.

Arguments against Computers in the Early Years

Many educational experts worry about rushing youngsters into the adult world of technology without fully understanding children's early development and the very serious limitations of the computer. They raise the following concerns.

1. *Young children learn best by direct, hands-on experience; computers present abstractions.* The richest learning takes place when preschoolers have concrete, direct experiences with objects and events. Yet the child at the computer cannot touch or physically manipulate the image on the screen; the computer only presents two-dimensional abstractions. For example, software designed to teach directionality (right and left, above and below) is far removed from the actual situations in which these concepts are best learned and understood, that is, when children move and orient their bodies and objects in space: "I'm above you on the jungle gym." "My truck is next to your car." As two computer educators put it, "Children need to play with Lego blocks *before* LOGO (a popular children's software program)."

2. *Computers limit experimentation and flexibility.* The computer's responses are programmed and, therefore, restricted. But in the world of children's play, anything is possible and the child can determine the outcome. Harriet Cuffaro, a Bank Street educator, critiques a graphics program which allows children to paint: "The experience is reduced and limited by eliminating the fluid, liquid nature of paint. There are no drips to control or spills to mop up. Neither are there opportunities to become involved in the process of learning how to create shades of color (or) . . . the effects achieved by rotating the brush and varying pressure".

Although computers offer some interaction, they can never be as responsive as another human being who can spontaneously pose a question to a child, extend an idea, introduce a new concept, or reflect back on what happened yesterday and think ahead to tomorrow.

3. *Some implicit lessons of computers are not beneficial.* Computers reinforce a particular learning style akin to TV viewing. Even if the computer is interactive, it never allows for the physical involvement characteristic of young children; rather, it requires a somewhat inactive, passive orientation.

Many computer experts praise the computer for its ability to lead a child to a precise, correct answer. But this is not the major lesson that young children need to learn. Instead, they need to experience open-ended situations, where there is no single right way to do things.

4. *Many software programs are inappropriate for young children: they present drills, are violent, or require too much reading.* Just as a good preschool program does not use workbooks, a good computer program should be more than an animated, electronic worksheet that uses pictures to teach colors, numbers, or letters. Puzzles, blocks, and other materials that can be manipulated are more effective (and less expensive).

Some software contains violent elements usually associated with the video games—disintegrating aliens or little creatures eaten by larger ones. There is evidence that computer violence may promote preschoolers' aggression.

Although many preschoolers can learn to read simple commands ("Go to," "Print") some programs contain lengthy written explanations that only frustrate young children and undermine their sense of mastery.

Are Computers Appropriate for Young Children? It Depends

Computers are an important feature of modern life, but there is no need for parents to rush out and install a computer at home just for the preschooler or seek out a preschool program with computers in the classroom. Computers can be an effective learning tool *if* they are used on a playful and limited basis, suited to a child's level of development. Computers can never replace first-hand experiences with real objects and events.

When computers were placed in one nursery school and the children were free to use them as they wished, the three-year-olds were moderately interested, but most of the five-year-olds were quite enthusiastic. Given a choice, most children will seek out experiences that are appealing and challenging to them. Hence, computers are most appropriate for children who are ready to make a transition from relying on actual objects and events to abstract thinking. In Piaget's terms, these are the children who are moving from preoperational to concrete operational thinking. Many children will begin this transition at the end of the preschool period. For others, it will come later. The important point is that computers will not help children "hurry" through the preschool period when direct, hands-on experiences are essential to development.

Nor will computers magically develop reading, math, or writing skills. They may be of some benefit in strengthening eye-hand coordination, discriminating details, recognizing symbols, and lengthening attention span, but the skills gained from the computer are only as good as the software being used. To date, little software is specifically geared for the learning style of the young child, and some even convey negative messages. In our opinion, the computer offers no learning experience nor fosters any skill for preschool children that cannot be experienced more meaningfully and less expensively in play at home and in good early childhood programs. The value of computers for learning comes later on, when children are older.

What Parents Can Do

Some general guidelines to using a computer wisely:

- Don't rely on the computer as a babysitter (just as you wouldn't use the TV that way).

- Participate when your child uses the computer. Make it part of the time you enjoy spending together.
- Be very selective about software. Look for programs that are developmentally appropriate for preschoolers. Don't expect your four-year-old to use a program geared for a ten-year-old.
- Differentiate between your own needs and those of your children. There will be many opportunities for your children to become computer literate. After all, the computer whizzes of today did not grow up in a computer culture; rather, they applied their ideas and insights to the new technology.
- If a preschool program offers computers, it should be just one of many activity areas. Five- and six-year-olds might stay at the computer for ten to fifteen minutes at a time; younger children even less, if at all. Children should be free to use or not use the computer.
- Let your children proceed at their own pace. Do not force time in front of the computer.
- Encourage your children to play and have a variety of hands-on experiences as the basis for concepts and abstractions. With this as a foundation, your children will be better able to use the computer in a meaningful, creative way as they grow.

Dependence and Independence

When I think about independence and dependence and preschool children, I think of how my own son, Philip, dealt with this issue. Like Picasso in the blue period, Philip at age four had a witch period. He drew evil witches and beautiful witches; he drew stomping, angry witches and dancing witches; he drew frenetic witches with menacing features and sedate witches.

In the way that children can express something at once profound and simple, his witches revealed to me the fundamental issue of the preschool years: adventure out into the world.

Witches and the Outside World

Philip's witches seemed to depict his vision of the world beyond his home. Though not quite human, the witches had arms and legs, eyes and ears. They were alien but familiar. They were also unpredictable as they stirred their cauldrons of toads and mice or took off on broomsticks into the dark purple sky.

His drawings represented moving out into a world of friends and strangers, and they reflected newspaper photographs that showed the faces of anguished men, women, and children at the scenes of fires, car wrecks, natural disasters.

Witches and Parents

Looking at his drawings, it was clear that I was the witch. Sometimes I was like the strong, thick-shouldered, stolid witch he so often drew. At other times I was as carefree as his witches who danced across pages and pages of drawing paper. But there were other times that I was transformed, the evil witch of the fairy tales who inexplicably yells or bears down on small, innocent children.

The Witch Within

The witch also seemed to portray Philip's tumultuous feelings. At one moment he was in control, then unhappiness with a drawing that didn't look the way he intended or tiredness or hunger could overcome all of his newly mustered control.

If he felt out of control, Philip would go into his room. He might punch a pillow or yell or draw scenes of combat between monsters and witches. Perhaps this was like the battle that waged within: to unleash his anger or to master it.

The Runaway Bunny by Margaret Wise Brown has been a favorite of innumerable two- and three-year-olds. Philip sometimes wanted to hear it again when he was four and five. The runaway bunny does all he can to leave home, but the mother, who understands this desire, protects the bunny by following him.

Fairy tales convey a similar message. Yes, the children wander through the woods or fields, scattering bread crumbs in the blackest of forests; yes, they meet terrible dangers, but in the end they are safely reunited with their families.

This witch-drawing phase was short-lived. Several years later, Philip became fascinated with *Dorothy and the Wizard of Oz*. On his green and white record player, he would repeat the part of the record in which water is thrown at the witch and she cries, "I'm melting . . . I'm melting."

At last there was a conquest. Philip had mastered the witches of his childhood; they melted away into memories. Not long ago, as he cleaned out his closet, he found the record of *Peter and the Wolf*. Dressed in a hat and a shawl, the wolf on the cover resembled the witches in his more frightening drawings. He ran his seventeen-year-old fingers over this picture, musing that it was amazing—how could he ever have perceived that drawing as scary?

It *was* amazing, I thought. But what faced him at four was not so different from what he faced at seventeen. He was cleaning out his closet because he was ready to venture out again, this time to college, and the same issue —of independence and dependence—reemerged.

Holding on and letting go is a lifelong process, one that stirs both the fears of the recluse and the imagination of the adventurer within us all.

Parents' Feelings about Independence and Dependence

The mother of a four-year-old says:

> ▪ ▪ ▪ *Last year we took Russell to the ocean. He took one look at the crabs crawling in and out of the sand and refused to set foot on the beach. He wanted me to carry him everywhere.*

How did you feel when you read about Russell? It is likely that your reaction centered on two dimensions: your feelings about your child growing up and your memories of your own childhood fears.

In general, parents experience a continuum of feelings that goes from a desire to stop time so your child remains a baby to the wish to advance into the future so your child will grow up as quickly as possible. In most of us, these emotions commingle—we applaud our child's growth with stirrings of nostalgia and loss. We also greet our child's cyclical return to more babyish ways with regret but understanding. If our response rests on either end of the continuum, we are in danger of preventing or prematurely pushing our child's growing up.

Our reaction to our child's fears also depends on our own memories. If we remember our own nighttime terrors, our fear of snakes under the bed or sharks in the toilet, we may be more sympathetic to our child. On the other hand, we may also exaggerate something that starts out as minor. However, if we have no recollection of being afraid, some of our child's preoccupations (from fears of escalators to daddy longlegs) may seem silly when, in fact, they are very real to the child.

Parents typically have flashes of fearful fantasies as their children take each new step toward greater independence. Seeing our child climb to the top of a slide, swing high on a swing, run ahead to the end of the block, visit a new place or person brings worries about the child's safety. We imagine our child falling off the swing, being hit by a car, or being insulted by other children. Knowing that these feelings are normal helps us see our own fears not as superstitious harbingers of dangers to come, but as the very real sorrow of letting go a little more.

How we respond to our children's push for independence may be colored by the exercise of autonomy in our adult lives. If we feel we have a say in our work, marriage, or community, then we are probably better able to grant autonomy to our children. We can understand their urges and recognize the satisfaction that comes from being one's own person. However, if we feel powerless or frustrated, these feelings can be reflected in attempts to thwart our children's strivings for independence.

RESEARCH AND THEORY ON DEPENDENCE AND INDEPENDENCE

If you spend any time standing back and just watching preschool children, the centrality of independence and dependence in their lives is clearly evident. Using these observable and normal swings of behavior as a base, researchers have concentrated on the question of extremes: What are the causes of one child's becoming more timid or more adventurous than another? One group of researchers has looked to child-rearing style, specifically to the mother/child relationship for answers, while another group has concentrated on the child's physiological makeup.

Over fifty years ago, John Bowlby, an English psychoanalyst, studied children being cared for in orphanages and hospitals. Even though the children were physically well taken care of—they were fed and bathed adequately—they did not have consistent, loving caretaking. Because they were deprived of the chance to form a strong attachment to another human, their development was arrested. They were slow to acquire language and motor skills, and their play was rudimentary. Bowlby also witnessed a breakdown of the abilities of healthy children when they were separated from their parents for extended periods of time. Bowlby's dramatic findings pointed out the importance of attachment to a child's later development.

Influenced by Bowlby's pioneering work, many researchers have looked for the roots of the preschooler's autonomy in infancy. Researchers Mary Ainsworth from Johns Hopkins University and L. Alan Sroufe from the University of Minnesota found that infants whose dependency needs were met by their mothers were more likely to become adventurous as preschoolers. (Mothers have been the focus of these studies because these researchers see the mother as the primary caretaker in infancy.) As Sroufe states, those children who have confidence in the mother/child relationship, that is, who have learned that the mother is there for them, can use her as a secure base. Often the infant or toddler literally does this, keeping the mother in physical proximity and returning now and again to her side. The older preschooler, who is now capable of symbolic thought, can call up the mother's comforting mental image when needed. Sroufe found that when children are securely attached in infancy, they are more likely later on to be "enthusiastic, persistent and effective in facing environmental challenges" and "confident, skilled, and positive in dealing with peers and other tasks of the preschool period." Thus, to those researchers, the inclination to be autonomous is predicated on a secure attachment to the mother.

But how does a mother establish this kind of relationship? Are there certain ways of relating that give the child more security than others? Ainsworth's studies of mother-child interaction indicate the importance of maternal sensitivity to the baby's signals and communications. This means that the mother seems to understand her baby's behavior, to understand the language of gestures, smiles, fussing, and cries, and gives the baby what he or she seems to need.

If children's dependency needs are met in infancy, won't the parent be conditioning or teaching the child to remain dependent? In fact, this does not seem to be the case. Meeting the child's needs does not mean always saying yes, it means being responsive to the child, including setting limits where necessary. As Sroufe and his colleagues say, the establishment of a secure attachment, "one in which the child's emotional needs are met effec- tively . . . paves the way for normal autonomy." But if one's dependency needs are not met in infancy, the need seems to remain, giving rise to later dependency.

Children are born with differences in sociability, proneness to anger, irritability, or activity level. These differences, called temperamental traits, affect their parents. (See the section on temperament, pages 170–181.) The attachment researchers believe, however, that a mother can adjust to these traits to fashion a good relationship. As proof, they note that attachment studies have included children who are lethargic and hyperactive, cuddly and not cuddly, cautious and impetuous. None of these characteristics de- termined the kind of attachment relationship the child formed.

Another group of researchers is less sure. In one fascinating group of investigations, a team of scientists that includes developmental psychologist Jerome Kagan from Harvard University found that some preschool children may be biologically disposed to inhibition. These are the children whose parents describe them as typically shy or fearful with unfamiliar children or adults and who take a long time to feel at ease. The scientists hypothesize that perhaps the locus coeruleus, a brain stem structure, produces more norepinephrine in the inhibited children and that this substance magnifies uncertainty and feelings of being upset in stressful situations.

Other psychoanalytic theorists have also probed for the meaning behind preschoolers' tendency to vacillate between independence and dependence. They, too, have concentrated on the mother as the first and primary figure in the child's life, although this notion is open to question in those families in which the father plays a greater role.

For instance, Margaret Mahler postulated that at birth the infant has no sense of his or her own separateness of self and moves from merged oneness with the mother to separateness. Between eight and fifteen months the child can become absorbed in activities and exploration but returns periodically to touch base with the mother. During the next phase, from approximately fifteen to twenty-four months, the child is increasingly aware that he or she is separate. Because this realization is scary, the child seeks reassurance and contact and holds on more. At this point, some parents worry that their child has regressed and become overly dependent. But by thirty months, the child once again accepts separation from the mother and now feels a strong desire for autonomy.

Daniel Stern disputes Mahler's interpretation that the infant and mother are symbolically merged. On the basis of carefully controlled experiments with infants, he shows that even very young babies know they are different and thus separate from their mothers. He says, "First comes the formulation of self and other, and only then is the sense of merger-like experiences possible."

Child psychoanalyst Erik Erikson has outlined major turning points in psychosocial development. In infancy, the child develops a basic sense of either trust in the world or mistrust. In the toddler years, the child develops either autonomy or shame and doubt, and in the later preschool years, initiative or guilt. While the baby has stirrings toward autonomy it is not until the second year that the child is ready for "a decisive encounter with his environment which will convey its own messages about how much the child is to express independence versus how much the child is to be controlled".

Overall, I think several conclusions can be drawn from the research and theory to date:

1. *Although some research efforts emphasize children's biological makeup while others stress the role of the mother and of the child's experience, it is impossible to separate nature from nurture.* All children in the preschool years swing back and forth between being brave and being fearful. Whether children are more or less timid may begin with their biology but can be shaped by the way they are raised by both their mothers and fathers.

2. *Children need a balance between familiar and new experiences.* Familiar experiences are like home base; they provide a sense of security while novelty makes children grow. The seminal work of Jean Piaget on how children learn reveals that new experiences can challenge children to explore. Too much novelty, however, overwhelms children, who need a balance between the known and the unknown in order to flourish.

3. *Interdependence is a more accurate concept, encompassing independence and dependence.* The American culture admires independence; most of us have been raised on the myths of such folk heroes as Davy Crockett and the pioneer families trekking across the wilderness. We tend to accept dependence in very young children but disapprove of it thereafter. For example, I recently conducted an exercise for corporate executives involving a series of case studies that concerned dependence: a woman is preoccupied at work because of her aging mother, a man must care for his ill

wife, a young man takes an unpaid leave to be with his new baby. The executives were asked to describe their initial reactions. They were somewhat supportive of the man caring for his ill wife, but he should "get his act together and hire someone to take care of her after a while." They were not particularly supportive of caring for the young and old. The woman with the older mother was described as a "bitch," while the man with the new baby was seen as a "wimp." Afterward, we discussed how difficult many adults find the notion of dependency.

For years, I have been suspicious of the developmental notion of separateness: that children proceed from dependence to independence, from oneness to separateness. In researching *The Six Stages of Parenthood* I found that for each step away from their parents, children find a new way to reconnect with them, and thus I call this process "separation/connection."

Likewise, in a series of investigations on children's dependence, young children were found to remain dependent (that is, they need others for nurturing, attention, and assistance) throughout their early years—but the focus of this need shifts from their parents to include age-mates and other adults, such as teachers. Furthermore, older preschool children learn to seek dependence in more socially acceptable ways. If they want attention, they can say "watch me" rather than whine or have a temper tantrum. As adults, we also need each other to survive and to prosper. We all have times of being sick and of being healthy, of feeling strong and of feeling in need.

4. *Moving between independence and dependence is a lifelong process.* Much of the theory and research makes it seem that once the child's dependency needs are met, that's it: the child becomes independent. It sounds as if parental influence takes place only in infancy; if parents don't do it correctly, it's all over—they have set their child on a course for life. These notions are inaccurate. Although the beginnings of parental influence are in infancy and these influences are very important, they do not end there. Over and over again as parents, we continue to provide a secure home base for our children as well as to teach them to venture out.

Many parents have observed that regression in children often precedes growth. Just before children are about to go to a new school, master a new skill, grow in a new way, they retreat. They may crawl back into our laps, suck their thumbs, wet their beds, cling, or ask to return to the stroller. We worry about what we have done to cause this. We resent going back to washing out underpants when we were so grateful that that phase was over. And then our children move ahead. The steps backward are perhaps an effort to harness energy for a surge forward. Growth is cyclical and does not proceed in an even, straight line. There are periods of calm, then upheaval, when the child's way of functioning is being reorganized. During the preschool years, when dependence and independence are central to children's development, we as parents play a crucial role in holding our children when they need it and giving them encouragement to move out when that is called for.

5. *In dealing with independence and dependence, we are teaching children how to cope with stress.* In the case of Russell, the four-year-old on the sandy beach, his mother was unsure what to do. Should she let Russell stay at the edge of the sand or insist that he manage? Would she be succumbing to his fears if she didn't push? On the other hand, she knew people who had been pushed too hard as children and had become fearful adults.

■ ■ ■ *At first I was furious at Russell. He was spoiling my vacation. I had had these wonderful fantasies of him dashing into the water, laughing and chasing waves, digging in the sand. But he wouldn't even step on the sand.*

Then I decided to see it as a challenge. I didn't pick him up, but realized that I could help him figure out how to deal with something hard. I asked Russell what he thought he could do to help himself. He wanted a path of towels to step on. So I put one towel in front of another and, like a little king, he marched across the beach to where we were sitting. He didn't stay on his towel for long—in a few minutes he was fingering the sand and by the end of the afternoon he was chasing the waves, just as I had imagined.

Russell had asked to be carried and his mother refused. At first her action may have seemed like a loss to him—the loss of the mother who would care for him in the way she had when he was younger. Yet she helped him take an appropriate developmental step in facing his own problem.

One five-year-old expressed this tug of war between parental protection and self-assertion when she asked her mother, "What would happen if you died?"

Her mother at first tried to reassure her: "I'm young. I'm healthy. I don't think I'll die for a very long time."

The child persisted: "But what would happen if you did?"

The mother finally answered, "Well, there would be Daddy."

"What if he died?" she asked.

"We have made arrangements with your Aunt Peggy to take care of you."

"And what if she died?"

"Then your other aunt."

"And what if she died, too?"

Finally the child asked, "What if everyone in the world but me died?"

To that, the mother replied, "Well, you'd be in trouble, wouldn't you?"

In the mother's words, "That satisfied her." This child wanted to know at what point she would be totally alone.

An almost-three-year-old had just given up her bottle. She was very proud of herself and kept announcing other new accomplishments: "I can turn on the light in my room" or "I can put on my clothes." But her nighttime dreams were populated with family friends who had moved away. One morning she said, "I don't have a bottle anymore. Soon I won't have a mommy anymore."

Her mother, like the wise mother rabbit in *The Runaway Bunny*, said: "No. You'll always have a mommy. When you get to be a big girl, you'll still have your mommy caring for you, but things are a little different now because you're growing up." And she went on to say, "There was a sadness on her part and on mine too, but both of us are so proud of her accomplishments."

VIEWPOINT: BONDING IS NOT A MAGIC MOMENT

At a call-in radio show, one parent said that she had missed bonding with her child because the doctor had taken him away on the delivery table. She worried terribly about the repercussions of this loss.

Much of the current interest in bonding stems from the research of Marshall Klaus and John Kennell in the 1970s. They found that when mothers and infants were kept together right after birth, they were more likely to be closely attached later on. Like many other professionals in this field, I dispute the notion that there is one moment to bond. I disagree that, as the word suggests, there is an epoxy-glue-like fusion binding together mother or father and child.

The attachment relationship is much more gradual and involves push/pull feelings from the very start. The new parent both desires to be with the child and to escape. As children grow, they, too, have ambivalent feelings—adoring and resenting the all-powerful parents.

It is in the everyday moments of infancy—of holding, feeding, exchanging smiles and looks—that the attachment relationship takes root. It is in the everyday moments of the preschooler years—of talking and playing together—that the attachment relationship grows strong. It is in the everyday moments throughout childhood that this relationship is formed through the inevitable periods of holding on, letting go, and coming together in new ways.

The process of negotiating dependence/independence is best revealed in the preschoolers' vacillation between being all-powerful and being afraid. Thus, questions we discuss next are focused on these two issues—superheroes and fears—and children's perennial solution, the "blankie."

Superheroes

Q *How do you deal with a child who is totally caught up with superheroes?*

Julia Smith says:

▪ ▪ ▪ *Scott is three now. When he was two and a half, my sister gave him a Superman shirt. Scott had never heard much about superheroes because he didn't watch much TV, but suddenly he was hooked. Now he knows everything about every superhero that ever existed. Sometimes he won't even answer to his own name but wants to be called Spider-Man or Batman. Scott wears his Superman shirt over his clothes every day.*

I just wish the whole thing would go away. My child is now a part of a world that I have no control over. I sometimes feel very sad that I can't shape his world anymore.

Giving up Some Control

Julia's realization that she can't completely control Scott's world, and her subsequent sense of sorrow, are normal feelings for parents of preschoolers. Knowing full well that the world isn't perfect, most parents still hope to create an enclave, an environment for their children that they can control. But whether or not their children watch much TV (Scott didn't), children of this age brandish guns, become television superheroes, and insist on the latest toy. Scott's interest in superheroes represents an independence from his mother that assaults her wish to stay in control.

Superhero Play as a Defense against Fear

Julia describes how Scott's interest in power grew out of a frightening experience:

▪ ▪ ▪ *We were away the summer before Scott was two, and he saw a fire. There were a lot of firemen, and they were screaming because there wasn't any water pressure. I think Scott was really frightened, but I also think he was fascinated, too. One thing about kids' fears is that they can be afraid of something but also lured by that fear. From that day on, for over a year, Scott played fireman.*

The way Scott dealt with this experience was to become the fireman—to save people from this new danger. That is, he was using play to comprehend and then gain control of a fear.

The same pattern holds for superhero play. As children become more independent from their families, they realize that their separateness holds the heady lure of becoming one's own boss. As one four-year-old said, "I'm in charge of me." But this also presents new and frightening possibilities ("I know I'm not really big enough to take care of myself").

Julia notes that "Scott becomes a superhero when he himself is feeling weak." He gives Superman rather than himself the credit for doing powerful things. Another child, Lisa, likes to play Darth Vader, identifying with a character who frightens her, and in this way working to overcome her fear.

Selma Fraiberg, in *The Magic Years*, stresses the importance of children finding their own solutions to anxiety—as Scott has done by playing Superman and Lisa, Darth Vader. As children pass back and forth between the urge to take care of themselves and to be taken care of, they face the developmental task of building up their own sense of autonomy. If the adult imposes solutions to all problems or if the child's own solutions are scoffed at or ignored, the child is learning "I can't really take care of myself." It is no wonder that Fraiberg describes this urge of children to solve their own problems as a cornerstone of their future mental health.

Superhero Play as a Means of Dealing with Good and Bad

In *The Uses of Enchantment,* Bruno Bettelheim points out that for centuries children have been attracted to classic fairy tales in which good triumphs and evil is foiled. These same themes appear in superhero fantasies—the bad person is caught so that good can prevail. Whether they pretend to be traditional heroes or modern superheroes, children are drawn to larger-than-life characters who clearly delineate goodness versus badness. In their play, they are attempting to dissociate themselves from their own "bad" impulses and stress the "good" within. (See pages 135–149 on moral development.)

Many people bemoan the fact that television presents children with a narrow range of heroes and that children's play, in reproducing these characters, is repetitive and frenetic, macho and even violent. While these criticisms are often valid, it must be noted that even without television superheroes, children would invent similar ones. Before TV, children played folk heroes like Robin Hood, whose power was pervasive and fantastic in their eyes.

SOLUTIONS

Setting Limits

Julia Smith decided that the best way to reconcile Scott's interest in super-heroes with her feeling that the play was consuming his life was to set limits. Limits would help him feel safe by imposing an order on his internal struggle—to be more independent, to be cared for, to sort out his good and bad impulses.

Figuring Out Which Limits to Set

Before she announced limits to Scott, Julia took time to decide which limits she felt comfortable with and could thus uphold. Other parents report that it is helpful to try out an imaginary conversation with their child, fantasiz-ing the child's usual protests and arguments to ensure that one is committed to his or her decision. In Julia's case, she decided that Scott couldn't wear his superhero clothes to school, out to dinner, or to visit relatives. Because wearing the clothes increased the possibility of his playing superhero, she based her decision on where it was inappropriate to play out his fantasy.

Presenting the Limits Positively

Julia told Scott about the new limits in a positive way, emphasizing what he could do as well as what he couldn't do. There are two ways of present-ing this: (1) "You have a choice: you can wear another shirt—not a super-hero shirt—to school or you can wear your superhero shirt under another shirt." Or (2) "Restaurants are not a good place to wear your Superman shirt, but you can wear it at home on Saturday." In addition, she announced the limits in advance. This way Scott could prepare and have clear expec-tations.

Articulating the Difference Between What's Real and What's Pretend

It was important for Julia to differentiate between fantasy and reality for Scott, to help *him* take credit for his own accomplishments. "I said, 'Scott, you were strong enough to lift that heavy box. *You* did it even though you're pretending to be Superman.'" At school, the teachers also insisted that Scott answer to his own name.

Extending Superhero Play

Some educators and parents have found constructive ways to engage chil-dren's interest in superhero play: for example, by helping children make costumes, a task that can include learning about different materials, how to sew and measure. Children can be encouraged to dictate (or write) stories about their favorite superheroes, thereby reinforcing pre-reading and pre-writing skills.

Introducing Other Comparable Interests

Parents can build on the preschoolers' developmental interest in strength and prowess by introducing other heroes whom they find more acceptable. Such heroes can be from the past. One father reads his son stories of knights and they visit the museum to look at displays of armor. Other parents have told their children about such people as Martin Luther King and Helen Keller. Julia takes Scott to the fire station every once in a while so he gets to know the firefighters—real-life heroes. Scott says he admires firemen because "they save people, are nice to me, and are all big and strong and smart."

Lisa's mother says:

. . . *I've read her stories and books about people who have heroic, brave, demanding jobs. Now she doesn't have to be a Darth Vader all the time. Sometimes she's an astronaut or a policewoman, sometimes she's the superhero who's helping the scientist who's helping the firewoman."*

Controlling Aggression in Superhero Play

In superhero play, children have the opportunity to learn about aggression in constructive ways. They learn what Kostelnik, Whiren, and Stein call "aggressive skills"—how to defend themselves, and "aggressive controls" —how to expend anger, to resist the temptation to attack, and to turn a conflict situation into a compromise.

They state that aggression is getting out of hand when:

- children stop having fun
- their voices become shrill
- facial expressions show fear, anger, or unhappiness
- talk changes from pretend into real threats

If any of these happen, the parents must intervene and redirect the play: "It's time to stop playing superhero because it's getting too wild. I'll read you a story now."

Emphasizing Moral Values

Parents can work on the moral issues that emerge in superhero play. When Lisa asked her mother, "Is Darth Vader the bad guy?" they discussed how a good person is different from a bad person and what makes a superhero a hero.

Superhero play is a concrete representation of the struggle children face between independence and dependence and between their good and bad impulses. With parental understanding and positive intervention, these experiences can provide children with the first of many opportunities to master these struggles.

Q *How do you handle young children's fears?*

When I last visited my hometown, I walked past a downtown building that I recalled as a huge medieval fortress. To my surprise, in fact it is a small, ordinary building—but then this building once housed my pediatrician's office. I also walked by the Woolworth's, where at age five I let go of my father's hand to pursue blue and green parakeets. When I looked up, I couldn't find him. I tried to find my way back to his office, but it seemed continents away, not the half block it really is.

These memories point to how very differently children perceive the world from adults. To understand children's fears, it's important to reconstruct the patterns of their perception.

The Toddler's Fears

A friend took her two-year-old daughter to an elementary school play her husband was directing. Because this play involved a masked character, he had brought the mask home for Alexandra to touch and play with beforehand. Yet at the actual performance, when the masked actor appeared on stage, Alexandra buried her face in her mother's shoulder and wept. The mask seemed entirely different to her onstage than in her own house.

In the second year, children begin to understand "object permanence"; that is, to understand that an object remains itself even if you look at it from a different angle or in a different context. The concept of object permanence was not well enough established in Alexandra for her to understand that the mask in her house was the same mask in the play. You may have noticed this phenomenon when your toddler treats you like a stranger when you wear unfamiliar clothes or have a new haircut.

Sometimes an adult comment or joke can frighten the toddler. Once when my daughter Lara was that age and refused to clean up her toys, I announced that I was not her mother anymore—my name was Genevieve and I was there to make sure she picked up her toys. The look of fear on her face told me instantly that this was not a joke to her. "Are you really not my mommy?" she asked. I told her how sorry I was to have made a dumb joke. The all-powerful adult can transform reality for a toddler.

Young children's fears can also be triggered by real events. One mother recounts:

> ▪ ▪ ▪ *When my daughter was almost two, she insisted on returning to being pushed in the stroller. My first reaction was, "Oh, she's being a baby." It took me a long time to realize she was afraid of something. She was frightened that walking on the sidewalk would make her vulnerable to the cars and trucks going by.*

This mother was disapproving until she saw a mail truck pull up on the sidewalk. She says, "For me that was a lesson that a lot of things that we assume are stubbornness or regressions are real fears."

Throughout the early years, the fear of abandonment or separation from loved ones is paramount. This fear takes many forms: some young children protest when left with a child-care provider, or are distressed when their parents simply turn the corner and walk into the next room, or do not want to be left alone to go to sleep.

Two- and three-year-olds can also be frightened by everyday objects onto which they project their own aggressive feelings: Dustbusters, lawn mowers, dishwashers, and toilets are menacing. Events or experiences that are discrepant with previous experience are also frightening. Marian Carey Hyson, a teacher who has studied children's fears, notes that children may become afraid when they encounter a doll with a missing arm or a slowly collapsing balloon.

Older Preschoolers and Fears

As the preschoolers' world continues to expand beyond the home, so do their fears. They see or hear stories about people dying, wars fought, robberies committed. These events are frightening to adults but can be even more so to young children who have no understanding of the issues involved and, of course, are powerless to do anything to stop them. Some child development experts note that a preoccupying fear of today's children is that their parents will get divorced. Even in well-functioning intact families, when parents argue in a healthy, constructive way, their children may worry and feel threatened. These events conjure up the basic fear of abandonment: that they won't be loved and cared for.

Some preschoolers' fears that are hard for adults to understand may originate in the concreteness of their thinking and/or their limited experiences. Upon hearing a neighbor say he put his dog to sleep and he died, four-year-old Brian was afraid to go to sleep for several days.

During the preschool years, children conjure up imaginary fears, witches (as my son did), and other frightening creatures. The appearance of these imaginary fears is related to children's intellectual development. Children can now form images of things they have never seen; while this ability to symbolize is an important aspect of learning, it also enables them to visualize shadows on the walls as monsters or to hear the wind beating against the windowpanes as an intruder. As adults we know that shadows are not monsters, but children find it difficult to distinguish between reality and fantasy. For this book, we interviewed groups of preschoolers, and a frequently recurring theme was the reality of their dreams. A child would begin telling a fantastic story—sounding dreamlike to us—and then would be unsure whether it had happened or not.

In the words of a parent, the child's way of dealing with fear seems to be "two steps forward, one step backward."

Adults as Reference Points

Robert Emde and his colleagues from the University of Colorado performed a dramatic experiment to illustrate the support that family members can provide. One at a time, thirty-six babies were placed on a "visual cliff"—a see-through plank stretching between two objects. The researchers told the mothers to look either positive or negative. With the seventeen mothers who looked fearful, none of the babies ventured across; with the nineteen mothers who looked approving, fourteen babies crawled across the plank. This experiment reveals that when anxious, young children use adults as reference points to guide their behavior.

The other day, I was on a plane with two families with preschool children. It was a stormy day, the plane and runway had to be de-iced before takeoff, and the flight was turbulent. Both mothers became frightened. One had her husband hold her hand while he read to the three young children, who remained quite calm. The other mother grabbed her son's hand, and he began to cry and covered his head with his coat.

It is obvious that children's fears come from within and without. It is also obvious that we can do a great deal to alleviate their fears. Telling children that their fears are silly or not real, however, is ineffective and denigrates their feelings. Their fears are real to them—just as the fear of the plane ride was real to the two mothers.

SOLUTIONS

Discovering the Cause of the Fear

The best course is to try to understand the cause of the fear. Begin by asking questions.

Has the fear been caused by a real event? Several weeks after the Fourth of July, one four-year-old balked at going to bed. It took a while for the father to figure out that his son had been awakened by firecrackers and had not understood what the booming noises meant.

Has the fear been caused by a change in the family's life? A mother of two who is a student reports that her children began having nightmares around the time of her exams. Her older daughter dreamed that her pet rabbit bit her, the younger one dreamed of being lost on the street. Because this mother was preoccupied with her own work during this time, perhaps her children felt her withdrawal as a rejection (being bitten by the rabbit) or a loss (being alone on an unfamiliar street).

By trying to probe for the cause of the problem, I don't mean grill your child. Young children are often unable to recall the source of the problem, or they don't want to resurrect troubled feelings. Think back to the events of the past few weeks to see if you can come up with a probable cause. A mother describes this process:

▪ ▪ ▪ *For the past few days, Cara has refused to get on the bus. I realized something must have happened. In talking to a friend who often brings her home I found out that one day she had stepped off the bus leaving Cara momentarily inside. The bus driver immediately reopened the bus door, but Cara must have been very frightened. Still, she didn't say a word about it.*

There may be many times that there is no discernible cause. Then, it's important to remember how normal children's fears are and how the pattern of fears changes as children grow up. Knowing this helps us respond more sympathetically.

Reframing the Problem

By sympathy, I do not mean that you should let these feelings overwhelm you or that you become undone by remorse, guilt, or the process of "if only": "If only I hadn't let my child go home with my friend" or "see that movie" or "listen to the TV news." Making mistakes goes with the territory of parenthood, and it's better to reframe the issue for yourself from "if only" to "what can I do differently next time."

Children learn a great deal from dealing with their fears. The mother with the child who was left on the bus says:

▪ ▪ ▪ *One day when I picked Cara up at school, she began to fuss. She threw her coat at me and announced she would not get on a bus. Because I didn't want to drag her out screaming, I talked to her until she calmed down. I told her I understood that she was afraid, that I would be with her and help her get over it, but that we lived in a city so we had to take buses.*

I turned the problem around so that it went from being overwhelming to being solvable. I feel good about it because it worked. She still grabs my hand tightly on the bus but I reassure her by saying, "The bus driver sees us and he won't close the door until we are both off."

Helping Children Understand That Fears Are Normal

It is helpful to children (just as it is to adults) to know that fears are a normal aspect of life. Many wonderful children's books address this issue. Ask your local librarian for suggestions. Some children find it more comfortable to talk about the characters in books instead of themselves. Others use books to open up about their own worries. The best children's books present problems as well as solutions that give strategies for coping that can stay with us into adulthood.

Several years ago when taping a cable television show on children's fears, I interviewed a group of five- and six-year-olds about what scares them most. The children asked to view the tape over and over. They were reassured to see that the biggest, seemingly toughest boy in the class had many fears (bears, snowstorms) as did the girl who appeared completely self-confident (dark rooms at night).

Parents' recollections of their own fears intrigue children. A son repeatedly asked his father to tell the story of how the father used to be afraid he'd wet his pants in school.

Modeling Coping Skills

Knowing that children look to adults as reference points, many parents consciously demonstrate how to cope. A mother who was at home with two children when a burgler tried to enter says:

. . . *I tried to stay as calm as possible. We called the police, and they came over. Together, we talked about what we'd do to prevent this from happening again.*

Other parents make a point of occasionally describing adult problems and how they were resolved: "I was nervous about giving a speech, but I picked a friendly face out of the audience and talked to him as if we were in the living room together."

Giving Children Control

Rather than saying "that's nothing to be afraid of," it's more helpful to give children techniques that put some control in their hands. One father told his children that their dreams are really their own—that they could think of them as television shows. When they went to sleep at night, they could imagine the dream they'd like to have and if they didn't like something, they could "switch channels." A mother whose child was scared of monsters suggested that she put those thoughts in a balloon and then pop the balloon.

In addition, parents can provide information so that children can anticipate what will happen in stressful situations: "When you go to the new school, here's what's likely to happen."

Of course, you should never deliberately frighten your child by saying, "The bogey man will come and take you away," or "That policeman will arrest you for being out of your seat belt in the car." Such threats create anxiety and undermine your child's self-confidence and self-discipline.

Providing Opportunities for Fantasy Play

Children's play offers them opportunities to master fears. If a child gets upset at going to the doctor, doctor kits can provide props for the child to be in charge of a drama about this episode. Similarly, a child with a fear of snakes, spiders, or dogs might like (but shouldn't be forced) to have small rubber or plastic versions of these animals to use in play.

Helping Children Solve Their Own Fears

One of the hardest dilemmas for parents is knowing when to nudge children and when not to. Do you make them secure by taking care of them or do you make them strong by giving them a push?

One way to deal with this is to involve the children in helping to solve their own problems. A parent whose four-year-old was afraid of going down the hall to the bathroom by himself asked him what he could do to feel better. He wanted his little sister, two years old, to go with him. She agreed. Here are some solutions that children have devised to ease their fears:

- a night-light in the bedroom for a child afraid of the dark
- a sword made of cardboard and aluminum foil in case a dragon comes
- an empty spray can of "monster spray" to get rid of monsters
- a happy face taped to the toilet

Parents can also ask children "What would you do if": if you got lost, heard a scary noise . . . As Marian Carey Hyson says, "The point is not to come up with a specific answer but to help children think of many solutions to problems." The fact of simply doing something in the face of fear builds children's self-confidence and coping strength.

Q *My child won't go anywhere without her blankie. Is this normal?*

In early childhood, many children form an attachment to an inanimate object (a blanket, an item of clothing, a stuffed animal). Carol Jordan's daughter Maggie, nearly three, is attached to her blankie.

▪ ▪ ▪ *Ever since she was born, she's slept with this blanket. I can't pinpoint exactly when she became attached to it, but when we went on a long trip when she was about nine months old, I realized she'd want her blanket. She held it most of the way.*

When she's tired or upset, she'll say, "I need my blankie." That means she really has to have it. She likes to finger one edge where the binding is ripped. She has to go to bed with it; sometimes she'll take it in the car. But, when she's involved in something else, she won't ask for it.

Carol has begun to worry about Maggie's attachment to the blanket:

▪ ▪ ▪ *My mother asked why my daughter needed a security blanket. That really got to me. I started to feel awful because I couldn't provide Maggie with enough security and comfort.*

Unfortunately, the term "security blanket" is used to suggest its opposite —insecurity. But in fact the child who has a blanket or other attachment object is coping well. About half of all middle-class American children use one to negotiate dependence and independence in the early years. The British psychiatrist Donald Winnicott calls such items "transitional objects." They are a transition from the present mother or father to the absent parent, from home to school, from waking to sleeping. In potentially stressful situations, attachment objects exert a powerful calming effect. For example, a four-year-old puts his "night night" (a piece of a quilt) on any part of his body that hurts. In one study, two- and three-year-olds accompanied by their blanket in a new learning situation performed as well as children who were with their mothers.

The transitional object has been called the child's first possession and creation. It belongs to the child who endows it with meaning, but it also belongs to the external world. Thus, it is a transition between the child's inner and outer worlds. At one level, Maggie's blankie is just a blanket, but it is really much more than that because of its emotional value to her. Very often these items become associated with a special smell, shape, or texture. Four-year-old Jeff uses two pacifiers in bed—one to suck on, the other to rest against his cheek because he likes its smell. Interestingly, Winnicott reports that creative artists are more likely than nonartists to have transitional objects or imaginary companions when young. Maggie's mother might view her daughter's blankie as an expression of her imagination and coping skills.

Because of its emotional significance to her daughter, Carol worried about Maggie losing her blankie:

▪ ▪ ▪ *When we were visiting friends in another state, Maggie went to a drop-in center for part of the day. On the way home, Maggie suddenly realized she had left blankie at the center. She panicked and began to cry. I said, "The center is closed, but we'll go back and check." Of course it was locked up, but we peered in the window. There was her blankie, on the edge of the couch where she'd put it after her nap. Maggie threw herself on the ground and cried, "I need my blankie." She was very upset, but I said, "It will be here for you tomorrow." Finally she accepted that and got distracted as we went off to buy cupcakes to bring to school the next day.*

I dreaded what would happen that night at bedtime. She cried and wanted it, so I explained again that she could get it tomorrow. Our friends' older daughter had a large supply of stuffed animals. I asked Maggie if she wanted to choose one of them to sleep with. She picked out a fluffy little dog and played with him for a while. I put her to bed but in about fifteen minutes she was up. She wanted her blankie. So this time, I asked her if she wanted to choose another blanket just for that night. She chose a fluffy child-sized one and took it back to bed, but she didn't really snuggle with it. Somehow we made it through that night.

The next morning she walked into the center, headed right for the couch, picked up her blankie, and then she got involved in play.

Other parents guard against the possibility of loss by having a replacement on hand. Brian Meyers recalls what happened when his son's toy lamb got lost:

▪ ▪ ▪ *When Tim lost his lamb in a park, I searched up and down with a flashlight but couldn't find it. I was upset because I knew how much the lamb meant to him. Tim kept saying, "You'll find it, won't you?" Finally, I had to tell him I couldn't. So we got him another lamb (plus a few spares). Last week he left this lamb at a skating rink. We went back and couldn't find it. He had a very long face and was very sad. Now it looks like he's picking up one of the spares. He has not forgotten the other lamb, and this new one is not the same, but he is dealing with it all right.*

Do blankets and stuffed animals belong in early childhood programs? Most child development experts say yes—they are a source of comfort when a child is under stress and represent something from home that can accompany the child into the new setting. Maggie's teacher's policy was that she could use blankie only in the rocking chair. Other preschools ask children to leave transitional objects in the cubbies except at nap time. We believe that programs should allow children free access to their blankets and stuffed animals during the day, especially in the first weeks. Children are the best judges of what they need when. Furthermore, because these objects are imbued with personal, emotional significance, children should not be made to share them.

Children will let you know when they are ready to abandon their stuffed animals and blankets. Carol has begun to see signs that Maggie's attachment to her blankie is waning:

▪ ▪ ▪ *Several times she's announced, "I don't need my blankie," and has left it at home. I'm so relieved because this blanket is looking pretty ragged and people must wonder why I let her drag it around.*

As children get older, most parents limit the time and place of the object's use. Carol wants to see if Maggie can save it for use at home or for very long trips in the car. Probably Maggie will be receptive, since she's already begun to take the initiative herself. But issuing ultimatums ("You can't have your blanket anymore") or being critical ("You're acting like a baby") would be counterproductive. They denigrate the child and intensify his or her need.

By five or six, most children have relegated these items to a shelf or closet. The surrender is usually gradual but sometimes dramatic—when one seven-year-old began to get a rash because his security blanket rubbed against his face at night, he suggested that it be burned, and it was.

If you worry that your child is overly dependent on a blanket or stuffed animal, early childhood educator Marie Jalongo suggests you consider the following:

• duration—has the attachment persisted beyond the age at which most children have begun to respond differently?

- intensity—is the child so involved that it interferes with his learning or being with other children?
- emotional distress—is the child under stress and struggling with a variety of problems?

If you answer yes, you need to look more closely at your child to identify any sources of stress and anxiety. Insisting that the child abandon the transitional object at this time will only make matters worse. If you are feeling stymied or frustrated, ask for help in assessing the situation from a teacher or other professional.

Those of us who had a favorite blanket or stuffed animal in childhood remember it well. Its special smell and feel are vivid; its comforting presence resonates. If we still have it, probably tucked in a box in the attic, we may enjoy taking it out every now and then and gently touching the blanket's frayed edges or the elephant's ragged body. We may even decide, as one father did, to pass it on to our own children—now his teddy bear accompanies his young daughter to sleep every night. These objects link us to our children, reminding us of their vulnerability as well as their capacity to cope in creative, meaningful ways.

Conclusion

Where the Wild Things Are by Maurice Sendak is a powerful symbolic treatment of independence and dependence in preschool children's lives. This classic children's story begins with Max making trouble. He is sent to his room without supper and runs away to a land where the wild things are. The wild things frighten him by roaring and showing their teeth.

The turmoil within Max, the struggle between his good and bad impulses, has led him into conflict with his parents, and so in his fantasy life he runs away. But what he confronts in fantasy is also frightening. Max is able to tame the creatures with his own magic and becomes the king of all the wild things. For the moment he has mastered his impulses and dealt with a world outside his own four walls. Now, he is free to return home where his dinner is waiting for him, still warm. *Where the Wild Things Are,* like my son's witch drawings, portrays the drama for us all to master adversity within and without.

The Social Life of the Young Child

Q *What are children's friendships like?*

Infants and Toddlers' Friendships

A mother of an eighteen-month-old says:

> ... *When I drop Adam off at day care, he looks for his best friend, Chris. They have a favorite ritual. One of them picks up the toy trumpet and they march around in a parade. On the weekend he'll ask, "School? Chris?" I think he really misses his friend.*

Until recently, child development experts assumed that infants and toddlers were too immature to relate to one another. But now that very young children are in playgroups or child care together, it has become apparent that they do interact successfully and sometimes form deep attachments.

What are the early interactions like? One-year-olds imitate one another, babble back and forth, and play simple social games. Toddlers are capable of more complex, cooperative play that involves taking turns and complementary roles. In one playgroup, the two-year-olds' favorite game was chasing and hiding behind a curtain. Still, much of young children's play is parallel—they play independently, but keep in proximity. They can also spend up to half their time just watching one another.

Toys and objects are vital to toddlers' interaction, and are involved in as much as 80 percent of their social exchange. Sometimes their interaction is friendly, as they take turns putting blocks in a pail, and sometimes there are struggles over the toys. But the great majority of toddler contacts are nonaggressive.

These young friendships have their roots in the parent-child relationship. The early commmunication skills like smiling and vocalizing that six-month-olds learn with their parents are subsequently used with one another. Many studies indicate that having a responsive, secure relationship with an adult lays the groundwork for social competence with age-mates.

Even in the first year of life, some children have distinctive styles of interaction. For instance, in a child-care group of 8- to 10-month-olds, Jenny, a responsive, adaptive playmate, was frequently approached by the other babies. Patrick, belligerent, was generally avoided. Toddlers with similar styles and temperaments tend to gravitate toward one another; those who are physically active may play together, as do the more quiet, reflective two-year-olds.

Are these early friendships important to children? Yes, judging by their frequency. In one child-care center, 71 percent of the infants had at least one friend and 100 percent of the toddlers did. Friends also make important contributions to development. Young children explore objects and the physical environment in more imaginative ways when together than they do when alone or with their parents.

Preschoolers' Friendships

A mother of a three-year-old says:

■ ■ ■ *For a long time, green was Sam's favorite color; he absolutely insisted on everything green. One day he announced blue was his favorite color. I asked, "Why?" and he said, "It's my friend in school's favorite color."*

A mother of a four-year-old says:

■ ■ ■ *Helen's suddenly aware that people can choose to play with her and choose not to. When they don't play with her, she feels totally rejected. She says, "I don't have any friends, no one likes me."*

A mother of a five-year-old says:

■ ■ ■ *My son is very opinionated about who will be his friends. His two closest friends live in our apartment building and he's known them since they were six months old. They were the only children he wanted to invite to his birthday party. He point-blank refuses to play with girls.*

Starting over fifty years ago, observational studies of preschool classrooms have provided a wealth of information on the social life of three- to five-year-olds. In a typical classroom, most preschoolers spend more time interacting with other children than with adults. Natural interests bring them together, whether it's playing out a family scene or painting pictures. Although toddlers tend to play in pairs, older preschoolers often play in groups. Sometimes a tight group of three to six children forms around favorite playmates and activities. In such a group, children try out their skills at leadership, cooperation, and self-assertion.

As twos and threes develop a gender identity ("I'm a boy," "I'm a girl"), many prefer same-sex playmates. Rather than being a rejection of the opposite sex, this more likely reflects a similarity of interests—boys tend to like boy activities (large muscle) and girls likewise (small muscle), although this is not always the case for individual children. By age five, the sex cleavage is usually quite pronounced in activities, and one sex may deliberately exclude the other from play.

What makes for a good playmate among preschoolers? Valued qualities are friendliness, outgoingness, giving praise and encouragement, being cooperative and empathetic, and accepting others. A degree of compliance also characterizes popular children; they are willing to compromise for the sake of keeping the play going.

Preschool friendships also include some conflict and disagreement. Child development experts consider this growth-enhancing, as long as the aggression does not get out of hand. Preschoolers learn that others have different points of view, and they are challenged to modify their own views. These experiences help them move from egocentrism to a more objective perspective.

Research indicates that the nature of friendship changes during the preschool years. One research team videotaped thirteen preschoolers at home, playing with another child their age. The three- and four-year-olds often asked each other about likes and dislikes and made "me too" assertions. They were creating a sense of solidarity and attachment. The five- and six-year-olds were more likely to differentiate themselves from their playmate by making a contrasting statement such as "I'm doing mine differently." They were laying the groundwork for cooperation, whereby friends can be different but assume complementary roles.

Many research studies have concluded that young children think about friendship in characteristically different ways than adults do. Starting at ages four and five, children define friendship as momentary and chance encounters: "We're friends because we share; we play together." Conversely, anyone who doesn't share or join in play is not a friend.

Young friends often seem manipulative: "I'll be your friend forever if you let me play with the puzzle, invite me to your birthday party," and so on. This concept of friendship derives from the preschooler's inability to understand fully that others have a different point of view and to coordinate that with their own perspective; the notion of mutual give-and-take is shaky. School-aged children's definitions of friendship broaden to include separate interests that allow tit for tat—"If you do this for me, I'll do that for you." By adolescence, friendship is seen as a more stable, enduring relationship based on an appreciation of each other's individuality and personal qualities.

Although preschoolers may say that all it takes to be friends is to play together and know each other's names, this is an oversimplification of what actually occurs. Preschoolers have favorite, long-standing playmates and intense feelings about these relationships. Their friendship behaviors are more sophisticated than their thinking about friendships probably because they lack the words to describe their social relationships in all their complexity and richness.

Why Are Friends So Important to Young Children?

Friends like to do the same things—whether it's jumping on and off a step twenty times or playing a pretend restaurant game. And they will sustain these activities long after an adult playmate has become bored. Friends also challenge each other at their own level—"Let's be fireboys and build a fire castle." They teach each other new skills and inspire confidence. A four-year-old who's never climbed to the top of the jungle gym will do it alongside a friend. Most of all, friends make a child feel special—someone who is liked and accepted, whose absence is missed and whose presence brings joy.

Q *When and how do children learn to share? It's an uphill battle with my child.*

Sandra Kane, mother of three-year-old Lillian, says:

• • • *Lillian used to have friends a year or two older, and they got along beautifully. But Lillian is reallly at an impasse with kids her own age. They do nothing but say "mine" and "no." It's just a standoff.*

When parents talk about the problems their young children have with other children, including siblings, sharing is at the top of their list. A father of twins puts it bluntly:

• • • *They spend so much time bickering over toys, even though there are plenty to go around. Sometimes I want to throw all the toys away, just to get them to stop fighting.*

Although playthings may be the most frequent battleground for preschoolers' possessive feelings, it's not the only one. They sometimes assert that a certain song is "mine and no one else can sing it." They also feel possessive toward other people. In the words of a mother of a four-year-old:

• • • *When my husband and I are talking to each other at the dinner table, David keeps interrupting us. He'll tell me, "Don't talk to him, talk to me."*

Many preschoolers feel especially possessive with the parent of the opposite sex; they want exclusive attention, unwilling to share the adult with the spouse or siblings. This phase, referred to as the Oedipal period (see the section on sexuality, pages 162–163), is normal and by five or six years diminishes in intensity.

Possessive feelings also characterize some friendships. A child-care teacher remarks:

■ ■ ■ *Preschoolers don't understand that you can be friends with many people at the same time. They tend to think it's all or nothing—if you're my friend, you can't be his friend.*

The Developmental Picture

What gives rise to these "grabby," possessive feelings? Some parents think it's because today's children are more spoiled, hence more selfish, than in previous generations or because so many are growing up as only children. Others insist that their children are just plain stubborn. These reasons may be partially true for some children, but possessiveness is so pervasive during the preschool years in all kinds of families that we must also seek a reason based on development.

Sharing is possible only when children are certain of possession, whether of a toy or a parent's attention. Children need to trust that if they let go of something, it will return and not be gone forever. Furthermore, sharing is difficult when children do not understand the relationship between an object and its owner—that you can own something even if it's not in your immediate possession.

Since two- and three-year olds are in the process of consolidating their sense of self, their toys, their clothes, their favorite drinking cup, even their favorite song are perceived as extensions of themselves. To part with them is like parting with a piece of themselves. For a young child to assert something is "mine" is not a sign of selfishness or weakness of character; rather, it's an important step in self-awareness. It's as if the toddler is announcing, "I can prove I'm Jeffrey because these are my blocks (not yours)." We see this behavior as a complement to toddlers' ubiquitous no; it reflects an understanding that they are separate beings.

In fact, being possessive about toys may be a first step in young children's social interaction. In a study by Laura E. Levine, toddler boys with a strong sense of self claimed their toys as "mine" in front of one another. Once this assertion was made, they could cross over these established boundaries and play together. In comparison, toddlers who had not yet achieved a strong sense of self did not claim ownership and were more likely to play alone.

Although you may be particularly aware of those moments when your child does not share, young children are capable of spontaneous cooperation and sharing. For instance, toddlers will roll a ball back and forth or play "chase me" and then reverse roles. This is the beginning of taking turns. Child-care providers and parents note that toddlers often want to share food—they'll pass a banana back and forth, each child taking a bite.

By the time many children are four and five years old, they have established a secure enough sense of self so that sharing is easier, especially with familiar playmates. They have learned that if their play is to continue, they must share, compromise, and negotiate. But in a new place with new playmates, it is understandable that initially they may claim ownership and protect their boundaries as a way of asserting autonomy and individuality.

SOLUTIONS

Sharing is not just an issue during the early years of childhood but follows us well into adulthood. How do we share our inner experiences? How do we share information and ideas so that we can work together and achieve common goals? How do we give and take in human relationships? When we think about the processes in children's learning to share, we see lessons to be learned at all ages.

Teaching Sharing

Because children need to hold on before they can let go, make sure that they have opportunities to assert their boundaries and ownership. Let them have things that need not be shared: "These are your very own sneakers that no one else can wear." Acknowledge their sense of self: "You are so big now that you can walk to the corner all by yourself." Keep in mind that research suggests that expressing possessiveness indicates a sense of self in two-year-olds and helps lay the groundwork for cooperative play.

With toddlers, you can indicate the idea of sharing by simple games. Take turns putting one block at a time in a pail; if there's another child nearby, encourage him or her to participate, too. You can also make a game of exchanging toys. You have a toy and so does your child; pass them back and forth. These are the rudiments of sharing and cooperation: "If I give this toy to you, I will get it back. If I take this toy from you, I have to give it back." In addition:

- Build empathy and consideration of others. For instance, the parents of David, the four-year-old who kept interrupting at the dinner table, told him, "You've had a chance to talk to Mommy today. It's Daddy's turn." They had to keep repeating this, but they were firm.
- Point out the consequences of not sharing: "When you pull John's toy away, he gets upset." This is called other-oriented discipline (see the section on discipline, page 15).

- Praise their efforts: "I like the way you let her use your new car."
- Enlist their help in problem-solving: "You both want to use this puzzle—how can we solve this problem?"
- Plan activities that require children to share their ideas and coordinate their actions, as in dramatic play. Encourage two children to string beads on opposite ends of a string—this teaches a different lesson than if each one has her own.

Above all, teach through your own behavior. Show how you share information: for example, telling a neighbor the street will be repaired tomorrow. Offer to share not-so-fun tasks with your children: "I'll help you pick up your room." In turn, this will make it easier for you to ask for their help.

- Think before you automatically say, "This is mine—you can't use it." Is this the message you want to convey? It's fine to have some things you do not want to share with your child but try to give your reasons: "It's an old necklace that Grandma gave me; it can break easily so I want to save it for special times."
- Fair does not mean treating everyone the same way: each child has unique needs. If one child has more playdough than the other, that may be okay with them. Let older preschoolers try to work things out between themselves. Do not insist on sharing unless a child seems unhappy or the situation is obviously exploitative.

Keeping Expectations Realistic

Many parents expect young children to share whenever the opportunity arises. Sometimes this comes from our own personality: if we dislike confrontation, we may be particularly pained to see our children fighting over toys or refusing to cooperate with their friends. If you believe that all two-year-olds should know how to share, you will be disappointed and frustrated most of the time. This was the case for Laura's mother:

. . . *When my daughter was two, I used to take her to the park. There would be so many squabbles in the sandbox, I would end up repeating "Share, share, share." Laura wouldn't share, and I would drag her home feeling like a failure. Finally, one day another mother said to me, "You know, I think it's okay if these kids don't share. They're too little to really understand." I felt reassured, like a big burden of guilt had been lifted. I realized that she wasn't ready. I sort of knew not to push when it came to things like toilet training, but this was a real revelation about sharing.*

Laura's mother realized that learning to share is a process which takes time.

Using Playthings

What kinds of toys encourage children to share?

- For two- and three-year-olds, it's easier to share things that there are a lot of: magic markers, books, Legos. One-of-a-kind items are the hardest to share. In many child-care settings there are at least two of the favorite items. This is not to say that you should rush out and buy duplicates of your child's toys, but it helps to have enough of the smaller, less expensive items to go around.
- Sometimes the attraction is not the toy itself, it's what's being done with the toy. Sharing the activity—not the plaything—is the issue. For instance, when Jeremiah saw Susan banging a pot with a spoon, he grabbed the spoon. What he really wanted was to join in. His mother handed him a ruler and a pail, and he could bang away, too.

Tug-of-War

When two children are grabbing the same block and screaming, "It's mine," should you let them fight it out? Young toddlers are too impulsive to work it out on their own. They are likely to bite or hit and can hurt one another. The adult must head off any physical confrontation. Asking "who had it first" in the heat of the argument will probably produce no response or contradictory stories. It's better to skip this question and move quickly toward a solution. You can try distracting and offer a substitute toy. You can set a timer—"In three minutes, you get a turn."

Instead of simply telling children to share, which is vague and moralistic, offer concrete solutions. For example: "One of you can ride the tricycle and pedal. The other one can ride on the back. Or you can each take turns riding around and then switch off. Which do you want to do?" With older children who can verbalize, try turning the problem over to them: "You both want this block—how can we solve this problem?" But it's important that you set the limits: "use words, no hitting or name-calling."

Some combinations of children share more easily than others. Your child may cooperate readily with one friend, perhaps someone he or she has known for a long time or who shares your child's particular interests. Sharing also tends to be reciprocal—if one child shares, the other is likely to as well. So if your child is having difficulty sharing with one playmate, there may be others who elicit more cooperative behavior.

Older versus Younger: Siblings

When siblings refuse to share, many parents believe that the older child should defer to the younger one. This, however, may end up increasing sibling rivalry. (See the section on siblings, pages 279–288.) You need to respect the older children's right to have possessions and to protect them from the ravages of younger ones. Talk with the older child and allow him or her to set some rules. For example, five-year-old Ellen agreed to share her toys with her younger brother "except for the new things I got for my birthday."

One father got so tired of hearing his sons fight over toys that most of the time he would just take the disputed object away. Although this solves the crisis at the moment, it is not a long-term solution. It is better to involve the children in working it out. As children get older, you can appeal to their sense of morality:

• • • *I say to my older daughter, "You weren't playing with it, can't he have a turn?" She's old enough to know that's reasonable. She responds well if it's stated this way.*

When Other Children Come to Visit: Preparing in Advance

Give the host child some say about which toys he or she wants to share. Children need not share each and every item. Put away the toys your child wants to keep off-limits. A parent has this advice:

• • • *I never make my son Chris share his favorites. If he doesn't want to share something, it goes into his closet, and no one can touch it.*

Children should never be forced to share their very special objects, like a blanket or stuffed animal that they use to comfort themselves. These things are so intimately a part of the children that they feel vulnerable if they're not in control of them. Of course, if children choose to share them, that's fine. One five-year-old handed his teddy bear to his younger brother, who was crying.

Q *What should I do when my child is bullied by other children?*

• • • *One afternoon I went to school to pick up Ben, my five-year-old. All the children were outside playing. Suddenly a bigger, older boy came up to him, smacked him on the back, and ran off in another direction. Ben was shocked. He didn't cry, but he just sort of looked at me, as if to say, "What did I do?" I asked him if he had caused it. He said no. The other boy's father was right there, but he didn't say anything. Should I have told Ben to hit back? Should I have spoken to the father? I wasn't sure what to do, so we just left.*

As I was driving home in the car, I got angrier and angrier. I felt so protective of Ben—he's no angel, but he doesn't hit like that. I really wanted to scream at both the other child and his father.

Ben's mother said Ben forgot about it, but she brooded about it for days afterward, angry at herself for not having done something. She and her husband considered giving Ben karate lessons. Her worries were reinforced when other parents told her that this particular boy tended to pick on other children.

Some aggression is normal in young children. Toddlers and preschoolers are learning how to control their impulses and to express themselves with words. They will hit, poke, and sometimes bite others in response to frustration. Such behavior must be curbed, but it does not mean the child will grow up to be a bully. However, when older children intentionally hurt or irritate others, the problem may be more serious. According to the latest research, elementary-school-aged children who frequently bullied others grew up to be adults who were more likely to abuse their spouses, punish their children more severely, and have more convictions for violent crimes.

SOLUTIONS

Parents are understandably upset when hostility and unfairness are directed at their children. Your responses should be directed first to the hurt child and secondly to the aggressing child.

Attending to the Hurt Child

Ben's mother did the most important thing—first, she asked him if he was hurt. In this case, he wasn't crying and seemed to be all right. She also expressed empathy, "Hitting is not okay." If you are at a park or another child's house and your child is being bullied, you can ask if he or she wants to leave. This is not running away; rather it illustrates your values—you will not permit hitting and, if it occurs, you will leave. Children who are bullying should know that one consequence of their behavior is that other children do not want to be with them.

Dealing with the Aggressing Child

Children need their parents to protect them, whether it is an unequal situation with an older child picking on a younger one or an equal one, with children about the same age and size. We think it's important to say something to the aggressing child: "If you want a toy, you have to ask." "If he was bothering you, use words to tell him. But you can never hit him." Such statements tell children that adult authority sets limits and will not allow hurtful behavior. Furthermore, you are also setting an example of how to handle hostility.

You will have to judge whether to involve the other child's parents. Whether or not you call in the parents, do not stereotype the aggressing child. Try to treat the child and the parents as you would wish to be treated in their situation. For instance, Ben's mother could approach the father in a nonthreatening way: "I didn't see what happened. Did you?" It would be useful to hear what he has to say and to assess how defensive he might be. Then she could empathize with him and let him know that his child is not mean or abnormal: "It's hard to teach children not to hit. It will be really nice when they've learned that lesson."

Ben's mother understandably wants to lash out at the other parent, but that would not be helpful because it would probably lead to a retaliatory or defensive action. The goal is to deescalate the bullying behavior and to help the aggressing child find other ways of communicating.

Understanding why a child is behaving like a bully can help your child cope: "This child has not yet learned how to use words to get what she or he wants." Because some children have a more physical style of interaction, they may express anger and affection in ways that can intimidate other children. If the other child means no harm, then explain this to your child.

Teaching How to Stand Up for Oneself

Help your child develop effective strategies to counter aggression. A few days after this incident, Ben and his mother had a talk:

■ ■ ■ *I asked what he would do if this happened again. He really didn't know. I said he could shout back, very loudly, "Don't hit me. That hurts. Leave me alone." I also told him that he could tell a teacher or adult. Ben listened to all this and then he said, "I could just go play somewhere else."*

After this conversation, Ben's mother felt somewhat reassured that her son had several plans and that next time he would not be as easily hurt.

A parent of a child now six says that teaching her son to assert himself was a gradual, ongoing process:

■ ■ ■ *When he first began nursery school, if somebody pushed him out of a chair and sat down in his place, he would just move and find another chair. The teachers encouraged him to say, "This is my place and you're not going to push me out of it." They worked on this for three years, but he learned to do it.*

Should young children be taught to hit back? We think not. Toddlers and preschoolers cannot make the distinction that it is all right to hit back in some circumstances but not others or to hit some people but not others. What they need is your help in controlling their aggression and putting their feelings into words.

Q *My child is very shy. How can I tell if this is a problem?*

Marilyn Christensen is concerned about Robbie, her three-and-a-half-year-old son:

> **. . .** *I took him to a birthday party and he stopped at the door and said, "We're going home." I said, "We can't, we've brought other people with us." Very reluctantly he went in. He stuck to my side for about ten minutes and then talked to a few kids. He wasn't interested in the magic show at all, so he went off and just played by himself. He always says he doesn't want to go to a party, and when we're on our way, he's very anxious and nervous the whole trip.*

Marilyn feels her own reactions aggravate the situation:

> **. . .** *I'm very tense around shy people. I don't want to shut Robbie out, but I feel like he's missing out. I love new things and meeting new people. It's very, very hard for me.*

Does Robbie's behavior indicate that he is overly shy? His parents should consider these points.

Shyness May Be Caused by a Lack of Social Skills

Perhaps Robbie holds back because he doesn't know how to initiate contact with others. Many shy children are inexperienced in social situations. Some ask to join in play so softly that other children simply do not hear them. Or once they do join in, they may not know how to cooperate and unintentionally disrupt the play. This frequently happens with Robbie. One day at school he wanted to build a tower but the others were building a railroad track; he couldn't find a way to complement their activity. His playmates got mad at him and he ended up building by himself.

Shy children are not necessarily unpopular or rejected by others, but they may be overlooked, especially in large groups. Psychologists have developed successful training programs for preschool and school-aged children that teach them the skills of friendship, such as what to say when they want to play with someone.

Extreme Shyness Has a Genetic Basis

Some children are born with a predisposition toward shyness and inhibition. They usually fit the profile of the temperamentally slow-to-warm-up baby discussed by Thomas, Chess, and Birch (see the section on temperament, pages 170–181). As infants they tend to show heightened wariness toward strangers. Physiological measures—heart rate, dilation of pupils, and levels of norepinephrine that amplify uncertainty and the excitability of stress reaction—differentiate them from non-shy children. They may also be prone to other symptoms of physiological arousal such as chronic constipation and allergies when toddlers, and nightmares and fears when preschoolers.

As a baby, Robbie had difficulty establishing a regular schedule. He always seemed sensitive to changes such as a new food or new people. According to his mother:

. . . *He's never been very loving and hugging, except with me or my husband, and once in a while his grandmother. If someone comes to the house and tries to talk to him, he pulls away.*

Robbie may have a biological predisposition toward inhibited or slow-to-warm-up responses. Even with a genetic basis, however, shyness can be helped. In one study, nearly one-fourth of the shy toddlers became less inhibited by four years of age due to parental efforts.

Shy Behavior Reflects the Child's Stage of Development

By about one year of age, infants show fear of strangers by withdrawing or protesting in their presence. This is an important behavioral milestone, indicating that the infant can distinguish the familiar from the unfamiliar. Somewhat older toddlers often exhibit a tension between exploration and wariness. They may approach strangers with interest but then stop and stare, keeping their distance. In older preschoolers shy behavior may be triggered by self-consciousness and an awareness that certain feelings or behaviors should not be revealed or that others will judge them. For instance, Robbie wants to go into the bathroom by himself and feels shy and modest about his body.

Most Shyness Is Not Abnormal

Psychologist Phillip Zimbardo surveyed 5,000 people on shyness; 80 percent described themselves as shy at some time in their lives. One-third of the children in a nursery school were rated shy by parents, teachers, and observers, and 42 percent of grade-school children considered themselves shy.

Most of us have felt shy. It is usually temporary, triggered by new situations or unfamiliar people. Once we feel more comfortable, these feelings generally dissipate.

The reactions of chronically shy individuals, however, are intense, pervasive, and long lasting. According to Zimbardo they tend to erect barriers in their contact with most people, whether friends or strangers. Their anxiety keeps them feeling isolated at work, school, home, and in the community.

SOLUTIONS

Building Social Skills

Some children prefer playing alone or with one or two friends, but this does not mean they are overly shy. What is important is that children be able to communicate effectively when they want to interact or if the situation demands it. No efforts (whether by parents, teachers, or more formal training programs) should attempt to make children popular. Instead, children should be helped to feel confident and capable in their social relationships, and individual differences should be respected.

In the case of shy children like Robbie who lack social skills, parents and teachers can work together in the following ways:

- Prepare them for changes. Preparation is almost always a good principle to follow with young children but is especially important with those who tend to hold back. Before going to a party, tell your child what he will be doing, how long you will stay. If necessary, call ahead for this information.
- Teach words and techniques for entering other children's play. "Can I help you do that?" and "I want to build, too—where can I put this block?" are effective openers. Using puppets for role-play can be helpful.
- Pair shy children with younger playmates who are less threatening than age-mates. Shy children will gain from higher status, and the lack of social skills will be less obvious.
- Provide one-on-one or small group activities. Many shy children, such as Robbie, feel overwhelmed in large groups.
- Organize special activities in which each child takes a turn.
- Provide large objects—such as a seesaw—that require cooperation.
- Try muscle relaxation exercises. When shy children become tense, one authority recommends "the floppy game." In a slow, soothing voice repeat several times: "Your whole body is loose and free, and you feel calm and quiet. Your arms and legs are just lying there all floppy, just like a

rag doll . . . Your face and neck, and even your tummy are all floppy too. You feel good."

- Remind children of previous successes. For example, Robbie's teachers note that over the year he has become more involved with other children; this is praiseworthy. When he's about to enter a new situation, Marilyn could say, "Remember when we went to Adam's house? At first you didn't want to go and you were very quiet when we arrived. Then you began to play with his toys and didn't want to leave."

Changing Parental Attitudes and Expectations

Marilyn never imagined that she and her child could be so different. If Robbie's inhibition is based on temperament, his reaction to new situations and unfamiliar people will tend to follow the same pattern in the years to come, and he is unlikely ever to be as outgoing as his mother. However, parents can use certain approaches to understand, accept, and encourage their temperamentally shy children.

- Try to stop blaming yourself. Knowing that shyness may have a genetic basis can be reassuring.
- Emphasize the positive. Robbie likes to build with Legos and to read books. He does not wander aimlessly at home or at school. He is not bullied nor does he suffer defeat when he fails to engage in play with other children. All in all, he is competent, self-reliant, and motivated. In fact, a more cautious, observant style in childhood has been associated with intellectual pursuits later in life.
- Avoid situations that require children to perform or show off. Robbie has learned a little Spanish in nursery school, but every time his mother asks him to say something in front of his grandmother, he clams up. As the parent of a three-year-old says, "During circle time, if the teacher asks who's wearing stripes, Ali will point to her striped overalls. But she won't speak up, and usually the teacher doesn't even see her. I tell myself that's okay, she's listening and responding in her own way."
- Avoid comparisons and reminders that others are judging your child. Marilyn admits: "I'm often tempted to say, 'Why can't you be like your little brother?' or 'How does your aunt feel when she's come all this way to see you and you won't even talk to her?' " A more positive approach is to discuss in advance what he could say to or show his aunt (a drawing, a new book).
- Avoid labeling. We all know about the power of self-fulfilling prophecies. Rather than saying that Robbie is shy, emphasize that he takes his time getting used to new situations.

Q *My child often plays with imaginary friends. What should I make of this?*

Marina Gleason, mother of Jonah, says:

• • • *Jonah, four years old, has invented three characters: Kahn, Min, and Mingo. Kahn is the name of his pediatrician. I think the other names come from "flamingo," a word he likes. He says they live in the city and take the bus back and forth to visit us. They're like real people. They get into fights, play games, and go to school. Sometimes they're about eight or ten years old, sometimes they're teenagers.*

Who Has Imaginary Companions?

Jonah is not unusual; it's estimated that a third to a half of young children have imaginary friends. They often come on the scene suddenly, usually first appearing when the child is between three and six. In fact, Jonah's parents cannot identify any precipitating event in his life.

Some parents worry that having an imaginary companion means that their child is lonely or withdrawn. However, several studies show that children like Jonah have as many friends and pets as other children do. A few studies, but not all, find that firstborns, including only children, are more likely to invent playmates than later-borns.

Research suggests that children who have imaginary companions are well-adjusted and creative. Psychologist Jerome Singer at Yale found that preschoolers who invent companions are less likely to be bored, use more advanced language, concentrate better, and are more cooperative. In another study, schoolchildren who scored high on standardized measures of fantasy (some of whom had imaginary playmates when younger) were more able to wait and to delay gratification, probably because they were able to provide richer mental experiences for themselves and thus make the time pass. Imaginary companions in childhood have also been linked to later "literary creativity" and have become immortalized in the writings of A. A. Milne, among others.

Why Do Children Create Imaginary Companions?

For the most part, children invent imaginary companions who are friendly, warm, and comforting. Children know that they are pretend but treat them as if they were real. They often represent the ideal companion, one who listens a lot and makes few demands. They may participate actively in the child's life—attending a pretend party or accompanying him or her on long car trips. They may help the child consolidate newfound skills. One preschooler says her pretend friends are teaching her how to button and to tie shoelaces; another four-year-old practices reading books to his imaginary companion. Some imaginary playmates help children meet challenges, such as moving into a new house or scaring away monsters at night. Other pretend companions represent an ideal self in which the child takes a vicarious satisfaction. If the child is shy, he or she may invent an outgoing companion; one hard-of-hearing child invented a companion with perfect hearing.

Imaginary companions can also mirror young children's struggles to become independent and develop a conscience. Just after her second birthday, Barbara invented Danny and Mary. Her mother explains:

■ ■ ■ *Mary doesn't do naughty things, but Danny hits and pushes. Sometimes Barbara prefers Danny to Mary. I think Danny reflects the negative feelings Barbara has but doesn't act out.*

Barbara's companions illustrate the psychoanalytic concept of "splitting." Very young children have difficulty reconciling the idea that good and bad impulses coexist within one person, and so they separate or split these qualities into "good people" and "bad people."

Similarly another child at age three viewed herself as good while her ever-present companion Genevieve was responsible for all wrongdoing: "Genevieve tore up the newspaper," "Genevieve went peepee on the floor." Thus the child affirms "I'm good and lovable; this other one is naughty."

With imaginary companions, children play out familiar parent-child scenes:

■ ■ ■ *Jonah will scold, "Mingo, you've been hitting Kahn, so you can't have any dessert," or "Mingo, I'm very disappointed in you when you hit Kahn."*

In fantasy, Jonah can do what he cannot do in real life. He can be a parent figure who punishes Mingo's aggression; he can feel strong and powerful when in reality he sometimes feels vulnerable and powerless.

Preschoolers also take on the role of a nurturing, loving parent with their imaginary friends:

■ ■ ■ *Eva tells her Tiger, "I'll be right back." Then when she returns, she says, "See, I told you I'd be back."*

Imaginary companions leave the scene when the child outgrows his or her need for them. This usually happens matter-of-factly, without any upset or drama. Most are gone by the time children are six years old, when school provides increased opportunities for new friends and interests. Coincident with this timing is a shift in the child's thinking processes, from less reliance on fantasy to a more orderly, logical orientation.

If your child has a pretend playmate, remember the words of noted child psychoanalyst Selma Fraiberg: "The child who employs his imagination and the people of his imagination to solve his problems is a child who is working for his own mental health."

SOLUTIONS

Most parents accept their children's imaginary companions and concur with the mother who says:

▪ ▪ ▪ *Her pretend friends are wonderful companions wherever she goes. They never get in the way of her playing; they expand it.*

Even so, many parents have questions of a practical nature.

How should I relate to my child's imaginary companion? Emilia's mother says she never initiates reference to her daughter's pretend friend Annie, but if Emilia mentions Annie, the mother acknowledges her:

▪ ▪ ▪ *I'll say, "How nice that Annie had a party today" or sometimes I'll challenge a bit: "It's amazing how Annie can change sizes like that."*

Emilia's mother does what many parents do: she talks directly to her child about the imaginary companion, but does not speak to the pretend friend. This acknowledges the child's fantasy as fantasy but not as reality.

What if the imaginary companion oversteps limits? If your child says, "Don't sit there, that's Beepo's place," tell him, "I'm sorry, that's where I usually sit. Tell Beepo to find another spot." If your child puts the blame on her pretend friend, handle it as you would other misdeeds: follow through on the consequences and explain why the behavior is unacceptable. But let your child act as the intermediary. For instance, if your child says, "Smithie dumped out the cereal," you can reply, "Tell Smithie that it has to be cleaned up and that you will do it for him."

It is important to respect your child's feelings about his or her imaginary companions. Never humiliate or make fun of a child who has an imaginary companion; invented friends are a constructive way to cope with developmental issues during the preschool period.

Allow the child to control his or her make-believe world. Do not suggest that the child set a place at the table for the pretend friend or make room for it in the car. If the imaginary companion can be controlled by others, it becomes a threat to the child, just as any other powerful "real world" adult can be.

Can having an imaginary companion ever be cause for concern? For some children, the imaginary companion may linger into elementary school, taking on a central role in the child's life to the exclusion of real friends and other interests. In this case, the imaginary companion may be a symptom of more serious issues. As a parent, you would want to look at your child's life at home and at school. Is she or he feeling anxious about something? It would be advisable to talk to your child's teacher as well as to other professionals who can provide you with an objective assessment. As an outsider, you cannot make your child's imaginary companion go away, but you can reduce the need for it.

Moral Development

Q *How do children learn what is right and wrong?*

Alison Fields says her five-year-old daughter, Heather, sometimes does things that are considered wrong:

∎ ∎ ∎ *She'll say she didn't take a cookie when one is missing and she's the only one who could have done it. Once she brought a toy home from kindergarten that belonged to another child.*

The other day I left some money on the kitchen table. I couldn't find it anywhere and I asked Heather if she'd seen it. She said no. Later, I found it in her drawer. When I confronted her, she denied taking it in the first place.

Parent's Reactions: Feeling Vulnerable

This incident made Alison question her ability as a parent:

∎ ∎ ∎ *My heart sank. Here she was, stealing from her own mother. Why didn't she just ask me? I would have given her some change for her piggy bank. I really felt at that moment as if years of trust between us had evaporated.*

Alison felt betrayed because she thought that she had communicated to Heather that stealing and lying were wrong. Now she wondered, "What have *I* done wrong?" Because parents tend to feel responsible for their children's behavior, they can end up feeling like failures when their children violate basic moral principles. Many parents worry—"Will they turn out to be good people?" They fear for the future—"Will they get into serious trouble as adolescents?"

With Stan Farley, the issue is his son's rudeness:

> ● ● ● *I want Peter to get along with people, but we're having a hard time with him. When someone approaches him, he'll refuse to talk or he'll block the front door and say, "Don't come in."*

When this happens, Stan often thinks that "Peter is out to get me" and feels a loss of authority as the parent. Stan is, however, uncertain about whether his son's behavior is entirely reprehensible:

> ● ● ● *I want him to learn to stand up for himself. Why should he have to say hello whenever adults say hello to him? But I also want him to be nice to people and to be considerate of their feelings.*

When parents like Stan are ambivalent about what is right in a situation, children pick up on this. This may be one reason that Peter usually refuses to be "nice" when his father tells him to be.

Other parents fear they have lost moral authority. They worry because their children are bombarded by values contrary to their own. Television programs glorify violence; "me-ism" and materialism are rampant. The father of a four-year-old voices another concern: "Now that Daniel is in nursery school and more on his own, he's going to see other kids hitting and swearing, things I don't approve of." Some parents harbor the impossible fantasy of isolating their children from negative influences.

A typical reaction of parents to these feelings of vulnerability is the desire to punish their children. This was Alison's response: she wanted to teach Heather a lesson "so that she'll never do this again." Despite feeling angry, parents may also feel protective. They want to shield their children from pangs of guilt or shame. This is sometimes the case with Stan Farley:

> ● ● ● *Sometimes when Peter is rude I'll make excuses, saying that he's tired or sick. I know those aren't the reasons, but I don't want other people to criticize him.*

Of course, Stan's excuses for Peter's rudeness also protect him from feeling criticized as a "bad father."

HOW MORAL DEVELOPMENT PROCEEDS

Although we may envision a child who takes a parent's money as a future troublemaker or a child who is rude as potentially antisocial, such acts in the preschool years do not necessarily mean the absence of a strong moral code. Developing a sense of morality takes time, and preschoolers are just at the beginning stages. As a first step, we can understand how our children's behavior is part of a pattern in the development of morality. Then when we explain rules or give reasons why children should act in a particular way, our knowledge of moral development helps us key into their level of understanding. Furthermore, when we have insight into how moral development proceeds, we usually end up feeling reassured that our children's behavior is normal. In the words of one mother, "I'm glad to know that my four-year-old will not be dishonest forever."

Four major strands in moral development are evident in the preschool years:

1. the formation of the conscience;
2. the development of guilt;
3. the ability to think in moral terms;
4. the tendency toward empathy.

These four aspects of moral development coexist in the child. They are normal developmental processes, the result of maturation and everyday experiences. A useful way to think about these processes is that they provide the framework or the structure while you, the parents, and the larger society provide the specific moral content. Families differ in their beliefs and values. For some, religion may be the source of moral principles; for others, the value of education may be primary. We will not discuss what moral principles or values to teach except in the general sense of instilling a respect for life and concern for others. But by understanding the processes of moral development, you will be more effective at passing on your particular values and beliefs to your children.

FORMING A CONSCIENCE

In everyday terms, having a conscience means that young children can repeat to themselves the instructions they have heard from their parents ("Don't hit," "Be gentle with the baby"). This process is well underway in the preschool period and by five or six years of age, the basic components of the conscience (also called the superego) are in place. Although Heather has the beginnings of a conscience, it does not function as effectively or reliably as it will in a few years. Faced with great temptation, Heather couldn't say no to her immediate wish—to take the money. At this stage, young children often take things because their desires are more powerful than their self-control. They simply cannot help themselves.

Heather's subsequent lying about having taken the money is an example of just how strong young children's fantasies are. She was not intentionally distorting reality so much as expressing her wish that this was the way it was. Preschoolers live in a magical world where wishing one did not do something is equivalent to believing that one actually did not do it. Sometimes children tell tall tales for the same reason, wishing that the fantasy were true.

From everything we know, love and conscience development go together in the early years. Babies' attachments to the people who love and care for them are their first links to the human community and to a set of standards and values. Numerous studies of young children reared in institutions where they were deprived of close bonds with a loving adult have found that these children failed to develop a conscience. By virtue of loving their parents and wanting to be like them, children begin to internalize parental standards and prohibitions. This is the process of "identification" that Freud and others refer to as the basis of conscience formation.

Because parental values and standards form the core of the child's conscience, the role models parents provide make a difference in moral development. Alison considers herself honest and sets an example for her daughter: "I pay the right fare for Heather on the bus." Stan Farley, Peter's father, treats other people with respect. Over next few years, Heather and Peter will more completely internalize their parents' values. At this stage of development, Peter's refusing to say hello is probably a statement of his independence—in effect, he's saying, "I'm my own boss."

How parents discipline can facilitate conscience building. According to Martin Hoffman, an authority on moral development, the best technique involves giving reasons and explanations about why a child should change his or her behavior or appealing to the child's emerging sense of fairness or empathy. Parents who assert their power ("Do it because I say so") or rely on physical punishment teach a morality based primarily on fear of detection and punishment. Another technique that parents use—withdrawing love, refusing to speak to the child until she or he apologizes—frightens the child into being overtly compliant and feeling guilty but it is not the best way to build a conscience. Children do need to be disciplined but not in ways that are punitive or scary.

Although preschoolers' conscience may seem primitive and self-centered to adults, young children generally want to be on the side of right. Several days after the incident with the grocery money, Heather told her mother, "I'm a good girl." When children, even two- or three-year-olds, begin to apply moral labels like "naughty" or "nice" to themselves and to others, this is a sign that they are developing internal standards of right and wrong.

DEVELOPING A SENSE OF GUILT

As part of identifying with their parents, children also adopt the parents' capacity to punish themselves. This is experienced as guilt. Young children are more likely to feel guilty after the fact; most have yet to develop a sense of anticipatory guilt that checks their impulses before they act. Thus, Heather could not think ahead: "If I take this money I'm going to feel bad later, so I won't take it." However, there were several indications that Heather felt guilty afterward. Her mother says:

. . . *She asked me repeatedly, "Do you love me?" She seemed unusually quiet during dinner. For the first time ever I saw her pinching herself, and I had to tell her not to hurt herself.*

Psychologists think that some degree of guilt is useful in guiding an individual's behavior. But because the conscience or superego of four- and five-year-olds is still primitive, they sometimes end up feeling overly guilty, way out of proportion to the offense. One parent describes her preschooler as "filled with remorse when she's done something wrong. I really have to help her let herself off the hook."

Sometimes children seem to egg their parents on, as if deliberately provoking punishment. Lyle Gunderson's mother describes a particularly horrible day when her son kept "pushing" her.

. . . *The first thing that happened was on our walk: he looked right at me and rode his tricycle into the street. I grabbed him hard. He grabbed at my blouse and yelled, "I'm so mad at you, I'm going to punch you right in the stitches." I had just had a cesarean.*

Back home, he began to throw blocks, and this is a child who doesn't hit or throw things. I knew he was just asking for it, so I told him to go to his room. When he came out, he looked relieved.

Lyle's anger had escalated to the point where he could not control himself. His mother was right to say he was asking for it—he was asking her to set the limits. He felt guilty over his aggression toward his mother, whom he deeply loved and needed. Most likely, Lyle did not think all this through consciously, probably all he experienced was a need to be punished, to be paid back for his wrongdoing and, as it were, to wipe the slate clean.

You may be tempted to spank your children when their behavior is exceptionally unruly. The problem with spanking is that it teaches the wrong lesson—if you are big enough, you can get away with hitting or anything else.

At other times, young children seem to show little sense of personal responsibility. They blame wrongdoing on others or even imaginary friends ("Wonka did it"). Stan Farley remembers:

> ▪ ▪ ▪ *One day Peter was climbing on a chair, which he wasn't sup-posed to do. The chair tipped over, knocking a lamp to the floor. Peter started to kick the chair and scream, "Bad chair." He never really owned up to the fact that he made this happen in the first place.*

At this age children are not aware that they could have acted differently. In Peter's mind, the only possible action was the one he took. This is why he did not feel personally accountable for his behavior. But as preschoolers grow, the seeming lack of guilt, or conversely, the excess of guilt, can come together into a healthy sense of guilt that serves as an internal monitor of behavior.

CHILDREN'S ABILITY TO THINK IN MORAL TERMS

Along with developing a conscience and a sense of guilt, preschoolers begin to do their own reasoning about what is right and wrong, good and bad, fair and unfair. The mother of Martin, four and a half, observes this process:

> ▪ ▪ ▪ *He'll ask, "Mommy, is it good to stick your hand out of the car when it is moving? Is it good to tie knots in your shoestrings? Is it good to hit Jake when he hits me?" He'll try things that he thinks are good things to do and things that are bad things to do.*

Being able to think and reason about moral issues is a great achievement, an outgrowth of intellectual maturation and social experience in the early years. Yet, at this stage of development, how children think about what is right and why a person should be good differs from adult thinking. The late Lawrence Kohlberg from Harvard University proposed a six-stage se-quence of moral reasoning; each stage has its characteristic ways of think-ing about right and wrong.

At the first stage, children around three and a half or four years of age reason from the perspective they know best—their own. They equate what is right with what they want, whether it is keeping a toy "because I found it" or thinking they should get the most pizza "because I like pizza." This first stage seems to be the epitome of egocentric morality and provides a convenient rationale for a fragile conscience to succumb to temptation. For example, Heather probably reasoned, "I want the money, therefore I should have it."

At the next stage, around age five, children tend to define what is right as doing what adults say to do because of their capacity to reward or punish. Their reasoning goes like this: "It's wrong to steal or lie because my mother says so. I better not do it because she won't like it." This second stage of moral reasoning represents something of an advance over the preceding egocentric stage for two reasons. First, the child now has the capacity to take another person's perspective (for example, a parent's) into account. Second, the child has a sense of future consequences instead of simply living in the all-consuming present.

The moral egocentricity of young children is obvious in many of their actions. For example, Elaine McFadden complains that her five-year-old cheats when they play Candyland:

■ ■ ■ *When it's Sean's turn and I'm ahead, he'll just move his pieces along the board without any regard to the rules. He does it with perfect ease, not feeling guilty at all. He'll just announce, "I want to win." Sometimes I find all of this amusing, and sometimes it really gets to me. Then I just want to end the game.*

As Elaine says, young children's cheating seems so obvious. They make no effort to disguise or deny it, unlike older children who know that cheating is wrong and something to hide from adults.

For children Sean's age, rules are not yet held as inner convictions and are not seen as having any intrinsic purpose except to serve their own interests—in this case, winning the game. In time, Sean will understand that rules are binding, unless everyone agrees to make changes. But right now Sean bends the rules to his own advantage without even being aware that's what he's doing.

Young children think about moral issues in terms of black/white, shoulds/should nots; they believe that the world is just—good is rewarded and bad is punished. So if something bad happens to them, they must have done something bad to deserve it. To their way of thinking, a cut finger or a lost toy could be punishment for a misdeed. This is like the adult who, after misfortune, asks, "What did I do to deserve this?"

Young children also typically focus on what can be seen rather than inferred. In his studies of moral development, Piaget described how children judge the rightness or wrongness of an act by its consequences, not by the person's intentions. In everyday terms, this means preschoolers often have difficulty distinguishing an accident from a deliberate act. When her younger brother stepped on her box of crayons and broke them, Heather got very mad and upset. It didn't matter that her mother explained it was an accident. However, like many preschoolers, Heather is also quick to excuse her own behavior and say "I didn't mean it . . . it was an accident." She thinks that automatically absolves her.

In the early stages of moral development, children also display magical thinking. They assume their parents can read their minds and know their "evil" wishes. When one mother found her son upset, she discovered it was because he had dreamed he had bitten his baby brother. He felt guilty for a deed he only imagined doing. In this case, his mother pointed out to him that his baby brother had no teeth marks and was not crying. She explained that a dream was not real and that dreaming of doing bad things sometimes keeps people from doing the bad things in real life.

As their cognitive abilities develop and their social experience widens, older children think about moral issues in different, more mature, terms. School-aged children consider many other points of view and define being good as living up to their own internal standards. Stealing or lying are considered wrong because they interfere with trust and mutual respect. But according to Kohlberg, it is not until late adolescence or adulthood that abstract moral principles such as the Golden Rule and respect for individual rights are understood. It has also been found that over the course of development, girls' sense of morality emphasizes interpersonal concerns, while that of boys emphasizes justice.

GROWING TOWARD EMPATHY

Although we tend to characterize young children as morally egocentric, they are capable of empathy. Being considerate and helpful toward others are important aspects of moral development. The mother of Maria, a five-year-old, is very proud of her daughter's sensitivity:

■ ■ ■ *When Maria began day care, another girl cried when her mother left. Maria would take her by the hand and say, "Don't worry, your mommy will come back." Then Maria would ask if she'd like to paint or draw. Usually the other child continued to cry, but I was glad Maria tried to make her feel better.*

Young children have many opportunities to observe acts of caring as their parents comfort, stimulate, and respond to their needs. And most parents also reinforce their children's acts of kindness. But empathy seems to arise from a deeper source than learning through experience.

Much current thinking indicates that we are born with the capacity to empathize and to respond to the distress of others. Babies display a primitive form of empathy when they begin to cry along with other crying babies. A two-year-old's empathy is still egocentric (he or she may offer a bottle to a crying mother), but by three or four years of age, children begin to show empathy in appropriate ways, covering the father with a blanket when he is resting or giving a toy to a crying child.

In one research study, preschoolers were asked which is worse—to hit someone or to break the school rule about where to eat a snack. Their reasoning was very similar to adults; the children made comments like "hitting is more wrong because it hurts someone" or "hitting makes people unhappy."

Parents may be baffled by these contradictory aspects to preschoolers' morality—their egocentricity alongside their consideration for others. The explanation is that young children are most likely to be egocentric when their own wishes are being frustrated. When they want a toy, a turn on the swing, another cookie, they cannot easily put themselves in someone else's shoes. On the other hand, if children are bystanders and neither the aggressors nor the victims, they are more likely to express empathy.

These four strands of moral development—developing a conscience and a sense of guilt, thinking about moral issues, and expressing empathy— represent growth in children's ability to understand right and wrong and to act accordingly. Although as parents of young children you may be aware of how much more they must learn about being good, you can appreciate the processes in moral development that are underway in the preschool years and look for ways to support them.

SOLUTIONS

Creating an Atmosphere of Mutual Respect

If children are to grow morally, they need to experience respect and reciprocity. Beginning early in life, how they themselves are treated will affect how they treat others. Stayton, Hogan, and Ainsworth found that mothers who were responsive to their babies' signals—for food, comfort, attention, stimulation—had babies who, in turn, were responsive to maternal requests and commands. Cooperation on the part of mothers seemed to engender cooperation from their babies.

The same principle holds true for older children. Parents need to respect toddlers' struggles for independence and help them find alternatives when there is a conflict. Morality involves balancing one's rights with the rights of others; young children can understand that principle in simple terms: "You can have a turn after Jonathan is finished"; "I'm going to rest until four, and then I'll play a game with you."

Help your young children learn how people live and work together by letting them contribute to the well-being of the family. Preschoolers can empty wastebaskets, set the table, put their clothes in the laundry basket. These efforts help counter their tendency toward self-centered thinking.

Keep in mind that moral development involves acting morally, not just avoiding wrongdoing. Praise children's acts of kindness, empathy, sharing, talking things over instead of fighting: "It's good that you put your sister's puzzles back. Now she'll know where to find them."

If religious values are important to you, be sure to share them with your children. As Thomas Lickona, an authority on moral development, says:

> *Religious faith alone will not necessarily make a child good, and there are many children who manage to be good without it. But faith can help a child grow up with positive moral values.*

Making Good Rules

As parents and children grow, parents must sort out where they stand on issues. Certainly children push us for a clear position, but during this time of uncertainty we can feel wishy-washy and that adds to the difficulty of this task. It is normal to go through a fumbling period before arriving at the dos and don'ts that are most important to you.

Part of teaching moral values is establishing rules in the family. Two guidelines can help you make rules that your children will respect:

- Set limits and ground rules that are fair and based on good reasons. Explain your logic: "The rule is that you cannot go outside the yard without telling me so I know where you are."
- Let your children participate in finding ways to respect and honor your principles. Elicit their ideas. "Let's think of a way that you and Johnny can remember not to fight at the dinner table."

Do not give your children a choice about rules unless you really mean it. They shouldn't have a choice about the rule for holding hands when crossing the street, but you could let them have a say about how to divide up household chores.

Some parents post their most important rules on the refrigerator or bulletin board for all to see: 1) no hurting anyone physically 2) no hurting anyone with words. Here are other rules parents have set:

■ ■ ■ *You can't call Mommy "dummy" because I hate that.*

■ ■ ■ *I told Matthew I will never buy him chewing gum and that he'll never see me chew it. But if a friend offers it to him, then that's all right with me.*

It is very important to tell children they must set their own rules and limits when being threatened or treated unfairly. Preschoolers can learn to say, "Don't take my toy because I'm still playing with it," or "I don't want Uncle Sam to pick me up and pinch my cheek." Recent public attention given to sexual abuse has made it clear to many parents that they should teach their children that their bodies are their own and they have a right to say no to what is uncomfortable or upsetting.

Developing Self-Discipline

One of the most important tasks of parenting during the preschool years is to help children develop self-discipline. At first, young children depend on adults to provide controls and limits for them. This is especially true for preverbal children who have no words to tell themselves "No, don't pick the flowers."

Yet even children who are four or five years old need a great deal of adult help because their internal voice or conscience is easily overruled by temptation. So, for example, you can remind your preschooler of the rules beforehand: "Remember when we go into the store, you can choose one book and no more." A useful technique is to ask the child to repeat the rule: "Tell me what the rule is about wearing seat belts." This will help the child remember the rule and feel in control of his or her own behavior.

If your child continues to break a rule (for example, against running around inside) use a problem-solving approach. Here is what one parent of a five-year-old did:

■ ■ ■ *I said to her, "How can I help you control your running? I'm tired of telling you to stop all the time." She said she should wear her slippers inside, because her sneakers made her feel like going fast. I thought that was a good solution.*

A critical aspect of self-discipline is a sense of personal responsibility. One of the most important techniques parents can use is to show how the child's action led to an event or someone else's distress. This is especially important for young children who may not see a connection between their behavior and an outcome. For example, Stan Farley could tell his son, "When you didn't say hi to Joseph, he felt bad. Then when you wanted to play with him, he didn't want to because you had hurt his feelings."

Using Guilt Constructively

Children need to learn how to handle their guilt feelings. They should not be left with a sense of overwhelming guilt after they have transgressed; rather, they need to find a way of "paying the price" and alleviating pangs of guilt. Sometimes saying "I'm sorry" is sufficient. You should also apologize to your children when you feel you have treated them unfairly. Finding reasonable ways to make reparations is helpful. For example, when Simone brought a toy home from the store without paying for it, her parents insisted she return it. But they went to the store with her while she handed it to the storekeeper without comment. This avoided humiliating the child but also presented her with the consequences of her action.

Reacting to Your Child's Behavior

Sometimes parents punish their children by saying things like "I'm not going to speak to you again" or "I don't love you." Even if said in jest, children can feel threatened with loss and abandonment. They may conform in the short run in order to win you back, but you will not be helping them build internal standards and self-discipline.

The best motivator is love, not fear. Reassure your children that you still love them even when you disapprove of their behavior. They may consider their misdeeds far more serious than you do and feel very guilty or anxious. Giving reassurance at this point is particularly important.

Teaching Honesty

When Alison found the money in Heather's drawer, she tried to extract a confession from her, but the more she pushed Heather into a corner, the more insistently Heather denied taking the money. Heather was not deliberately being dishonest as much as she was trying to avoid punishment and expressing the wish that she had not taken the money.

Instead of trapping Heather in a lie and ending up in a no-win situation, Alison could have said: "When I couldn't find the money, I checked your drawer, and there it was." This shows Heather that her mother values honesty because she is being forthright with her child. When you get the truth right out in the open and avoid any hidden agendas, everyone can save face.

Appealing to Children's Desire to Be Good

Preschoolers want to be good and this generally means doing what adults tell them to do. You can build on this tendency by making positive requests to elicit their cooperation. For example, one psychologist describes how his son would protest when told, "It's time to stop playing. We've got to go home." When the father rephrased his directive, "This is a chance to obey ... Let's get ready to go home," his son was much more agreeable. You can also make obedience a challenge: "By the count of five, let's pick up the red blocks."

Building Empathy

Although we are probably born with the capacity for empathy, certain child-rearing practices foster it. According to research, parents with the most empathetic children do the following:

- give children affection and respect
- are helpful themselves
- call attention to the child's feelings ("Are you feeling lonely because Sandy can't come over and play today?")
- call attention to other people's feelings ("He's sad because he lost his dog"), and to their own feelings ("I'm happy that Grandma called on the phone.")

In one study, mothers who talked to their firstborns about the needs and feelings of younger siblings ("He's cooing because he's happy") had older children who were more friendly and affectionate toward the younger children later on.

Other ways to build empathy:

- Give reasons for rules or prohibitions that involve consideration of others: "When you pick up your toys, no one will fall over them and you'll know where to find them."
- Point out the implications of children's behavior for other people: "You hurt his foot when you did that," or "She wants to play and when you say go away, she feels angry."

It is also important to provide opportunities to develop empathy in a nondisciplinary context. One family sponsored a child through CARE as a way of sensitizing their children to other peoples' needs. Another family spends one day a month at a shelter for homeless people; their preschooler helps by setting the tables, peeling carrots, and performing other useful tasks.

Moving Away from Moral Egocentrism

Kohlberg and other psychologists who describe stages of moral thinking suggest that there are two ways to relate to a child's moral stage: (1) "go with the flow," that is, respond to their present level and help them use the reasoning ability they have, and (2) "challenge," in other words, ask them to look at the world in a new way.

At home, when preschoolers equate what is fair with what they want, offer incentives for following rules and requests: "When you're done picking up your room, we can go to the toy store." This reinforces the idea that if they do what they are asked, they may get what they want. This approach meets them at their level. At the same time, challenge their egocentrism: "Think of other reasons why I should buy this toy. Because you said so is not reason enough for me." Saying something like this will stretch their thinking.

The objective is to expose children to a point of view different from their own, *not* to rush them into the next moral development stage. In time, they will be comfortable with a new way of thinking about moral issues.

Promoting Interaction with Other Children

One of the most important stretching experiences that parents can offer their children is contact with other children. As children play and learn together, they encounter differences: "They eat with chopsticks . . . We don't." "It's fair because I say so . . . No, it's not." Such experiences challenge children's egocentric perspectives and help them learn to accommodate to the views of others. Among friends their own age, children are on equal footing (more or less), unlike with adults. This gives them the chance to learn how to disagree, work toward consensus, and find resolution. Child development experts say that experiences with other children lay the groundwork for learning about cooperation, equality, and fairness, which are important ingredients of morality.

Parents can value this interaction with other children and take advantage of its inherent opportunities for moral growth.

- Encourage your children to take their friends' perspectives: "Why do you think she wanted you to do that?"
- Help your children problem-solve with their playmates: "You seem to be arguing and not really playing. Let's try to find a way that is fair to everyone."

Holding a Family Forum

Moral issues come up every day in families because families are made up of individuals with different needs and wishes. You can make potentially difficult situations an opportunity to stretch everyone's moral reasoning by examining different points of view. A father explains how this happens in his family:

... *When my kids (two, five and seven) are not getting along, we call a family council. Each of us has a turn to talk and say what's on our mind. We each have a "talk ticket" and everyone else has to listen. Afterward, each of us talks about what the others said, and how it's different from what I felt. Then we try to find some resolution.*

Discussions like this, at home and at school, foster understanding and empathy and challenge egocentric tendencies. Another family has a regular get-together on Sunday night to review the week and to think ahead to the next week and how to make it better for everyone.

Seeing the Lighter Side

Finally, although we tend to think of moral development as very serious business, it is important to maintain a sense of fun and play, too. One father explains how his four-year-old makes up a game:

... *He asks a serious question: "Is it okay to wash my face with shampoo?" I answer and he asks again, this time getting silly, "Is it okay to wash my face with shaving cream . . . with soap for the washing machine?" We keep on going like that. It's a litany, one we both enjoy.*

This activity, in the spirit of fun, builds the child's confidence in distinguishing right and wrong. Also, by asking outrageous questions whose answers he already knows, he feels good about himself and his knowledge.

Another parent capitalizes on children's love of rhyme and language by making up rhyming rules: "Toys left out make parents mad, toys picked up make parents glad."

As parents, you are at the center of your children's moral development. You are their first moral teachers and exemplars. Your children identify with you, eventually incorporating your values and standards into their own moral system. Yet, developing a strong conscience and self-discipline takes time. It will be years before your children understand right and wrong and the meaning of rules in the same way you do. The foundations are laid in early childhood in the ways you discipline, explain rules, show affection, and convey respect for your children.

Sex Roles

Q *How do children develop a sense of their own masculinity and femininity?*

Sex role development is fraught with controversy. Impassioned forces work both for and against change in attitudes and behavior. As more mothers are employed outside the home at earlier stages in their children's development and as more fathers share in household tasks, sex role expectations have changed. The women's movement has challenged traditional sex roles, and national legislation (Title IX) prohibits sex discrimination in federally funded school programs. But strong currents also work against change. Some parents strive to maintain traditional sex roles and, for the most part, the media tend to present traditional sex stereotypes.

We side with the forces for change because we believe that individuals develop best when numerous options are available. Boys and girls need to learn how to take care of themselves and to care for others. Both sexes need problem-solving skills. To the extent that traditional sex-typed roles restrict personal and professional fulfillment for males and females, we need to question them. At the same time, we side with parents who want their sons and daughters to grow up feeling good about being male or female. These goals—providing options and promoting a strong sense of gender—are not incompatible. It is our intention to help parents find ways to accomplish both of them.

As society has changed, so has research on sex role development. Compared to ten years ago, much more is known about sex differences. Nonsexist child-rearing methods have been studied as well as the effects of mass media on sex role attitudes. We will first review the relevant research and then look at some of the issues that concern parents and the ways they deal with them.

Developmental Processes

Child development experts talk about three aspects of sex role development that emerge at different ages. The first to appear is gender identity, which is the self-awareness of being either male or female. By two years of age children will proudly announce "I'm a boy" or "I'm a girl" and will often label the sex of other family members. The second aspect is the acquisition of sex roles (also called gender roles), which is well underway between three and four years of age. At this time, children begin to adopt the socially defined behaviors and attitudes associated with their sex. They are interested in "boy things" or "girl things." This is the aspect most influenced by culture and changing social values. The third and final aspect is the acquisition of patterns of sexual behavior in adolescence and adulthood.

At first, young children do not understand that gender identity is constant and stable. Many preschoolers assert that a girl can be a boy (or vice versa) if she wanted to be or if she played boy's games or had a boy's haircut. Little boys will insist that they can grow up to be "mommies." By the time children are five or six, they know that one's gender is permanent and unchanging.

It may come as a surprise to parents that their three- and four-years-olds already know the sex stereotypes for clothing, tools, household objects, toys, games, and work. They typically choose to play with toys associated with their own sex, and they generally prefer same-sex playmates. They are acting in ways that are consistent with their sense of who they are as male and female. During middle childhood, both sexes recognize that sexual stereotypes are not absolute, and that exceptions are possible.

According to psychodynamic theories of development, one of the important motivations for children to acquire sex-typed behaviors and attitudes is their identification with the same-sex parent. Young girls imitate their mothers, and boys their fathers. Because parents are their children's primary models for learning about what it is to be male or female, the kinds of examples they set are important.

Sex Differences in Early Childhood

Parents notice gender differences in boys and girls, as do teachers and child-care providers. Children themselves remark that "boys are like this and girls are like that." Among all these generalizations, it is important to sort out what is known about sex differences and what is myth.

The answers depend somewhat on the academic discipline. Medical researchers who consider hormonal and physiological factors tend to conclude that "girls and boys differ from each other in a multitude of ways—physically, psychologically, and behaviorally." On the other hand, psychologists and child development experts tend to be more conservative, emphasizing that there are more areas in which no sex differences have been found than vice versa. Furthermore, they point out that the differences among members of the same sex are far greater than the average differences between the sexes. Many women and girls have characteristics more like those of the "average" male. Many men and boys feel and act in ways that resemble the "typical" female. There is a wide range of "normal" masculine and feminine behavior.

After surveying the research on sex differences in young children, developmental psychologist Jeanne Block concluded:

- Boys are more aggressive, physically and verbally.
- Boys are more active and more exploratory.
- Girls tend to have more impulse control and to be more tolerant of frustration.
- Girls are more compliant to adults.
- Girls and boys are equally persistent and motivated, but in different kinds of situations and under different conditions.

As children get older, other sex differences emerge that are related to self-concept, basic social orientation, and academic achievement. For example, boys are more likely to excel in math and visual-spatial abilities, girls at verbal tasks. Females tend to be more interpersonally oriented than males, who have a more individualistic, instrumental orientation to the world.

Debate continues about the role of nature versus nurture in sex differences. Differences in boys' and girls' intellectual abilities have been attributed to differences in the development of the hemispheres of the brain, but most psychologists think the evidence is inconclusive. Higher levels of the male sex hormone testosterone predispose boys toward more aggression. Yet even if aggression is a sex-linked characteristic, how and when it is expressed are influenced by social and cultural factors.

The Power of the Label

The mother of a four-year-old girl says:

> ▪ ▪ ▪ *Even when boys and girls do the same thing, I think that adults react differently. My daughter has very short hair; most people think she's a boy. When we're at the park and she does something daring, like jump off the top of the jungle gym, people say, "Oh, what a strong fellow!" But if she's in a dress, strangers warn her, "Be careful, you might fall."*

Usually the very first question asked the parents of a newborn is "Is it a boy or girl?" To most of us, this information is critical. Once we know that, our biases about sex roles often come into play and shape our behavior. This is well-illustrated by research that experimentally manipulates gender labels. In one study, the same infant played with different adults. When the baby was introduced as a boy, the adults encouraged more motor activity; when the very same baby was introduced as a girl, the adults offered more interpersonal stimulation. In a similar study, adults watched a videotape of a nine-month-old baby playing with toys. When the baby was labeled a boy rather than a girl, both men and women attributed more pleasure and fewer fears to the child. Such studies leave no doubt that gender labels affect how babies are treated.

Are Boys and Girls Raised Differently in the Family?

A mother from Iowa says:

• • • When our son was a baby and cried in the night, we used to let him be. Now when our one-year-old daughter cries, my husband and I take turns sleeping in her room. I think of her as being more tender and sensitive than he was at that age.

Research shows that during the first year of life sons receive more physical stimulation and gross motor play, especially from their fathers, than do daughters. The results are inconclusive as to whether daughters receive more verbal stimulation. There are no sex differences in smiling and touching and other forms of social interaction between parents and their infant boys and girls.

By the time they are toddlers, differential treatment of the sexes becomes more obvious. Most studies report that parents give more praise and criticism to boys than to girls. In addition, parents respond favorably when their young children engage in sex-stereotyped behaviors, such as girls playing with dolls or boys playing with blocks. Clearly, parents send messages to their children about how boys and girls should act.

In one study, parents were asked to encourage their preschool child to construct squares the same size as a model. The parents pressed their sons to do the task well, but expected less from their daughters. However, when parents have high expectations for achievement and independence in their daughters, their daughters show more of those behaviors.

Starting at an early age, boys experience more freedom and fewer restrictions than girls do. In one survey, parents were asked at what age children can be allowed to take on a variety of independent tasks, such as using scissors without adult supervision, crossing the street, tying their shoes, taking a bus ride. The parents of sons were willing to let them do these tasks earlier than the parents of daughters were.

Summarizing results from many studies, including cross-cultural research, Jeanne Block concluded that such differences in how boys and girls are parented affect their ego and cognitive development. Boys, more than girls, develop a sense of mastery ("I can do it"), independence, and innovation as they deal with new information or tackle new problems. Block concludes that this gives them a considerable advantage in learning tasks, and eventually, in work-related situations.

What are the respective roles of mothers and fathers in sex role development? In most societies, fathers, more than mothers, enforce traditional sex-typing, particularly for their sons. In one study, mothers were more tolerant of their son's playing with typically female toys than fathers were, but in general, parents were more accepting of their daughter's cross-sex play than that of their son's.

As might be expected, the sex-typed behaviors that show up at home are also reinforced in schools and child-care settings. Teachers give boys both more positive and negative attention. In an observational study of toddlers and preschoolers, it was found that the teachers tended to reward boys who chose toys and activities of high complexity, but did not do so for girls. Thus, boys were being encouraged to engage in intellectually stimulating activity more than girls were.

Much more has been noted about the positive male experiences that girls can miss out on than vice versa. We believe that there are typically female experiences that would promote boys' development. For example, boys would profit from being around and caring for younger children and playing games where cooperation, not competition, is stressed.

The Wider World—Toys and TV

Parents rightfully complain about the sex role stereotypes perpetuated by toys. As one father said, everything for boys is "dark, gloomy, army green" and for girls, "light, pink, and airy."

But parents themselves may promote sex-typed choices. They often select toys for their sons that encourage physical activity and exploration and toys for their daughters—household-type items, dolls—that promote imitation and nurturing. To some extent, these choices may reflect the inherent interests of their children; far more parents of boys report their child's passionate attachment to cars and trucks than do parents of girls.

Given that the average child spends a great deal of time watching TV, parents are understandably concerned about the sex roles presented in the media. A mother of a four-year-old daughter says:

■ ■ ■ *She loves to watch Dance Fever where all these eighteen-year-olds are dressed up. She imitates them, putting on a sort of "sexy" vamp number. In TV ads she also sees ten-year-olds acting like forty-year-olds. They wear makeup and glamorous dresses, and she's hooked on this.*

Despite efforts to the contrary, TV shows have perpetuated sex role stereotypes. The statistics are shocking:

- In a mid-1970s analysis of children's Saturday morning programs, males more often displayed activity, independence, and problem-solving. Females in the programs showed more deference and passivity.
- Fewer than 20 percent of TV's married women with children are employed outside the home compared to well over half in real life. As early as age three, heavy TV viewers in the United States have more stereotyped views of sex roles than do light viewers.

Commercials for toys also promote sexual stereotypes to sell their products. Researchers at the University of Kansas found that commercials for girls' toys used more fades, dissolves, and background music, while those for boys' toys used more action, frequent cuts, sound effects, and loud music. What these commercials are doing is directing boys and girls toward different types of merchandise without ever bringing the message of sex typing out into the open.

Parents' Own Life-Styles

Where do parents' ideas about sex roles come from? For many, the patterns learned in early childhood as a result of identifying with the same-sex parent persist into adulthood and are then passed down to the next generation. A father of three looks back upon his own childhood with deep appreciation for the kind of man his father was:

. . . *He was hard working, a real pillar. He wasn't a lot of fun, and he was distant. But he was a good father, and that's how I want to be.*

Other adults have consciously chosen to be men and women in ways different from their own parents. An employed mother of a preschooler and toddler says:

. . . *I'm trying to do it all— raise children and pursue a demanding career. When I was growing up, none of the women I knew did all of this. They chose to have a family or they went out to work, but not both. Now my generation is trying to set a different example, and it's tough.*

For men who want to follow new paths, few models exist. As one father said, "When I became a parent, I had to create new patterns of fathering for myself."

One consistent finding over the last twenty-five years is that having a mother who is employed broadens children's ideas about sex roles. However, we believe that mothers at home who consciously want to present an equally broad view of sex roles can certainly do so. There also seems to be a similar loosening of stereotyped concepts when fathers engage in nontraditional activities, such as child care.

The popular press debates whether androgynous parents (what psychologists call those who embrace both masculine and feminine qualities) make better parents. To date, the research findings are inconsistent. One major study of school-aged children reported that whether or not parents were androgynous seemed to make little difference in the children's overall competence. Another study found that adolescents with androgynous parents scored higher on self-esteem. Jeanne Block's research shows that androgynous parents pass on their values to their children, who grow up to become adults with a similar outlook.

Sex role development involves a complex interplay of many factors—biological, familial, and cultural. These strands come into play in infancy and by the preschool period greatly influence the behavior and psychology of boys and girls. Yet we still have much to learn about the differences between the sexes and their origins, information that would be useful as we raise our children.

Q *How can I help my child develop a nonsexist orientation when so much of the world reinforces sex-typing?*

Explaining Stereotypes

It is important to help children understand why stereotyping in any form (sexual, racial, ethnic) is harmful. One parent explains why stereotyping is unfair to people:

■ ■ ■ *I tell my children that if you're a boy and you're not supposed to play with dolls just because you're male, then you don't have a choice. This is something my children can relate to, because they know they like to have choices.*

When children are in the process of consolidating their own identity, they often react negatively to other children who are different. For instance, preschoolers may tease a boy who plays with a doll or a girl whose best friend is a boy. It is important to help your children learn to respect other people and accept differences. You can say, "It's okay for Sammy to play with a doll. He's learning how to be a good father," or "Remember how much you like to hold your kitty? It's also nice to hold a doll."

What can be done about the stereotypes on TV, short of banishing those programs from your household? One of the most effective strategies is to discuss what you see with your children. You can refer to their own experience: "You know, this soap commercial always shows the mother washing the dishes. That's not the way it is in our house, is it? Daddy does the dishes." You can also point out the nontraditional sex roles portrayed on TV. When parents take responsibility for teaching their children from TV, children learn to think critically about what they watch.

Giving Examples of Nonstereotyped Roles

One parent describes a conversation she had with her daughter:

. . . *At the age of four, Alexis already knows the stereotyped roles that men and women have. So my husband and I point out the various jobs that women can have. For instance, every time we see a woman working for the telephone company or driving a truck, we say, "Look, there's a woman working there."*

Integrating Activities and Friendships

During the preschool years, many children prefer playmates of the same sex. The nature of the activity brings children of one sex together. They do not set out to be exclusive in their playmates, but it ends up that way because boys are more likely to prefer typically masculine activities and toys and girls traditionally feminine ones.

Parents and teachers can make a concerted effort to integrate activities: "How can Tommy join you and Lucy in the house corner?" Encourage your children to have friends of both sexes. If your daughter says, "I don't like boys, only girls can come to my party," first ask for an explanation. If she says, "The boys will just run around," use this as an opportunity to break down stereotypes. For example, suggest some outside games for everyone at the party and explain that most children, not just boys, like to play outside. But in the end, it's preferable to let your children invite whom they want to their parties. You will be showing them that their choices are respected, even though you may disagree.

Q *My preschooler engages in the most sex-stereotyped play imaginable. Is this normal?*

Joyce Eggar is the mother of five-year-old Pam:

. . . *When Pam was three years old, she adored nail polish and frilly dresses. Now that she's older, it's escalated to makeup. First she used mine. I thought the whole thing would go away, but then she asked for her own makeup. All the other girls in class were doing this, too. So we bought her some play makeup. She used it all up in a week.*

> *This bothers me because I don't want her to think of women as decorative objects. I was very much a part of the feminist movement in the 1960s, and now I have a daughter who looks and acts a lot like what I stood against.*

Why does Pam want to be traditionally feminine when her mother presents such a different image? Part of the answer is that Pam is very close to her grandmother, who, in Joyce's words, is a "stereotypically feminine woman":

> **. . .** *She likes perfumes and she crooks her finger just so when she holds a cup. When Pam was about three years old and really impressionable, we spent Christmas at her grandmother's house. She had a dressing room filled with jewelry and makeup, high heeled shoes and long gowns. Pam's eyes were popping. I'm sure she was thinking, "This is heaven."*

The explanation for Pam's superfemininity at this point is also strongly tied to her developmental stage. At this age, children are attracted to potent, concrete gender symbols. For them, the essence of a thing is in how it looks: to be girls, girls must look like girls. When boys think about what it is to be a boy and grow up to be a man, they think about being big, strong, powerful, and active as their fathers and other men appear to them. By adopting exaggerated ways of dressing and behaving, the child makes a clear statement about his or her gender. When Pam's behavior is thought of in this way, it becomes a means of solidifying her femaleness. As children get older and can think in more abstract, relative terms, their definitions of masculinity and femininity focus more on internal, psychological qualities and less on superficial appearances. As a twelve-year-old said, "It doesn't matter what you look like, you'll always be a boy." With parents who model different values, children will also move away from rigid sex stereotypes and become more flexible in their thinking.

Playing with makeup on the part of girls is not too different psychologically from the superhero play of boys (see the section on superheroes, pages 103–107). Julia Smith, the mother of Scott, three and a half years old, echoes the concerns of Pam's mother about sex stereotyping in her child's play:

> **. . .** *He is hooked on superheroes. The thing that bothers me the most is his "macho" stance. He runs all over the house and captures all the bad people. He is this big dude who is taking care of everything for me. Even though I stay home with Scott, I don't see myself as a traditional woman, nor is my husband*

a traditional man. And we try hard to raise him in a nonsexist way.

Although it is normal for young boys and girls to embrace sex stereotypes in their play and behavior, their own unique personalities have a role, too. For example, Joyce offers insight into why Pam is attracted to superfeminine symbols:

. . . *As long as I can remember, one of her major interests was costumes. She loves to put on performances of Cinderella and fairy queens. So being fascinated with makeup was a natural extension of this.*

One way that Joyce has come to terms with her daughter's sex stereotyping is to look for positive signs in Pam's behavior:

. . . *She is independent and has a mind of her own. She does not fit the stereotype of the submissive, dependent type. She refuses to be persuaded by me not to wear makeup.*

As Joyce has said, Pam's brand of femininity goes against the principles she herself stands for. Although she recognizes that Pam's behavior is "normal," she has decided to set some limits:

. . . *When I bought the makeup for her, I made it clear that this was for play. I don't allow her to wear it outside or to a birthday party.*

Scott's mother also set limits—he could not wear his superhero shirt to school. By setting reasonable limits, these parents accept their children but also assert their authority as parents and convey their image of what is appropriate.

Parents who try to raise their children in nonsexist ways are understandably puzzled when their own children act in sex-stereotyped ways. This is a normal part of development. Yet it's important to present your personal values to your children while respecting their interests. In the words of one parent, "It takes a long time to grow, and there are many stages in becoming men and women."

Sexuality

Q *Young children often show an interest in sexual matters. How can parents deal with their questions and feelings most effectively?*

At a parents' meeting a group of mothers and fathers talked about their young childrens' sexual behaviors and feelings:

• • • *I caught my four-year-old son playing "doctor" with his little girl cousin.*

• • • *My daughter follows me into the bathroom and bedroom. I never have any privacy.*

• • • *I'm pregnant and my preschooler asks, "How did you get the baby?"*

• • • *My daughter has her hand between her legs a lot. I know she's playing with herself.*

• • • *My son insists he's going to marry me when he grows up.*

• • • *My daughter gets furious when my husband and I are affectionate with each other. She wants him to hug only her.*

The parents reacted to these episodes with varying degrees of shock, concern, amusement, and understanding. But all expressed some bewilderment, asking, "What is going on here and how should I handle it?"

First, parents should know that these situations are common among young children. Much of preschoolers' sexual behavior stems from curiosity about themselves, their bodies, and how they function. Other people's bodies are fascinating, too, especially when different from their own. Preschoolers are also very attached to their parents, and at this age, their affection can take on romantic and sexual overtones. It can be reassuring to know that these patterns are normal and indicate healthy sexual development.

Wanting to Do the Right Thing

Some parents in the group were dissatisfied with the sex education they had received from their own parents. One father admitted:

... *I remember a lot of don'ts ... don't touch yourself, don't say dirty words. I never heard any dos ... do feel good about your body ... do feel good about being a boy.*

A mother of two young girls remembered:

... *When I was twelve, my mother handed me a book. By then I knew a lot from friends, and I was too embarrassed to ask her the questions I had.*

Both these parents hope to be better sex educators for their own children—they want to be sensitive to their children's physical needs and desires; they do not want to threaten them or make them feel ashamed, but are wondering how to proceed.

Our Own Discomfort

The parents' group explored why they felt uncomfortable as sex educators. Some related it to their own background or personality, while others feared revealing their own sexual anxieties or ignorance. Carolyn Hahne, mother of a four-year-old, said:

... *When my son asked, "How does the daddy's sperm get inside the mommy?" I really got nervous. I felt that his question invaded our sexual privacy.*

As the group talked, she realized that her son's question was legitimate, but she still did not know how much information to provide.

Several of the parents viewed childhood as a time of purity and innocence. They envied this time in their children's lives and felt very protective; as one father of a preschooler half joked, "I'm going to chaperone her until she's married." Another parent said that seeing her toddler masturbate for the first time was a shock—"as if she had been thrown out of the Garden of Eden." When children's sexuality challenges our basic notions, we may want to deny it or look for something or someone to blame (too much sex and violence on TV, other children who are leading our children astray).

However, being curious and interested in sexual matters is part of normal development. Even if we did not exhibit overt sexuality as children, we had sexual fantasies; because some of these fantasies, especially vis-à-vis our parents, were guilt producing, we may have repressed memories of our own early sexuality. Consequently, our children's sexuality may seem alien and baffling to us, and we think, "I was never like that."

Society has changed; discussion of sexual issues is more permissible. There is more openness about sexually transmitted diseases and contraceptives; nudes are featured on magazine covers at pharmacies and newsstands, and blatant sexual behavior is broadcast during family TV hours. Not surprisingly, some parents feel adrift in a world so different from the one they grew up in.

From the Child's Perspective: Being Sexual

Martha's father cites behaviors that make him uneasy:

■ ■ ■ *She is fascinated with my penis. When I pee, she wants to watch. She wants only me—not her mother—to read her a story at night. She likes to curl up in my lap. The way she squirms, trying to get into a certain position, I feel like she's sort of pushing her genitals against mine.*

The mother of Simon, a four-year-old:

■ ■ ■ *Simon is too much in love with me. If he crawls into bed with us on a Sunday morning, he tries to get between my husband and me. He says, "Daddy, you go fix breakfast. Mommy and I will just lie here."*

Children are born sensual. Their existence centers around their bodies and their sensations. They are constantly being fed, bathed, rocked, and caressed. These bodily feelings are intense and often pleasurable. Since it is primarily parents who take care of the baby, many of these early feelings are associated with parents.

During the preschool years, children's sensuality is expressed overtly. They delight in making their bodies feel good—everything from running fast to dancing to splashing in water. Touching one's genitals is also pleasurable and soothing and is normal behavior for boys and girls at this age. Often children will masturbate at bedtime or when they watch TV or play quietly. One father observed his four-year-old daughter masturbating before she fell asleep and gently asked her what she was doing. She simply replied, "I'm doing my work," without any trace of guilt.

Preschoolers are also intensely curious about all aspects of life: "Where did I come from?" "What happens to people when they die?" They enjoy stories about when they were babies. At this age they recognize the differences between the sexes and correctly label themselves boys or girls. Doctor play is often motivated by curiosity—what does someone else's body look like? This is what lies behind preschoolers saying such things as "I'll show you my vagina if you show me yours."

Preschoolers' sensuality is also directed toward their parents. Although some children do not express their feelings in obvious ways, many girls declare they will marry their fathers, and boys their mothers. Like most children their age, Martha and Simon feel attracted to and possessive about the parent of the opposite sex and competitive with the same-sex parent. Even in households with absent fathers, children can express these desires, directing their possessive feelings toward a relative or teacher of the opposite sex. In Freudian theory, this family triangle is called the Oedipus complex. Whatever one's belief about the origins of these behaviors and fantasies, they are a normal phase of growing up. Eventually the feelings of competition and exclusivity are replaced by a strong identification with the parent of the same sex.

Parents should not attribute adult motivation to children's sexuality. Preschoolers are not sexually mature and lack the sexual drives and capacity for sexual experiences associated with adolescence and adulthood. For young children, sensuality is associated with bodily pleasure that comes from self-stimulation and from tactile contact with other people. Nevertheless, the intensity and passion of children's longings can surprise parents.

From the Child's Perspective: Sex Differences

It takes time for young children to understand their bodies and how they function. Debra's mother describes what her daughter went through, trying to understand her own anatomical makeup.

■ ■ ■ *When Debra was two, she saw her cousin take a bath. That was the first time she saw a penis. She made a big deal out of it. Who has them and who doesn't? Why didn't she have one? Once she asked for a bottle and stuck it between her legs. She smiled and said, "Big penis." I explained to her that girls are built differently and that a womb is inside her body.*

Another mother said, "Since young girls have no breasts and no pubic hair, it's hard for them to understand that their bodies are female like their mother's. It is also hard for them to understand that what makes them female is way inside of them." Some parents feel that explaining male sex characteristics is easier because they are more visible. Thus, girls may need reassurance that their bodies are beautiful and special.

Boys sometimes worry that they will lose their penis when they see that little girls do not have one. Anxiety may be expressed via masturbating, as if saying to themselves, "Yes, my body is still intact." Boys, too, need reassurance that this is the way bodies are and that they too are special and beautiful.

Adults may have difficulty understanding children's confusion about sexual differences, because to us they are just the facts of life. But children's reasoning is different than ours, characterized by magical and wishful thinking. They think it's possible for someone's body to change: boys might grow up into mommies and girls into daddies. Over time, however, children learn that sex characteristics and gender are permanent and unchanging. What is important to convey at an early age is a positive attitude about being male or female.

From the Child's Perspective: Where Do Babies Come From?

Max's parents describe his first inquiry about the facts of life:

■ ■ ■ *When we were at the aquarium, we saw two otters mating. Max kept asking, "Are they wrestling?" We chickened out, because we weren't prepared to handle it in front of all those people.*

But the questions did not go away. Some time later, Max saw a pregnant woman and asked, "Why is she so fat?"

Children base their theories about where babies come from on observations of their own bodily functions, like eating and eliminating. To children it makes perfect sense that babies emerge from the same opening they use to go to the bathroom, or that by eating a watermelon seed they can "grow" a baby.

Even when young children use accurate terms, their understanding of the processes is limited. A four-and-a-half-year-old offered a typically concrete, anthropomorphic description:

■ ■ ■ *The sperm goes into the mommy to each egg . . . I think it makes a little hole and then it swims into the vagina . . . it has a little mouth.*

According to one study, it is not until eleven or twelve years that children can explain the physiological basis of reproduction.

As Selma Fraiberg says in *The Magic Years*, adult's explanations of reproduction strain children's credulity. They are asked to believe in a sperm and ovum that they cannot see, while at the same time they are told not to believe in ghosts or monsters that also cannot be seen. And then to be told that *you* did not even exist as *you* before conception verges on the fantastic. So it is not surprising that it takes children a long time to assimilate the facts of life in a way they can understand.

SOLUTIONS

Teaching Sex Education

The goal of sex education is not only to teach the facts but also to instill positive attitudes. We want our children to feel good about their bodies, to be comfortable with who they are as males and females, and to be able to express their sexuality in deep human relationships. Looked at this way, sex education is broad, encompassing parents' attitudes toward children's physical abilities, curiosity, and sex role behaviors.

Sex education begins in infancy, with the way we hold, touch, and kiss our babies. It includes nurturing, comforting, and stimulation—all the ingredients that establish trust in others and a positive sense of oneself.

Parents also teach sexuality by the ways in which they express affection with each other. Parents who are loving say one thing to their children; parents who withdraw from one another convey a different message.

All sex education experts emphasize that parents must show that they are interested and available to talk with their children. How you talk about sexuality—openly, nonjudgmentally—is more important than knowing the right answer. As the mother of two preschoolers says:

■ ■ ■ *If we discuss sex now, before strong adolescent emotions get involved, that will make it easier. If I keep avoiding it, I'll either get hit with everything at once or nothing at all. I want to keep the door open, starting when they are young.*

Expressing discomfort is all right: "This is hard for me to talk about . . . When I was young I didn't have a chance to talk about these things, so I'm new at it."

Sex education is a continuing process; children will ask questions and wonder for a long time. It is reassuring to know there will be many opportunities to talk with your children.

Finding Out What You Are Comfortable With

There is no single right way to deal with childhood sexuality. Some parents feel uncomfortable being naked in front of a child; others don't care. You should do what you are comfortable with; children will sense when you are not. However you respond, never punish or shame the child for what is normal curiosity and exploration.

Many parents say they have a sense of when to draw the boundaries, taking their cues from the children's behavior. One mother stopped letting her four-year-old and six-year-old take baths together when they "got very giggly about each other's bodies."

Another mother describes how she feels when her six-year-old son watches her change clothes:

■ ■ ■ *He looks at me differently now than when he was younger. He pays attention to how I am. That makes me want to be*

> *more private. I told him that he should knock before he comes in and that sometimes I want to be alone.*

Her son understands this limit because he also asserts his right to privacy, wanting to close the door when he is in the bathroom or playing in his room.

Martha's father decided to draw the line when his daughter wanted to sit on his lap during her bedtime story:

> ■ ■ ■ *I just didn't feel comfortable with her trying to snuggle up against my genitals. I told her she could sit next to me but not on me. That seemed to be all right with her.*

When parents feel young children are becoming too "sexual" or too "intimate," they should set firm limits. This can be done in a straightforward, nonjudgmental way, as Martha's father did. He is also teaching his daughter an important lesson: All people—children and adults—have the right to decide under what circumstances to show our bodies and allow intimacy. That is one of the most important messages in preventing child abuse and in laying the foundation for responsible sexuality during adolescence and adulthood.

Helping My Child Feel Good about His or Her Sexuality

Feeling positive about one's body and sexual identity is an important aspect of children's self-concept. We want boys to feel good about being boys and girls about being girls. Here are some of the ways you can help your children develop positive attitudes toward their bodies:

- Appreciate their bodies and their physical skills. "Look how tall you are." "You are so graceful when you dance."
- Make bathtime (or changing diapers) a pleasurable time. Play games in the water, wrap children in a big towel, let them know that it is okay to make their bodies feel good in these ways.
- Provide dolls with anatomical features. Seeing one's likeness affirms one's own identity.
- Talk about body parts—the child's, the doll's. Use accurate or at least nonderogatory terms.

We want to help children accept the fact that boys' and girls' bodies are different. It may take repeated assurances that they were born this way and that it will not change. Eventually Debra's mother decided to explain sex differences in a very graphic, direct way:

• • • *We held a mirror up to her vagina and it began to make sense to her. I said, "Your vagina is like the hallway and your womb is like a room at the end of it." I showed her pictures of when I was pregnant and said, "You were growing inside my womb." Later that day, she came up to me and said, "I have a womb." It was an incredible mixture of joy and wonder.*

Handling the Family Romance

When your child expresses great love for one parent ("I'm going to marry you when I grow up"), you can respect the child's feelings while offering a dose of reality. "I love you too and I'll always be be your mother, but I'm already married to Daddy." Thus, you are reassuring children that they can always count on your love and on your being their parent. If you say, "When you get older you'll find another person to marry," keep in mind that young children do not understand "getting older." It could refer to tomorrow or to their next birthday. Your explanation may sound like rejection or may arouse fears of having to leave you. Emphasize and respond to the child's expression of affection in the present and do not be overly concerned about setting the record straight for the future.

Dealing with the rivalrous feelings can be complex. Try to defuse the competition—"I want to hug Daddy and you—let's all do a bear hug." One mother turned to Grimm's fairy tales when her almost-six-year-old daughter was especially critical and hostile toward her. Together they would read about wicked stepmothers and witches, which helped acknowledge the child's fantasies in a safe, nonthreatening way. Parents should remember that this stage is temporary and is followed by a period when children generally identify more closely with the same-sex parent.

Answering Their Questions

As you respond to your children's questions, be sure to convey that sexual expression includes loving and caring about someone. Let them know that one way for adults to be close to one another is to be sexual. If you are comfortable talking about yourself, you can say something like, "It makes me feel loved and really good when Daddy holds me."

Use the names of body parts and processes that you feel comfortable with; however, avoid slang and euphemisms that have to be unlearned and may connote something shameful. Some parents worry that the correct terms are too technical, but if children can learn the names for shoulder and ankle, they can just as easily learn words like penis, uterus, and clitoris. A parent who enjoys playing a naming game of body parts with her two-year-old says she gives "equal treatment" to genitalia.

Take cues from your child. Notice what he or she says or observes. For example, if your child's cat has just had kittens, your child probably has a lot of theories and questions. Before you offer your explanation, ask, "What are your ideas about where the kittens come from?" Carol Hahne could first ask her son, "How do you think the sperm gets to the egg?" In this way you elicit your children's ideas and you have a chance to clear up their misconceptions.

Child development experts agree that factual explanations are best. After eliciting her son's ideas, Carol could have said something like: "When a boy grows up to be a man, sperm grow inside his testicles. The sperm comes out through his penis when it gets hard and it is put into the mommy's vagina. From there, the sperm goes into the mommy's uterus. If it meets with an egg, a baby grows."

Giving children (and adolescents) accurate information about human sexuality helps them make sound decisions and makes them less vulnerable to peer pressure or misinformation.

By the time most children are four, they have expressed some curiosity about where they came from. However, some children may be reluctant to ask questions because they feel embarrassed. One girl told her mother that another child told her sex was a bad word and so she could not talk about it. If your child does not initiate a discussion, you can. One way to do this is to visit a litter of new puppies or a friend who has just had a baby. You can also read together. There are many good picture books about animal babies as well as photo essays on human sexuality, but use your own judgment here.

Explaining Adoption

Adoptive parents frequently wonder when and how to tell their children about the adoption. The Smiths adopted Ryan when he was one year old:

■ ■ ■ *He never questioned his origins until he became aware that babies grow inside mommies. Then he started to say, "When I was inside you . . ." At that point, I would say, "You did grow inside a woman, but you did not grow inside Mommy." He would get very confused. We had been talking about staying away from strangers, and he would say, "I grew in a stranger." He was right, in a sense. I said, "Well, she is a stranger only because I didn't know her."*

The most important consideration is your child's developmental ability to comprehend this idea. Sandra Panetta, a researcher on adoption and an adoptive parent herself, has found in some preliminary studies that by the age of five, children begin to understand that they were born before they were adopted. Parents, however, may be surprised by some of their children's theories about the sequence of events:

■ ■ ■ *My mommy and daddy lost me and my other mommy and daddy found me.*

■ ■ ■ *My mommy threw me away.*

Child development experts suggest eliciting discussions about adoption throughout the children's growing up years. Children's books or made-up stories are good stimuli for such discussions. When children ask why, you can say, "Your birth parents gave you the gift of life; your adoptive parents are giving you the gifts of love and a home," or "I'm not your birth mother. I am your mommy because I love and take care of you."

Responding to Doctor Play

Most young children engage in doctor play, expressing interest in how people are made. You may not know until it happens how you will react. If you are upset, try to calm down before saying anything to your child. Waiting is better than making your child feel ashamed, dirty, or naughty.

Most parents want to limit doctor play. You can simply say, "Let's end this game; we're going to do something else." This puts parents in the legitimate position of limiting and redirecting sexual behavior, just as they would other behavior. Acknowledging the child's right to be curious is important, but parents can encourage children to express curiosity in acceptable ways: "I know all children wonder about how other people look. Most children want to look at other people's bodies. If you want to know how other people are made, ask me and I'll explain it to you. Tell me what you want to know."

Despite our best intentions and appropriate reactions, young children often end up feeling guilty about exhibiting themselves or exploring someone else's body. One woman remembers when she and a neighbor boy (both about five) undressed in front of each other; they were out in the woods and no one caught them. During her bath that evening, her mother joked, as she did every night, "This is the dirtiest water I've ever seen." But the young girl felt *she* was the dirty one. If you suspect your children have played doctor, reassure them that most children want to look at other people's bodies and this is normal.

Dealing with Masturbation

Masturbating is common in early childhood. Most parents know not to scold, threaten, or punish. Nevertheless, they want to limit masturbation in public. One mother describes how she acknowledges her child's sexuality and also circumscribes its overt expression:

■ ■ ■ *When my son began to masturbate around the age of four, I asked if it felt good. He said yes. I told him, "I know." But I also told him, "That's for when you are by yourself." He accepts that and goes into his room.*

Psychologist Lawrence Balter, author of *Dr. Balter's Child Sense*, offers a practical suggestion if your child is masturbating in public: give the child something else to do with his or her hands. In a grocery store, ask him to hold a bag of apples. At a friend's house, suggest looking at a book or doing a puzzle. Generally, by the age of five or six, most children are embarrassed to be seen masturbating and do it privately.

Not everything that we call masturbation is actually that. Sometimes young children repeatedly touch themselves when they are anxious or frightened. If this is the case, then try to get to the source of your child's concern.

"This is new for me," said a mother at the parent meeting. "I came here thinking there was one right answer to each of my child's questions about sexuality. I thought everyone else knew these answers. Now I see we all are figuring out what to do, but the exact words make less of a difference than the way we express them—with affection and respect."

Temperament

Q *I live with an intensely dramatic, active child and although I hate to use this word—he's difficult. He's always been this way and I'm not sure why.*

Martha Wilson describes her son:

• • • *Alex is only four, but everything is life and death to him. It doesn't matter what it is—it could be a hole in his sock that sends him off. When he went to bed last night, he insisted on having the light on, so I left it on. A few minutes later, he wanted it off. I told him that he could turn it off himself. He got out of bed, stood at the top of the stairs, and screamed for half an hour.*

He is constantly demanding interaction, and it's a drain. When I'm doing housework, he'll come to me, saying he wants this or that. But he really doesn't want anything, he just wants the interaction. When I try to do something with him, he is so intense and impatient that everything seems to fall apart.

He's always craved stimulation. When he was a baby, the

only way to get him to sleep was to put him on his stomach and vigorously rock him. He rarely played—two seconds in a swing, two seconds in a stroller. Now he's got a longer attention span, but until a month ago he could not sit still long enough to watch TV.

Even when he's joyous, he's intense. He sings a song thirty times over, all very loudly. How I wish he would mellow a bit.

What Makes Alex Tick

A number of parents describe their children as "intense, demanding, or difficult." We've also heard other parents describe their children as "inhibited" or "easygoing." Even parents of newborns frequently note that their babies are characteristically active, quiet, or content. What these children all seem to have in common are very strong biases in how they approach and deal with the world.

In trying to understand her son's behavior, Martha wonders:

. . . *Maybe this is just the way Alex is. Maybe he was just born intense and high-strung.*

In fact, there is evidence that such profound and pervasive qualities like Alex's do reflect temperament.

In the 1950s, Thomas, Chess, and Birch initiated the New York Longitudinal Study, the first extensive look at individual differences in temperament. They described temperament as an "inborn behavioral style," the broad pattern of how a child behaves, rather than the particular details of what a child does. Based on parent interviews and observation of 133 children in everyday situations from infancy to preadolescence, the researchers identified nine dimensions of temperament: activity level, rhythmicity, approach or withdrawal, adaptability, intensity of reaction, threshold of responsiveness, mood, distractibility, and attention span/persistence.

These nine characteristics clustered into three patterns. The most common pattern, seen in about 40 percent of this sample, was called the "easy" child (high rhythmicity, positive mood, high approach, high adaptability, and low intensity). The opposite pattern, characteristic of 10 percent of the sample, was called the "difficult" child. These children, like Alex, were often negative in mood, slow to adapt, intense, and had unpredictable biological patterns. More recently these categories have been replaced with a single continuum: "easy to difficult." About 15 percent of the sample was termed "slow to warm up"; the remaining 35 percent did not appear to fit into these three groups.

The concept of the "difficult" temperament has come under attack. Parent educators criticize labeling children as "difficult" and suggest more neutral terminology such as "active," "persistent" or "intense." Researchers also have qualms: for example, J. E. Bates has suggested that these categories are a function of adult perception more than objective descriptions of the child.

Although the exact meaning and description of temperament are still fuzzy, the notion that children do exhibit inborn characteristics is now widely accepted by child development experts. Knowing that temperamental differences exist is important for parents because it leads them away from the view that they completely mold the child to an understanding that from the very beginning the child brings certain predispositions to the parent/child relationship.

For example, Beth Newton, the mother of Anna, now two and a half years old, was relieved to find out that temperament, not bad parenting, was shaping her baby's behavior:

▪ ▪ ▪ *Anna would awaken four or five times during the night. You expect this to happen for several months with a baby, but when it goes on and on, you're really beside yourself. My husband and I kept asking, "Are we doing something wrong?" The doctor gave her a thorough exam and found nothing the matter. He told us that she was probably born an irritable and sensitive baby.*

As might be expected, innate tendencies of infants persist into childhood. Beth, for example, notes the extent to which Anna's disposition has endured:

▪ ▪ ▪ *She still has difficulty unwinding and tuning out the world enough so she can fall asleep. Even then, she is a restless sleeper and awakens to noises that we sleep through. When she gets up in the morning, she's very irritable and grouchy, although she's certainly had enough hours of sleep.*

Several longitudinal studies report that children continue to manifest certain traits into late childhood and adulthood, particularly their ability to inhibit or not inhibit their emotions. But these studies also point out that children change over the course of development. For example, what makes a baby irritable and how he or she expresses that will change by the preschool years. Although children display inborn dispositions, their temperaments are not permanent and unchanging.

What Makes Temperamental Dispositions Change?

Children's experiences do. For example, children tend to grow away from extreme behavior, such as aggression or withdrawal, probably because other children reject them when they behave this way. Martha attests to this, saying that, in general, Alex's behavior is less difficult at school than at home.

Parents, too, influence the expression of temperamental characteristics. One researcher, Jerome Kagan from Harvard University, says that middle-class American parents who tend to value a degree of boldness and extroversion in their children may consciously and successfully encourage less fearful approaches to new situations.

What is important for parents like Martha and Beth to realize is that temperament is an aspect of a child's individuality, just as physical characteristics and abilities are. Although parents can direct their child's temperament in positive directions, they are not responsible for creating the child's predominant temperamental disposition.

Feeling Effective as Parents

Since Alex was their first child, his parents wondered if their own lack of experience caused his behavior. As Martha says, "We worried that we were doing everything wrong and were terrible parents." When parents doubt their worth as parents, their sense of satisfaction in parenthood is undermined. In one study, parents' perceptions of their infants' temperaments were the primary determinants of their difficulty in adjusting to parenthood.

Parents of children like Alex report being under a great deal of stress. In one study of 149 such families, 89 percent of the mothers felt they were not coping, 69 percent reported strains on the marriage, and 92 percent said their discipline style was ineffective. All of these factors can contribute to a vicious cycle—the parents feel ineffective and frustrated, they try to change the child's behavior, they meet resistance, and the cycle continues.

Isolation

Related to feeling ineffective as a parent is the isolation that Alex's mother experiences. Her husband sometimes criticizes how she handles their son; generally he has an easier time with Alex than she does. Research indicates that this is a typical pattern. Children like Alex tend to have the most intense relationship with their primary caretaker.

Alex's behavior is hard for others to handle, and that, coupled with his reluctance to enter new situations, makes it difficult for Martha to take him places:

▪ ▪ ▪ *When Alex was a baby, we would manage to get out with him, but now I really have to think twice. The arguments and constant demands embarrass me.*

Not surprisingly, Martha complains of "feeling burned out and needing to be recharged." Being around children is demanding and especially so with a child who presses for constant attention.

Martha's sense of isolation is further reinforced when she talks with other parents. All parents deal with difficult behaviors some of the time, and while Martha has found some very sympathetic mothers, she has yet to find someone who has a child like hers:

▪ ▪ ▪ *One mother called to say she'd heard our sons were so much alike. By the time we were through talking, she said her son was a piece of cake compared to Alex. She felt embarrassed that she'd complained to me.*

Martha feels uncomfortable talking about Alex's behavior with her pediatrician, whom she expects will blame her (even though she tends to blame herself much of the time). Feeling that she is wrestling with a unique situation adds to Martha's doubt and frustration about parenting.

The Match Between Parents and Child

In talking with parents about their child's dispositions, one aspect becomes clear: how parents react depends on their own characteristics and expectations. Thomas and Chess emphasize the matches and mismatches that contribute to the "goodness of fit" between a child's temperament and environment. Parents who are easygoing may find themselves at odds with an intense child. The temperamentally quiet child who plays alone for hours on end may have a hard time fitting into a gregarious, active family. In one study, patterns of sleeping and waking that were regarded as a major problem by some parents seemed normal to others.

In Beth Newton's family, there is something of a mismatch:

▪ ▪ ▪ *My husband and I are sort of low key and quiet. We can be stubborn, but we're not intense the way Anna is. That's half the problem. If we were very active and on the go all the time I can see that we would flow with her better. But we like to sit down and read a paper once in a while.*

Different styles, however, do not automatically lead to problems. Stella Chess further defines goodness of fit as the parents' readiness to accept their child's individual behavioral style.

The Wider World

Many experiences that most children find exciting and satisfying may upset children like Alex or Beth. Going to a birthday party or to the circus can elicit their most intensely negative reactions. For example, Alex was reluctant to start nursery school, and even several months later, he often preferred to stay at home than go to school. He has always resisted leaving his mother, even to the extent of refusing to go to the store with his grandmother. As a result, Alex and Martha are very seldom apart.

Alex insists on repeating the same routines day after day, such as the familiar route to the store, one kind of snack, and the same bedtime stories. His temperamental traits include being slow to adapt to changes and transitions and being "locked in" to certain patterns. One concern his parents have is his missing out on new experiences, yet they want to protect him from unhappiness and are reluctant to push him.

Giving In

Faced with Alex's intensely negative reaction to many situations, his mother admits, "I often take the easy road and just let up." One day last summer the family went to a community swimming pool. Alex had never been there before, but he wanted to go swimming. Martha had great hopes for a wonderful family outing:

. . . *When we got to the pool entrance, Alex had a tantrum. He pulled back and screamed. Nothing we said made a difference. I guess the newness and the stimulation of so many other kids were too much and he freaked out. His father and I ended up taking turns swimming while the other parent sat outside the gate with him. Alex never got wet. This was not at all what we had planned, and I think in a way Alex was disappointed, too.*

Although parents, when embarrassed or meeting resistance, understandably just give up, several studies have found that when socialization pressures against aggression and impulse control are reduced with children like Alex, the children become more difficult; a circular process is set in motion. Generally, parents' "backing off" is counterproductive in the long run.

Susceptibility to Distress

To his parents and his teachers, Alex is a "driven" child. He overreacts to minor incidents such as not being able to find a puzzle piece. More severe stresses elicit even stronger reactions. When Alex moved to a new house, his mother says, "he'd take out wires and strings and make intricate web-bings so that no one could get through"; he was consumed by this activity.

Recent research suggests that temperament is an important factor in how children cope with family stress, such as moving. Children's reactions to stress represent their efforts to gain control in what may feel like an over-whelming situation. The immediate consequences of Alex's vulnerability to stress are that he has less energy, interest, or "staying power" for other activities or learning experiences. Although he is bright and capable, his mother is concerned about his future adjustment to school.

SOLUTIONS

The First Task—Asking If This Is Temperament

Martha and Beth must figure out which behaviors are temperamentally based. In *The Difficult Child*, Stanley Turecki writes that if "a behavior stems from temperament, the child in a sense can't help himself." On the basis of the studies of Richard Abidin at the University of Virginia and Stanley Turecki, we have developed a set of criteria so parents can begin to assess if their child's behavior has a temperamental basis.

Adaptability
- Does your child have difficulty in changing from one task to another?
- Does he or she react strongly to changes in sensory stimulation?
- Does he or she avoid new situations?
- Does he or she become upset if there are changes in routines? Once upset, is your child hard to calm down?
- Is he or she often resistant or defiant?

Distractibility/Activity Level
- Is your child extremely active, always on the go?
- Is he or she restless?
- Is it difficult to distract your child?
- Does he or she have a very short attention span?
- Is it difficult for him or her to listen?

Moods/Regularity
- Does your child have intense reactions—whether angry, happy, or sad?
- Does he or she complain a lot? Is he or she never very satisfied and hard to please?
- Does he or she frequently have long, out-of-control tantrums?
- Is he or she unpredictable—do his or her moods change suddenly?

In each of these areas, children's behavior can range from "not at all" to "nearly always." If you have answered affirmatively to most of the questions in any category and if these characteristics have been present in some form since birth, then your child's behavior is likely to be a result of temperament. Recognizing that a behavior is temperamentally based can help you be more sympathetic to your child, respond more objectively, and not blame yourself.

Recognizing Typical Behaviors

Knowing what preschoolers are generally like, parents will feel reassured that their children are "normal." For example, preschoolers typically want other children's toys and resist sharing. Sometimes Martha gets annoyed with Alex's barrage of questions—"Why is that truck going there?"—but such curiosity and a belief that everything has a purpose are typical for this age. People who work with young children—parents, teachers, pediatricians—can help you recognize typical aspects of preschooler's development.

Investigating Other Possible Sources

Difficult behavior in children has also been linked to food sensitivities and food allergies. Martha took Alex to an allergist who tested him but found nothing. Other parents, however, report that what they thought was temperamentally based behavior turned out to be a physical reaction to eggs, wheat, chocolate, sugar, food additives, and so on.

To find out if your child is allergic or sensitive to certain foods, first play detective. Observe when your child seems to fall apart, behave frenetically, become exhausted, get puffy or red eyes. Is it a long or short time after eating? Write down what she or he ate. Do certain foods reappear on your list? If so, experiment with these foods. Avoid them and see if the behavior improves. Provide them and see if the behavior deteriorates.

Another clue to allergies is a craving for a particular food. Studies of allergies indicate that people become addicted to what disturbs them most. If you suspect your child is food sensitive, you can either try eliminating such foods from the child's diet and note changes in behavior and/or you can have your child tested by an allergist.

Establishing Routines

Intense children often have a hard time establishing patterns on their own. As babies, they may have had irregular cycles and been easily irritated by environmental changes. As preschoolers, they may need help developing routines around daily tasks. Alex, for example, seemed to get lost between the time he awoke and ate breakfast. His father made a chart with pictures in sequence of what he was to do: wash his face, brush his teeth, and so forth.

For children who have difficulty adjusting to changes, disruptions of routines can be very upsetting. Advance preparation helps them function better; remind them before it is time to start or stop an activity.

Giving Limited Responsibility

Alex enjoys taking responsibility for certain tasks. Although his parents generally feel overwhelmed by what he does *not* take responsibility for, they try to build on his competence. Alex likes to shop with his mother. She lets him hold the grocery list and tells him his job is to locate certain items (cereal, yogurt). As with most preschoolers, Alex's behavior is more manageable when he is given limited choices that allow him to exercise a degree of autonomy.

Getting Time Away

Both Alex and his mother would profit from some time away from each other. His intense reactions—whether sad, curious, angry, or happy—constantly involve her. Martha thinks her most important step in their new neighborhood will be to find a consistent, understanding care giver for Alex. She also thinks Alex will more easily accept someone coming into their house than his going elsewhere. Beth, Anna's mother, gets time to herself by going to exercise classes at the local Y while Anna stays in the drop-in center there.

Since you and your children need time outside of home, it is important to make such visits part of a regular routine. First, plan a short visit to a grandparent or a good friend. Prepare the children ahead of time, telling them what to expect, and giving them some control over what they can do there (play with toys, draw, eat a snack). As the children get used to this routine, you can try doing it more often.

Deciding Which Experiences Matter

Children who find change difficult tend to be sheltered from new experiences. Rather than running the risk of overwhelming such children with a lot of new things at once, carefully select the most important new venture. This year, for example, Martha decided that Alex should attend nursery school. She stuck by her decision in spite of Alex's difficulty in adjusting. It would probably be too much if she also enrolled him in a gym or swim class. As parents, you are the best judge of which experiences will interest your child and provide a supportive environment. Martha made a point of selecting a nursery school where the staff would be sensitive to Alex's needs and allow him to adjust at his own pace.

Responding to Crises

Of course, sometimes it simply is not possible to forewarn a child or plan in advance. Turecki notes that these are the most difficult situations for a child who by temperament is slow to adapt. Probably the first response is to judge whether the situation can be remedied—perhaps by distracting or by allowing an active child to run around and blow off steam. For example, one mother had to stop unexpectedly at the pharmacy for medication. Her daughter, a temperamentally active and intense child, protested loudly before they were even out of the car. This mother decided she had to get the prescription—that was absolute—but she let her child run up and down the stairs of the building before they went in. The child still whined, but her reaction was somewhat diminished.

Tantrums

Parents of intense children say that what bothers them most is their children's tantrums. Martha describes such an event:

. . . *When we bought him a new pair of jeans in the store he loved them, just the right design with neat pockets and snaps. But when he put them on at home, he screamed "I hate them. I won't wear them." He was still worked up even after he took the jeans off.*

In this case, Alex's tantrum was temperamentally based. He is very sensitive to sensory stimulation and dislikes the way new clothes or shoes feel on his body. He cannot help himself and gets out of control. Martha ended up washing the jeans several times before Alex would put them on again. Even then, it took a while before they were comfortable. Martha could also reassure Alex by saying, "I know new clothes are hard for you. You'll get used to them . . ."

Another example of a temperamental tantrum is the active, excitable child who gets "revved up" and dissolves into tears and anger. At this point, parents need to offer sympathetic understanding, "I know you're upset but it will be okay in a while." Sometimes physical comforting or distraction will help. But remind yourself that the child cannot help what he or she is doing.

Stanley Turecki distinguishes the temperamental tantrum from the manipulative tantrum in which the child deliberately throws a fit to get his or her own way. When your child can't help it, as is the case with a temperamental tantrum, the best tactic is sympathy, understanding, and firmness. "I know you are upset and want to throw things but I'm going to hold you until you feel better." Avoid falling into a battle of wills with this kind of situation—that's clearly a "lose-lose" scenario.

Feeling Positive about the Child

It can be very hard for parents of children like Alex to maintain a positive view of their children yet that is critical for the children's self-image. Alex is an articulate, curious child—he can spend a day taking apart a clock in school and then putting it together again. His persistence and determination at age four have also helped him learn to print his name. When Alex's parents identify his assets and show him how much they recognize and appreciate all the special things he can do, he also begins to value those abilities.

Avoid vague statements such as "you're wonderful." Specifics are more helpful and meaningful to the child: "You know how to do very difficult things like putting on your rubber boots." It is tempting for Alex's parents to lavish praise when his behavior is positive because his behavior is often so difficult to manage. But overpraising overwhelms a child and may even engender a sense of guilt. Keep your comments direct and matter-of-fact.

Anna's parents engineer situations in which she can respond well. Since she enjoys being with other people, her mother takes her out whenever she can:

■ ■ ■ *She's happy in the grocery store or at the park, walking down the street or riding the bus. If we take her to a new place, she struggles out of her coat to meet people. It's amazing how much improved she is when she's out.*

When parents concentrate on their children's strengths, they are more likely to feel effective as parents.

Avoiding Labels and Stereotypes

Related to parents' feeling positive about their child is the importance of not labeling. When children like Alex or Anna are called "difficult," such a categorization can become a self-fulfilling prophecy. We prefer "difficult to manage," which emphasizes the interaction of temperament with environment or a more neutral term like "determined."

Furthermore, do not let others stereotype your children. For instance, Anna's parents have found they must reinforce her positive qualities with relatives who are very critical and sometimes compare Anna to their own children. Parents must find a balance between telling others about their child's abilities and strengths and being honest about the difficult aspects as well.

Accepting the Child

Martha says:

■ ■ ■ *We're coming to the conclusion that Alex is who he is. He has his own biology—he's high-strung and intense. We can't change him much. He hears a different drummer. If he can channel much of that energy into positive behavior, he'll be a terrific person. Someone once told me that wild colts make the best horses, and I try to remember that when things get rough.*

Hal, Anna's father, has also come to this view:

■ ■ ■ *This is just the way Anna is. There's not much we can do about it. We don't see it as a problem; we're not looking for a solution. Our two daughters have different styles and we try to adapt.*

Wanda, the mother of a very shy and inhibited five-year-old boy says:

■ ■ ■ *I'm more outgoing and social than my son, John. My husband is more like him. I get impatient and want to push John into situations, but my husband is more sympathetic. So on the first day of school, we decided that his father would take him and help him ease into the group. It worked out really well.*

Most parents accommodate to the inborn biases of their children. Although living with some temperamental dispositions is easier than with others, parents must accept their children's style of dealing with the world.

Getting Help

When making the decision to seek help, parents wonder, "How do I know if this is a serious situation?" In our view, the issue can be reframed: "If I act now, I may prevent future problems." With Alex, an indication that preventive action may be helpful is that his parents feel ineffective and isolated with no one to relieve them or help them. Such feelings can lead to a vicious cycle, intensifying Alex's difficulties in adapting. Ask yourself:

- Is this situation straining our family's ability to cope?
- Do we generally regret how we react to our child and do we tend to see ourselves and our child negatively?
- Do we feel isolated and alone in dealing with this situation?

Local parent support groups can provide help, as can psychologists and social service agencies. Some hospitals and clinics offer programs specifically for families with temperamentally difficult-to-manage children. The goal of any program should be to help parents direct the behavior of their children in positive ways and to reinforce good feelings about their children and themselves.

Death

Q   *My child has become frightened of death and dying. How can we help him?*

Rebecca Witts, mother of Keith:

▪ ▪ ▪   *When Keith was nearly four, we had two deaths in the family in one year. First, his grandmother died, and it didn't frighten him much. Then his Aunt Nancy, a woman in her early 40s, died. That really shook up the whole family. She was terminally ill for a couple of months, and my husband Peter went to see her every day. He hadn't gotten over his mother's death and now his only sibling was dying. The phone rang constantly — everyone was very upset. Keith certainly knew what was happening.*

I debated about whether Keith should see his Aunt Nancy in the hospital, though it was a supportive, cheerful environment. When she planned a birthday party there, I finally decided that would be a suitable time to take him because he'd be distracted by the balloons, the party, and the people. He had been told that she was very ill and in a wheelchair. When we were there, Nancy dropped something. He asked if he could help her and went to pick it up. I was really surprised by his sensitivity. She died two or three weeks later.

It was so hard to explain what had happened. With his grandmother we told Keith people die when they get very old and sick. When his aunt died, I said she was very, very sick and that she died from her illness. He listened and didn't say anything. Then he said, "I wish we knew another Nancy who looked the same as she did, talked just the same, walked just the same." Then he started to cry. I said, "Does it make you feel sad?" He said, "I feel very sad." I said, "So does everybody else. She is dead, and that's the way it is."

After these deaths, he was very different for a few weeks. He held back a lot; he was quieter, a bit withdrawn. He was not his usual happy, outgoing self.

How Parents React to Loss

When adults lose their own parents, they are confronted with the irrevocable loss of loved ones as well as with the loss of the childhood fantasy that they will be protected and taken care of by their parents forever. Along with this comes the realization, as one forty-year-old said, "I'm next in line. Now there's no one between me and adulthood. I'm it."

For Peter Witts, it was particularly difficult to lose his sister, the one remaining person who shared his life history. Her death knocked the stability out of his family, particularly coming so soon after the death of his mother. His sister's death intimated his own, and this realization added to his depression.

When Parents Lose Control

Rebecca tried her best to be sensitive and empathetic to her husband and son. Yet she, too, grieved. She admitted, "Eventually I realized I needed a change of scene or else I was going to explode under all the stress." Two months after Peter's sister died, while her husband was away on a business trip, Rebecca took Keith to visit a cousin in Florida.

• • • *When we got to the Orlando airport, he said, "I feel sad because Daddy's not here." He'd never said that before. I said, "We're going to go to Disney World," and he said, "Yes, but I'd feel better if Daddy were here."*

At the end of the week Keith went into a complete tantrum when I tried to wash his hair. He said I was a horrible mommy —he hated me, he wished I were going to die, I always did horrible things and I never did anything he wanted.

I'm fairly psychologically oriented but that really got to me. I screamed, "I'm never taking you on a vacation again. You can get yourself another mother!"

Keith was so horrified he didn't talk the rest of the day. When we got home, his hands were peeling. The pediatrician gave him some cortisone and said children's skin around the fingers and nails can peel from tension. Of course I remembered all the screaming in Florida.

That evening when I put him to bed, I said I was really sorry that I'd been so angry in Florida, that sometimes mommies lose their tempers, but that I loved him even when I was angry. He looked at me with this hesitant smile and said, "You really, really do love me?" "Of course." "Well, you know, I didn't think you did," he said. Evidently, at that point when I screamed at him, he thought I'd stopped loving him. In the next few days, his skin condition cleared up.

Saying things that one later regrets is inevitable as a parent, but the consequences need not be long-lasting. When Rebecca recognized the intensity of Keith's anxieties, she talked with him about what had happened in Florida. No doubt Keith felt guilty at provoking his mother's outburst and was frightened by his own power to drive his mother away. After the two deaths, losing his mother was a frightening possibility. It was a relief when his mother told him that no matter what he said or did, she would always love him. Although losing control can be upsetting to parents and children, it can also lead to increased understanding and closeness.

The Child's Fears and Anxieties

As Rebecca said, Keith's initial response to the deaths was similar to the adults'—sorrow and depression. Yet his reactions also reflected the typical fears of young children. The deaths of his relatives intensified his anxiety over separation. His mother describes the changes she saw:

> ▪ ▪ ▪ *He no longer wanted to go to nursery school. He said he felt sad there. Probably he was worried that while he was gone, something might happen to me.*
>
> *He didn't want me out of his sight in the house. He would play upstairs in his room as long as I was nearby, but if I went downstairs, he would stop what he was doing and follow me. If I went outside to hang up laundry, he'd insist on coming. He was like a shadow. He had been quite independent before this.*

Young children frequently equate death with loneliness or abandonment, wondering, "Who will take care of me when you die?" Keith's reluctance to go to school, as well as his sadness at his father's absence in Disney World, reflected his fears about being left behind on his own without the safety and security of the adults who loved him. Even his own familiar house felt a little scary. Because Keith's father expressed his grief by withdrawing and turning into himself, this compounded Keith's sense of loss.

Young children may have difficulty distinguishing a brief separation (a parent's trip away from home) from a permanent separation (divorce or death). When his mother told him that they would be home in a week and that his father would be there, Keith blurted out, "How do you know— maybe we won't see him again, like with Aunt Nancy." Keith was understandably confused and worried. He had to face the reality of never seeing his grandmother and aunt again, while maintaining his trust that his parents would return to him.

The deaths brought to the fore another aspect of Keith's anxiety. Preschoolers tend to believe that their parents are all-powerful and all-capable. Yet when his grandmother and aunt died, Keith was confronted with his parents' helplessness—they could not "make things better." One way that

Keith dealt with his anxiety over his parents' impotence was to escape into fantasy. Rebecca says:

> **• • •** *For the first time, television became a big part of his life. Keith wanted to stay home to watch shows, especially those with happy endings.*

At other times, Keith tested the limits of his parents' capabilities. He would put himself in scary or dangerous situations that demanded their help. One day he climbed to the top of a jungle gym, froze, and began to cry hysterically. Rebecca had to climb up and guide him down. She felt he had been intentionally reckless (which was unlike him) and forced her to rescue him. Events like this bolstered Keith's belief that his parents were able to take care of him and protect him.

What Do Children Understand of Death?

Most children are exposed to death and dying; they see it around them, ask questions about it, and make their own observations. Often the first death that young children experience is that of a pet, either their own or one at preschool. In cartoons and TV shows, characters die. Themes of illness or death begin to appear in preschoolers' play. There are shouts of "bang, bang—you're dead," slayings of monsters and creatures from outer space, and deathbed scenes in hospitals.

Rebecca had heard that at his age, Keith would understand nothing about death, but she thought otherwise:

> **• • •** *I read him a book about a bird that dies and we talked about his grandmother's death. Within a few minutes he said, "Are you and Daddy going to die also?" I said, "Not for a very, very long time. When you're very old. It's so far away that you don't have to think about it." Then he asked if he was going to die—he made the connection. I wasn't prepared for that at all, thinking that would take him at least another year or so to ask. I answered as best I could: "Everybody dies some-day, but usually when they get very, very old. In the mean-time, you can think about the fact that you're going to be four years old soon." I kept trying to focus on his age, his youth. But it's not easy to deal with when your kid confronts you point-blank.*

Keith's questions were especially distressing to Rebecca when they focused on his death and that of his mother and father. Clearly, he was expressing his concern about being alone without the care and protection of his parents. Young children often have very concrete questions: "Will it hurt to be buried?" "Will Grandma miss us?" Keith wondered if his aunt would get hot in the coffin. These questions can best be understood as legitimate attempts to make sense of something that is scary, overwhelming, and new to them, but their bluntness may shock or anger adults.

Of course, young children are unable to understand death in the abstract, complex terms that adults do. Preschoolers' thinking is magical: for example, they think the dead can be resurrected (e.g., "by keeping them warm"). Children think of death in very personal terms: one child said Jesus died because "he ate too many Easter eggs." Children also tend to equate death with punishment for wrongdoing and thus believe that "bad" people die and "good" people do not. Children's questions and ideas about death reflect their literal thinking as well as their belief that others' experiences are identical to their own.

How Do Children Mourn?

It is generally agreed that young children grieve and that this process is similar to that of adults: they need to deal with the reality of the loss and the pain in order to continue loving, trusting, and growing.

Keith initially expressed his grief as his father did. He was withdrawn and enervated. His mother gave him other ways of coping. She verbalized her own pain, anger, and fear and helped Keith express some of his concerns. To some extent, Keith was borrowing the grief responses of both his parents in order to manage his anxiety and to integrate the experience in a positive way.

Sometimes young children express their grief differently than adults do. Their sadness may be short-lived, giving the false impression that they are indifferent or uncaring. When her grandmother died a five-year-old said, "Oh, now I can wear the necklace she promised to give to me." Children's immediate wishes or egocentric concerns may not be inhibited in times of crisis to the extent that adults would like.

Grieving children are sometimes outwardly mischievous, angry, or noisy, which may be offensive to adults. These children are reacting in age-appropriate ways when they express their feelings through physical activity. Children also use play to cope with their feelings and anxieties about death. One group of kindergarten children repeatedly reenacted a fatal accident they had witnessed. They took on the roles of the victim and the medical staff and played out the rescue and death for months afterward.

SOLUTIONS

Grief is a normal and predictable response to loss. It is important for bereaved children to experience "good grief," which strengthens coping skills, prevents the development of emotional problems, and keeps children psychologically healthy.

Sandra Fox, director of the Good Grief Program at Judge Baker Guidance Center in Boston, outlines three tasks that children must accomplish to experience good grief: 1) understanding the death; 2) grieving; and 3) commemorating. How any one child will undertake these tasks depends on the child's stage of development, his or her own personality, and the particular circumstances. Although the death of a parent from cancer may involve different issues than the loss of a playmate from a car accident, the bereaved child still needs to understand the event, mourn the loss, and remember the person.

Helping Children Understand Death

Children wonder what has happened and why. They need simple, clear information about the specifics of the situation: "Johnny ran after a ball in the street and didn't see the car coming. The car couldn't stop. He went to the hospital where the doctors and nurses tried to help him, but they couldn't make his body work. He died last night."

Young children are sometimes afraid of a sick or dying person because they think the sickness is "catching." Parents should distinguish the cause of death and, where appropriate, reassure children that they will not catch any germs.

Children also need information about what death is. According to Sandra Fox, most preschoolers seem to understand that death means that your body stops working—you do not breathe or eat anymore, you cannot play or talk. Nevertheless, what may seem like simple, straightforward explanations to adults may be confusing to a young child. One boy had trouble falling asleep after a newborn died of respiratory distress; he thought that anyone who sleeps might die and therefore dared not close his eyes. He began to feel reassured when he was reminded that a sleeping person can still hear and feel and that he often woke up when there was a loud noise or when he felt thirsty. Similarly, young children are understandably confused when a pet is "put to sleep." A better explanation is: "Banjo was in a lot of pain and would never get well. The vet gave him a special shot, only for animals, not for people. It made him stop breathing and he died." It is very important to distinguish death from all other events in the child's experience.

Although different families have various beliefs about what happens after death, your children can be told that they will not see the dead person the same way as when he or she was alive on earth. Religious explanations, while comforting to many older children and adults, sometimes add to the confusion of preschoolers. "How can someone get to heaven when he is buried in the ground?" "If God loved Grandma so much that he wanted her to be with Him, why doesn't He love and want me?"

You need to arrive at explanations of death and dying that you are comfortable with and that take into account the child's developmental level while simultaneously laying a foundation for later, more sophisticated understandings and concepts.

Participating in Formal Rituals

Rebecca Witts was uncertain whether Keith should attend the funeral.

. . . *One person said, "You must expose him to everything." Another said, "Don't traumatize the child, don't take him." I thought it was probably not a good idea for him to go. Yet I didn't want him to feel left out, because I remember when my grandparents died, I was not allowed to go and developed a fear of funerals.*

In times of loss, family rituals can serve as familiar supports for children even though they may not fully comprehend the significance of the occasion. Here again, parental attitudes make a difference: if you want to include your child, it is more likely to be a meaningful experience for him or her than if you really do not want your child to attend.

Rebecca Witts decided to give Keith a choice:

. . . *I said to Keith, "We're going to something called a funeral where they're going to play sad music and talk about your grandmother. Do you want to come, or should we arrange something else for you to do?" He said he'd rather play with a friend. That way he knew where we went and it was not a big secret.*

When they are given information about rituals (what they are like, what people do at them), most children can articulate their preference, as Keith did. When young children participate in formal rituals, take into account their shorter attention spans and provide adults who can take them aside or take them away.

You can also create your own rituals. One family told their children—a six- and four-year-old—that if they wanted to, they could have a "good-bye" visit with their dying grandfather. Judith S. Rubenstein describes how she prepared each child for this visit with frank but reassuring explanations: "Grandpa looks very tired. He's going to die soon. He may cry, but he's still your grandpa who loves you." The children were told that this would probably be the last time they would see him.

Another family held a Quaker memorial service in their home when the mother died of cancer. Families, including young children, were invited. Adults gathered in one room to share memories of this woman. The children were in another room with food and drink or outside playing. In yet another room were scrapbooks of photographs of the mother and a notebook in which the guests could write something. This way the children will have many memories of their mother to return to as they grow up.

Providing a Forum

Give your children a chance to talk about death and loss whenever they need to. Sometimes just spending time together will give children an opportunity to express their feelings or fears. Rubenstein noted that her children would ask questions about their dying grandfather while she was cooking or driving to the store. If discussion becomes difficult, you can say so: "We've talked about it enough for today, but when you have more questions you can come ask me."

Sometimes children need to be encouraged to talk. For example, "I think Johnny was very quiet today in the hospital. What do you think he was feeling?" or "I was thinking about Grandma and remembered how much she liked to read with you. I bet you miss those special times with her."

Acknowledging a Range of Feelings

When someone dies, children (like adults) experience sadness, often mixed with anger. Although rage seems distant from grief, it is normal to feel angry and abandoned when someone you care about is gone. When a child's parent dies, reassure the child that people will still take care of him or her. Let children know that their feelings are acceptable and that you will help them find constructive ways to express them. Encourage bereaved children's pretend play since this is a domain in which they can take charge and make events go the way they want them to.

Here is how one father helped his three-year-old son cope with his mother's terminal illness:

■ ■ ■ *The nursery school teacher told me that Drew was running around the classroom, shouting at the other children: "I don't like you, I don't like you." The teacher and I talked with him and helped him understand that he really felt angry at his mother who had just been hospitalized. He really missed her at home. Because he loved to draw and paint, we suggested he make pictures to hang in her hospital room. Sometimes the pictures seemed to convey a happy mood; at other times, a sad mood. We accepted whatever he did and let him decide which ones to give to his mother.*

Commemorating

Keith wished for another Aunt Nancy just like the one who died. Parents can honor that impossible wish by commemorating the life of the deceased. They can make a book with photographs of the family and the person who died. Young children can also draw and dictate stories about the person. They can plant a tree or flower that the person particularly liked. By creating something—a book, a photo album, a picture, a memorial—children and their parents alike can begin the process of healing. It is by cherishing memories and making them a part of ourselves that we accept and adapt to loss.

After the spaceship Challenger tragedy, many school classes collected articles and pictures about the astronauts and the space program and wrote letters to the astronauts' families. In one school, the upper grades drew pictures and wrote stories depicting the lives of the astronauts and their adventures in space, then shared their work with the lower grades. This experience generated a sense of community among children of different ages.

Enjoying Time Together as a Family

One of the best things a family can do to ease the pain of loss is to spend time together, doing things they like (visits to the playground or to a special place, like the zoo). What is important is that the family members share good experiences that reinforce their love for each other and their capacity to enjoy life.

When to Seek Professional Help

A death can precipitate a crisis that threatens to overwhelm the survivors' coping skills and their capacity to resume living; in this case, special assistance may be needed. When a parent or sibling dies, children are particularly vulnerable.

Children who are having difficulty dealing with a loss may show it in a number of ways. Some may continue to grieve long after others have resumed normal activities. They may go over and over the details of the death or repeat the same questions again and again. Others may be unable to talk about it, may regress, or show prolonged disturbances in sleeping, eating, or playing patterns.

When a child's response to any death is this intense, it is a signal to ask for help in assessing what is going on. Many communities offer a range of professional services and resources. We urge you to use them when you or your children are feeling vulnerable and overwhelmed in dealing with loss.

THREE

At-Home and Away-from-Home Routines

Introduction

After many years of working with parents and their young children, I have come to believe that a battleground emerges in almost every parent/child relationship—these skirmishes are about sleeping or eating, stalling in the morning or at bedtime. If dressing is the issue in your family, rest assured that if it weren't clothes, it would be something else. In the preschool years these battles over routines reflect the contradictory forces of dependence and independence. Children are struggling to assert themselves—to be more grown-up and in control over their bodies. At the same time, they feel vulnerable and want to be taken care of. What more appropriate place for young children to express their contradictory urges than over the necessary routines of daily life?

Dressing

Q *My problem is getting my child dressed. I hate starting the day with a struggle, but that's what is happening. Are there ways to reduce this conflict?*

I turned this parent's question back to the parent's group that I was addressing at a nursery school: Do any of you have a struggle over dressing your child in the morning. If so, what happens?

I heard the following stories:

■ ■ ■ *My problem is over the outfits my child wants to wear. He wants to put on the same orange shirt every day. I finally went out and bought three more just like it, but I'm sick of seeing him in the same shirt day after day. And I wonder what his teacher thinks.*

• • • *I'm going through something similar, but at least she'll wear different clothes. It's the layered look—one shirt over another, over another. Nothing matches. She'll wear orange plaid with pink ruffles. When we're out in public, I feel like pretending she's not my child.*

• • • *My daughter is extremely particular about the kind of clothing she wears. She's disturbed if it's not fancy enough. She would love to be in a dress 24 hours a day, whether it's practical or not.*

• • • *I wish my child cared about the way she looks. She doesn't. She is so busy drawing or looking at books that she refuses to put on her clothes. I have the kind of schedule that we have to be out of the house at a certain time, so I end up running after her, pushing her arm into a sweater, pulling on her pants.*

• • • *My child stalls in the morning. He's very crabby. From about six-thirty to seven he relaxes on my lap while I drink my tea and wake up. Then starts the battle of getting him dressed. Some mornings, I have to wrestle him down to get his clothes on.*

• • • *We put out the clothes the night before, but in the morning, he hates those choices. He'll want his striped shirt, and of course it's filthy dirty and in the hamper. Nothing else will do. He insists that he won't go to school unless he can wear that shirt.*

The parent who asked the original question was surprised and somewhat relieved that so many of the other parents in the group had similar conflicts. Perhaps because she had never discussed it, she had assumed that the other parents were having smooth mornings and arriving at nursery school without any scars from an earlier conflict over dressing.

In the quest for greater autonomy, dressing is one area over which many children want to exercise control. They want to determine what goes onto their bodies and when. Their taste is their taste, even if the children look outrageous in adult's eyes. Clothes can also represent security (the same orange shirt) or a powerful identity (a superhero shirt). At the same time that children want to exercise control, they want to be cared for. So even when they are fully capable of dressing themselves, they may refuse, saying "dress me."

Preschool children are still young and engage in the kind of magical thinking in which they believe that their powerful parents can change events —to make a cool day warm enough for sandals, a dirty shirt clean in time for school, a tight schedule leisurely enough to play before dressing, or a roughhousing day right for wearing a fancy dress.

The here and now predominates, and playing before school may seem much more alluring than going to school. In fact, a number of children find the transition to school difficult. The mother who described her child as needing cuddling in the morning before she "wrestled him into his clothes" had just given birth. Her son, she later revealed, did not want to have his mommy and baby stay home without him, so dressing became the symbol of separation and departure.

In addition, morning is the time in which temperamental differences may be most evident—the child who is slow to get going clashes with the mother or father who is fast paced. Or the child who is crabby clashes with the parent who is also crabby. Furthermore, clothing feels different to different children. I thought that my son was obstinate when he resisted clothes with big buttons or zippers until I saw that his skin was very sensitive and actually turned blotchy from these fastenings.

As parents of preschoolers, we are likely to judge ourselves and feel judged by our children's appearance. When our children wear outfits that clash with our standards, we feel that we aren't firm enough. When our children refuse to part with the sweatpants that seem fit only for the rag pile, we feel that we aren't caring for our children adequately when they go out in public looking like waifs.

The following solutions have worked for parents with dressing problems:

- Select clothes that are comfortable and durable. If they are easy for children to put on or off by themselves, all the better.
- Put out clothes the night before. If your child rejects the choice once morning comes, discuss that possibility in advance: "You change your mind in the morning and then it's always a hassle. I don't want this kind of fight every morning. What would work for you in making dressing more peaceful?"
- Leave enough time for the morning to be as calm as possible. One parent lets her three young children sleep in the socks, underwear, and shirts that they'll wear the next day. The peace she gains in the morning is worth the wrinkled clothes.
- Think back to a time in which clothes selection and dressing went smoothly. What principles can you deduce? Try them out again.
- Pace the morning to your temperament. If you are irritable in the morning, leave enough time so you feel good before you see your child. Forewarn your family so children don't take it personally. Figure out a schedule that fits your style.

- Pace the morning to your child's temperament. Perhaps breakfast should come before dressing.
- Let your child select clothes if and when possible: "Would you like the green or red pants?"
- Pick your battles. Wearing clothes that are inappropriate for the day's activities is a more important issue than questions of taste.
- Don't threaten unless you mean it. Saying, "You're going to have to stay home unless you get dressed" should be avoided unless that option is realistically possible. Some parents have kept their children home from a special event, but if you do so, make sure that you don't resent this action and don't take it out on your child the rest of the day.
- Problem-solve with your children. Do not reject their solutions out of hand without considering them.
- Don't expect your child to go automatically from being dressed to dressing himself or herself. Work on one skill at a time.
- Use books and games that teach dressing skills. "How many numbers do you think I'll count before you get on your socks?" You can also use a kitchen timer.
- Use charts with stickers as rewards for learning new dressing skills.
- Above all, keep a sense of humor. I remember going into a restaurant with my daughter dressed in a feather boa and a sundress with the straps tucked in so it was strapless. Heads turned as we walked in. Rather than feel embarrassed, I decided to enjoy her sense of style.
- One parent sent a note to her child's teacher: "My daughter's choice in clothes do not reflect the taste of the management."

Eating and Mealtimes

Q *How do I deal with a picky eater?*

Adele Green-Williams is the mother of three-year-old Phoebe:

• • • *Phoebe is not a great eater. She likes cheese, dairy products, and fruit. She has never eaten meat or vegetables.*

Generally, Phoebe won't try new things, and she'll go through periods when she'll want to eat the same thing morning, noon, and night. Occasionally if she sees somebody try something she might taste it, but she'll just kind of lick it.

For the past two years Phoebe has been spitting her food out a lot. I've taken her to the doctor and he couldn't find any

allergies or anything wrong with her gag reflex. It really both-
ers me to see the food I've cooked spit all over the table.

The battle over food can take on significance in parents' minds because of some underlying assumptions.

Assumption: My Child Doesn't Love Me If He or She Doesn't Eat Well

Adele Green-Williams says, "I feel like Phoebe is rejecting me when she doesn't want to eat what I've cooked." For many of us, food is a gift we give to those we love, a pledge of our commitment and caring. We fantasize about our family members enjoying what we have prepared and appreciating our efforts. To have Phoebe not only reject food but spit it all over the table feels like a slap in the face to Adele, so it's not surprising that she becomes angry. What possibly started as Phoebe's limited food preferences has turned into a contest of wills between mother and daughter.

Assumption: My Child Is Not Well Cared for If He or She Doesn't Eat Heartily

Feeling insecure as parents, we look for signs that our children are well and healthy. Joan Lombard worries about her daughter:

. . . *Jessica eats only popcorn, corn on the cob, hot dogs, and peanut butter. That's it. No vegetables, no fruit, no other kind of protein. I feel that she must be malnourished in some way but you wouldn't know it to look at her. She's a gymnast. She climbs on the high bars, hangs by her arms and somersaults . . . I don't know where she gets the energy.*

Contributing to the feeling of failure is the fact that others—mothers, mothers-in-law, even strangers in restaurants—feel obliged to point out the disastrous results of your child's not eating meat or vegetables. Standing up to the criticism of others is hard, as Joan Lombard reports:

. . . *My mother says, "How can you let Jessica eat that stuff? What kind of terrible mother are you?" I try to tune it out, but it drives me crazy anyway.*

Assumption: We Have Done Something Wrong If Our Child Is a Picky Eater

This assumption may be reinforced by other parents whose children love to eat. Barbara Farmer is such a parent:

• • • *I've been very successful in feeding Ralph. Other parents say, "Why don't my children eat anything except peanut butter, hamburgers, and hot dogs?" I answer because you give them those things. If you'd never given them "children's" food, they wouldn't ask for it. I have given Ralph sprouts, avocado, spinach, and greens ever since he was little. He loves them because he's never even had a pizza. He'll get food like that soon enough, but only after I've established a preference for healthy food.*

Parents of picky eaters often feel guilty when they hear from someone like Barbara. They should know, however, that many parents who share Barbara's philosophy report that while it worked for the first child, the second one rejected bean sprouts and avocado.

Parents ask themselves, "Have I caused my child's eating problems?" The answer is complex. Eating problems can be related to the child's inborn disposition and experience. Some children are by nature more sensitive to taste, touch, and smell and may react to foods more strongly than others do. Furthermore, it is also clear that eating problems are normal in the preschool years. According to English researcher Judy Dunn, between 10 and 30 percent of parents of preschoolers say their children are picky eaters, a characteristic which is generally outgrown as the children mature.

Our own attitudes make a difference. If we are enthusiastic and unambivalent about good food, our pleasure will probably be transmitted. Conversely, if we worry about food, we can aggravate the situation. Adele Green-Williams feels, in retrospect, that she has intensified Phoebe's problems with eating: "I wish I hadn't been so uptight about food."

Assumption: Children Need to Eat When Adults Do

Problems may occur because of a mismatch between when children are hungry and when we traditionally eat. Of course it is much easier to serve scheduled meals and not be short-order cooks; however, some children want to eat small amounts every two to three hours. There is accumulating evidence that this is a healthy pattern of eating for adults as well.

Try to note the times when eating difficulties occur with your child; perhaps your problem comes from the timing of meals.

Assumption: Every Meal Should Be Balanced

Many nutritionists dispute the notion that every meal must contain all the food groups. Think in terms of eating over a several-day period rather than getting all the essentials into each meal.

Assumption: Children Should Finish Everything They Are Served

How many of us grew up with such dictums as "You have to finish all of your food because children are starving in Asia or Africa," and how many of us replied, "Then send them my dinner"? Jane Hirschmann and Lela Zaphiropolous, who treat people with eating disorders, make the important point in their book *Are You Hungry?* that teaching children to clean their plate can obscure the child's own hunger. They write, "The message of the Clean Plate Club is that there will be an *external* reward for eating." Thus, eating becomes dissociated from the actual physical hunger. Eating for external rather than internal reasons can be reinforced by the many games that parents play with children at the table: "Open biggie like a piggie and take a bite for Daddy." As amusing as these games are, they can teach children to eat to please others rather than to satisfy their own hunger.

Along with these assumptions, parents can fall into two traps over food.

Using Food as Punishment.   It is not very effective to threaten: "If you don't pick up your toys, you can't have any dinner." When children are hungry, they are less capable of coping well. If children are running around at dinner or throwing peas across the table, they can be sent from the table for a short time "until you can manage."

A corollary of this idea is that "you can't have any dessert until you eat all of your chicken (or pot roast or beans)." This tactic makes desserts even more appealing than they need to be and presents the idea of good foods and bad foods. Try to avoid serving anything that you don't consider nutritious. You can freeze juice into frozen pops for dessert or, with ice cream makers, quickly make frozen desserts out of bananas, fruit, or yogurt.

Using Food as Reward.   The complement of using food as punishment is using food as reward. When I was young, children were given bread-and-brown-sugar sandwiches or other treats if they did something noteworthy. Having a special treat to celebrate a happy occasion is wonderful. If, however, food is always used to comfort, then children learn to eat not because they are hungry but because they need a crutch when they are upset.

Child's-Eye View of Food

Because their experience is primarily grounded in their senses, young children are much more attuned to the textures and smells of foods than adults are. So they may reject food for reasons that adults find strange: "The pepper looks like bugs," "The eggs smell like throw-up." They may insist on having each portion of food on a plate clearly separated from the others; if the peas are touching the meat, they won't even taste them. This is not perversity but rather reflects children's affinity for ritualistic, rigid ways of doing things. In time, most children learn to enjoy a variety of sights, smells, and tastes.

Think back to your memories of childhood meals: were you ever forced to eat? If so, little else matches the feeling of violation to your body and your dignity. Was the food delicious, plain, or tasteless? Was mealtime pleasant or something to be endured and ended as quickly as possible? These memories influence how we think about mealtime for our own children. Despite differences in upbringing, however, most parents have similar goals: we want our children to eat when they are hungry, stop eating when they are full, and enjoy what they eat.

These parental goals find support in a longitudinal study conducted by Lois Barclay Murphy and her colleague Alice Moriarty. They found that infants' ability to regulate their own feeding in the sense of making their hunger known and terminating when full was associated with their later development: as preschoolers they were more adept at coping with problems and frustrations.

SOLUTIONS

Figuring Out What Food Means in Your Family

Pretend you are videotaping your family's mealtimes for a documentary on "America's Ways of Eating." What patterns do you notice? If there is a conflict, when does it begin? Why? How do you respond? How does your child, in turn, react to you? What does this problem really mean to you? How would you explain the patterns in your family to someone unfamiliar with this culture?

Solving Problems

Once you have identified the reasons for the conflict, think creatively about the solution. For example, Adele Green-Williams decided to deescalate her conflict with Phoebe by giving her an acceptable way to spit out food:

■ ■ ■ *I've concentrated on having Phoebe spit into a napkin. If I'm sitting with her I'll remind her to use the napkin and try not to lose my temper. Now she usually spits only when she doesn't like the food and doesn't want to eat it. She gets a lot of reinforcement with the napkin bit. I told everybody about it, so every time my parents see her do it, they say how nice it is. I always say, "I'm so proud of you, you remembered to use your napkin."*

In the Feminilla family, the conflict was over which foods were permissible. Five-year-old Donna demanded supermarket cookies that her mother,

Mary, thought were junky. To resolve this problem, Mary told Donna the cookies contained a lot of chemicals, but they could buy cookies at the bakery or make some cookies at home. Donna chose to make cookies and they had a good time selecting different recipes.

Checking with Your Pediatrician

If you are concerned about malnutrition, consult your pediatrician. Do not, however, threaten your child: "I'm going to check with the doctor because you never eat." This sort of comment can only intensify the battle between you and your child.

If your child sticks to one or two foods, he or she might have allergies. If there are allergies in the family or if you note disruptive behavior after eating certain foods, check with an allergy specialist.

I found, through trial and error, that my son was allergic to eggs—a food he craved. After eating eggs, he would race around or fall into a deep sleep; once he stopped eating them, his energy level evened out, and his moods greatly improved.

Planning Meals Together

Let each family member select one food for dinner. You can post the menu on the refrigerator so everyone is reminded of the upcoming meals. This way, meal planning is shared and family members can look forward to favorite foods.

Shopping Together

Many families post a marketing list on the refrigerator or bulletin board. Young children can cut labels from favorite foods and tape them to the list —a good exercise in prereading. You may want to limit the categories or kinds of food: cookies, vegetables, or fruits. Using the list you have made together, you can take your children shopping. The younger ones can use the labels they have cut out to identify the items (see the section on shopping, pages 223–229). If there are hassles about certain items you don't want to buy, provide alternatives: "You can select any cereal except those with sugar as one of the first three ingredients or that have the letters BHA on the ingredient list."

Keeping a Plate of Snack Foods

Keep a supply of acceptable snack foods—carrots in a glass of water, pieces of cheese, plastic bags full of popcorn, celery, or apples with peanut butter —readily available so that children can get them when they are hungry. You will feel comfortable knowing they are eating healthy snacks, and it will matter less if they don't eat as much at dinner. According to Hirsch-mann and Zaphiropolous, saying, "You'll spoil your appetite," teaches children to ignore their own hunger: "The child who has to wait too long will be so hungry that she may overeat at dinner, unable to recognize fullness when it comes. It is difficult to know when you are full if you sit down to eat feeling 'starved.' "

These authors suggest that whenever children ask for food, they be asked, "Are you hungry?" Thus children will learn to respond to their internal signals. Then I suggest you provide a limited choice, "Would you like crackers or carrots?" And finally ask, "Are you full?" This last question helps children assess their internal state. The goal of this approach is to teach children to eat when they are hungry and to stop when they are full.

Letting the Children Help You Cook

Nothing helps children become more adventurous eaters than cooking themselves. It's hard not to try something if you have helped to make it. My own children particularly liked to make biscuits (almost like playing with play dough) and were willing to experiment with adding different ingredients to muffins or pasta.

Presenting Food Attractively

Children like to see food presented in interesting ways—sandwiches cut with cookie cutters in the shape of hearts or Thanksgiving turkeys. A mother of a toddler says: "If I feed my son with chopsticks, he eats everything." Other parents have colorful spoons, plates with the child's name on it, and so on.

Having the Children Set the Table

Many children enjoy decorating the table for mealtime. They can color on napkins or make place cards. You can also try the technique that family restaurants use. Use a big roll of paper as a tablecloth and have a can of crayons on the table. Children can thus design the tablecloth, and mealtime will be more of a celebration.

Having Interesting Games or Conversation at Meals

A single father who raised three children passed on this idea. Every night at dinner time, each member of the family would take a letter of the alphabet and think of something beginning with that letter. For example, if you have B, you might think of "bakery." Then you would tell everything you know about bakeries. Then the next person would do the same for the letter C.

My daughter invented her own ritual. She wanted us all to hold hands and say one thing we liked about the meal.

Conclusion

As the mother of a child who ate only spaghetti and water when she was three, I can report that if you don't fall into the pattern of letting food become a battle that continues to escalate, your child will grow up to like much more than spaghetti and water or hot dogs and pizza.

Bottles

Q *When should my child give up bottles?*

This is a subject about which experts and parents have strong feelings, both pro and con. Research evidence is scant and inconclusive.

Before beginning to wean your child from the bottle, ask yourself two questions.

Are You Ready?

Are you ready to give up holding your child with a bottle? Are you tired of carrying leaky bottles around? Are you retaining this routine because you don't want your child to grow up, or do you suspect you want your child to grow up too fast? It's important for you to be ready to wean because if you aren't, it will be harder for you to communicate a clear, unambivalent message to your child.

Is Your Child Ready?

Does a bottle comfort your child in a good way, or is your child disappearing out of the sight of other kids when he or she wants a bottle? Is your child becoming too dependent on bottles, lacking other ways to provide self-comfort?

How the bottle is given up is also important:

It's Not All or Nothing

The general assumption is that giving up the bottle is done cold turkey. This isn't necessarily the case. Many families limit the number of bottles or confine them to certain times of day as a first step.

The Child's Involvement Is Critical

Most parents see giving up the bottle as something you do to a child. I see it quite differently for the verbal child—as an opportunity to *begin* to learn how to handle the more difficult aspects of life. For this reason, I advocate making a plan with your child about when and how he or she will give up the bottle.

The following stories from parents in a group I conducted illustrate this approach:

> ▪ ▪ ▪ *My son Andy (almost three) was drinking ten or more bottles a day. He would have to go to the bathroom all the time, which I think was an embarrassment to him. Once when his friend John was over to play, he wanted a bottle but didn't want John to see him, so he went into his own room and shut the door to drink it. That night I said to him, "It seems you aren't so comfortable about your bottle anymore, so it's time to start thinking about giving it up." I asked him when he wanted to do it, and he said he wanted to do it after his birthday. I asked him if he wanted something special for giving up his bottle, and he said he wanted Lego blocks. So I went out and bought the Legos.*
>
> *In the meantime, I said it would be easier if he cut down on bottles during the day and just have them at mealtimes. So he tried that and it was fine—especially because he didn't have to go to the bathroom so often.*
>
> *One day, about a week before his birthday, he came to me during the morning and said, "I want a bottle." I said, "Remember that you decided that you were going to have bottles only at mealtimes." He said he remembered, but this bottle was going to be his last.*
>
> *So I gave it to him. He drank it with great relish and then threw it in the wastebasket. He asked for the Legos and we had a family party to celebrate the event.*
>
> *He never asked for his bottle again until about a year later—after his sister was born. I gave him one of his sister's bottles, and he tried to suck it. He had forgotten how. He handed it back and asked for a glass of milk.*

The mother of a two-and-a-half-year-old describes how her daughter changed her mind about her decision.

> ▪ ▪ ▪ *Sasha picked Wednesday to give up her bottle, but as the day approached she changed her mind. She said, "I didn't mean this Wednesday. I meant another Wednesday."*
>
> *She had just started nursery school and I had been away, so I did think it might all be a bit much, but I still wanted her to keep some commitment to Wednesday. I said she could give*

up her daytime bottles but have one at night. I said, "Maybe you'd like something special to drink out of during the day. Let's go to the store and pick out a really special cup for you." We chose a cute one with a top like an ice cream cone. That satisfied her for a while. Then we were in the store several days later and she asked for little Dixie cups. I bought a package—she loved them. Her new cup and the Dixie cups got her through this difficult transition.

Two other children—Barbara and Amy—decided to give up their bottles together. Barbara's mother describes it:

■ ■ ■ *Barbara and Amy decided to give up their bottles one week after Barbara's birthday. On the particular day they had selected I forgot about it, but as we were leaving to go to school, Barbara said, "Don't forget my bottle, I have to throw it away." So I gave it to her and she and Amy went into the bathroom at school and threw their bottles into the garbage can. That was the end of that for Barbara.*

Amy's mother, however, found a more gradual approach was necessary:

■ ■ ■ *Because it was her decision, Amy gave up her daytime bottle easily. At night she wouldn't ask for her bottle, but she could not fall asleep, and she was up for hours. She didn't know what to do with herself. She would cry, but she would never say to me, "Mommy, I want my bottle." She tried so hard. This went on for a week. One night my husband said to me, "This is terrible." The next day we said, "Okay, Amy, we're going to go out and get you a special bottle just for nighttime." She was another person—so much happier. We'll work on giving up the nighttime bottle later on.*

Barbara, on the other hand, seemed to be fine for several weeks. In fact, her mother had forgotten all about the bottle when Barbara's behavior began to change. Barbara's mother described this change:

■ ■ ■ *Barbara's just driving me crazy. She's got to have everything her way, and if she doesn't, she'll just shriek or start crying. But it's really a phony cry, a whining kind of cry.*

I suggested that perhaps this behavior had to do with her giving up the bottle. Her mother replied:

... *Now that you bring it up, I realize that whenever she had a fit like this, the first thing I'd do was give her the bottle and that would calm her down. Now there's nothing that really comforts her the way the bottle did, but I don't want her to develop another crutch.*

I said:

... *It might be interesting to ask her what helps her feel better when she's upset: maybe it's being held or snuggling with a stuffed animal or rubbing a blanket. Then the next time she feels upset, you could steer her to this way of comforting herself.*

This method of handling problems gives the children increasing control over their own growth; it teaches them skills for handling problems. As Barbara's mother stated:

... *I'm glad that I didn't just take the bottle away from Barbara. If I had insisted, "We're throwing the bottle away," it would have been a struggle. Because she decided to do it, she feels wonderful. But you're right—now she has to find a way to do without the bottle and yet get comfort when she needs it.*

Toilet Training

Q *What should I do about toilet training?*

Joan Dean, mother of Melissa, says:

... *I feel like I've done all the right things: I bought underpants and put them in the bottom drawer so Melissa (age two and a half) could look at them all the time. I bought potty seats and put them around the house. Then I waited for clues from her to show me she was ready. Nothing is happening. What now?*

When a parent has problems with toilet training, that parent is generally harboring some unrealistic expectations. Here are the most common:

Assumption: There Is a Correct Age to Toilet Train

This expectation usually comes from subtle or not-so-subtle hints from others. Grandparents might say, "She's almost two and you haven't even started training. Is there something wrong with her?" A neighbor might boast, "My child was trained easily by one and a half." The school in which you have enrolled your child might require that all toddlers must be trained, or your pediatrician might announce that it's time to start.

There is no one correct age to train your child. Rather, there is a range when the child is mature enough to learn: generally between the child's second and fourth birthday.

Because the external pressure is so strong, pediatrician Berry Brazelton says he forewarns parents of this at the time of their child's first birthday. He believes that one-year-olds are too young to be trained and helps parents in his practice prepare a response to the pressure.

Assumption: There Is a Recognizable Moment When Your Child Is Ready

If there is no one correct age to toilet train, then when should parents begin? Most child-rearing books advise parents to wait until their child is "ready." Yet the parents I have worked with over the years aren't sure what "ready" means. Many expect it to be more obvious than it usually is. So they wait, perhaps beginning to resent the child or worry that their child is "developmentally delayed" or "slow."

Vicki Lansky, in an excellent pamphlet on this subject, spells out the signs of the child's readiness:

- is aware of going to the bathroom and lets you know by verbal or non-verbal signs (such as crossing legs, pausing, looking around)
- can understand words that refer to toileting such as "wet," "dry," or whatever words you use
- can use these words
- can imitate you or others in various ways
- seems uncomfortable after going to the bathroom in diapers
- stays dry for increasingly longer periods of time, maybe two hours or more (This may not be the case if your child drinks constantly.)
- can put on or pull off loose-fitting shorts or pants
- seems aware of yours and other people's feelings and wants to please you
- tells you that he or she is about to go, is going, or has gone to the bathroom
- shows an interest in using the toilet by watching you or others or asking or trying to use it herself or himself.

In order for toilet training to proceed smoothly, both the child and parent should be ready. Sometimes this may require introspection on the part of parents. When her daughter began to show signs that she wanted to use the toilet, Joelle Hymes didn't respond. She recalled her own childhood:

• • • *I was born right after my older brother. And it was hard for my mother to have me around, I realize that now. But she pushed me to grow up fast and she had very high expectations for me. I've never wanted to do that with Janice.*

In her attempt not to duplicate her mother, Joelle realized that she was ignoring Janice's interest in being trained:

• • • *I wanted so much to be babied that I was overbabying Janice —but it was for me, not for her.*

If you're not ready yourself, it is difficult to muster the resolve to teach your child to use the toilet. Here are some clues:

• You are tired of lugging bags of diapers around, tired of the expense, tired of the changing table.
• You want to do this for the child and for yourself—not because others are saying "you should" or "it's time."

Joan Dean realized she had to gear up to begin toilet training:

• • • *I hadn't wanted to make a big deal out of it, but now that my daughter is almost three and beginning nursery school in the fall, I've realized that I'm going to have to approach it in a more pronounced way. It's time for her and it's time for me.*

Once you are both ready, here are some suggestions for setting the stage.

Providing Role Models

It is helpful to begin talking about the process of going to the bathroom; you might note how you recognize the signs that you have to go. Other children can also serve as models. One of my children became very eager to use the toilet because a friend had just learned how. Resist the temptation, however, to compare your child with another. Statements such as "Rachel just learned so quickly—why are you having so much trouble?" merely undermine the child's feeling of competence.

Helping the Child Become Aware of His or Her Own Patterns

You can also articulate how you know that your child has to go to the bathroom: "I can tell you have to pee when you get fidgety," or "You cross your legs," or "You always go off in a corner."

You can show the child that bowel movements go into the toilet by dumping them from the diapers into the toilet. Some children find flushing upsetting—their body products are being thrown away—so be alert to your child's response when deciding whether to flush or not. You can also put the child on the toilet at the times when he or she is most likely to go. Berry Brazelton suggests setting your child on the toilet fully dressed for a week or so before beginning toilet training.

Some parents let their children run around naked or bare-bottomed to help the children become more aware of when they need to use the toilet. "This worked well for us," said one mother, "but of course you have to be prepared for accidents on the rug with this method."

If your child drinks a lot of fluids, it will be harder to train him or her, so many parents cut down on the number of bottles or drinks before beginning the actual training.

Buying the Right Equipment

You'll need to get attractive underpants and either a toilet adapter seat that slips over the toilet or a stand-alone potty chair. The potty chair should be sturdy enough not to slide across the floor; it should also have an easily removable receptacle that you can fit with plastic bags or rinse out after use.

Children's books about toilet training can also help prepare children for beginning toilet training. Once you have set the stage and all has gone well, move into the more active part of toilet training.

Bringing the Child into the Process

As always, it is more effective for the child to feel he or she is accomplishing something than to feel acted upon or forced into it. You can create a partnership by asking in the morning, "Would you like to wear underpants or diapers?" or "What day will you wear panties, Tuesday or Wednesday?"

Several months after I first interviewed Joan Dean, she called to tell me how this approach had worked with her daughter:

• • • • *This solution worked like magic for me. Instead of asking Melissa if she'd like to sit on the potty—which was a clear no most of the time—I gave her a choice between wearing diapers or pants. That made her feel more in control of the situation. For the first three days, she chose diapers. Then coincidentally we got a birthday package from relatives that had three pairs of frilly underpants in it. The next day I asked her if she wanted to start wearing those or diapers. The answer was "underpants." And we never went back.*

You don't have to hope relatives will send a package of appealing underpants if you use this method—you and your child can shop for "special, big-kid pants."

Another mother found that asking, "Do you have to go to the bathroom?" consistently produced a no answer from her son. She now says, "It's time to go to the bathroom." Some children establish a ritual, as Paula Phillip's daughter has done:

. . . *As soon as I put her on the toilet, she says "sssss" and she pees. I say "Good, Judith. Are you finished?" And I give her toilet paper. She says no and she goes again. I say, "Are you finished?" And she says no and then she goes again. It's like she's holding it for deposits. She's certainly in control this way.*

Using Positive Reinforcement

Paula Phillips praised Judith by saying "good" when she used the toilet. Children appreciate acknowledgement when learning a new skill, but lavish praise ("You are the most wonderful, terrific, smartest child in the world") often leads to an unintended result. Children suspect that they don't match that description and guilt may ensue. Thus praise is more helpful if it is specific and describes the action: "You used the toilet!"

There is controversy about what terminology to use when describing body parts and the process of elimination. Some experts advise using only scientific terminology. My belief is that you should use whatever words you are most comfortable with, from "poop" to "bowel movement," from "tinkle" to "urinate." However, avoid negative terms such as "stinky," which imply that going to the bathroom is an unclean, shameful act.

Many parents use a reward system for the child's accomplishments. One I often hear about is a calendar-like chart. Every time the child successfully uses the toilet, he or she selects a special sticker and pastes it on the chart. One parent keeps a fishbowl full of penny toys that the child can select each time the toilet is used. If you decide on the gift-giving approach, set a time limit: "There will be prizes for a few weeks when you are first learning how to use the toilet."

If you've begun toilet training and are encountering difficulty, you may have some other mistaken expectations.

Assumption: Toilet Training Is an All-or-Nothing Process

If your child shows little progress, stop and try again in a few weeks. Even when children are making progress, it is not all or nothing. In fact, most children take a long time to acquire this skill, and accidents are commonplace. The sequence of learning is usually daytime, then nighttime control. Some children go through an intermediate stage, such as urinating in the toilet but asking for a diaper for their bowel movements. Most parents find their daughters are trained younger than their sons.

It's not only parents who have an all-or-nothing expectation: children do too, as Paula Phillips discovered:

■ ■ ■ *After Judith had two perfectly dry days, she demanded to sleep in her panties. We tried for two nights and she was flooding two and three times a night. So I called her pediatrician, and he suggested that I put a diaper on her at night. When I told her about the diaper, she became hysterical. She was dry all day, why must she wear a diaper at night?*

We explained this wasn't a punishment. We were very proud of how she had taken care of herself all day and gone to the bathroom like a big girl. We said that we weren't trying to make a baby out of her, but until she could wake herself up at night and go to the bathroom, she needed to wear a diaper.

After about twenty minutes of explanation, Judith seemed satisfied. She asked if Joshie's mother had said the same thing to him. I said yes. "Well, then, it's okay," she said.

Over these next few years, there will be periods of going backward as well as periods of progress. While it's upsetting to find your child staining underpants, regression is commonplace. A change (a vacation, a new teacher, or even a cold) can trigger a loss of control. Look for the underlying cause and be very supportive. Sometimes there is no clear cause. If you suspect a serious problem, consult your pediatrician. As one parent stated:

■ ■ ■ *It's two steps forward and three steps back for a very long time. That's the normal pattern for children when they learn something new.*

Assumption: Your Child Is "Out to Get You" When He or She Has Problems with Toilet Training

Being supportive about accidents is one of the most difficult aspects of toilet training for parents. Because parents feel powerless (the child is ultimately master of his or her own elimination), the process can feel like a battle of wills. Warner Schmidt describes this feeling:

• • • *We started out doing great. We got some new books and Elliott loved them. We were very accepting, very calm at first, but then we got impatient, especially when Elliott had an accident on the floor. It was a mess, so we yelled and spanked him.*

   One time my mother was babysitting and he had an accident. He said, "Will Mommy hit me?" He was frightened and my mother told us so. That was the end of our spanking and we're back to trying to be supportive.

   Now Elliott is afraid and nervous when he has a bowel movement and I'm on a guilt trip about it. But the real trouble is that when he has accidents it does make us angry.

Warner Schmidt's feelings are shared by most parents sometime or another during the toilet training process. As discussed on pages 35–47 in the discipline chapter, parental anger is often the result of feeling out of control ourselves and not knowing what to do. In addition, toilet training our children can arouse strong feelings from our own childhood.

As Warner discovered, what looked like defiance in his son was really fear and nervousness. Another parent, Kim Schubert, also found that her son's seeming rebellion had a different origin:

• • • *Jeffrey's almost two and a half and he's been trained since the beginning of the summer. But the last two days he's deliberately been making any place. Today he did it in the kitchen closet. I said, "What did you do?" and he laughed. Sometimes I think he does this just to get me upset.*

Kim was a member of a parent group I was conducting and her story spurred others to tell of similar experiences. One parent's account of her son peeing from an apartment porch (feeling like he was on top of the world) jarred Kim's memory:

• • • *A few nights ago, Jeffrey had overalls on and couldn't get them off. I laid the baby down to help Jeffrey, but he couldn't hold it back. He peed all over the baby. I laughed. So now I realize that he got a laugh last time, so why aren't I laughing now?*

Whether children are testing you, expressing their anger, or simply having an accident, they don't start out "to get us." Only the adult can turn it into a battlefield.

Furthermore, I've never spoken to a parent who felt, in retrospect, that coming down hard on a child during toilet training was ultimately effective. So if you are feeling angry, find a way to cool off, such as walking away until you are calm enough to respond. Calm doesn't mean wishy-washy. You can have expectations for your child while still being supportive. As Kim said to Jeffrey, "We use the toilet for going to the bathroom."

Making mistakes is a part of growing as a parent. If we regret how we've handled an accident, we'll have another chance. Elaine Dumont describes how she and her daughter made up:

● ● ● *One day, Lilly peed on the couch. I just blew my top. Afterward, she asked, "Do you love me?" I said, "Of course. I'm sorry I got so angry, but it's hard to get stains out of the couch and that upset me."*

In *Childhood and Society,* Erik Erikson postulates that the muscular maturation associated with toilet training allows the child to learn how to hold on and let go psychologically:

> *To hold can become a destructive and cruel retaining or restraining, and it can become a pattern of care: to have and to hold. To let go, too, can turn into an inimical letting loose of destructive forces, or it can become a relaxed "to let pass" and "to let be."*

Inherent in this process is the individual's development of a sense of autonomy versus shame or doubt. Guiding the child toward a sense of autonomy means giving him or her some control within the safe confines of knowing that the parent is in charge. Erikson's message to parents is profound. Toilet training is an opportunity to teach our children self-control and to inculcate a positive attitude about their own abilities that can last a lifetime. In Erikson's words:

> *From a sense of self-control without loss of self-esteem comes a lasting sense of good will and pride.*

Sleeping

Q *How do I get my child to bed?*

The issues around bedtime and sleeping are complex for parents for many reasons. First and foremost, when our children are asleep, the sometimes overwhelming responsibility we feel as parents is momentarily diminished. It's as close as we come to the nostalgically remembered days without children: once again we have a little time for ourselves, our spouses or friends. Yet we can feel ambivalent about this time off: it seems unnatural to admit that we want to get rid of our children, yet we need this time to rest and to be renewed. Thus bedtime can take parents back to the dilemma they first encountered when their children were born—the push/pull feelings of wanting to be with their children, yet wanting to escape.

Conversely, we may miss our children when they go to sleep so that we are eager to see them if they cry for us. In parent groups I've led, this has been especially true for parents who are employed or who have recently separated or been divorced.

Another reason for difficult bedtimes is that at night our energy is often waning. We are tired, our children are tired, and so we may want to avoid conflict and go along with whatever is easiest.

We also identify with our children. They look small, fragile, and all alone in their beds. We want to protect them, to shield them from danger and stress, and so we hook into their nighttime fears and concerns. Furthermore, we have our own memories of bedtime, our own experiences with separation that are rekindled when we deal with our children on this issue. It's important to try to identify our own responses so that we do not impose these unthinkingly on our children.

For children, bedtime represents a separation—from their parents and from the activity of the day. It is moving away from the sounds of family members, the telephone and television, from bright lights into darkness, stillness, and isolation.

Finally, some children are lighter, more restless sleepers than others. After years of research on this subject, Richard Ferber writes in *Solve Your Child's Sleep Problems:* "It is true that children differ in their ability to sleep. Some children are excellent sleepers from birth—other children seem inherently more susceptible to having their sleep pattern disrupted."

Out of these complex factors, patterns around sleeping emerge. Some problems can be traced back to the child's infancy. This was the case for Penny Weber:

• • • *When Daphne was born we lived in a very small apartment.*
Daphne was not the greatest sleeper to begin with. When she
woke up in the middle of the night, so as not to disturb my
husband, I'd put her in the carriage and take her into the living
room. I'd lie down on the couch and fall asleep, and nine times
out of ten, I would end up spending the whole night on the
couch and she would spend the whole night in the carriage.
This went on for about five months until we moved into a
larger apartment and she had her own room.

For others, problems begin after a child's illness or during a summer
vacation when bedtime is more casual or when it stays light until late.

Many families use strategies that are counterproductive. For Penny
Weber, using the carriage was ineffective:

• • • *Daphne liked the carriage; it was cozy and small, a nice secure*
place for her to be. I think she got so used to sleeping in the
carriage that she never developed any attachment to her crib.
As she got older, she was too big for the carriage. I would have
to rock her to sleep in the carriage (which was terrible), pick
her up and put her in the crib. And if for any reason she'd open
her eyes for a split second and realize she was not in her
carriage, the whole scene would start all over again. I was a
zombie. I said to myself, "If I have another child, that child is
not even going to see the carriage." I gave it to somebody who
had a baby and said, "I don't want it back."

Penny assumes that her job is to put her child to sleep, not to bed. The
problems have arisen because Daphne has learned to associate going to
sleep with being rocked in the carriage. When she wakes up and the carriage
and rocking are no longer present, Daphne is distressed.

Another common solution is lying down with the child. Still other parents let their children fall asleep while the family is watching TV or in the
parent's bed and then carry the children back to their own beds later on.

Problems can arise when using all of these approaches. First, the parents
make the assumption that getting their children to bed and to sleep are one
and the same, while in fact they are not. It's the *parent's* responsibility to
put the child to bed; it's the *child's* responsibility to fall asleep.

Second, the child associates certain conditions with going to sleep that
are out of the child's control. These conditions depend on the parents, and
when the conditions are no longer present—the TV is off, the child is not
being rocked or the bottle falls out of the child's mouth—the child has no
means of going back to sleep. In addition, the child may become wary that

these comforts will disappear and fight sleep so as to guard against this occurrence. Richard Ferber explains this process by using the analogy of an adult who always goes to sleep with a pillow. He says,

> *Think . . . what it would be like if you had a normal waking during the night . . . and found your pillow gone . . . You would wake more completely and begin to look for your pillow . . . But what if your pillow was really gone? . . . What if someone were stealing your pillow every night? . . . Each time you started to fall asleep you might catch yourself and become alert in an effort to prevent this loss.*

Effective bedtime methods must meet two criteria.

- They work for the child. They enable the child to go to bed calmly and safely and to fall asleep on his or her own.
- They work for the parent. They don't make you feel trapped or resentful.

Children function best with a familiar ritual at bedtime. You, too, probably have regular ways of going to bed that may become apparent when they are changed. The purpose of these rituals is to end today peacefully and to anticipate tomorrow. Here are some suggestions from parents:

- I give a warning that it's time to get ready for bed in ten minutes. This seems to give Jack time to finish up what he's doing and to switch into a bedtime mood.
- My daughter knows that when the big hand gets to the top of the clock, it's time for us to go to the bathroom to wash her face and brush her teeth.
- We have a song we sing at bedtime: "This is the way we walk upstairs, walk upstairs, walk upstairs. This is the way we walk upstairs so early in the evening." The next verse might be about taking off shoes or brushing hair or whatever he does next.
- We play a game with Kristin's special dinosaur sheets. On one side of the pillowcase is an awake dinosaur. At bedtime we always turn it over to the side where the dinosaur has closed its eyes. We both say "Night-night, dinosaur," then I say "Night-night, Kristin," and I tiptoe out of the room.
- I made a chart with Polaroid pictures of all the things that Beth does before she goes to bed. She loves the chart, and it helps her manage in a more independent way.
- We call bedtime "special time." My husband and I take turns being with Drew for special time—one night it's me, the next night it's him.
- Rachel takes Ernie and Bert, Kermit and Miss Piggy to bed. She comes

into the living room, gets Ernie and runs in and throws him on the bed and then she does the same thing with all the others. After that we tell a story.

- We find the time before bed a nice time to chat about the day. I have a song I sing, "What did you do today, do today, do today? What did you do today, dear little girl of mine?" She doesn't like to answer general questions, so then I ask a specific one: "Did you have a peanut butter sandwich for lunch at school?" This reminds her of her day and she'll tell me about whom she played with, what her teacher said, or even what upset her. It's also a time to talk about any special plans for tomorrow: "You're going on a trip to the zoo, so you'll have to remember to wear warm clothes."

- We made a rule that we have three stories and two songs. Sometimes Eric stalls by asking me to pick out the stories and then rejecting all my selections. So we made a different rule that either he selects or he can pick any three from the six I've chosen.

- My child used to keep popping out of bed; so I said she should stay in bed. I'll come back every five minutes to check on her.

- I read the newspaper outside my child's room. She calls out if she wants me and I answer back.

Pediatricians say that, on average, children between two and three years of age need about twelve or thirteen hours of sleep (including naps) and that four- and five-year-olds need somewhere around ten to twelve hours. Clearly there are individual differences—and you have to be the judge. Does your child seem well rested when he or she gets up in the morning? How irritable is your child during the day? Does her behavior change if she has had more or less sleep?

How Children Get Themselves to Sleep

The criteria for a strategy that works are that the child can use it independently and that you feel comfortable with this procedure. Children use many ways to fall asleep. They cuddle their stuffed animals, they rub their blankets, they listen to music, they sing to themselves, or they look at picture books until they fall asleep.

What about bottles or pacifiers? One problem with a bottle is that the child can't refill it when the bottle is empty. Furthermore, over the years there has been controversy about children going to sleep with milk or juice on their teeth—some doctors object while others don't. A pacifier can fall out of bed, and the child is dependent on you to retrieve it. If, however, your child uses a bottle or a pacifier successfully and you don't resent your role in this process, then you have a strategy that works for you—until the child outgrows these aids and you have to help your child develop other ways of falling asleep.

What about lying down with a child? The pitfall is that you must be present when your child falls asleep and sometimes that is impossible—you are going out or you have too much to do or you don't want to risk falling asleep yourself. Again, the criterion is your level of comfort with this strategy. If it really works for you, then that's what's important. However, like a bottle or pacifier, in the future you will have to help your child learn different methods.

What about putting your child in your own bed? This method has strong defendants and opponents. The well-known pediatrician Berry Brazelton once told me about an article he wrote against the family bed. He said he got more mail on this topic than for anything else he had ever written— predominately in favor of the family bed. So he conducted an informal poll of his friends and found that about half took their children into bed with them.

People opposed to this tactic feel it violates the parents' privacy and may stimulate Oedipal or Electra fantasies (the child replacing the same-sex parent in the parents' bed). Those who favor this method argue that the family bed is a respected element of many cultures and enjoy the closeness it brings. So your own values are critical here. At some point, however, you will want to teach the child to stay in his or her own bed.

You can ask your three-, four-, or five-year-old child for suggestions that will help in falling asleep. For example:

- My daughter did not want to sleep in her room alone, so she asked for gerbils.
- Suzanna has her stuffed animals in her bed. We turn the light off, but she wants to leave the fishtank light on. She can see everything in the room and there are no weird shadows.
- After two stories and a glass of water, Ben always asks for a little cotton ball to hold. He also asks me to sit in his room for a little time while he gets settled down, about a minute or two.
- My son did not want to sleep alone, so he asked me to move his baby brother into his room.
- Seth wants a flashlight beside his bed.
- Robert made a sword out of cardboard and aluminum foil. He keeps it beside him in case there are monsters.

In *The Interpersonal World of the Infant,* Daniel Stern describes the fascinating example of a two-year-old child who talked to herself after her father said goodnight. She often re-created his tone of voice as well as the bedtime dialogue they had had "in order to reactivate his presence and carry it with her toward the abyss of sleep."

In addition, here are some recommendations from professionals:

- Berry Brazelton suggests a kind of self-hypnosis. If a child has a sleep problem, the parent speaks to the child and says in effect: "When you are falling asleep at night, don't think upsetting thoughts like how mad you are at someone. Think about something that you don't care about and think about it over and over. That will help you fall asleep."
- If a child is afraid of monsters, Stanley Turecki suggests helping the child think up a character who will be a protector during the night.
- I tell children who worry about scary thoughts to think about putting those thoughts on a TV and then switching channels. My daughter came up with the idea of putting her scary thoughts into a balloon in her mind and then popping the balloon.

Q *If our method of putting our child to bed makes us feel trapped, how do we get out of it?*

This parent's question was once mine. I had fallen into a pattern of reading in my daughter's room until she feel asleep, but if it took a long time for her to fall asleep, I felt simultaneously angry and guilty. The method I used has worked successfully with numerous other parents. It involves several steps.

1. *Decide that you are really committed to making a change.* If you pull back from your decision, it will be all the harder to begin again because your child will assume you can be swayed and will redouble his or her efforts to return to the familiar pattern.

2. *Explain to your child what you are doing.* Sometime before bedtime on the day you are making the change, briefly explain your reasoning to your preschooler: "I'm not going to lie down with you tonight because I end up falling asleep and I have trouble falling asleep later on," or "I'm not going to read in your room tonight because I have work I need to do."

   You can ask your child to plan this time with you: "What will help you manage?" You can also give specific suggestions: "When Jon's mother stopped lying down with him, he decided to take his stuffed clown to bed. Would taking your bunny to bed help you?"

   At bedtime, explain what you will do: "I will come by your room and check on you, but we're not going to talk."

I then checked in on my child every ten minutes. Richard Ferber suggests lengthening the time between each subsequent visit—five, ten, fifteen, twenty, then twenty-five minutes.

3. *Keep a chart of your child's progress.* If your child fusses or cries, it's hard not to give up on the first night. Some parents find it useful to write down what is happening.

A parent of a two-year-old describes how this method works:

■ ■ ■ *Alice kept getting out of bed for "one more story . . . or glass of water." We were up until eleven with her. I told my husband this bed thing has gotten totally out of hand. It's not her fault—we encouraged her, we set it up, we taught her exactly what she's doing, so we have to undo it. Undoing a habit is so hard sometimes that parents don't bother.*

On the first night, I told Alice it was bedtime, got her washed, and read one story. She asked for several, but I said no! I told her I was going to rub her back for five minutes and then I was going to leave the room and I'd come back and check on her in a few minutes.

Well, she followed me out of the room eight times. Every time I put her back in the bed and went through the same exact procedure and left. Again, I told her I'd be back in a few minutes to check on her. It took an hour and a half of the same thing, but the next night it took twenty minutes. We wrote all this down, which helped us see that the second night was better than the first, and so on. At the time her fussing seemed eternal, but in looking back we saw that it really tapered off after a week.

Q *What do I do about a child who wakes up at night or gets up very early in the morning?*

Joan Levinson, mother of Barry, age four:

■ ■ ■ *In the middle of the night, my son gets out of bed, walks down the hall, and stands outside our door crying, "I need you, Mommy." I get up and sit with him because I feel he does need me. I don't want to visit an emotional trauma on this kid.*

Roxanne Smith, mother of Amy, age four:

■ ■ ■ *Amy has awakened almost every night for the past several weeks and come into our bedroom. Every morning I've found her in the bed next to me. I've been so tired I haven't even heard her. I've got to put a stop to this.*

It is normal for children to awaken at night. There are distinct patterns of sleep throughout the night—beginning with drowsiness, proceeding to REM (named for the rapid eye movements that occur during a dream state) and then light and deep non-REM sleep. Much of the night is spent alternating between light and REM sleep interspersed with brief awakenings. In the morning, there is more deep sleep and dreaming.

Children who do not get up during the night have learned to get themselves back to sleep during these brief awakenings. Children who get up may depend on someone or something else to fall back to sleep. Or by nature they are irregular sleepers or more easily disturbed by external stimulation, such as the crying of a sibling or their parents' conversation. Another cause of night awakening is bad dreams.

If your child does awaken, first try to assess the cause. If your child sounds very agitated or upset, a bad dream may be the cause, and your child will need you for comfort. One mother said, "Jennifer (three) on rare occasions has night terrors, where she cries and screams hysterically, doesn't even recognize us, and fights us off when we hold her. Eventually she comes out of it and goes back to calm sleep." If your child is only fussing mildly, you may want to stand by for a moment or two to see if he or she will fall back to sleep. If not, you can use the same method you used at bedtime: explain the procedure, help your child find some way to comfort himself or herself, and come back to check on the child in increasingly longer periods.

These strategies do not "visit an emotional trauma" on your child. In fact, if you overreact to protect your child, you may be communicating that the child was right: his or her room is unsafe.

If your child is truly afraid or has had a scary dream, you can stay until he or she calms down or feels better. If you feel your child needs you but you don't want to establish a new pattern, you can say, "Just for tonight, you can bring a sleeping bag in my room." It's helpful to comment on your child's progress in dealing with this issue: "Two nights ago you got up five times and last night it was only three times," or "You used to need the sleeping bag right beside our bed, but now you feel comfortable sleeping in the hall outside our room."

For the child who wakes up very early, here are some suggestions from parents:

▪ My husband and I take turns getting up early so each of us can sleep a bit later every other morning.

- I am resigned to getting up early because my son wakes up so hungry. I fix him breakfast, then I lie down on the couch while he plays.
- My daughter is allowed to turn on the TV if she wakes up early. We've picked out the station she can watch.
- I keep a pile of old magazines by Susanna's bed. She likes to look at them when she wakes up early.
- Lauren picks out some cassettes the night before so when she wakes up, she can listen to music.

Q *Naps are my problem. I have a three-year-old who bounces off the walls at nap time. Should I try to get him to sleep or not?*

Mary, Jeremy's mother, brought this problem to a parent support group.

▪ ▪ ▪ *When I send Jeremy to his room to nap, he makes so much noise that he wakes up his sister. So I'm in a double bind. If I push him to go to sleep, he resists so much that I end up a wreck, he ends up a wreck, and the baby ends up a wreck.*

Most of the other parents had faced similar problems and were sympathetic. As Nan Arnold said, "You can make kids go to their rooms, but you can't make them sleep."

The following are principles that make nap time less of a contest of wills.

Changing the Name
Young children respond more positively to the concept that everyone, old and young alike, needs a break in the middle of the day. If you call this period "rest time," "quiet time," or "alone time," the child understands that it is acceptable to play quietly or sleep, but the intent is to take a rest.

Developing Rituals
Children need to wind down for quiet time just as they do at bedtime. Listening to a story or a record helps calm them down. Thus, many families develop routines for rest time.

Designating Acceptable Rest Time Activities
If the children are to sleep, they need to develop ways to fall asleep as they do at night. If they are to rest, then they need quiet activities that will occupy them so that they don't "bounce off the walls." As one of the mothers at the support group said:

. . . *I need this time as much as my child. Sometimes my daughter sleeps and sometimes she doesn't. Sometimes I take a nap, sometimes I read, and sometimes I work, but we all feel better at the end of the day if we've each had some "alone time."*

Q *Can shopping with a child be made enjoyable?*

A mother of two, Karen Cook provides some insight into what happens when parents and children go shopping. When her children were young, Karen was a full-time student and would stop at the grocery store after picking Nicky up from his child care-center.

. . . *At four and a half, Nicky was an active curious child and going to the supermarket with him was always an adventure. When I put him in the cart, I'd have to watch him; he was so quick that he'd reach for items on the shelves and put them into my basket. Once I ended up with fourteen boxes of Tetley tea. Another time he grabbed a box of pretzels and ate them all. He was always interested in paper products. He would take rolls of paper towels from someone else's cart and put them into ours. Another time he just chucked all of the rolls out of our cart onto the floor.*

One day I just wanted to pick up a few things for supper. Nicky was walking alongside my shopping cart. For about the hundredth time he asked for Twinkies and for about the hundredth time I said no. Next thing I knew, he threw himself on the floor and started screaming, "You're killing me. You're killing me."

I was absolutely stupefied. I couldn't believe it. Somewhere, something inside me clicked. I said, "Who told you to say that?" He stopped, looked at me and said, "Oh I saw it on TV. How do you like it?"

Parents can enumerate many problems with shopping expeditions:

Child's Needs versus Parents' Needs

. . . *In retrospect, I think some of Nicky's behavior in the supermarket was an attempt to involve me. We would finally be together after a whole day of being apart. The strain of having to share my attention, even in the grocery store, was hard for him.*

This makes a lot of sense. At the end of a day, when parents and children are tired, it may be difficult for children to tolerate one more intervention or demand. Karen also thinks that Nicky's pleas for attention stemmed from more than just the fatigue and separation of a long day:

• • • *Although I love to cook, grocery shopping is pure drudgery for me. To make the task bearable, I used to think about my courses at school. Now I'll think about my job. Sometimes I see a woman wearing an interesting sweater and imagine how I'd knit that pattern.*

When Karen self-protectively withdrew in the face of an odious task, Nicky would try even harder to reach out to her.

Although many parents do not loathe grocery shopping as Karen does, they may feel tremendous pressure to be organized and to keep tabs on prices. As one parent says, "I see shopping as a huge responsibility for the family's well-being. For my children it's just another time to play and have fun."

"The Gimmes"

Surrounded by tempting items, Nicky often got into a power struggle with his mother. He wanted something, she would say no, and he would insist. Even when she offered him an alternative (fruit instead of cookies), he continued to press for the thing he could not have.

• • • *I shopped mostly in a local store that didn't have magazines or toys; but he still wanted everything. Even now, we'll pass by the olive oil and he'll say, "Don't you need this? Let's get some."*

One study reports that on an average, two-and-a-half-year-olds demand items once a minute in the supermarket. When I cited this at a parents' meeting, everyone laughed and said, "That's too low—it's more like once a second."

Sometimes parents buy treats for their children to make up for real or imagined injustices they have inflicted on them. A mother who feels guilty about something, like a fight she has just had with her child, may assuage her anxiety by succumbing to her child's "gimmes." This way she feels she is taking care of him.

Being on Display

One mother says:

> ■ ■ ■ *When Randy falls apart in a store and starts crying or yelling,*
> *I'm so embarrassed. People must be saying "Oh, look at that*
> *terrible mother."*

Being judged by the general public when your child is at his or her worst can be embarrassing and lead to anger toward your child and condemnation of yourself as a parent. In these circumstances, try to remember that your child is ordinarily delightful and you will never see most of these people again.

Other Frustrations and Pleasures in Shopping

Crowds, lines, and noise can make everyone irritable. Routines that adults take for granted can confuse children. As Karen says, "When Nicky was young, he thought I just threw things into the cart—he would imitate me and toss things in, too."

But a shopping expedition can also be an opportunity for fun. A mother of a three-year-old enjoys pointing out the vegetables and fruits to her daughter and discussing various ways of preparing them: "It's a real learning experience." At the end of a hectic day at work, another mother looks forward to talking with her toddler who is seated in the grocery cart:

> ■ ■ ■ *When we're outside, I'm usually pushing her in the stroller and*
> *we can't really talk. But I love the face-to-face interaction we*
> *can have in the supermarket!*

SOLUTIONS

Involving the Child

Karen gave Nicky his own shopping list:

> ■ ■ ■ *At four, he could identify the labels on many products. I*
> *showed him how to pick out the word "sugar." I would tell him*
> *he could choose a cereal, but that sugar could not be the first or*
> *second ingredient.*

For very young children, you can draw pictures for the shopping list: a bag of apples, a carton of milk. Many parents let the child add an item or two to the list.

Other parents pose problems:

- Can you find a vegetable that is orange and begins with a C?

- I want you to find a drink whose name rhymes with "silk" and bring it to the shopping cart.

Controlling the Gimmes

Here are suggestions from parents:

- Decide in advance on something the child can get and stick to it. "You can have a Popsicle but no cookies." "Will it be cheese or crackers today?" "You can buy one thing if it costs less than two dollars."
- Steer down the middle of aisles and bypass tempting displays.
- Pack a snack for your child. One parent always brings a small bag of raisins for her five-year-old when they go shopping.
- Establish a ritual. One mother explains: "He really wanted something special, and that meant something I bought in the store. At first he wanted bubble gum. I said, no, we need to decide on something else! We agreed that he could get a bag of banana chips. He eats them as we shop and then he gives the nearly empty bag to the checkout clerk to ring it up. He likes that little ritual."
- Let your children pick out a treat. A mother of two preschoolers shops at a supermarket with a bakery: "I let each of them pick one cookie and then we shop. They're entertained because the cookies are decorated. I can shop easier and faster and they don't ask for this or that."
- Give children some control. Some parents give children a sum of money to spend in the store.
- Teach them to be good consumers. A parent says: "I talk to my children about how I figure out what to buy—for example, how I judge how well made a product is or how fresh the meat is. I want my children to be able to shop well."

Making Realistic Promises

When children ask to buy something, many parents say, "Not today." Then the children think, "Okay, then tomorrow I'll get it." You can get stuck if you say, "Yes, another day," and not really mean it because your child may remember what you said. It is better to be honest and to give a reason: "I'll never buy that cereal because it has too much sugar," "I'll buy you another book when you've read the one we just got."

Teaching About Money

Although young children do not understand the value of money, they can begin to learn that people must think about what they buy and that some things are more important than others: "First, we'll pay for the milk and eggs; if there's money left over, we can buy ice cream."

A father sets limits for his two children:

> . . . When I took them to a special toy store, I said, "You can go to where they have the little things and each of you can pick out two things." They understand that they're getting something, but we stay away from the expensive, big stuff.

Parents' attitudes and values about money also influence how they react to their children's requests. One mother on a limited budget approaches the issue this way.

> . . . Willie, my five-year-old, will say, "This looks like a good comic book; this is the new GI Joe." His grandmother will say, "My God, you paid a dollar twenty-five for this comic book—they used to cost only ten cents!" But I can't think of why I should say no to my son. If I don't have the money with me I would have to say no, but since I do, why not? He's interested in trying to read, it's something he likes. That's important to me.

Most parents do some mental accounting, weighing expenses against pleasure or the potential for learning. A parent of four:

> . . . I've had to make a lot of hard decisions about how to spend money on my children. I realized long ago that I'd rather go to a thrift shop to buy used clothes than spend a fortune on brand-new things. With the money I save, I take them places like the circus or the movies. I want to use what little we have to buy them experiences they can enjoy and remember.

One parent describes her philosophy as "giving in some of the time, not because my daughter is having a fit in the store but because she is behaving so well."

Ways to Handle a Tantrum in a Store

Take a break. A father whose three-year-old had a temper tantrum on the floor of a department store says:

> . . . She was tired and cranky and one more stop in the housewares section just pushed her over the edge. I talked to her quietly and rubbed her back. When she calmed down, I picked her up

and said, "Let's get an ice cream cone." I thought we both deserved a treat and a change of pace.

One family shops at a suburban mall on Saturdays. Every hour, they take the children outside to run, walk backward, jump. They make a point of walking up and down the stairs or escalators, thereby avoiding the crowded elevators.

Leave the store. A mother of a four-year-old says:

• • • *When she's whining, I put her in the cart and hold her still so I can talk to her. I explain why what she's doing is not a good thing to do right now in the grocery store. If she continues to crab, we go sit in the car. As much as anything else, she's tied to the attention of people looking at her, so if she's in the car and nobody sees her, that's the worst thing that can happen.*

Keep a sense of humor.

• • • *My son had a temper tantrum in the store. I started to pretend we were in a TV sitcom and it made this tantrum a lot easier to take.*

Stores can be tempting, exciting, boring, and all of us inevitably spend time in them. There is no one answer for all children all the time in all stores, but here are a few final guidelines:

• Involve your child by giving him or her something to look for or carry.
• Before you begin to shop, set limits and articulate your expectations for appropriate behavior.
• Be flexible and seize opportunities to have fun, to teach, to play games: "What would we need to buy if we had a pet elephant to feed?"

PARENTS SPEAK: BUY ME TV TOYS

Ruth Cohen is the mother of a five-year-old son, Donald:

• • • *Donny craved some of the junky toys they advertised on TV. I tried to explain about how cheaply these toys were made, they were a waste of money and would fall apart, but this conversation only intensified his desire.*
    I was in a quandary. I was saying no, saying it with convic-

tion, but I was only making these forbidden objects more appealing. He became preoccupied with them.

So I finally decided that I needed a plan that would preserve my values but take some of the mystique out of these TV toys. I told him that I did not want to spend my money for the toys because I did not like them but he could spend his money. He had some birthday money saved up. I also told him I'd pay him for certain chores—not the chores he is expected to do every day but special chores. We went to the five-and-dime and priced the toy he wanted. It cost $9.95. He had about seven dollars, so he needed to save three dollars more. It took him about eight weeks to earn that three dollars and then he couldn't wait to buy it.

Two days later, it broke. I did not say one word—it would have been mean to make a comment, but I sympathized with him and we fixed it as best we could.

Then they started advertising another toy on TV and he began saving for that one. This time it took a couple of months. He bought it and took very good care of it. He actually used it with more imagination than I thought possible, used it for all kinds of dramatic and creative episodes.

Having him save up and buy his own TV toys was a good solution for us. I could express my opinions but at the same time allow him his. In addition, he has learned something about the value of money. Of course, there were times when I simply said no to such things as interactive war toys because it stretched my values too far. The TV toys Donald bought were within the realm I could accept.

Safety

Q How can I teach my child to be safe away from home?

As a mother of a five-year-old says:

. . . Safety is the bottom line. If a child's not safe, nothing else matters.

Today, perhaps more than ever before, parents are worrying about how to keep children out of dangerous situations and how to help them handle danger if it occurs.

Here are some important principles:

- Teach children strategies so they learn the beginning steps of taking care of themselves. Adults are completely responsible for children's well-being, but children can begin to learn some skills such as crossing the street.
- Teach children to trust their instincts. Even young children can sense when things are "wrong"—for example, when they want to say no. If they can listen to their inner voice and speak up, they are beginning to learn skills that you will continue to teach them as they grow.
- Teach safety without fear. Scare tactics do not help children learn to be responsible. If you say, "Don't take candy from strangers because it might be poisoned," your children might think that the stranger—the clerk in the market—is poisoning food there. If you warn, "Don't wander away in the store because I won't be able to find you and you might get locked inside," you're conjuring up a very negative image of the world in which scary things are inevitable. Instead, communicate rules straightforwardly: "We don't take food from people we don't know, but we do buy food from people who sell it in markets," or "Stay close to me in the store so I'll know where you are."

Teaching about Strangers

A mother of a three-year-old describes her concerns:

• • • *My child is very outgoing. She'll walk up to any stranger and start a conversation. I don't want to instill fear in her by saying that a person could be dangerous, and I don't want her to cling to me all the time, but I do have to teach her how to be cautious with strangers.*

A father of preschool twins says:

• • • *When I warned my twins not to get into strangers' cars, they became frightened that strangers would stop their cars, pick them up, and drag them off the street.*

We must teach our children to be careful, but in a way that does not scare them or make then feel paranoid. After all, most people want to be friendly and kind to young children. We also must find ways of communicating at the child's level so our messages will be understood.

A number of strategies will protect your children from strangers. The first step is to explain who a stranger is. You can say: "A stranger is someone you do not know. Even if the person says 'hello' to you or says he or she knows your mom or dad, that person is still a stranger. Only if someone you know introduces you (like your mom, dad or teacher) does that person stop being a stranger." Children often have stereotypes of strangers; they're mean-looking or they dress funny. Explain that "Strangers often look and act very nice, so you can't tell a stranger by the way he or she looks."

Preschoolers are almost never out of sight of known adults, but if by chance this should happen, Sherryll Kraizer in *The Safe Child Book*, gives four rules that tell children exactly what to do in such situations:

1. Stay an arm's reach plus away from people you don't know. Convey this rule by practicing it: "Show me how far away you would stand if you were out of my reach."

2. Don't talk to someone you don't know. We want our children to be polite and respectful, but this doesn't mean they should respond to a stranger if they're alone. Being safe is more important than being polite. If they are with you, that's different, although most safety prevention experts recommend that under no circumstances should children be forced to be affectionate with relatives or friends of their parents.

   Sometimes strangers will use a child's name and this makes the child think the person is okay. Make it clear that knowing someone is more than just knowing his or her name. If an adult asks for help or directions, it's not your child's responsibility to respond. Adults should ask other adults for assistance.

3. Don't take things from strangers. Children tend to think this means treats like candy, toys, or animals. But it also applies to their toy left at the playground. Children are in conflict because they don't want to get in trouble for leaving their things behind. Tell them this rule is more important. They can come and tell you if a stranger has something that belongs to them.

4. Don't go anywhere with someone you don't know. Strangers can make up believable stories: "Your mother will be late and she told me to pick you up." Rehearse with your children what would happen in an emergency: "Mrs. Jones, our neighbor, would get you."

   Don't use code words with preschoolers. They're easily tricked into revealing them ("I bet you've forgotten your code word" whereupon the child replies, "No, I haven't, it's . . . ")

One of the best ways to help your preschoolers develop solutions to safety problems is to play the "what if" game. You or your children can pose the questions. Your questions should reflect possible situations your child might face: "What if our house was locked and we didn't have the keys?" "What if our dog ran away and we couldn't find him?" "What if a lady came to school and said I should go home with her?" The "what if" game can reveal what your children are thinking and feeling. Respect their ideas before you comment about their validity. You can say, "What do you think would happen if you tried that idea?" Most children are enthusiastic and eager to reply. If they hold back, you can answer first and then ask, "What do you think of my idea? Is it a good one?"

You and your child can also role-play—you can pretend to be the lady who comes to school and your child can be herself. When you play this game, do *not* frighten your children. Fear can block learning. As the author of *The Safe Child Book* says,

> The "what if" game helps children to anticipate and plan. It is this aspect of the game that makes it the single most valuable tool you have for teaching safety to your children.

Children have fantasies about how to protect themselves. The mother of a four-year-old recounts:

- - - *My son heard about a stabbing on TV. He worked out what he would do if a man came after him: he was going to put ice cream on the man's head so he couldn't see where he was going and couldn't stab him.*

It's important to respect a child's wish to protect himself or herself and not dismiss the plan as "silly." At the same time, you can reassure your child that such an event is most unlikely and that it is your job as parent to take good care of him or her. By playing the "what if" game, you can also help children think of ways to handle situations they consider scary, especially in relation to strangers.

Getting Lost in a Store

When children are lost, they may need to turn to strangers for help. How can you apply the rules about strangers in these situations?

Tommy's mother describes what she did:

- - - *Last year when Tommy was three and a half years old, he got lost in a large department store. Eventually a store clerk found him crying under a rack of clothes and took him to the lost and found. That's where I found him.*

I realized we hadn't made any plans about what he should do in this situation, so when it happened, Tommy was really in a panic. For a long time afterward he was so scared, he didn't want to talk about it.

I began to approach it indirectly, reading a few children's books (e.g., My Mother Is Lost). I made up a story: "Yesterday I was talking to a mother whose little girl got lost in a store. The girl was scared and didn't know what to do. What do you think she could do?" At first he didn't respond and I had to make suggestions. Then he came up with the idea that she should know her phone number and address so she could tell someone. I thought that was very smart because it was something he had just learned himself.

Tommy and his mother also thought of these suggestions:

- Look for a person who works behind a counter or who wears a uniform. These are safe people. Young children can make the distinction between people who are shoppers (e.g., people wearing a coat, carrying a purse) and those who work for a store.
- Call out the parents' first names. If a child just calls out mommy or daddy, anyone might respond.

Safety in the Car
Children who are not buckled into a seat belt will be thrown forward if the car stops suddenly—the impact is equivalent to a one-story drop for each ten miles per hour the car is traveling. Most children do not understand why they must be in a car seat, but they do understand that under no condition will you drive if they are not seated safely. If you compromise on this rule, your children may test you or resist. For safety's sake, enforce this rule strictly. In addition, be a good model and point out that you're buckled up, too.

Teaching the Meaning of Dangerous
Young children don't fully understand what danger means. Sometimes they deliberately take risks even after repeated warnings. A mother of a two-and-a-half-year-old had told her daughter that only an adult could plug in her record player; otherwise, the outlet had to be covered.

■ ■ ■   *One day I walked into the room and she was trying to pull the cover off the socket. I screamed, "What are you doing?" She said, "I'm pulling this out of the wall because I want to get a shock. I want to get a boo-boo."*

Although this parent had previously told her daughter that shocks hurt, the words didn't make much sense to her. At two and a half, she hadn't understood what a shock was and her curiosity propelled her to find out. The mother responded by removing her daughter from the room and not allowing her to listen to the records. Wisely she gave her child a clear consequence for her behavior.

Another parent has tried to explain to her toddler how dangerous busy streets are:

> • • • *But at times he just runs toward the street. I immediately tell him, "We can't stay out if this is what you're going to do." We go right inside.*

By using a logical consequence, this mother conveys the seriousness of her son's behavior.

Another mother describes how she resorts to the final no:

> • • • *My son was playing in the yard with a group of children. He was tired and excited and kept racing around. He ran into the street. I stopped him and said, "Gabe, you cannot do this. It is dangerous and you could get really hurt." He just laughed and ran in the direction of the sidewalk.*
>
> *A few minutes later he did the same thing. So I stopped him, held him tightly, and yelled, "No, you may not do that!" He broke into tears and I thought, "I'm glad I got through."*

Young children have different playground styles ranging from timid to intrepid. Some children seem to put themselves in greater danger, while others are instinctively more cautious and know where their bodies are in relation to the equipment. Rules must be made clear to every child and repeated often: "No running behind the swings," "Wait until the seesaw stops before you climb off."

In general, children like obeying safety rules. It's a way of identifying with grown-ups as well as showing that they know right from wrong. One six-year-old explained the rules to his younger brother, "These are rules to make you safe so you can play. They're not rules to be mean."

As parents we want to protect our children yet give them room to grow and learn. We look for the balance between keeping them close and letting them go. A parent of a kindergartener explains how she found this balance:

> • • • *He wanted to walk to the school bus stop all by himself, but he has a busy street to cross. So I gave him a choice: either he and I could walk together until the block before the stop and then*

he could go alone, or he could walk with our neighbor, a teenager, the whole way. He decided we could walk together.

Teaching your children about safety will lessen your anxiety about giving them appropriate freedom and allow them to grow with the freedom.

Child Sexual Abuse

Child sexual abuse is best treated as a safety issue. Just as your children need to know what to do if they get lost in a store, they need to know what to do in an abusive situation. Although we may worry that such information will frighten children, informing them in a developmentally appropriate way means teaching them positive safety skills. Furthermore, young children's fantasies about danger may be far more terrifying than a factual, straightforward discussion. For instance, a six-year-old whose parents had not discussed this topic heard about it from other kids and believed "sex maniacs take off your clothes, murder you, and cut you up into about a hundred pieces."

We need to teach children some basic skills: to value themselves, to communicate feelings, and to make decisions consonant with their developmental level. Children must have these skills to help them begin to take some responsibility for their own well-being in all kinds of situations, not just in sexual abuse.

"Talking about Child Sexual Abuse," a pamphlet for parents published by the National Committee for Prevention of Child Abuse, recommends that young children learn the following:

- *Their bodies belong to them and no one has the right to touch them without permission. Children have traditionally been taught to comply with adults' requests, but they need to know that with regard to touching, they have the right to say NO, even if the touch seems accidental or even if the person touching is a relative or trusted adult. Obviously, children need to know the names of parts of their bodies, whether the correct words or euphemisms are used among the family. One way to explain private parts is to say that they are the parts of the body covered by a swimming suit.*
- *There are different kinds of touching. Talk about touch that feels good (hugs, comforting), touch that feels bad (hitting, pinching), and touch that makes children feel "funny" or uncomfortable or scared or that gives them a feeling of "uh-oh."*
- *They can trust their feelings about kinds of touching and always ask a trusted adult if they're not sure. Most children, even young ones, can tell*

when another person's touch or request or behavior makes them feel scared or "funny" or uncomfortable. They need to be encouraged to trust those feelings so that they can recognize behavior that can lead to sexual abuse.

- *They can tell their parents or a trusted adult about anyone whose behavior makes them uncomfortable or who touches their private parts or who asks them to touch someone else's private parts and they will be listened to. Children must be free to ask about adult behavior that confuses them, even when the behavior is not related to sexual abuse. For example, the child who is told not to ask about Aunt Sue's whiskers also learns not to ask why Uncle Steve wants her to sit on his lap when he's alone with her.*
- *Being asked to keep an unpleasant secret may mean danger of sexual abuse. If there is one central clue to the possible or actual sexual abuse of your child, it is the child's withdrawal into secrecy. No adult or older child has the right to ask or tell your child to keep an unpleasant secret. Explain to your child the difference between a good secret and a bad secret. A good secret is something pleasant and fun and exciting when shared later with others—for example, a surprise birthday party, or when Daddy secretly brought the puppy home. But a bad secret feels like a burden, it doesn't make a person feel good, and it is intended never to be shared with others. Your child can say, "No! My family doesn't allow bad secrets."*

Although we believe in teaching preschoolers how to begin to take care of themselves, children are not ultimately responsible for their own safety. We—their parents—are. We are responsible for taking good care of them when we are together, and for making certain that the other adults to whom we entrust our children are decent, caring people.

FOUR

Happy and Sad Times

Q *How can we celebrate holidays and birthdays so they are happy for everyone, including me?*

From time immemorial, people have held celebrations—religious, seasonal, family—to renew their sense of living and sharing with loved ones, the community, and the wider world. Celebrations provide meaningful ritual and affirm our values. Above all, they grant a sense of security and identity that we carry with us through the years. Looking back, most adults cherish memories of special events—lighting the Hanukah candles or seeing the cousins at Thanksgiving. We want to make such events part of our children's legacies, but many parents ask, "How do I keep the fun in and the hassle out?"

Great Expectations

We want a special occasion to be "perfect"—the best food, decorations, gifts. We expect everyone to get along. We expect the children to be well behaved and to appreciate their presents. As one parent said, "I have visions of a Norman Rockwell Thanksgiving—the whole family joining hands to say grace over the turkey."

Reality doesn't always live up to these expectations. The turkey can be overcooked, it rains during a July Fourth picnic, and people get on each other's nerves. Children unwrap their presents so quickly they hardly notice what is inside or they refuse food that has taken weeks to prepare. When expectations are great for a special occasion, disappointments can be commensurately great.

Keeping the Meaning in Holidays

One mother wistfully confessed her fantasy of living on a mountaintop between Thanksgiving and New Year's—far from newspapers, radio, and TV—to avoid the barrage of commercialism. Most of us share her outrage and wonder how we can sustain spiritual and aesthetic values in our holidays.

One father has resigned himself to the inevitable:

> ▪ ▪ ▪ *Living in this society, my daughter is going to be exposed to as much commercialism as anyone, and she will have to deal with it. My role is to expose her to a "People Christmas": a real Christmas, with quiet, peace, warmth, and home.*

How much harder it is for parents to convey other values when they themselves feel caught up in the materialism. Competition among adults over giving the best Christmas gift or the best party can ruin the good times. A divorced mother, for example, finds herself competing with her ex-spouse over whether Santa Claus, the Easter Bunny, even the Tooth Fairy is better at her house or his.

When Parents Disagree About How to Spend Holidays

One of the most difficult aspects of holidays is when parents disagree about how to celebrate. A father, Bruce Guarino, says:

> ▪ ▪ ▪ *I like making the holidays a peaceful homey time, but my wife likes being on the go all the time—parties, seeing the store windows, going to the Christmas movies with the kids. The sight of the crowds makes me feel ill.*

In multicultural families, differences are built in. How are the December holidays to be celebrated when the mother is Jewish and the father is Catholic? What about Easter when the mother is Greek and the father English?

When Families Get Together

Going home for the holidays with one's children can be a very special time, bringing memories and an opportunity to share traditions with one's children. For some adults, however, being with their own parents is a return to childhood. They complain of being treated as if they were young children again, or they find themselves reverting to childlike ways. Some also feel their childrearing is under scrutiny or attack. Delores Jones describes the first Thanksgiving she spent in her own home:

> ▪ ▪ ▪ *I was really looking forward to inviting my relatives. My father said things to my three-year-old like, "We chew before we talk." In principle I go along with that, but at age three my son*

is better off expressing himself than getting hung up on table manners.

In hindsight, Delores realized how much she had wanted her mother's and father's "seal of approval." When it was not forthcoming, she was resentful. And her parents probably unconsciously had hoped she would fulfill their fantasy of perfect wife, mother, and daughter. When their expectations were disappointed, they became critical.

One frequent concern is "turf": whether to stay at home, visit the grandparents—and if so, which set of grandparents—or go to a neutral setting such as a restaurant. Feelings run high around this issue. Grandparents may feel forced to give up their old traditions. Their own children—now parents themselves—may want to establish different traditions.

It can be hard to find a balance, retaining what one likes about the past but changing it to suit one's own needs and preferences. Still, many families have found ways to integrate different traditions in their celebrations.

When Families Do Not Get Together

In our mobile society, young families may live far away from their relatives. The cost of traveling and limited time off from work can make visits infrequent. A mother from Missouri wishes her own children could be with her extended family for the holidays:

■ ■ ■ *My family and relatives still live on the West Coast and my favorite memories are when all of us would gather at my grandparents' ranch. It was something to really look forward to. We do manage to take our children out West every few years.*

Carrying on traditions is one way for families to share the holidays when separated by miles. One family, who now lives abroad, has a St. Patrick's Day party every year, an event that began when the parents were children. Not only does this celebration link them with the past, it also give them an opportunity to share their heritage with friends from other countries. Another parent remembers making fresh peach ice cream every July Fourth; now she does that with her own children.

How Children Experience Big Events

Children love ceremonies and special occasions. They are entranced by rituals—decorating Easter eggs, singing Christmas carols, watching a parade on Memorial Day or July Fourth. And they protest if changes are proposed: "We always have Thanksgiving here—we can't go to Aunt Ann's."

Holidays can bring on tensions between us and our children. When we are hurried, frantic to get things done, our children are moving slowly. When we need peace and calm, our children's excitement is boundless. Susan Gleason, a mother with three children, describes what happened with her four-year-old:

> **. . .** *I was doing some Christmas cards and Alison made some, too. I suggested she sign hers and we could send them to all of our relatives. She was thrilled with the idea and eagerly picked up her marker and went to work. But she was so slow, making little designs around her name and all. I could just feel myself starting to push: "Just write your name . . . we have twenty of these to do."*

Eventually Susan was able to pull back and say to herself, "If she just sends three cards, that's great." Susan realized that for Alison the *doing* mattered, not the final product. Although children's involvement in the activity for its own sake may be frustrating and time-consuming, it also serves to remind us that the spirit of the holiday is what counts.

Preschoolers focus on what is concrete and readily experienced, not on an event's deeper significance. Aunt Mary's hand-knit sweater, representing effort and love on her part, may be dismissed in favor of an electronic toy from a distant relative. But parents need not worry that their child is callous and unappreciative. Understanding what lies behind the exchanging of gifts takes time to develop and is enhanced when parents explain how hard Aunt Mary worked on her present. This message, however, may be lost if a parent tells the child, "You're ungrateful," or "You're spoiled."

On the other hand, children may take pleasure in what, to adults, are insignificant aspects of a special occasion. A mother planned a special weekend for just her and her six-year-old daughter. They went to a mountain resort that offered a zoo, park, and train rides for children. On the way home, when asked what she liked best about the weekend, the girl replied, "The zoo and all was nice, but I liked sleeping in a double bed best." Sometimes children help us keep a balanced perspective.

Anticipation drives many parents and their children crazy. Days in advance, children wake up wanting to know, "Is today Christmas (my birthday, the picnic at Grandma's)?" We must remember that young children's understanding of time is different than ours. To a child, "only ten days away" can seem like an eternity.

Novelty contributes to the attraction of holidays, but can also cause anxiety and fear in children. Noise and crowds at a party or in a busy department store can make children feel overwhelmed and scared. Costumes and masks can terrify children whose grasp of reality is shaky. How

many parents of young children have eagerly anticipated their child's intro-
duction to Santa Claus only to be disappointed when the child refuses to sit
on his lap or talk to him? As one mother said, "What I thought was going
to be a great photo opportunity was just a disaster."

Birthdays—the Day of Days

To children, birthdays are probably the most important occasion of all.
This is the day when the child is celebrated as the most special person and
when family and friends demonstrate their love. Reaching a new number
means being more grown-up: "I'm a big girl. I'm five today." A birthday
generates great excitement but also moments of disappointment. Children
may become overstimulated and end up cross and teary. Party games can
lead to chaos, a birthday present can get broken.

Since most parents have limited budgets, space and time, they must make
decisions about how to celebrate their children's birthdays.

Lisa Sayer, mother of three, says:

> ▪ ▪ ▪ *I always have mixed reactions to my children's birthdays. It's
> a great day for them, but not always for me. My five-year-
> old is at the age where one day she wants to invite the entire
> kindergarten class; the next day she wants to invite just the
> girls, and then the next day, only her best friends. I think she
> wants to invite a lot of kids because she'll get more presents. I
> want her to be happy, and yet I know I have to put my foot
> down to keep the party manageable.*

Lisa raises another concern, having to do with how parents' needs can
interfere with keeping the focus on the child:

> ▪ ▪ ▪ *Birthday parties can be real competitive in our neighborhood.
> Parents sort of out-do one another, trying to offer the best
> entertainment, the best party favors. There's also a lot of talk
> about which children to invite, depending upon whether their
> parents are in or out of favor. Sometimes the birthday child
> gets lost in all this maneuvering among the adults.*

As Lisa Sayer says, keeping one's perspective is difficult but important
to do.

Not Being the Center of Attention

At a three-year-old's birthday party, her five-year-old sister was bossy and
mean. She insisted on sitting on a chair when all the other children were on
the floor. She grabbed one of the presents—a pretty headband—put it on

and announced that she was the queen. Some of the other children wanted to open the presents themselves, and some just wanted to hold on to the gift they were supposed to be giving. Even though the birthday child is meant to be the center of attention, other children want some of that acclaim.

Competitive party games can also lead to hurt feelings. Watching from the sidelines is hard for the "losers." A mother described a scene at a family party:

> ▪ ▪ ▪ *My four-year-old nephew was losing a game of musical chairs. He had to sit out, and he began to cry. His father got mad at him, which made him cry even more. The rest of us felt really uncomfortable.*

In this case the child's reaction, which is typical for his age, clashed with his father's expectation that this activity was "fun." This father also thought that "boys shouldn't cry"; when his son's vulnerability threatened his image of what kind of son he was raising, that fed his anger.

SOLUTIONS

Clarifying Your Expectations

Much of the tension and hassle of holidays derives from unfulfilled expectations. Share your expectations with your children: "At Thanksgiving dinner at Grandma's, let's be sure to . . ." "It's important to me that you . . . " Likewise, encourage your children to talk about their visions. For example, who will be invited to their birthday party, what food will be served, what games will be played? Knowing what they expect will help you plan. If some of their wishes cannot be fulfilled or must be modified, tell the children beforehand.

Because special occasions involve so much novelty for young children, prepare them for what lies ahead. The mother whose children balked when visiting Santa Claus had given them little idea of what to expect. She had decided not to say much for fear of spoiling their spontaneous reactions. She hoped to capture their first look of wonder and delight when they saw Santa up close; instead, she encountered tears.

Many parents say that one of the best ways to deal with gift-giving is to help young children make a list. Even three-year-olds can dictate their list to you. Let them put down whatever they want, then read and talk about the list together. In this way both you and the child can begin to figure out what you want most, so your expectations are more likely to mesh than conflict. In one family, Christmas lists are posted on the refrigerator door so each person can revise his or her own list and others can see the changes.

A family with three young children has come up with a clear principle for birthday parties: Each child can invite one more guest than her age. The children accept this as part of the birthday ritual.

Keeping the Tasks Manageable

There is always too much to do and never enough time or money. This becomes even more true during holidays and celebrations. A few simple guidelines are helpful:

- Decide what is essential and eliminate what is not. Consider which aspects of special occasions are most meaningful to you (sending cards, visiting special friends, preparing certain foods). Be sure to set aside time for those things.
- Be flexible, especially with children. If they show great interest in one activity and not another, switch your plans. Remember the legacy you want to give your children.
- Keep your sense of humor. When your children decorate Easter eggs like Halloween pumpkins, enjoy it instead of trying to correct them.

Long-Range Planning

Some parents function best by planning ahead. One family managed the Christmas holidays by allocating one week for each activity. One week was designated "cooking week"; most of the food was then frozen. Other weeks were for shopping, decorating, housecleaning. The last week was reserved for special requests, such as last-minute shopping or seeing store windows in the city. This scheme helped organize all activities and put things in perspective. Shopping was only one activity among many, and the parents managed to enjoy that one week.

Resolving Family Differences

If you and your spouse (or your parents, relatives, or in-laws) disagree about how to celebrate holidays, a first step is to consider what is most important to you. Alissa Nelson says:

. . . *My husband associates Christmas with family quarrels. I told him that it mattered a lot to me that Christmas be a pleasant time. He agreed to support me on the condition that I didn't drag him into things. He didn't want me to assume that he would come to the Christmas caroling party, for instance—he might decide to come, he might not—but he would help make Christmas Day a peaceful time.*

A Jewish mother and Catholic father decided to incorporate the essence of each of their religious beliefs into their children's observance. They gave presents for Hanukah and told the Hanukah story, but they also put up a Christmas tree and went to Mass on Christmas Day. They invited friends and relatives to a special meal for each holiday. In effect, these couples were agreeing when to agree on the issues most important to each.

Being Aware of Your Own Style

Families who plan ahead and do all of their holiday shopping during the summer can be infuriating to the parent who, one week before Christmas, has not even started. It is important to identify your own style. Do you need an orderly plan or do you like the excitement of coming right under the wire? The participants at the seminars I conduct feel most successful if they determine what works best for them and then follow it.

One family living in New York City found pre-Christmas an intolerable shopping hassle. Now they exchange stocking stuffers on Christmas Day, but set aside a day after Christmas to shop together for one big present for each of them. This also allows them to take advantage of store sales. Another couple discovered that they disliked selecting presents for one another; now they shop for gifts together.

Keeping the Tasks Enjoyable

Find activities that give children a sense of accomplishment. They take pleasure doing simple things—making a Halloween mask or drawing on a pumpkin with magic markers. Assembling a fancy costume taxes their energy and patience.

Enjoying Other Activities

Take time to enjoy seasonal and outdoor activities such as ice skating at Hanukah or Christmas. This helps keep the spirit of the holidays alive and provides a balance to the hustle and bustle of preparations.

Scheduling Breaks for Yourself

Many parents function better if they pace themselves during the preparation and culmination of a big event. Set aside "unplanned time" in the midst of all the scheduled activities. One family makes a point of spending the day before Christmas at home: "We all sleep late, eat a big breakfast, read or play quietly. It's a wonderful family time. Then we're ready for the round of afternoon and evening parties." Another couple arranges child care for a weekend in December. They spend the night in a hotel and take in a concert and Christmas sights in the city—activities their children are too young to enjoy.

Scheduling the Children

Give children time to wind down. The stimulation and anticipation of special occasions can overwhelm them, leaving them hyped-up and over-tired. Help your children find quiet, restful activities that restore their sense of equanimity. Listen to records and read stories about the holiday.

Children may get tired and cranky when their routines are disrupted. Some changes are inevitable, but it helps to maintain the important ones, such as morning and bedtime rituals.

One parent makes a calendar for her four-year-old that depicts the daily events leading up to a holiday:

• • • *In the morning, she's playing at nursery school; in the afternoon she's shopping or baking. I draw a picture of myself with her, or if I'm going to do something away from her, I draw a picture of that too. This way she can tell what's going to happen. I draw very simple stick figures.*

Bringing out the Meaning of Holidays

Holidays are special because they link us with people in other parts of the world. Young children enjoy hearing the Thanksgiving story, and that can lead to other stories about feasting, harvesting, and hunting. Many Afro-Americans celebrate Kwanza, a time to honor their heritage and traditions. Expose your children to the festivities of different ethnic groups in your area in age-appropriate ways.

To emphasize that Christmas is a time of giving, one family made presents and took them to a shelter for the homeless on Christmas Eve; the next day they helped prepare a meal there. Many school groups and civic organizations collect toys for poor children or sing Christmas carols in hospitals and nursing homes. Similarly, Easter represents renewal and hope. In that spirit, after their neighborhood Easter egg hunt, a group of parents and children donated their decorated eggs to a local shelter. It is important that children experience the good feelings that come from helping others and giving them pleasure.

Making Your Own Traditions

Many parents establish their own rituals:

- A New England family celebrates the first snowfall and the first day the crocuses bloom.
- Many adoptive parents celebrate the day that their child came to live with them as well as the child's birthday.
- In one family, the children make something special for their parents every holiday: Valentine collages, a letter for Santa Claus, a Christmas tree ornament, or a welcome home sign for a family member who was away. These homemade gifts are carefully saved and brought out again and again for holidays and birthdays.

Vacations

Q *How do you handle vacations with preschoolers?*

Whether you are going back to the seashore cottage where you spent your own childhood or driving across country for the first time, vacations are special. You can relax and have fun with your family at a different pace. Vacations are also an opportunity for adventures together that you will remember for a long time.

How can you, as parents, make the most of your family vacation? These guidelines can help get your vacation off to a good start.

Involving Children

The more your children actively participate in the planning and the doing, the better it will be for everyone. If there is a real choice about where to go, perhaps you can solicit their ideas about what they most like to do. Whether you decide to spend a vacation fixing up your home or traveling, let each family member select something special to do (where to eat dinner, which park to go to).

Creating a Balance between Following Routines and Leaving Room for Adventure

Children feel secure when patterns are predictable and familiar. But if you're far from home, it may be difficult to eat and sleep at the usual time. Do not stretch your children's tolerance for change beyond their limits. If you plan to eat later than usual, give them a late afternoon snack. Even though the pace may be slower during vacations, young children may be very excited about all that is happening and need more rest, so daytime naps or rest times may be a good idea for everyone. Bring along familiar comforts: a blanket, stuffed animal, pillow.

Anticipating Problems

One parent who drives long distances every summer to visit relatives attributes the fun and ease of their travel to her basic philosophy:

> ... *When we're in the car, my agenda has to be the children's agenda. You have to foresee what the difficulties may be and try to prevent them in order to help the children manage as best they can.*

Wherever you may be—at home or on vacation—try to foresee your children's needs and help them find ways of dealing with them so that they will be developing self-discipline and problem-solving skills.

Setting Limits

Communicate the rules before you start: "Use your seat belt," "Don't throw anything out the window." Even though it's a holiday, children will need limits in order to feel comfortable and safe: "In five minutes you have to get out of the ocean and rest—we can build a sand castle." Of course, it is fun to play games with your children when you're on a trip, but you may need a break too: "We'll play 'I Spy' until we come to the next exit on the highway."

If you are visiting others, it's important to let your children know what to expect. A mother says:

. . . *I told Sarah, my four-year-old, that every house has its own rules. In my cousin's house you can't put your feet on the table or on the furniture. I told her this before we went because I knew it was very important to our hostess.*

Making the Time Pass When You're En Route

Here are some ideas from parents:

- I make sure my daughter always has a pair of sneakers in the car for trips. She loves to take them on and off and lace them up, over and over again.
- Before we left, each child made address labels so they could mail post-cards back to their friends.
- I think that children need to know what's going on, where they're going, how long they're going to be in the car, and what the next stop will be. So we made a calendar, writing down or drawing a picture of what we were going to be doing every day. We would update it as we went along.
- We use a rimmed cookie sheet for a desktop in the car; it's flat and easy to draw on, plus it keeps the pencils and markers from rolling all over. I put bathroom decals on the bottom so it doesn't slide off laps. I avoid crayons—once they melted into a gooey mess on the back seat.
- My five-year-old will start a story line and then I will add another. We go back and forth to the very end. Or if someone else is driving, we'll take turns adding on to a drawing.
- My four-year-old has a Fisher-Price tape recorder that she can work herself. She has a little suitcase that has all the tapes in it, and she can choose what she wants. We also sing songs.
- I'm a neat person and I don't like my kid's stuff all over the car. A Pampers box or a plastic milk crate is good storage.

- "I Spy" is my family's favorite. An adult starts off with something like, "I spy a thing that is red and has four white letters on it. What do I spy?" Then everyone searches for something of that description. Whoever guesses "a stop sign" first gets to play the "I Spy" role next.
- From *What to Do after You Turn Off the TV* by Frances M. Lappé: "When you're traveling with children who do not know the alphabet or numbers, you can make up a bingo game using pictures of things they are likely to see . . . a stop sign, a green car, a white house. They can check off whatever they see. You can make up a color dot bingo too. The driver can call out colors 'green car, yellow house, red sign' and the players can mark their cards. Keep going until everyone wins."
- If my children are restless in the car and someone else is driving, I take them on a lion hunt. I begin, "We're going on a lion hunt [keep time clapping your hands on your knees] and . . . we're bringing a lunch." Then make motions of preparing the lunch, buttering the bread, etc. As you go on the lion hunt, you can "swim the river, crawl through the grass, climb the tree," and do the appropriate motions. Your children can add things, too. Finally, you see the lion ("oops, it's time to go home") and then, as the lion chases you, repeat all the actions in reverse order until, "Whew, we made it back safe."
- We look for license plates that begin with a 1, then a 2, etc., or we search for an A, then a B, etc.
- I make up a mystery box with some old toys and some new ones, each one individually wrapped. Every day, they chose one. We do this after lunch on a long car trip, because that's when they're getting tired and bored.
- On a sparsely populated country road, we try to guess the color of the next car or the next house.
- On a bumpy plane ride, my children and I were quite scared. A fellow traveler really helped us out. He told us, "Pretend you're in a big boat. The air is like waves in the ocean. It will hold you up and you won't fall down." Hearing these words and visualizing this put us all at ease and made the rest of the trip pass more quickly.

Using Travel as a Teaching Opportunity

Traveling can open up new vistas. Parents who are experienced travelers say they seize the opportunity to help their children learn. A mother who drove cross-country with her two children explains:

- - - *I care that my children have a good time, enjoy being a part of the family, and have an adventure. But I also want them to learn about what we're seeing, like the different kinds of hay and how it's baled across the country. So I try to get them excited about the new and different things.*

Aaron, our eleven-year-old, was in charge of lists. We made lists of everything—the bridges we crossed, the kinds of ice cream we ate, the different states we were in. This got the whole family involved. Each place we stopped, we bought several postcards and put them in a scrapbook. We used roll-on glue so that Marcea, who's four and a half, could do it herself. She's just beginning to read and write, so she could also write a little in the book. That was good practice for her, and it made her feel happy that she'd created a book.

As another parent said, "Traveling is an opportunity for creative interaction with my children."

Varying the Pace

Young children are active and have shorter attention spans for some activities, like visiting museums or souvenir shopping. It is a good idea to take breaks when children can go outside or at least be active. Children also need breaks from a fast-paced schedule so they can slow down. One family who likes to camp has this philosophy:

. . . *When we go on a hike, we never go for more than two hours without a "reward." It could be a swim in a lake at the end of the trail or a refreshment stop where there's a beautiful view across the valley. These rewards refresh all of us.*

Appreciating Your Children's Perspectives

Traveling with children can open you up to new sights, sounds, and smells that you might otherwise overlook. Who but a two-year-old would notice the colored rocks on a path? Isn't it typical for a four-year-old to ask, "Why does the owl stay up at night?" and thus inspire you to find the answer? Your children will also help you meet people, both young and old, who can enrich your experience.

Handling Some of the Practical Matters

- Pack comfortable, easy-care clothes. Bring clothes to mix and match so that you don't get so tired of your wardrobe.
- Let each child pack a special carry-on or backpack that contains his or her favorite things. A rule of thumb for airplane travel: If they can't carry it, they can't take it.
- Eat healthy food. Keep your children well supplied with cheese, crackers,

fruit, yogurt, and other nutritious snacks. Young children may not be adventuresome eaters when it comes to new or foreign cuisine but encourage them to try a new taste—a bite of yours.

- Keep a small medical kit handy, including Band-Aids, thermometer, antiseptic cleaner, and any special medicines. Depending upon where you're traveling, you may want to bring along a roll of toilet paper or Kleenex and Handiwipes for the bathroom stops.
- Pack a fix-it kit with essentials like safety pins, needle and thread, glue, and tape to repair toys.
- It's too stressful for young children to have to wait to go to the bathroom. Stop as soon as possible, even if it's not the most socially acceptable place.

Commemorating the Vacation

There are many ways to preserve your memories. Children often want to collect special things: seashells, pinecones, paper napkins with restaurants' names, postcards. Scrapbooks are a handy way to save mementos. One family in Chicago sends a Christmas letter to friends that includes drawings and descriptions of their summer holiday written by the two older children.

Moving

Q *We're going to move. How can we do it in the best possible way?*

According to national statistics, about one out of five American families moves every year; that means about 34.5 million children under the age of twelve are affected.

The Circumstances of the Move

The reasons for moving can be both positive and negative—job promotions or unemployment, an increase or drop in income, marriages or divorces, births or deaths. Whatever the specific reasons for the move, they color your outlook.

For some families, moving means fulfilling a lifelong dream—enjoying a big backyard or restoring an old house. For others, moving signals the end of some dreams. This was the case for Derek Graham, father of an infant and preschooler, who was suddenly transferred from Boston to Atlanta. One of the hardest aspects for him was coming to terms with his expectations:

. . . *I was really invested in my newspaper job in Boston. I wanted to stay there the rest of my life. My wife and I loved our house and our neighborhood. The baby was just born, and we were feeling very settled.*

At first I tried to hold on to my life there. I looked for another job, but couldn't find one. Then, I tried to refuse the transfer. But that would have meant a dead end in my career.

Eventually I had to start my new job in Atlanta. I ended up commuting back and forth for several months. It was a terrible time; it wore me out. I kept asking myself, "Why are they doing this to me?"

Derek's feelings of frustration, disappointment, and anger all point to a loss of control. Feeling that he had no say in what was happening to him, he was under great stress.

On the other hand, a father of a three-year-old was enthusiastic about an upcoming move because it gave him more control:

. . . *We had been renting for a long time and were tired of having to conform to the edicts of our landlords—like no pets. We wanted to own our own house. When we finally found this house, I felt like a new person.*

Sometimes one member of the couple wants to move while the other does not. In the Williams family, Bruce had always wanted to live in the country while Brenda loved the city. They moved to the suburbs and now Brenda becomes very angry whenever she gets stuck in traffic commuting back to her old job. Likewise, Anita Graham resented the move to Atlanta and blamed her husband. Derek says:

. . . *We rented a floor in a house. It was quite nice but it didn't have a washing machine. Listening to my wife, it sounded like the washing machine was indispensable to life. There was a laundromat a block away. I've always been the laundry person, so I figured it was more my problem than hers. But she made me feel very bad, as though I had done the wrong thing.*

The relocation policies of employers can hinder or help the transition, too. In Derek's case, they were virtually nonexistent:

. . . *The personnel interviewer at the newspaper asked me how old my children were, and when I told him, he said, "Oh, that's easy. When they're young, you can move them around like pieces of luggage."*

Adults' Attitudes toward Change

Despite what this personnel officer thinks, it takes families a while to get settled, to learn where the nearest grocery store is, which pharmacy is open late, which school is right for the children, and how to make new friends. According to the Employee Relocation Council, the average transition time for adults is sixteen months.

Moving is a significant change. It involves saying goodbye to people and places. We tell ourselves, and mean it, that we will come back to visit, that our friends can visit us in the new place, that the past will not be forgotten. These thoughts are reassuring, but we still may have anxieties. In part, they are residues from childhood, when separations threatened our very existence and when a change—a new sibling, starting school, even a haircut—could temporarily shake our world. When we move as adults, these fears may resurface.

Coupled with these feelings is uncertainty about newness. Will my neighbors and colleagues accept me? Will I like them? How do I feel about the change in climate? Will I end up spending the rest of my life here?

Whether or not we moved as children can make a difference in how we react to the situation as adults. For some people, frequent moves during childhood were so disruptive that now the overriding wish is to put down roots in one place. Others have learned to enjoy change. A parent who moved only once as a child is glad that her husband's job involves numerous moves:

... *I don't regret our life-style for a minute. I really do not want my children to be as isolated as I was growing up in one community.*

Children's Perspectives on Moving

Children may also feel the stress of moving. They do not have the words for abstract concepts like homesickness or loneliness, but they may have many of the same anxieties that you do. It is certainly *not* true that children can be moved around like "pieces of luggage." Yet we may be so caught up in our own feelings about moving that we don't notice the effects on our children. In a survey of kindergarten-primary teachers, the majority thought that coping with a move was more difficult for young children than adjusting to the birth of a sibling.

When faced with a move, young children tend to take their cues from adults. If you are generally enthusiastic, they are more likely to see the positive. But if you are angry, resentful, or negative about the move, that may affect their reaction. In addition, some children seem more comfortable with change, others less so. A very typical pattern is for young children to regress under stress. Children who are toilet-trained have accidents, children who were adventuresome become clingy. These are normal behaviors, children's ways of saying they are adjusting to the change. Given time and understanding, most children will adjust to the move and resume their more mature behaviors.

Even if you and your children look forward to the move, they may still have some worries and concerns. Children like stability and routine, and when they move, they lose the concrete landmarks that help them orient themselves, such as the big tree in the yard or the grocery store down the street. It takes great energy to learn about a new environment and find one's place in it.

Your children may have many questions: "Will I have the same room? Will my dog come? How will I know which house is ours? Will Mrs. Jones still be my teacher there?" Underlying these questions are some of the fears of childhood.

- *Who will take care of me?* When Virginia's parents went house-hunting in another state, they left her with her grandmother. Despite their reassurances that they would return soon, three-year-old Virginia was upset and angry, not fully understanding when and if her parents would really come back for her. If the move entails a major change in the family's lifestyle, such as a mother going to work or a father living apart, fears of abandonment may be even more intense.
- *Where will I stay?* When a three-year-old visited her new house prior to moving in, she was worried. She thought this house would remain the way she saw it that day—no bed for her to sleep in and none of her toys to play with.
- *Will I still be me and will you still be you?* The child's concerns echo the adult's who fears a loss of identity without familiar surroundings. One two-and-a-half-year-old who had moved from Connecticut to Massachusetts three months earlier told her mother, "I want to go back to my other home where my real mommy lives."
- *Will I have friends?* Preschoolers who move miss their friends. The children who stay behind also feel a loss. One four-year-old continued to dream about her friend who had moved away several months before.

At the root of children's anxieties is their sense of losing control. As one four-year-old said, "Whose idea is it to move? Not mine." Adults decide to move for reasons sometimes beyond the understanding of young children. Being told that the new neighborhood or school is better than the old one may make little sense to a child who has only the beginnings of a basis for comparison or who may have really liked the old situation. One parent thought she was consoling her children by saying, "We're only going to rent the new house for two years, then we'll move back"—she had a two-year consulting contract. But to a child who is only four years old, two years may seem like a lifetime.

To another child, the explanation that her single-parent mother needed a roommate to share the rent did not justify the arrival of another woman and her child. Her mother explains:

■ ■ ■ *Laura was the child being "moved in on." She really resented having to share the general living space in the apartment, even though she kept her own bedroom. She started to have temper tantrums and became really stubborn.*

How do children cope? They often use play to work through their feelings. According to Derek Graham, his four-year-old daughter created a happy ending to her family's upcoming move:

■ ■ ■ *She had a Barbie doll in Boston and she said that the Ken doll lived in Atlanta. She said that when we moved there, Barbie and Ken would get married.*

Other children enact moving scenes: pretending to be packing up suitcases or driving a moving van.

Once the move is made, children may exhibit new anxieties. They are the newcomers—in the building, on the block, at school, in the park. Some may initially become clingy, others may rush in and push other children away. Underlying these behaviors may be a fear of being rejected and a desire to be accepted. Sometimes the new place seems scary. Children may not want to go upstairs or downstairs without you. A child whose bedroom was on the second floor of a new house repeatedly asked his mother, "Do burglars have ladders?" In many ways, children who move wonder, "Am I safe here and will you take care of me?"

SOLUTIONS

What Is the Best Time of Year to Move?

If you have a choice, conventional wisdom has it that summertime is ideal. The weather is better for outdoor play, there is more time to pack and unpack. But neighborhood children may be away vacationing with their families, and it may be harder to find activities for your children. However, if your children are there for the beginning of the school year, they do not stand out as "new kids." On the other hand, moving in the middle of the school year means that some friendship groups will already have formed, and it can be more difficult for newcomers to break in. But being the new child in the class can also be special. There are pros and cons for whatever time of year you move, and parents can make the best of it.

Anticipating the Move

Giving Your Children Time to Adjust. You may think it is better to wait until the very last minute to tell your children about the move so they won't worry. In fact, it is better to give them sufficient warning so they will have time to adjust. You should tell them as soon as there are family activities involving the move because they will sense that something is going on. If you do not tell them, their fantasies may be more frightening than the reality. For instance, they may think that you will be leaving them behind. Keep in mind that the move is an event in your family's life and that it needs to be dealt with by every member.

Explaining the Reasons for the Move. Young children often think that the world operates in magical, arbitrary ways. Even though they may not fully grasp your explanation, they will at least understand that moving was not a casual decision, designed to cause discomfort in their lives. No matter why you are moving, try to frame your reasons in concrete terms they can understand. A widow told her children, "We need a smaller house for just the three of us."

Expressing Your Own Feelings and Helping Your Children Express Theirs. Talking about moving helps to anticipate and relieve the stress. Patricia C. Nida, author of *Families on the Move*, says the key to successful moving is working together as a team to ensure that each family member has the clear support and understanding of the others. She recommends that families take many opportunities to talk together about how they feel about the move.

As a start, you and your preschoolers can talk about:

- What are you really looking forward to with this move?
- Whom will you miss? How can you stay in touch with them after we move?
- How will you make new friends?
- What things will be different because of the move?
- What do you like best about the old place?
- What things will you be glad to leave behind?

With older children, you might add other topics to your family discussion, such as:

- What do you know about your new place so far? What positive things have you heard about it? What negative things?
- What difference do you expect this change to make in your life?

During family discussions you as parents need to share your own feelings, and listen in a nonjudgmental, accepting way. Moving may trigger a lot of emotion. It is natural for you and your children to feel ambivalence. Spending time talking about the move—before, during, and after it occurs—will smooth the transition for all concerned.

Remember also that your children may be more resilient and adaptive than you expected. They may focus more on the concrete details of the move rather than the long-term implications. Furthermore, what children consider the pluses of a move may surprise you. According to Derek Graham, his daughter was thrilled with her new bedroom because it was carpeted, which meant that it was very fancy.

Just Before the Move

As the move draws closer, involve your children. One mother who has just moved her three young children halfway around the world summed up her philosophy:

> **. . .** *I did everything I could to change moving from a passive situation into an active one for my children. Even the youngest one, two and a half, was able to peel off the new address labels.*

Encourage your preschoolers to play "moving"—give them boxes and other materials. There are many good books about moving for preschoolers. Ask at your library or local bookstore.

If possible, take photos of the new house or apartment, inside and outside. This will help make it a reality. You can subscribe to the new local newspaper before you move so that your family will have a better sense of their new community. Whenever reasonable, elicit your children's ideas about the new place: Do they prefer to have separate bedrooms or to share a bedroom and then have a playroom?

Maintaining Links with the Past. Parents say this is one of the most important ways to help children deal with moving. Children worry that their friends will forget them or that they will not be able to remember what their old house looks like.

- Make a photo album of people and places. One family took two Polaroid pictures of each member with his or her best friends—one to take with them, the other to leave behind with the friends.
- In a first-grade classroom, children draw pictures of the child who is moving: "The Things That Sybil Likes to Do," or "The Things I Like About Johnny." They are put into a book and given to the child.
- The parents of two four-year-olds who were best friends helped their

children write a book about their shared times. A copy was made for
each child.
• Hand out pre-stamped and pre-addressed postcards to your children's
  friends. They can write or draw on the cards. This way your children can
  get mail soon after they move.

Encouraging Your Children to Say Goodbye.   By saying goodbye to
people who are special, your children will acknowledge the reality of the
move and their feelings of sadness. Some children may want to leave behind
something special they have made (a drawing, a card) or buy a small gift.

Preparing Children When Their Pet Can't Come Along.   If your pet
cannot move with you (for example, your new landlord does not allow
them) discuss with the children what would be best to do—is there someone
who can adopt this pet? Let them be present when the transfer is made and
see the pet's new home, if possible. They can leave a self-addressed postcard
so the new owner can write to let them know how the animal is doing.

Involving Children in the Sorting Out.   Children may be attached to
possessions that you consider junk, so avoid sorting out their things without
consultation. Set limits, but within these limits give your children some
choice: "We only have enough room for one box of books—you choose
which ones to take and which ones we'll give to the library." If something
must be left behind—a plastic wading pool, a jungle gym—tell your children in advance, and if they are special items, take photos of them.

Involving Children in Packing.   If possible, let them help pack their
things. At the very least, they can draw pictures on the packing boxes.

Moving Day

Tell your children in advance what is going to happen: "The moving van
will come. All the boxes and furniture will go inside. It will take three days
for the moving van to get to our new house."

Some parents want their children to be out of the way and arrange for
them to play with a friend. Others try to involve their children by giving
them tasks like checking the closets.

It is a good idea to pack the children's belongings last, so they will be
the first unloaded. At least make sure your children have some of their own
things ready for the first night in the new place.

After the Move

Those first days after the move, it seems like there are a thousand and one
things to do. But pause and celebrate the occasion. Children love ceremony,
and you can make this a special moment—adults can open a bottle of
champagne and children can have their favorite treat or everyone can go
out for dinner.

You can ease the transition in several ways and help your children adjust by:

Giving Children Some Control over Their Room.   Even young children can have some say over where their toys go. Many parents report that their children want to set up their new rooms exactly like their old ones. You can go along with this, recognizing that it is their way of making the new place familiar and comfortable. Eventually, they may try out a new arrangement.

When Laura's mother decided to take in roommates, she realized that her five-year-old daughter was feeling a loss of control over her space and her time with her mother. So they set aside special time just for the two of them alone in the apartment. They also designated special shelves in the kitchen and bathroom where Laura could keep her things.

Helping Children Make Friends.   A mother of two sons describes what she did in a new neighborhood:

. . . *I got them involved immediately in a preschool and a group at the Y, so that they would meet other children. Then we would take walks in the neighborhood and look for Big Wheels. Once, I have even got up enough nerve to knock on someone's door and say, "Hi, do you have a kid here?"*

Other suggestions from parents:

- Ask a neighborhood child to take your family for a walk. This way you will learn a lot about where other children live.
- Encourage your child to invite other children over.
- If you are involved in activities, you will begin to meet other parents. And of course, the more involved you are in the new community, the more at home you will feel.
- The appearance of a moving van often draws other children. They want to see if there will be a "new kid on the block." If possible, welcome them with a snack.

Preparing Children for the First Day of School or Child Care.   At any age, the first day of school or child care can be frightening. Try to talk with the teacher before the first day about your child's previous schooling and bring your child to show him or her what the school will be like. Alert the teacher to the fact that you are newcomers to the area and that your child may still be adjusting to the move.

Often the best facilitators are other children. A parent of a child who moved halfway through her kindergarten year says:

. . . I thought the new school would be traumatic. But Margot had met other children in the neighborhood the weekend we moved in. They helped her—they sat next to her on the bus, they walked her to her class and even hung up her coat.

Affirming Your Familyness. Everyone in the family is affected by a move. Keep communication open by making time to do things together and to talk together. Explore the new area and identify the "pluses" of moving, whether it is walking to the public library around the corner or making biscuits in the new kitchen.

As much as possible, maintain your familiar routines; they provide children with a sense of security.

Recognizing That Moving Is Stressful and That It Takes Time to Adjust. A mother of a five-year-old says:

. . . A few months after we moved, I went on a field trip with David's kindergarten class. I couldn't believe what I saw. He stayed by himself and never joined in. He was a totally different child. I had no idea this was happening. I had taken his silence to mean that he was adjusting well. But in fact he was under a lot of stress.

David's mother talked with the teacher, who agreed to help David mix with other children. At home, the family talked more about the move, the new school, and making new friends. They encouraged David to invite other children over to play.

There may be times when you or your children feel overwhelmed by nostalgia. You may wish you had never moved. These feelings are normal and usually diminish as you begin to make a life in the new place. A mother who has just moved from Vermont to Florida says:

. . . This will be the first Christmas we've spent without any extended family and that's upsetting. We're writing a family Christmas card to send to our relatives and friends back home. We're making Christmas tree ornaments out of sand dollars. This is something we could never have done living in the mountains, and so it's really special.

Q *How can I make trips to the doctor or dentist bearable?*

Most children resist going to the doctor or dentist. They may vehemently protest—"I'm not sick," or "I don't want a shot," or "I promise to get better tomorrow"—or they may withdraw, keeping their anxieties to themselves.

It is important to prepare your children for the visit. Explain in simple, direct language the reason for the visit: "Your cold is making it hard for you to eat and sleep and play. The doctor will find out what's wrong so we can help you."

A father of two preschoolers says:

> ▪ ▪ ▪ *I try to associate visits to the doctor or dentist with being healthy more than with being sick. I say, "Just like your nursery school teacher teaches you songs and how to play, the doctor and dentist teach you how to have a strong body and grow big and how to have good teeth."*

Explain what will happen. Young children focus on the concrete, visible aspects of events: "The doctor will listen to your heartbeat with a stethoscope. It will probably feel very cold when it first touches your chest." What upset a three-year-old most about a doctor's visit was having to take her clothes off; her mother hadn't thought to tell her that was expected.

Some things to help the visit go smoothly:

- Let your child bring a blanket or stuffed animal for comfort, if he or she wants to. Your doctor should never tease your child about this.
- Encourage your child to participate in the procedures, if possible. A mother says: "My daughter has to have a lot of blood work. She sits in my lap and puts one hand under her elbow to keep it straight. She feels like she's helping instead of being hurt." The principle here is to turn a passive situation into an active one. Children's cooperation is more easily elicited if they have some control over what is being done to them.
- If the waiting room does not have children's toys, bring along books, stickers, or other quiet activities.
- If you anticipate a long wait, bring an easy-to-eat snack: raisins, dry cereal.

Play helps children understand and gain control over what frightens or puzzles them.

- Encourage your child to play doctor, nurse, dentist, or other medical roles. If your child makes frequent trips to a doctor, it might be helpful to encourage his or her play before the next visit. In this way, you might gain insight into his or her anxieties or concerns.
- Provide props. Sometimes toy replicas are good; familiar objects will do too. Most three-year-olds are like Claire, who loves to give "shot-ties"

(with a plastic straw) to her teddy bear. You can get realistic props like eyedroppers and tongue depressors from the pharmacy.

- Dolls and puppets allow children to play out scary, unpleasant parts.
- Books about visits to the doctor also help children understand and prepare for check-ups.

In a study of how children of different ages think about illness, Bibace and Walsh found that preschoolers' explanations are prelogical and egocentric and reflect a belief in external, "magical" causes: You can get a cold from the sun or from trees or from outside "when someone else gets near you." When kindergarteners were asked about a stethoscope, they said it tells if you're alive or dead, happy or sad. They didn't believe that there could be medicine in a syringe because "only the needle goes in and it pushes your blood." Because they thought a procedure either made you better or killed you, any procedure that made them sick before it made them well was very frightening.

It is normal for preschoolers to be concerned with their body's intactness. Taking a blood sample may be perceived by a four-year-old as "making a hole for all my blood to fall out." Thus children will often insist on a Band-Aid, something concrete, to close off the hole. It's reassuring if you show them how old cuts have stopped bleeding and healed.

Because preschoolers have different views of bodily functions, health, and illness than older children and adults do, we should try to understand and empathize with their perspective:

- Elicit your children's ideas and listen to their responses. "Why do you think you're going to the doctor? What do you think the doctor and nurse will do?" Sometimes out of our own anxiety we impose explanations without giving them a chance to offer theirs. Explain at their level of understanding in simple, concrete terms.
- Reassure your children that they are not going to the doctor or dentist because they're bad. Sometimes children associate sickness with punishment.

If Your Child Is Going to be Hospitalized

- If possible, ask for a pre-admission tour. Many hospitals have tours specifically designed for children, including puppet shows and films.
- Inform your child's preschool program. Ask the teacher to read books, supply play materials, and talk with your child. If your child is going to be absent for a while, the other children will want to know what is going to happen to their friend. Tell them.
- Your child will be most interested in the concrete, visible aspects: the

uniforms that staff wear, the instruments to be used, what will happen to the parts of his body he can see. Detailed physiological explanations will mean little.

- Many aspects of the hospital will seem strange and frightening. Explain that there will be other sick children, they may be crying, your child will not "catch" their illness, etc.

Sometimes parents wonder if it wouldn't be better to take their child to the doctor or dentist or the hospital without advance preparation. Won't preliminary talk or play simply increase his or her anxiety? To the contrary: giving children information and providing them with opportunities to express their feelings helps them cope with stress. They may have misconceptions that your more realistic explanations will alleviate. Whatever you can do to ease their fears and anxieties is good parenting.

Finally,

- Choose a doctor or dentist who's sympathetic and "tuned in" to children.
- Be aware of your own reactions. If you are apprehensive about going to doctors or dentists, you can communicate this to your children. It is normal for you to be worried when your children are sick, but reassure them that you and other adults will figure out what's the matter and help them get better.

FIVE

Family Relationships

Parent/Parent/Child Relationships

Q *Our marriage has changed since we've had children. Before we got along wonderfully; now we fight, usually about the kids. Is it possible to stop this cycle before it gets out of hand?*

Amy Zucano lives in Southern California with her husband Stan and their two preschoolers, Robert and Roy. Amy feels her husband is too hard on the children:

• • • *If there are toys on the floor, Stan is bothered. Toys around aren't a mess to me, but they are to my husband. It's the different way we see things that's so hard; I say if you can't live with Legos on the floor or cookies in the TV room, you don't understand children because that's the way they are. My feeling is Stan has to do something about his problem because our sons are becoming negative and tense.*

Stan and I get along so well as grownups. We like the same music, the same movies, to do the same things. But we often have very different ideas about how to parent.

Having Children Changes the Marriage

In 1957, the sociologist E. E. LeMasters interviewed forty-eight couples and concluded that for 83 percent, the birth of the child precipitated a crisis: these couples had to reorganize their lives very rapidly to accommodate the baby. Since that time, numerous studies have investigated how marriages are affected by the transition to parenthood—is this a crisis or a normal turning point? While several of these studies consistently found a decrease in marital satisfaction after childbirth, the researchers concluded that the concept of a crisis was an overstatement.

In the most recent studies, the research methodology has been improved to capture a fuller picture. Rather than cross-sectional studies that would deal only with groups of new parents, the new studies are longitudinal, examining the marital relationships before and after the birth of the child. They also include comparison groups of nonparents. In one study, researchers Susan McHale and Ted Huston found that it wasn't just the parent group that showed a decline in love and satisfaction with their marriages; the nonparent group did as well, reflecting the changes that occur as marriages evolve from a romance to a working partnership. "Parents and nonparents alike reduced by about one-third the extent to which they say and do things that bring pleasure to one another."

Other studies reach a different conclusion: Some of the changes in a couple's relationship are specific to becoming parents.

This is a view I strongly support for the following reasons:

1. Having children brings an increase in the amount of family work. Women tend to take on more of these new responsibilities, creating a greater disparity between the amount of work that husbands and wives do. In addition, couples tend to move to more traditional sex-stereotyped roles —women care for the children and prepare meals while men handle household repairs. There is evidence, however, that men become more involved in the household when a second child is born.

2. The centrality of the marital relationship decreases when couples have children. In a fascinating exercise conducted by Carolyn and Philip Cowan and their colleagues from the University of California at Berkeley, prospective parents and nonparents were asked to list the main roles in their lives by dividing a "pie" (an eight-inch circle) drawn on a piece of paper so that it reflected the importance given to each aspect of the self. This exercise was repeated twenty-one months later. For the thirty nonparents in the sample, the space given to "lover" and "spouse" grew larger, whereas for the ninety-four new parents, it decreased. Furthermore, the importance of the parent role was greater for women than men. Being a parent occupied 20.3 percent of the men's pie and 39.1 percent of the women's. This change can cause jealousy. The time and attention formerly spent on the husbands is now directed to the children.

3. During the transition to parenthood, conflicts can be evoked. Research has revealed gender differences in dealing with conflict. Men tended to become authoritarian and controlling with the children, while women became more child-centered. Women tend to want to plunge in and grapple with the problem, while men are more likely to want to turn away. Some experts have traced this pattern to the different socialization for boys and girls in our culture: females are raised to pay more attention to emotional and interpersonal issues than men. Other scientists find physiological causes: e.g., it is more difficult for men to regulate emotional arousal. In addition, men generally take longer to recover once upset. The Cowan study notes: "When women raise issues in order to bring them to resolu-

tion, men 'stonewall' in order to avoid what they experience as a stressful interchange."

In Selma Fraiberg's phrase, there are "ghosts in the nursery." For example, those who have been raised to see anger as a harbinger of abandonment find interpersonal problems more threatening than those who see anger as a normal emotion between two people who care for each other. I also believe that temperament plays a part in our response to conflict. Those who are particularly sensitive to experiences of any kind might find a fight more abrasive and disturbing than those without that sensibility.

Conflict—even conflict over child-rearing—can serve many purposes in a relationship. It can represent a discharge of built-up tension. It can also represent a bid for intimacy. In addition, it can create distance in the pendulum swing between separation and togetherness that occurs in normal relationships.

Overt conflict is not the only response to differences within a relationship. One common reaction is denial. Still another is reaction-formation: blaming your partner for your own problems. For example, when Amy accuses Stan of making the children too negative, underneath is the fear that she is responsible.

For most couples, parenthood necessitates a renegotiation of the relationship, but change also brings opportunity. The differences that emerge between men and women are not problems per se; it all depends on how they are handled. Couples who learn how to resolve differences constructively adapt well to parenthood. As George Levinger from the University of Massachusetts observes, "What counts in making a happy marriage is not so much how compatible you are, but how you deal with incompatibility."

Books for parents usually stress the concepts of togetherness, consensus, and consistency. In my experience, two parents will inevitably be different. These differences can be healthy or unhealthy. Healthy differences reflect respect for each other, a desire to communicate well, sensitivity to each other's needs, and skills in problem-solving. Furthermore, children generally benefit from learning to deal with different sets of rules (e.g., those set by grandmothers or teachers or by your spouse).

SOLUTIONS

Understanding Conflict

As a first step in dealing with marital conflict, ask yourself the following questions:

- What is my part in this conflict?
- Who are the "ghosts in my nursery" and what are they saying?
- What am I really expecting? Is it realistic?

- At whom am I really angry and why?
- Do I want to change or do I have a stake (hidden or not) in maintaining this conflict?

You've undoubtedly noticed that instead of talking about how to bring your spouse into line, I've focused on you first. Change always starts with oneself.

1. Pick a time and place conducive to discussion. It may be best to wait until the heat of an argument has died down or the children are out of earshot. Some couples schedule time to air conflict so it doesn't build up. For example, one couple holds what they call "bitch time." Once the children are asleep, they spend twenty to thirty minutes talking together; each person has a chance to "bitch" about what has gone wrong during the day without advice or comment from the other.

2. Be specific. Deal with one issue at a time and don't use a problem as an opportunity to dredge up old grievances or insults.

3. State what's important to you and ask your spouse to do the same. Try to agree about which differences are acceptable and which are not. In other words, agree when to agree and when to disagree (see the section on discipline, pages 50–52).

4. Plan thoughtful gestures for each other. A couple from California regularly arranges a mystery date, each taking a turn planning the surprise for the other. They have dinner with friends, go to movies, take bike trips, and have picnics. Small gestures are also meaningful: A handmade card, a greeting card or flowers signify a lot.

5. Find a new parents' group in your community. Such groups can help couples learn to improve communication and problem-solving skills.

Siblings

Q *How do you help a preschooler deal with the birth of a baby?*

The birth of a second child is very different from the first. The procedures are now known; labor and delivery are not the mysteries they once were. You can remember the up-and-down nights, the feedings in the still-dark dawn, and the addictive smell of the baby's hair. The unknown is your older child. How will she or he react?

Is It Mainly the Presence of the Baby That Affects the Older Child?

That's how we tend to think about it: The older child has been on center stage, standing alone in the spotlight. Along comes the baby and pushes the older one to the wings. But how accurate is that perception?

First of all, the change begins with the pregnancy. The mother may be more tired and want to nap. Roughhousing may be less acceptable. If she is having any problems in her pregnancy, the mother may act guarded, worried, and withdrawn. Family conversation now includes the prospective newcomer.

In the last months of pregnancy, parents report changes in their children:

- "She asks me twenty times a day if I love her."
- "He has become more and more directive about who can take care of him."

Nadelman and Begun, from the University of Michigan, studied a group of children before and after the birth of a sibling. Some children in this study showed more negative behavior before the birth and improved once the baby arrived; clearly they were responding to prebirth changes in their parents.

Immediately after the birth, changes in their parents' behavior may affect the older child more than the presence of a newborn. Specifically:

- Parents, especially mothers, are frequently tired.
- Mild depression after childbirth is common.
- There are usually changes in household routines.

Parents, too, frequently view their older children differently. The older child needed protection before the birth; now he or she becomes the potential aggressor. A mother says:

■ ■ ■ *I used to worry about Joseph's safety; now I wonder how to keep the baby safe from Joseph.*

The new baby engenders possessive feelings within the parents, the stance that "I am the only one who can really protect my newborn." With these competitive emotions comes the desire to push others away. Mothers and fathers may race to see who gets to the crying baby first, the father's hand on the baby feels like an intrusion to the nursing mother, as does the grandmother pushing the carriage. The older sibling may be included in this unfavorable new light. One new mother had the desire to slip away, just the baby and her:

> ... *The pediatrician suggested that I spend more time alone with Abby, my four-year-old. I thought it was a good idea, but I haven't done it. Instead, I've gotten sitters for Abby because I'd really rather be with the baby by myself.*

One study of forty-one couples who were interviewed beginning in the third trimester of pregnancy until twelve months after the birth of their second child found that the primary source of stress for mothers and fathers was their relationship with their older child. Parents expected more grown-up behavior and were less tolerant of infractions.

An extensive study of the birth of the second child, conducted by English researchers Judy Dunn and Carol Kendrick, supports this point. Forty mothers and their children (approximately one and a half to two years old) were observed and interviewed in their homes during the last weeks of the mother's second pregnancy, during the first month after the birth, again when the baby was eight months old, and finally when the baby was fourteen months old. These were among their findings:

- The time that the older sibling and mother spent together playing and focusing on a subject of common interest decreased markedly after the birth of the second child.
- The number of conversations initiated by the mother to the older child substantially decreased.
- Before the second child's birth, very few glances from the older child went unreturned by the mother. After the birth, the children looked at their mothers often without having these looks reciprocated.

At fourteen months, all of these patterns persisted. In addition, there were other short-term changes:

- The number of conversations between the mother and older child that concerned the control of the child's behavior increased.
- There was a striking rise in the amount of confrontation between the mother and the older sibling.

Thus it appears that the changes older siblings have to adapt to involve their relationship with their parents and are not merely centered on getting used to the presence of the baby.

Is the Older Child Predominately Negative after the New Baby's Birth?

In the English study, Dunn and Kendrick report that 93 percent of the older siblings were negative, especially to the mother. Almost all children became defiant and demanding when their mothers, grandparents or fathers were paying attention to the baby.

Mary Elizabeth Kirkpatrick describes her son:

> **. . .** *When the baby was born, Danny would insist that only I do things for him. He became adamant. He also got into a period of telling people "You're not nice," "I don't like you," or "You're stupid."*

Older preschoolers' hostile feelings against the mother and the baby can be guilt-provoking. Like Danny, many children will then deflect their anger outside the family. Children can also be withdrawn and clinging. They may be listless, wandering about, seemingly at loose ends.

In the Dunn and Kendrick study, 70 percent of the mothers reported that their children regressed to more babyish ways. Furthermore, approximately one-fourth of the children had trouble falling asleep or awoke during the night. Children who were toilet trained also regressed.

Studies have shown that age, sex, and temperament make a difference. Children under two tend to be more clinging, while three- and four-year-olds become more demanding. Boys tend to become more withdrawn, while girls regress. The child who has been slow to warm up in a new situation will undoubtedly react this way to the new baby.

The children's behavior can also be positive—they become more independent and helpful. In fact, Dunn and Kendrick report that 95 percent of the children in their study were extremely eager to help with the baby. Often the very same child who is defiant will also be friendly and helpful. In other words, children's reaction to the changes in their lives is complex, both positive and negative.

Does the First Meeting between the Siblings Affect Their Future Relationship?

The first meeting between older child and infant is often regarded as significant. Parents speak of it as a kind of "bonding" and react with understandable apprehension if older children stick their tongues out or say, as one child did, "Go back into the uterus, baby."

In my view, the first meeting, whether it takes place in the home or hospital, is much less a harbinger of the developing relationship than the patterns that become established over the first few weeks and months. The first meeting, according to Dunn and Kendrick, was not predictive of the feelings between the two children eight months and again fourteen months later. They say:

> Anna Freud gave some wise advice on this issue of preparation and introduction to the baby: she pointed out that however well prepared a child was, and however clearly he seemed to understand what the arrival would mean, he might easily be emotionally overwhelmed by the real event.

Are Children Especially Negative when Their Parents Are Caring for the Baby?

Parents notice that as soon as they settle down to feed or bathe the baby, the older child needs or demands something, whines, or becomes more abusive, particularly to the parent. Carefully timed observations of mothers and the older sibling corroborate this parental observation. There are exceptions, however: When the parent comes prepared with activities or diversions for the older child, he or she tends to be more cooperative.

Are Parents' Fully Responsible for the Kind of Relationship That Develops between the Siblings?

Parents have an important effect, but the ensuing relationship depends on other factors, too. Most important, it depends on the personality and temperament of the older child. The match or mismatch between the two children—their interests and their behavioral styles—seems to be crucial. An analogy to cooking comes to mind: The ingredients for the relationship are fixed, but how they come together makes a difference.

Before the Birth

Preparing Your Child.
- Initiate discussion and be responsive to questions such as "How did the baby get inside you?" Some parents describe how men and women have babies in anatomical detail, others simply say, "When mothers and fathers love each other, they make babies." (See the section on sexuality, pages 160–170.) Remember that children can confuse the stomach and the uterus, so make that distinction clear: "Babies grow inside a special place in the mother called the uterus."
- Bring your child to the prenatal checkups. One mother always weighed herself and the child at each checkup so that her child felt a part of this process from the beginning.
- Discuss pregnancy and birth by talking about women who have had babies. Spend time with new babies, if you can, so that your child can see

that a newborn is not a playmate, has a realistic view of the capabilities of newborns, and can observe nursing and caregiving first hand.

- Talk about what babies are like when they are first born. One mother made a scrapbook with her four-and-a-half-year-old. They looked through magazines and the child cut out pictures of babies and pasted them in the book. The process led to a great deal of discussion about babies.
- Show the child pictures of himself or herself just after birth.
- Avoid saying the baby is a "gift" to the older child "so you won't be lonely," or "You're going to love the baby." Discuss the birth in terms of "you'll soon be a big brother" or "big sister."
- Find children's books about the arrival of a sibling.
- See if your hospital or birthing center has a preparation program for siblings. Find out if they have a visiting program for siblings after childbirth.
- Discuss your expectations of childbirth, specifically what will happen to the child and who will care for him or her. Remember that childbirth is not predictable—you may have a C-section or stay in the hospital longer than anticipated, so when preparing the child, describe these as "plans."
- In her booklet *Welcoming Your Second Baby,* Vicki Lansky suggests taping yourself reading, giving the child a photograph or something else that the child selects to remind him or her of you while you're away. One child chose his mother's shoes to keep near him during her stay in the hospital.

After the Birth

Introducing Your Child to the Baby.
- If possible, arrange for your child to visit you at the hospital or birthing center.
- Make a movie or take photographs of the first meeting.

Acknowledging Your Child's New Role.
- Give your child a present because now she or he is a big sister or big brother.
- When friends and relations come to visit, try to ensure that the older child is not shunted aside. Suggest that they bring something small for the older sibling or keep a supply of gifts yourself.
- Make sure the guests pay attention to the older child.

One mother accompanied her older child to nursery school, bringing the baby. She asked the older sibling to demonstrate how to hold a baby to the class. The response from the other children increased this child's pleasure in being a big sister.

Another day-care center always celebrated the older child, making hats and badges that read "I'm a big sister" or "I'm a big brother."

Having Realistic Expectations.   Expect your child's reaction to the new baby to be ambivalent. Total acceptance exists more in fantasy than in reality. It is also helpful to know that when your child plays baby or imitates the newborn, this is positive. Studies have linked this behavior to a friendlier relationship later on.

Minimizing the Changes in Your Child's Life.   Children in the preschool years are usually ritualistic, especially around separations as well as the more difficult aspects of everyday life such as bedtime. Maintaining their routines during this time can help them adjust more easily.

Furthermore, this may not be the time to push new skills. As Mary Elizabeth Kirkpatrick says:

> **. . .** *I am very conscious of expecting too much from Danny. I'm trying hard not to use these first weeks to pressure him to do new things, like dress himself.*

Avoiding a Large Drop-off in the Attention Given to the Child.   It's important to attempt to maintain your relationship with your older child, especially finding fun time together. Despite the fact that the relationship between most parents and the older sibling had moments of conflict, Dunn and Kendrick found that the children who developed the most positive relationships with new siblings had mothers who were able to enjoy their older child. These mothers were "more likely to enter the child's pretend games by making verbal suggestions and comments." They also used language in complex ways with their children. These maternal behaviors reflect a parenting style, the researchers suggest, in which the mother enjoys the child's world.

- Share the care of the children to the degree possible. Many parents find their roles shift after the birth of the second child. Fathers frequently get more involved with their firstborns.
- Plan time alone with the older child. You can take the child out to dinner, to a movie, to the library for story hour, or just for a walk. Many families plan a regular "special time" activity for parent and child before bedtime.

Providing Safe Opportunities for Your Child to Express Negative Feelings.
- After listening to "Hansel and Gretel" with his mother, Danny announced that they should leave baby Mark in the woods.
- Joseph, age three, said things like "I hate this baby" while he pounded his fists on the counter.

- Rebecca, age two, yelled loudly in the baby's ear when he was sleeping.
- Simone, age three, deliberately splashed water on her nursing sister.

Parental reaction to such episodes is usually dismay. Our impulse to say "You should love the baby" is obviously unhelpful. In family relationships, love commingles with anger and animosity. Thus it is important to do as Simone's mother did: she stopped negative behavior and sympathized by saying, "Sometimes it's hard to be a big sister."

We can put limits on behavior while accepting the emotion: "I know you feel angry at the baby and you can say so. But I'm not going to let you hurt her."

Maintaining Positive Discipline Techniques. Hostile feelings toward the new baby and mother can make older preschoolers feel guilty; some seem to push their parents to punish them—the children's way of temporarily diminishing the guilt. Yet, if parents fall into a pattern of punishing, a cycle of bad behavior relieved by punishment is set up. Parents who can accept the negative feelings, while stopping and then redirecting negative behavior, have children with better sibling relationships later on.

Planning for the Caregiving Times. When you feed, bathe, or change the baby, your older child may become more disruptive. Here are some suggestions from parents:

- When you feed the baby, it's inevitable that the older child is going to barge in, especially to ask for something to eat. So bring food and a cup of juice for the older child so you don't have to interrupt the feeding.
- Children love to play in water, and if times get tough around five or six at night (as they do with most babies), the sibling can take a bath; mommy and baby can sit in the bathroom and feed or play or whatever. The two- or three-year-old can play in the bathtub for an hour and have a wonderful time.

You'll have to decide what to do when your older child asks to nurse or drink a bottle. Here's what Mary Elizabeth did:

• • • *I gave Danny formula in teaspoons and in a bottle but I wasn't going to let him nurse. Danny didn't like the taste of the formula. He also wanted to suck on a pacifier and play with baby toys, and this was okay with me.*

Discussing Caring for the Baby as a Joint Enterprise. Dunn and Kendrick found that mothers who encouraged their children, especially their boys, to help (95 percent of the children initially showed signs of wanting to be involved) had siblings with more positive relationships at fourteen months.

Kara Lewinson says:

■ ■ ■ *Right after we brought the baby home from the hospital, David came over, put his hand up and said, "Mom, can I pat her head?" The baby was one week old and my reaction was to go, "No, don't touch her." But I bit my tongue and I said, "Sure. Pat her this way." Then I praised him and said, "You did a really good job." He said, "That's because you taught me how," and he patted her again.*

Gina Robinson says:

■ ■ ■ *Suzanna helps me with the baby's bath. She washes the belly button on down and I do the belly button on up. She takes a great deal of pride in this.*

Mary Elizabeth says:

■ ■ ■ *I told Danny that he taught the baby to smile, and I encourage this game. In fact, no one else can get such a big smile from the baby as Danny.*

Including the child encourages independence and a growing sense of competence. But when your child is ready to turn to his or her own interests, that should be accepted. As Kara Lewinson concludes:

■ ■ ■ *When David has had enough of being a helper, I remember that it is not his sole purpose in life to assist me. I encourage helping primarily to ease him into his role with his sister.*

Discussing the New Baby as a Person.   This, in my view, is extremely important. Many parents instinctively discuss the baby's feelings: "Rachel seems hungry," or "Do you think that Ryan wants to burp?" Dunn and Kendrick found that differences in the way the mother discussed the baby were associated with differences in the quality of the siblings' developing relationship. If the mother referred to the baby's wants and needs, the two children were more likely to form a better relationship.

It could be argued that mothers who use such a technique have older children who initially show more interest in the baby; however, this was not the case—mothers did this with children who were hostile at first as well as those who were friendly. When mothers described the baby's behavior to the older child, he or she became more attuned to the baby—a seemingly small step that can pay dividends in the future relationship between the two siblings.

Q *What would help my children fight less and get along better?*

Recently my daughter beckoned me to watch a psychologist on an early morning television talk show discuss how to handle problems between siblings. He said the parents had to remain emotionally neutral. "It works for me in my office," he stated. Lara turned to me and said, "He doesn't have his own kids—that's for sure."

The fact is that we as parents often know how to handle a problem between our children, but we don't do it. We get pulled into the conflict. Rather than pretending these emotional hooks don't exist, I think it is more constructive to try to unearth them.

CHILDREN'S BEHAVIOR HAS SYMBOLIC MEANING TO PARENTS IN A VARIETY OF WAYS

The First Child Sets the Standard

A mother with a precocious first child realizes, in retrospect, that she has pushed her second to be like the first:

... *I expected too much from my second at every stage because I simply did not take the time to watch and see what he was ready to do—whether it was being on his own in a nursery school situation, being ready to be toilet trained, or enjoying fairy tales.*

Parents Tend to Classify Their Children

Sue's mother sees her as easy and reasonable. By contrast, Donald is seen as more difficult and hypersensitive. Children can be cast in black and white terms: if one is good, the other is bad; if one is tough, then another may be vulnerable.

Sue's mother says:

... *I can leave Sue anywhere and she'll say, "Goodbye, Mom," and that's it. When Don says, "Goodbye, Mom," my heart cracks in half. He's so easily hurt that I worry about him.*

Although most of us think of the younger child as the more vulnerable, that's not always true. Donald, for example, is older than Sue. Furthermore, we are not the only ones who create these categories: relatives do, too.

Children also take on roles: the clown, the appeaser, the provoker. These roles can be extremely powerful as our children develop. Unfortunately, they have the potential of becoming self-fulfilling prophecies—the child seen as bad begins to see himself or herself that way.

Our Children's Roles Reflect Our Own History

Our overall reaction to our children's behavior harkens back to our own childhood—we are reminded of features in ourselves or others that we dislike or admire. Sometimes children become assigned to one or the other parent as "his" or "her" child. In the process, the symbolic meaning of the behavior can overshadow reality. For example, a toddler's typical fussiness reminds a father of his older cousin who was always taunting and teasing him. Since his cousin has led a desolate life, the child's normal behavior is seen as a harbinger of problems to come; thus it must be stopped at all costs.

The problem with roles is that they are self-limiting. If the child is the tough one in the family, then it becomes hard for him or her to show fear or dependency; the "good" girl or boy may feel trapped and prevented from exploring unconventional avenues of self-expression. The pain of these confining definitions can last a lifetime:

• • • *I went to visit my mother, who is eighty-one years old, when she was ill. In my family, I was always the one who could do nothing right. And there I was again, at age fifty, still doing it. I didn't call the doctor soon enough. I fixed the wrong lunch. My sister was the golden one: "Look at the beautiful bed jacket she bought," or "Look how your sister got my plants to grow." I've struggled against this all my life—it's been a slow process of trying to convince myself that I am a capable person.*

UNFULFILLED EXPECTATIONS

The second category of emotional hooks that draw us into the fray with our children has to do with expectations that do not come true.

The Sibling as a Gift

As children, many of us longed for a close sibling relationship—a confidant, a friend to spend hours with, a companion who shares our history. But that closeness eluded us then, perhaps because we and our siblings had divergent interests or seemed too far apart in age. Perhaps we were only children. Starting in childhood, we fantasize about the family we will create. Then our children don't act accordingly; they insult or hurt or ignore each other. A mother with three daughters says:

• • • *As an only child I wanted nothing more than to have a sibling, so on some level I feel as if I've given my children a gift by providing them with each other. I had always thought if I had a sibling, things would be so wonderful and I would love that person so much. So there is tremendous disillusionment because of the way my children fight with each other. I'm trying not to take it personally or as a failing on my part, but I wish it weren't that way.*

Siblings Should Love Each Other and Not Fight

This expectation comes from a variety of sources:

"*I was taught not to fight.*"

• • • *I grew up being told that if you fought with someone, something was terribly wrong. If you argued or disagreed, that was okay, but don't raise your voice or slam the door. It is extremely difficult not to revisit those sins upon my own children.*

"*My children didn't fight when they were younger, so why now?*"

• • • *We were so pleased that our children got along so well. Now that Jill has turned eighteen months, she's into Charlotte's things, and the honeymoon is over.*

"*Other people's children don't fight.*"

• • • *There's another family in the neighborhood with children the same ages as ours, so we see them quite a bit. Their children seem extremely considerate of each other—compared to mine who are always grabbing toys out of each other's hands.*

Despite our expectations of having families like we see on television or read about in books like *Little Women*, children—even "other people's children"—do tease each other, hit, bite, pinch, and take each other's toys. As Seymour Reit says in *Sibling Rivalry*, battles between brothers and sisters are "normal and natural." Observational studies of siblings show fighting is commonplace. Yet as parents we may overestimate the time our children spend bickering as compared to the time they spend as friends.

Over the past several years, a group of Canadian researchers has been conducting naturalistic studies in the homes of twenty-four pairs of same-sex siblings and twenty-four pairs of mixed-sex siblings with either a small (one to two year) or larger (two and a half to four year) interval between their ages. The siblings' behavior to each other is coded as "prosocial" (verbally or physically cooperative, helpful, or friendly) or "agonistic" (verbally or physically aggressive, threatening, or teasing). The researchers conclude:

> *This study has shown that siblings are important individuals in each other's lives, and that the importance is not mainly in terms of negative feelings. Our siblings spent a great deal of time playing together, interacting in a variety of ways. . . . The point is not to deny that siblings are often competitive but merely to note that it is probably a mistake to think of siblings' relationships, at least during the preschool years, as primarily competitive or negative.*

The research on sibling relations reveals that, well before age three, children are remarkably adept at understanding their younger brother's and sister's feelings. The older siblings also function as teachers, explaining or showing the younger ones new skills.

Children Should Be Treated Equally

This is another parental expectation: "If I give attention to one, then I must give the same amount to the others." "If I let one stay up late, then the younger ones are entitled." "If I bring one a present, then the others get gifts too." In their book *Siblings Without Rivalry*, Adele Faber and Elaine Mazlish point out the ridiculous extremes to which this strategy can be carried: one child's curls are cut off so her hair will be more like her sister's. The authors remind us that "equal is less" because it always involves a comparison rather than a focus on what the individual child needs and wants.

An irony emerges from the research on siblings. Despite our intention to treat our children equally, we are much more likely, consciously or not, to treat them quite differently. Because siblings are in fact different to begin with, we create what psychologists have termed microenvironments for each child. In a fascinating, nationally representative study, 348 siblings, ranging in age from eleven to seventeen years old, completed various assessments of their experiences within their families. For example, individual siblings reported how much say they had in decision-making, the chores they were expected to do, or how close they felt to their mothers. The mothers answered the same questions for each of their children. The researchers found that two siblings often experienced the same family life very differently from each other, almost as if they lived in separate homes.

In reviewing this research, it is evident that differing treatment of siblings is customary. Rather than denying or camouflaging it, we should attempt to understand how we respond to each of our children. Problems arise, in my view, not when children are treated differently, but when they are compared positively or negatively to one another or when they are valued more or less than the other.

Given, then, that a certain amount of conflict exists in every family and that we do treat children differently, what promotes closer sibling relationships?

Is it the Spacing of the Children?

Some experts say the interval between children is critical to their development as well as to their feelings about each other. The parent educator Burton White has claimed that if children are less than three years apart they won't adjust as well. Jeannie Kidwell from the University of Tennessee argues for a very short interval (one year) or a long one (over four). With the short interval, she states, older children are not dethroned—they have almost always had to share their parents' attention. With a longer one, they have established more independent interests, more relationships outside the family. Therefore the new sibling is less of an intrusion.

Numerous studies have investigated the impact of different age spacing. In research conducted by Rona Abramovitch and her colleagues, spacing children one to two years apart as opposed to two and a half to four years made no difference in the friendliness and cooperation of the preschool-aged siblings. Similar results came from the English study conducted by Dunn and Kendrick in which the majority of the children were a year and a half to two years apart. It may be, however, that these intervals are not sufficiently different to reveal the effects of various spacing patterns, although they do represent common spacing intervals.

The effects of spacing may not appear until the children are older. In a study of seven- and eight-year-olds, Helen Koch found that with an interval of two to four years between the children, competition was more intense, but so was affection. These children often sought out each other's company. With a larger age gap, the children did not play together as much and were thus less influential in each other's lives at that point in time.

From the studies conducted thus far, it seems that the age spacing of children is not as potent a force as some experts claim. At most, it plays a minor role.

Does the Sex of the Siblings Matter?

Common wisdom would answer yes, at least in the early years. Most assume that boys would prefer to be with boys, girls with girls. The data on this subject, as with age spacing of children, are inconclusive. The two most thorough observational studies came up with slightly different results. In the Abramovitch study, at the first assessment the younger siblings were approximately eighteen months old, the older ones ranged from three to four and a half years old. At these ages, the sex of the child did matter:

pairs of brothers were more physically but not verbally aggressive; pairs of sisters more nurturing. However, in comparing mixed- with single-sex pairs, they found that the children were equally friendly with each other. When Abramovitch and her colleagues reassessed the same children eighteen months later, they found no difference in the frequency with which children were friendly or unfriendly to each other in the same-sex or mixed-sex pairs.

By contrast, the Dunn and Kendrick study of slightly younger children found that the older was increasingly friendly to the younger one if they were of the same sex, but more hostile if they were of the opposite sex. These researchers speculate that the increasing hostility in the mixed-sex pairs might be related in part to much greater disparity in the manner in which they were disciplined compared to the same-sex pairs. It may be that this differential treatment intensified the rivalry.

The findings on the importance of the sibling's sex in influencing their subsequent relationship, while inconclusive, reveal that mixed-sex siblings are not predestined to be less close than pairs of same-sex siblings.

What Else Makes a Difference?

Does the birth order matter? Not much. In reviewing the research on birth order, Brian Sutton-Smith states it has "relatively little power in accounting for psychological outcomes." The effect of birth order depends on whether the family is large or small; it also depends on the temperament of the children. Judy Dunn notes that while studies show that first children are more likely to be the dominant ones in the early years of the sibling relationship, they are not more likely to be more friendly or aggressive: "The closeness, intimacy, support, and affection a child feels for his brother or sister is not clearly linked to whether he is a firstborn or a laterborn."

In studying family relations, researchers have identified the concept of "goodness of fit"—that is, the match between the parent's and the child's temperaments. There is also, I believe, a goodness of fit between siblings. If they are similar in activity level and other characteristics, they are likely to get along better, at least when they are young.

What Part Do Parents Play?

The findings on this subject are ironic. When parents are depressed, hostile, or remote, the children tend to band together to find comfort and sustenance from each other. Fortunately, positive relationships can also promote closeness. When parents treat each child as an individual and build on the positive overtures that the siblings make toward each other, the siblings are more likely to be close.

Carefully controlled observational studies indicate that children pay a great deal of attention to how their parents treat their siblings. In some families in the Dunn and Kendrick study, the older children showed an interested response (such as moving closer to listen) to as many as 78 percent of the interactions between mother and the younger sibling. Thus, the parents can be a model for how to behave and treat the younger sibling.

Most parents recognize that the children fight less if they themselves are not present. Abramovitch and her colleagues recorded the amount of fighting that took place in the mother's presence or absence. They concluded that when mothers were in the same room with their children, the children did not interact as much with each other. Furthermore, the interaction that did take place was visibly more negative. Perhaps, as many parents suspect, sibling fights represent bids for parental attention.

Does this mean that parents do better to remove themselves from sibling quarrels if the children are in no danger of hurting each other?

In one experiment, twelve families were taught not to intervene in sibling fights. Eight months later, a follow-up study revealed that the amount of bickering had decreased. Another study found that when parents spend "special time" alone with each child, especially those who were having difficulty with siblings, the amount of fighting is reduced. A third study employed both strategies: Parents intervened in fights less often as well as reinforced their children for playing cooperatively. This third strategy was also successful.

In conclusion, parents can and do help shape the kind of bonds that brothers and sisters form, but not in a vacuum. The children themselves play an important role in the kind of relationship they have with each other.

SOLUTIONS

Forming a Positive Relationship with Each of Your Children

Children's behavior toward others is affected by the parent/child relationship. You can sometimes glimpse this transference in the way that older preschoolers discipline their dolls or pets (but, also, don't take all play literally). Spending time alone with each child is a prelude to good sibling relationships.

Valuing the Individuality of Each Child

Put negatively, this means that if you compare your children, they are more likely to compete. If you want your daughter to pick up her toys, it is more effective to say, "Time to clean up," than to say, "Your brother is so neat, why aren't you?" I've found it helpful to explain to my children, "Fair doesn't mean the same. I do what I think is right for each child."

Avoiding Stereotyping

We do see children differently, but don't let those views confine or limit your child. If one of your children is bold, describe specific behavior: "You went to a new place all by yourself!" rather than assign roles, "You are the brave one in the family."

As parents we tend to identify with one or another of our children more than the others. As they grow, children learn that "I'm like my dad." The process of being like the parent is wonderful as long as children don't get narrowly divided up: "This child is the mother's," and "This child is the father's." Most children undoubtedly exhibit behavior reminiscent of both parents, and that can be acknowledged.

Understanding the Children's Point of View

One expert suggests understanding how our children feel about a sibling by thinking how we would react if our spouse came home and said, "I love you so much that I've decided to get a second wife (or husband)." This puts into perspective statements like, "Don't be mean to your sister," or "Of course you'll share your toys with your brother."

Before you intervene in a sibling dispute, imagine how you would feel if this were a conflict between you and a rival wife or husband. How would you like to be treated? Treat your children with that same kind of respect.

Reinforcing Friendliness without Forcing It

I think that it is important to allow children possessions that they need not share. These can be acknowledged by the family: "Katie does not share her fuzzy rabbit." If one child taunts another with a possession, then have the child remove it: "If it is too hard to be around Brian without making him want your fire truck, then put it away."

In addition, there can be communal spaces and possessions that the children agree to share. My children merged their individual collections of small rubber animals and table blocks and eventually negotiated a system for taking turns sharing them.

Viewing Conflict as an Opportunity for Learning Social Skills

When I realized that all siblings fought, I began to change my perspective. I realized that very few adults have learned to deal effectively with conflict —most of us escape, become defensive or retaliatory. Think of how many marriages are troubled because adults have never learned to fight in constructive ways. I began to see the sibling relationship as the perfect opportunity for my children to learn these skills with each other. Thus, I say, "I'm more interested in how you solve this problem together than in who started it."

Teaching negotiation skills involves several steps:

Allow each child to say how he or she feels. You can do this alone with the child or in a family meeting in which the children listen and then have a turn to speak. Giving the children opportunities to express feelings, contrary to what we think, helps create better sibling relationships. In the workshops that Adele Faber and Elaine Mazlish conduct they discovered an important paradox:

> *Insisting upon good feelings between children led to bad feelings.*
>
> *Allowing for bad feelings between the children led to good feelings.*

Reflect back children's statements. A parent, Michelle Wells, describes how this works:

. . . *You say to Abigail, "Carol says you hit her." Then Abigail responds, "Well, Carol hit me first." Then you say to Carol, "Carol, Abigail says that you hit her first." You just tell each child what the other child is saying, you reflect it back. Either the children realize how ridiculous this is and they ought to be talking to each other, or it gives them enough time to take it all in and calm down.*

By using this technique, you're not passing judgment or taking any sides. This strategy is practical with older preschoolers who can step back with some objectivity; toddlers are too young to understand the reasoning.

Try to understand the family dynamics. Double-check your impressions of what is going on. For example, I found that I was jumping in to protect my younger child without noticing how she was quietly instigating sibling wars. She would tease her brother, and when he got upset, he would get in trouble. I didn't learn this until I gave both my children a chance to talk about their feelings.

Help the children devise solutions. During the fight or afterwards say, "How can we solve this problem?" Each child can suggest solutions. Between them, they must agree. My children have, for example, come up with sensible solutions for getting along in the back seat of the car (putting a pillow in the middle, taking a tape recorder to interview each other) and for determining who gets to listen to which radio station (each child gets one day).

This technique becomes progressively more effective as the children grow older. Michelle Wells says:

. . . *I find it difficult to problem-solve with Abigail. Three-year-olds don't go by the rules. It's very frustrating for Carol (seven* *years old) because she would like to work it out, but her sister doesn't abide by what she says. Abigail's too young, but she is learning.*

Withdraw when you can. Try an experiment. If you are in another room and hear your children start to squabble, resist the temptation to rush in. Listen instead and see if they can work it out. Of course, intervene if they are hurting each other, but as much as you can, let them learn how to resolve their differences. Praise their attempts without setting up comparisons: "You both came up with an interesting idea about sharing the Legos."

We asked some young children to talk about their brothers and sisters. Here are the good things they said about having siblings:

doing things together
giving presents
saying "you're nice"
making up after a fight

The bad things:

fights
getting hurt
insults
wanting to watch different programs on TV at the same time

Only Children

Q *Will my only child turn out to be selfish and spoiled?*

Despite the fact that the number of only children has been increasing, negative stereotypes about the only child resist change. Since the 1950s, national surveys have asked whether being an only child is an advantage or disadvantage; the majority say it's a disadvantage. Only 1.7 percent of the respondents said that the ideal family has one child. The only child can seem like an aberration, even to his or her parents. A New York City mother describes Christmas morning:

▪ ▪ ▪ *Alexis woke us early. Jim and I were exhausted so after Alexis had opened her presents, we went to lie down. When I got up* again she was in the middle of the living room floor with her dolls and toys, playing all by herself, alone. It struck me to my heart. It didn't seem right that she should sit there all by herself, but she's an only child, and that's what her life will be like.

Parents of only children have many particular worries:

"My child will be all alone in the world later on." Jo Anne Gelman says:

■ ■ ■ Not only is Dara an only child, she has no first cousins nearby. My brother is important to me. There is no one else who has known you that long, who knows how your parents raised you. I worry about Dara's not having that sense of connection.

Even in today's world, blood is thicker than water. For instance, David's uncle just died. His aunt is one of five children and they all swooped in to take care of her. They made all of the arrangements for the funeral, called the relatives, got the food. Then they all sat around saying things like "Remember when we did this or did that." Listening to them, I felt very worried for Dara. I do think that people take care of their own, and she won't have that.

"My child will be too adult-focused." A father became concerned about this when his son was asked whom he would like to invite to his birthday party. His list consisted of adult friends of the family.

"My child will be spoiled." A Chicago mother says:

■ ■ ■ My mother and I took Sally shopping and she wanted me to buy her everything she saw. I know that kids this age do that, but Mother gave me a look that means "This child is too indulged." It frightened me. I know we give Sally a lot—not only material things, but time and attention. I keep wondering if she won't grow up to be selfish and demanding.

"My child won't learn to get along with other people or to stand up for herself because she has no brothers or sisters." A father says:

■ ■ ■ Lucy is shy. If we go into a social situation, she stays close to us. Yes, she goes to nursery school, but she has no experience in the rough and tumble of childhood.

"I worry that I'll pressure my child to achieve." Jo Anne Gelman says:

• • • *I don't want to pressure Dara to excel, but I'm afraid of doing it unconsciously. I've got all my eggs in one basket. If there were another child, my expectations would be spread out.*

"I worry that I'll be paranoid about my child's safety." A mother says:

• • • *Every time I read in the paper about a child dying young, I cry. I'm afraid that I hold on too tightly to my child.*

Alexis's mother describes a visit to her sister who has several children:

• • • *These kids have breakfast and then walk out the door. They don't have to say where they're going; they watch out for each other. I must admit that I'm terrified that something will happen to Alexis. She's never been out of the sight of an adult, but she'll have to do it sometime.*

Before discussing what the research evidence has to say about these fears, I think that it is important to put them in context. Virtually every parent I've ever interviewed has an "it's because" theory. Whenever the child has a difficult moment, this emerges as the cause. For instance, the child has a severe fight with a friend: adoptive parents feel, "It's because he's adopted"; single parents think, "It's because I'm divorced"; working mothers say, "It wouldn't have happened if I stayed home"; and parents of only children say, "It must be because he has no brothers and sisters."

Sometimes the child's behavior *is* linked to one of these circumstances, but other times it merely represents a normal phase of growing up. So the next time you think, "It's because—," step back and ask yourself if other children your child's age with siblings are acting this way.

Perhaps because of parents' concerns with "how will the only child turn out," research on this complex subject has focused on adults. The early studies simply compared groups of adults who had been only children with those who had siblings. Any result (the only children achieved more, for example) was attributed to their being only children. Current studies recognize that other factors come into play, particularly demographic differences among parents. Higher achievement for the child might result from the parents having more education rather than to the lack of siblings.

In one reanalysis of the data from seven national surveys, Norval Glenn and Sue Keir Hoppe took those demographics into account. They found that the stereotype of the maladjusted only child is false—only children were not different from children from larger families on a variety of measures of well-being. In fact, in this study, white adult males who were only children were more likely to be happy than those with siblings.

Are only children smarter? In a study that controlled for demographic differences, Claudy, Ferrell, and Dayton found that only children have IQs slightly higher than or similar to children with siblings. As to achievement, some studies show no differences between only children and those with siblings, while others show that only children are more likely to excel. Only children may get more attention from their parents, who also have higher expectations for mature behavior.

In a review of the research on only children, Toni Falbo reports that as adults only children are more likely to seek out others in stressful times, perhaps because they had their mothers' full attention growing up and learned that people are comforting in the face of problems. Under ordinary circumstances, however, studies have found that only children have a less intense social life as adults but are also more likely to be cooperative rather than competitive.

Thus, the picture of the only child as disadvantaged is simply not true. But it is not the lack of brothers and sisters that is the sole determinant—some of the other important ingredients are the family's economic situation, how the parents feel about being parents and having one child, and the other experiences and people in the child's life.

Separation and Divorce

They meet, fall in love, marry, have children, but the scenario is now far from "and they live happily ever after," if it ever was. They grow in different directions, they fight, they hurt each other with words, actions, and even their fists. She or he meets someone else or becomes hurt, depressed, angry, and they separate and divorce. This is the projected scenario for close to half of all marriages in the United States today.

Parents Speak: Breaking Up Is Hard to Do

Carolyn Martin, a parent of two children, lives on the West Coast:

▪ ▪ ▪ *Marshall and I met when he was five and I was three. We dated through high school, had no connection in college, then remet and eventually married. First we were friends and then lovers.*

I have been feeling very hopeless about my marriage for many years. We no longer give each other anything. For instance, I'll ask for support in some diddley sort of way, like, "Will you help me out and feed the cats." He'll respond very

*negatively. I'll swallow and we'll go along and there'll be sev-
eral more of these incidents. Then something will happen,
maybe involving the children, and I'll blow it all out of proportion. Consequently I'll feel bad about myself because I've lost it
in front of the children. It's a cycle in which there's a reconcili-
ation period, then the building of tension, then this incredible
blow-up, and then huge remorse and the cycle starts again.*

Marshall Martin:

• • • *Everything I seem to do is wrong. Carolyn is always finding
fault with what I say and do.*

Carolyn Martin:

• • • *The other night we were pulling onto the freeway and Marshall
pushed the accelerator to the floor and the engine really
screamed. Patty (five years old), in distress, said something
like, "Don't do that. That's scary." All he heard was that tone
of voice and he snarled back. So I said, "Who do you think just
talked to you?" And he said, "Well, you did, of course." I said,
"No, that was Patty." And he said, "Oh, Patty, I'm so sorry."
He was real soothing to her, real gentle. Obviously I'm not
five, but that nurturance, that tenderness is never in his voice
for me and that's why I'm so needy.*

*I have backed myself, over a long period of time, into a
situation in which there is no exit. I feel like I'm in a room with
no doors.*

*We've been in family therapy for over a year. I don't know
whether it's too late or whether I can hang on to rebuild.*

Marshall Martin:

• • • *Carolyn talks about separation and I'm absolutely opposed to
it. I say, "If you want to do something, you do it, but I'm going
to stay here and fight for the house and the children." I don't
think you throw away a marriage because there are problems.*

Q *How should I tell the children that we are separating?*

Children are the physical representation of the union: their very presence
can be a reminder of happier times, of a commitment to one another, a

trust in the future of the couple relationship. Telling them that this relationship is possibly—if not definitely—over can be extraordinarily difficult. No wonder a study in California that has followed sixty families from divorce through the next ten years found that the parents of preschoolers often did not discuss the impending separation with the children. The directors of the study, Judith Wallerstein and Joan Berlin Kelly, write in their book *Surviving the Breakup:*

> *Four-fifths of the youngest children studied were not provided with either an adequate explanation or assurance of continued care. In effect, they awoke one morning to find one parent gone.*

During a time of such crisis, our views about how to parent and how to meet our children's needs can be at odds. Common assumptions we hold have proven erroneous:

Assumption: The Children Already Know

Some parents feel that the children will not be surprised by the separation since there has been so much conflict and since so many people split up these days. In some families, children are shielded from the conflict; in others, despite our intentions, all it takes is one word or even a look from our spouse, and a battle erupts. The children watch in silence, retreat to their rooms, set up a distracting outburst, or try to throw themselves between us. One four-year-old would cover her mother's or father's mouth and start to cry, saying, "Don't talk. Don't talk." She would keep it up until one of her parents left the room.

In a longitudinal study of children at three, four, and again at eleven years old, Jeanne Block and her colleagues were able to go back to their data to assess if there were differences in the children whose families subsequently divorced and in those who stayed together. They found that boys whose parents ultimately broke up were more aggressive and more easily upset, even many years prior to the divorce, presumably as a result of family tension.

Yet, even when children witness conflict, the news that their own parents are separating is usually shattering. As Wallerstein and Kelly write:

> *The children considered their situation neither better nor worse than that of other families around them. They would, in fact, have been content to hobble along. The divorce was a bolt of lightning that struck them when they had not even been aware of the existence of a storm.*

Assumption: The Children Won't Be Upset

Many parents assume that the children will be less upset by the separation because there's been a good parent/child relationship up until now. Studies such as Wallerstein and Kelly's have found little correlation between children's preseparation relationships with their parents and their response to the news that their parents are breaking up. In order to understand how young children react, it is important to consider their developmental stage. Preschool children have not fully developed the capacity to comprehend that others have different perspectives from their own. In a highly unfamiliar situation, such as the announcement of an impending separation, the research to date shows that younger preschool children (two years old to four) tend to respond in egocentric ways—they focus on how it affects them. While there is a range of individual responses, younger preschoolers are likely to use the following logic:

"My parent left me." If it is the father who moves out, the child feels, "I won't have a daddy anymore." The complexity of the husband/wife relationship is beyond the child's comprehension; it is behavior that matters: "Daddy has gone." For some, it can take a while for the magnitude of the change to hit them. In the meantime, they focus on the details: "Does Daddy have a playground at his new apartment?"

"It's because of something I did." Young children are likely to see themselves as the cause of the separation. Often incidents that we don't even remember loom large in their explanations: "I broke the glass and spilled the milk on the floor. Mommy and Daddy started to fight. Then Daddy moved to a different house. If I hadn't dropped the glass, Daddy would still be here."

"If one parent leaves, the other one might leave, too." Many parents notice that just after a separation, their child becomes clingy. A four-year-old who enjoys going to nursery school will plead to stay home. Even a parent's trip to the laundry room can cause anxiety. One father whose child moved in with him said:

• • • *Rich began to guard the car keys. If he heard me take them off the hook in the kitchen where we keep them, he'd be there in a flash, saying "Where are you going?" I guess he was afraid I'd disappear.*

Children also worry that other important figures in their lives might disappear: grandparents, friends, favorite child-care providers.

"Whether or not I see my other parent depends on my behavior." Some children do not even mention wanting to see the parent who has moved out but assume that the frequency of contact is related to their own behavior: "Daddy did not show up today because I hurt my sister."

Many children will maintain their best behavior with the noncustodial parent so as not to be rejected. Grievances or concerns may go unspoken during the visit but are voiced vehemently once the child returns home: "I don't want Daddy to take me to his girlfriend's house when I visit."

"My parents will replace me with a new child." The child fears that he or she will be forgotten, cast aside for a new son or daughter. Especially as a parent begins to date, the child may worry that the parent/child bond is tenuous and easily broken.

The preseparation family is the only one the child knows intimately. For better or for worse, it represents stability and safety. When it seems to be disintegrating, children can become bewildered, vulnerable, fearful, angry, and lonely. They often feel rejected and worry, "Who will take care of me?" Nightmares and regression to more babyish behavior are common.

Even adults can have trouble initially understanding why a couple is separating. In my neighborhood, any time a marriage breaks up the air swirls with the hum of discussion as neighbor talks to neighbor trying to figure out why. The separation of a couple is threatening to the mature onlooker; it is even more threatening to a child caught up in it.

Assumption: It's for the Best

That children will understand that the separation is for the best is another erroneous assumption that parents may make. What adults consider for the best is not usually perceived that way by children. In the Wallerstein and Kelly study of sixty families, most of the children reacted to the idea of separation with hostility and anger at the time. Only the adolescents from families in which there had been unusual violence responded with relief. A year and a half later and even five years later, the majority of the children still wished their parents had stayed together. Their longing for the old family persisted even when their lives were actually much improved.

Children do not necessarily recover from the separation quickly. Neither do adults. In a very comprehensive study conducted by E. Mavis Hetherington from the University of Virginia and her colleagues, it was found that separating adults took between one to two years to regain their equilibrium.

Assumption: The Children Are Doing Very Well Right Away

A parent's interpretation of the children's recovery from marital breakup is frequently influenced by whether or not that parent instigated the split. Those who initiated the separation are more apt to see their children initially as doing very well—sometimes despite strong evidence to the contrary. Those who have been left are likely to see their children as being in terrible pain.

Numerous researchers have noted a temporary diminishment of the ability to parent at the time of the separation. We tend to become self-absorbed, rubbed raw. We concentrate on our own survival, thus for a limited period we are more likely to project our own needs onto the children and not attend to them.

Assumption: My Child Is Just Like My Ex-Spouse

During this time, we are particularly prone to see our children as stand-ins for the departed spouse. A manner of walking, or of shrugging shoulders, or a spoken phrase reminds us of our ex-spouse. This behavior can be like a red flag signaling that the ex-spouse is somehow still present. Wallerstein and Kelly write of such children as victims, the son being made a scapegoat by the mother, the daughter by the father:

> *There is evidence in our findings that many mothers were more responsive to their daughters than their sons, and that there was a significant preference for daughters in their parenting at this time.*

Furthermore, the tendency to label children as "his" or "hers" became more pronounced.

Assumption: The Children Are Helping Me Manage

In this state of self-preoccupation, the need to turn to others is pronounced. Sometimes the most accessible person is our child. The children can slip into a role of parenting their parents. Yet at this time, more than ever before, they need us to care for them.

SOLUTIONS

Explaining the Separation

As soon as activities in the household make it obvious that one parent is leaving, tell the children. If possible or productive, both parents should be present.

The reasons for the separation are hard for young children to comprehend. No matter what you say, children can find a reason to argue against it: "If Daddy and Mommy don't love each other anymore, then they should start trying." Thus some parents simply say, "We are going to separate." One mother and father told their four-year-old: "Mommy and Daddy both love you. We will both always love you and take care of you, but we aren't going to live in the same house anymore. Daddy is moving to an apartment near the stores where we shop."

It is very important to tell the child who will take care of him or her. Also describe the specific arrangements for seeing the other parent.

Explaining That the Separation Was Not the Child's Fault

It is important to state that the child is not the cause of the split-up, even though your child may fantasize otherwise. You will have to repeat this more than once.

Explaining That It May Take a While to Feel Better

Telling the child that there is a healing process gives him or her permission to express feelings. It also can provide a framework for understanding your own moods when you are at a low ebb. As long as you don't place the responsibility for your well-being on your child's shoulders, you can share your feelings: "Today was an awful day for me," or "I'm having a hard time since the separation." Such statements are best kept succinct, and shouldn't impugn the other parent.

Keeping the Door Open for Further Discussion

Children's books can provide a nonthreatening vehicle for the child to give voice to his or her feelings. Ask your local librarian for suggestions.

Providing as Much Continuity as Possible

The less the children's actual world is disrupted, the less problematic this transition may be. This means maintaining the rules already in place to the degree possible. Children need the safety of an adult who cares enough to set reasonable limits.

If you move to a new home, try to preserve a sense of the familiar. In one family, the child helped arrange her new room exactly as it had been, with the major difference being that the new room was blue, the old one yellow.

If friends have been left behind, try to arrange for the children to stay in touch by phone or letter. Just because children don't mention old friends doesn't mean they're not on their minds. One parent discovered this when her son tried to push through the bushes in the backyard to his friend's house, even though this friend now lived many miles away.

Providing Support for Your Children and Yourself

You are more important to your children than ever before. Give them all the support you can.

There is clear evidence that parents function best when other people are available to support them as adults and as parents. Find people you can call for practical help and for talking through problems. Many single parents say they feel they don't deserve help: "I've made a mess of my life. I can't ask anyone to rescue me." Yet those who could and did lean on others found this transition time much more bearable.

Things to avoid:

- One parent leaving without saying goodbye.
- A promise to the child that "you'll like this new arrangement better."
- An assurance that you and your spouse will reunite. If you don't know what will happen, don't share your wishes or fantasies with the children.
- Surprises, such as moving without prior communication to your child on a day when he or she's away from home.
- Guilty compensation, such as buying presents.

Q *What can I expect after the separation?*

The words "separation" or "divorce" connote specific events, markers in time. Yet, as E. Mavis Hetherington has noted from her research on the impact of divorce on families, separation and divorce are a "sequence of experiences" rather than discrete occurrences. As such these experiences typically bring about profound changes.

Postseparation Changes

Financial Change. The income that supported one family must be stretched to cover two households. In general, this means a short-term decline in the standard of living for both. Over time, however, men's income tends to increase while women's declines.

Changes in Status. The financial changes cause shifts in class status, in particular, a downward spiral for women. There are also changes in social status, from being married to being separated, divorced, and single.

Moving. Following separation, fathers and mothers are likely to move repeatedly. In the Wallerstein and Kelly study, two-thirds of the children moved, many of them three or more times in the first five years.

Changes in Social Relations. People who have been friends of the couple may also shift, some taking sides, others dropping away. The loss of a social structure can be very difficult. A newly separated woman says:

. . . *People kind of forget about you. They sympathize, they want to help, but Saturday night rolls around and they're all off at their parties. I have tried to have families over for cookouts, but they don't always reciprocate. It's not that they're not nice. They're not sure what to do, so they do nothing.*

Many separated parents work hard at seeking out new friends in similar circumstances.

Changes in Work Status.   Many women go back to work after separation. Thus their roles expand from being parent to being provider as well. No wonder researchers note that "task overload" can occur.

Changes in the Husband/Wife Relationship

One member of the couple may want to separate; the other is opposed. Even in the most oppressive of relationships, one person may want to stay; the security of the known can be far less scary than the unknown.

For those convinced they want to end the relationship, it is still not easy. There are ties that have held them together, ties of enmity perhaps. A woman, recently separated, describes the feelings she has:

> **. . .** *I'm so alone. It's what I wanted, but now that I'm left with myself, there's no one to fight with, to blame. If I'm in a rage now, I'm in it by myself. I can't blame him. So I'm trying to understand why I'm so angry.*
>
> *There are times when I'd like to throw tar on him and then pump him full of bullets. It's different from the form my anger used to take: that he'd be killed in a car accident. Sometimes I laugh at the things I want to do to him.*
>
> *I wouldn't be feeling these things if I weren't still so passionately attached to him. That's what's hard to let go of—the love and hate.*

For several years, the Laboratory of Community Psychiatry at Harvard offered a program of eight sessions called Seminars for the Separated. In working with these men and women, psychiatrist Robert Weiss found that:

> *There persists after the end of most marriages, whether the marriages have been happy or unhappy, whether the disruption has been sought or not, a sense of bonding to the spouse.*

Parting couples experience "separation distress." They feel enraged and panicked. At times, too, they feel euphoric, which, according to Weiss, comes from the sense that "I can manage alone." Ex-spouses seek each other out, calling on the telephone just to hear the other's voice, driving past the ex-spouse's home or holding fantasy discussions:

Richard Cohn:

> **. . .** *In the beginning, I would call Carol and say "Come on, stop torturing yourself. Accept that our marriage is over. Stop hurt-*

ing yourself and the kids." But when I did call, we'd end up with the same fights. So now I fantasize about conversations in which we reach some consensus.

Anne Atwell:

• • • *When Bob and I left each other, one of the most upsetting things to me was that we had different stories about why the relationship ended. I didn't want to take full blame, nor did I want him to. Not being able to agree about why we separated represented the most profound rupture of all—we simply could not communicate.*

Dealing with alimony, child support, and visiting rights are potentially explosive issues. In some families, the living arrangements and child support are hotly contested, in a few to the point of kidnapping and ugly court battles. In others, the ex-spouses can agree—to the benefit of all concerned.

While many couples think of separation as severing their relationship, this is not at all the case when children are involved. In the place of the old relationship, a new relationship must form—at best, a co-parenting relationship.

Changes in the Parent/Child Relationship

A multimeasure longitudinal study of forty-eight divorced and forty-eight married men and women with preschool children by E. Mavis Hetherington and her colleagues found that during that first year divorced parents showed less affection and used more erratic discipline techniques than the married parents. The children, furthermore, were more disruptive and disobedient. The parent-child relationships improved markedly in the second year.

The Custodial Parent and the Child.   The parent with whom the children lives most of the time bears the brunt of the change. She (typically women are the custodial parent) or he must be everything to the child: provider and nurturer, comforter and disciplinarian. This parent is also the major recipient of the child's joys, angers, and sorrows.

It is discouraging to try so hard to manage and to be told by the child, "I hate you. You're not a good parent." Knowing that the child is angry about the separation and that you are the safest and most accessible target can be some comfort. But when the child puts on her best manners and clothes to visit the noncustodial parent and comes home with chocolate stains on her shirt, french fry grease in her hair, and a bad temper, life seems devastatingly unfair. As one divorced mother put it, "There's little escape from living in the child's world." And yet it is rewarding, too—to see how the family can coalesce to ride through the storm.

The Noncustodial Parent and the Child.   Researchers studying divorce have hypothesized that the preseparation relationship between the noncustodial parent and the child would predict the postseparation relationship. That is, fathers who were close to their children would make every attempt to stay close. That was not the case in a California study and others. Some fathers, for example, who had been the full-time parent edged out of their children's lives, while some remote and distant fathers became very involved. Women who were the noncustodial parents were the same as men in this respect.

Another surprising finding was that mothers who discouraged the child's relationship with the father did not necessarily deter his visiting. For those fathers who did pull away, Wallerstein and Kelly found that with intervention counseling, custodial parents could inform their ex-spouses of how important regular and reliable visiting was to the child's mental health. They posit a sensitive period, right after separation when visiting patterns are established, during which the noncustodial parent and the child should try to develop a positive relationship.

The visiting relationship is complex. Coming and going can be emotionally wearing. The timer ticking off the duration of the visit is always on, so to speak, and some parents withdraw under that tension. Some are unaccustomed to being fully in charge of their children while others fear rejection or find being thrust back into the tempest of the old marriage, via their children, difficult to handle.

This relationship between the child and the noncustodial parent is very important to the child. Young children yearn to see this parent. Even parents who are late, who break dates, who pick fights when they walk in the door are eagerly awaited by preschoolers and older children.

Laura Baumgarten speaks of five-year-old Joseph:

· · · *If anything happens to the time he has with his dad he gets upset. When Carl [her ex-husband] went on a business trip a few weeks ago, Joseph began to act like he did when Carl first left: screaming every minute. It finally occurred to me that this was bringing back the pain he had felt when we separated, so I mentioned it to him. He said, "The pain never went away."*

According to Wallerstein and Kelly, the noncustodial parents who established the best relationship were able to:

· be flexible about the logistics of visiting
· deal with the anger of their children and ex-spouse without retreating

- get over their own anger, depression, or guilt
- involve the children in planning for the visits

The Ironies of the Post-Separation Period

In most experiences of parenthood, the parent and the child are more or less in sync. Separation and divorce can throw the whole relationship temporarily off track, leaving a number of difficult issues.

The parent has inflicted this pain on the children. As a parent, you want to protect your children from harm. Yet now, as one parent aptly stated, you are "the perpetrator":

▪ ▪ ▪ *Whether I wanted it or not, my child has had a terrible experience, and I am responsible. A few days ago, my son got a shot at the doctors. It hurt, but I could say, "It will be better soon." This morning we pulled off the Band-Aid. But I can't take the Band-Aid off the pain he suffers from the divorce.*

The parent's task is to deal with the separation, while the children's objective is to reunite the parents. It is excruciating to try to divest yourself of the relationship, to stop being preoccupied by it, especially when your child cries, "I miss Daddy," or "I want you back together." A parent reports:

▪ ▪ ▪ *One time I said, "Sandy, you don't want it the way it was before when Mommy and Daddy were so unhappy." She said, "Yes, I do. I'd rather have it that way."*

Parents are preoccupied with their own distress when children need them most. Children crave time with their parents while the parent wishes to be alone; children need solace while the parent may have only enough reserve to minister to herself or himself. Children need warmth and discipline at a time when the parents' control seems shaky; they require nurturing and care, yet their own anger and grief may erupt aggressively, which further drives their parents away.

The social structure fails to accommodate the needs of separated and divorced parents. Friends may feel threatened, loyal to one spouse or the other, or simply uncomfortable. Your relatives may take sides. Schools often do not acknowledge that a child has two parents living apart; only one newsletter will be sent out. As common as divorce is, we still have few systems to help parents through this transition, but more continue to develop: separation counseling, divorce mediation, parent support groups like Parents Without Partners. Some communities are even developing support groups for kids.

PARENTS SPEAK: ELEVEN MONTHS AFTER SEPARATION

Laura Baumgarten, a single parent with a five-year-old child, says:

. . . *Carl left me for another woman. It's been excruciating. At the time, I felt there was a knife turning in my heart. Now the knife is still there, not twisting but dangling, and someday I hope it will come out.*

We went to talk to a mediator. Carl recently told me there was a lot of conflict between him and his new girlfriend. I said, "I don't want Joseph around that, but since I'm not there, I'll have to trust you to keep Joseph out of a bad situation. The problem is I don't trust you but I have to trust you with the person who is the most important to me."

If I'd been able to trust Carl, then maybe we wouldn't have split up. A few months ago, I told a friend I wanted to murder Carl. She said, "You may want to murder him, but you don't want to murder Joseph's father." I have to learn how to relate to Carl as Joseph's father. To do that, I have to make one person into two people.

I wish Joseph had not had so painful an experience in his young life. I'm trying to mirror to him that adults can deal with hard things. Maybe he'll learn that—but I do wonder how he has been affected.

Q *How are children affected by divorce?*

The answer is, it depends. Some children emerge strong and well functioning, others appear more wounded.

What makes the difference?

Developmental Age

The sixty California families were reassessed ten years later. The children's recovery followed a pattern: Children of all ages had the greatest decline in adjustment at the time of the separation. Eighteen months later, half the children had made great strides; however, at five years, that number had dropped to approximately a third.

At first the youngest children seemed to fare worst. Just after the breakup of the marriage, they were visibly suffering. Wallerstein and Kelly write:

> *Their immature grasp of the events swirling around them,*
> *together with their difficulty in sorting out their own fantasy*
> *and dreams from reality, rendered them especially vulnerable.*

Five years later, the youngest children in the study did not look very different from their older brothers and sisters, but ten years later they did. They now seemed better adjusted than their older siblings.

However, age alone cannot account for these findings. The researchers found that upon separation, parents treated younger and older children differently:

> *Young children, especially preschool children, were the chief*
> *beneficiaries of their mother's concern, and when there was*
> *little attention to go around, they got almost all of it.*

Again at eighteen months, younger children were treated with more compassion than their older siblings. Thus, it is possible that this extra attention, while not mitigating the immediate distress, did help the younger children cope well in the ensuing years.

The Sex of the Child

In the Wallerstein and Kelly study, in the first eighteen months, girls predominated among the children who had recovered the most easily. This finding has been confirmed by others. Like the age of the child, sex is not a simple determinant; the difference appears to reside more in the treatment of boys and girls than in their biology:

- Boys are exposed to more fighting before and after divorce.
- Boys tend to respond to parental conflict with more overtly aggressive behavior. This is undoubtedly both learned (perhaps modeled on their fathers) and a result of inborn constitutional differences.
- Boys are more likely to be disciplined in harsher yet more inconsistent ways.
- Boys long for their absent fathers more than their sisters do and see the men's move away from the family as more rejecting.
- Boys are also likely to remind their mothers of their ex-husbands and thus become the targets of criticism.
- Boys may also be buffeted by more conflicting loyalties between their fathers and mothers.

In sum, boys seem to experience more pain, to express it in less acceptable ways, to be perceived more negatively, and ultimately to receive less support from their parents, friends, and teachers than girls do.

Temperamental Differences

As the research on temperament makes evident, children are not just passive victims of fate. Their own behavior shapes the way people respond. Thus, children who are less adaptable to change tend to be more vulnerable to strife. E. Mavis Hetherington writes:

> The difficult child is more likely to be the elicitor and the target of aversive responses by parent, whereas the temperamentally easy child is not only less likely to be the recipient of criticism, displaced anger, and anxiety but also is more able to cope with it when it hits.

SOLUTIONS

Parents can help the child during separation and divorce in three important ways.

Reducing the Conflict in Co-parenting Roles

Robert Hess and Kathleen Camara compared married couples with divorced ones. They found that the level of conflict or harmony between the parents was a more influential factor than whether the couple was married or divorced. Children with harmonious parents were less aggressive, had fewer problems with friends, were less stressed, and functioned better in school. Furthermore, in the divorced families, the child's relationship with the noncustodial parent was as important to the child's well-being as the relationship to the custodial one.

The implications of these findings are as follows:

- Understand that it is desirable for children to maintain a relationship with both parents (unless one parent refuses or is abusive or disturbed). Children will ultimately resent you if you keep them away from their other parent.
- Be reasonably sensitive to the other parent's needs.
- Establish a predictable schedule for visiting.
- Allow the child to control access to the other parent by telephoning or arranging visits.
- Make sure the child has time alone with each parent.
- Separate your past couple relationship from the present co-parenting relationship to the extent possible.
- Avoid demeaning or criticizing the other parent in front of the child.
- Above all, try not to use the child as a pawn in your relationship.

It is important for children to see their parents together periodically. In the words of Florence Kaslow, director of the Florida Couples and Family Institute in West Palm Beach, "Children of divorce feel safer when they see that their parents can be in the same place without fighting. It lets them know that in an emergency they can rely on both parents to help them."

Maintaining a Positive Relationship between You and Your Child

Through careful statistical analysis, Hess and Camara explored a fascinating question: what affects the child more—conflict between the parents or between the parents and child? In other words, how do children fare when parents have an antagonistic relationship with each other but close and positive relationships with the children? What about children under opposite circumstances: the parents cooperate but are distant with the children? They found that variations in children's aggression, social relationships, and effectiveness at school were related even more strongly to the relationship between parent and child than to the degree of parental harmony.

The implications of this research are the following:

- Spend time with your child in activities that she or he especially likes.
- Keep up-to-date on your child's interests, concerns, and worries.
- Spend time talking and playing with your child.
- Express affection to your child.
- Try to avoid being critical, sarcastic, hostile, or withdrawn.

In general, make yourself available to your child.

Providing a Secure and Predictable Home Life

E. Mavis Hetherington states:

> Young children have more difficulty than older children in exerting self-control and ordering their changing lives and thus require more external control and structure in times of stress and transition.

- Children need rules.
- They need warmth and encouragement.
- They need predictable routines.

In other words, like all children, children undergoing divorce function best with the discipline style we call "authoritative" (see Chapter One: Discipline).

Q *How can I handle my anger at my ex-spouse?*

The most chilling finding in the research on divorce is the tenacity of anger. In the California study, four-fifths of the men and even more of the women walked away from their marriage feeling betrayed and furious. The passage of a year or more did not dull these feelings for over half of the men and two-thirds of the women. By five years, one-third of the men and half of the women had still not recovered. Even at the ten-year marker, 40 percent of the women and close to 30 percent of the men remained outraged at being exploited and rejected. Only a few admitted they had played any part in ending the marriage—divorce was blamed on the ex-spouses ("She never liked men," or "He was afraid of intimacy") or on external causes ("He traveled too much").

While the large majority of men and women eventually viewed divorce as beneficial, and most improved the quality of their lives and their self-esteem, entrapment in anger is frightening. Thus, we interviewed people who had recovered to examine how they had managed:

PARENTS SPEAK: RECOVERING FROM ANGER

Nicole Federstein, a mother of two in the Midwest, says:

. . . *What was significant in my family was that I initiated the divorce.*

That night I told my husband Tim two things. First, our marriage had become unworkable and hurtful to both of us, and second, that I had met a man, Arthur, who had been a part of my life for the last year and a half. I said that Arthur had not ended our marriage, that it had been dead for me for a long time before that.

About ten days later I moved out. When friends called, Tim portrayed it as "Nicole has left her family." He conveyed that to the children, who had come with me: "Your mother has deserted her family."

At the time, my action gave everyone—Tim, my family, and friends—license to be very angry with me, but I was not supposed to be upset in return. Society was saying there was a bad guy—me—and a victim—Tim.

I never expected my family, including my mother, with whom I had had a good relationship, to become so politicized.

It was clear that the majority of this big group of people that had been close were sympathetic to Tim and upset with me. My own mother refused to speak to me for over a year.

I tried to be thick-skinned about the criticism and put my energy into doing well by the kids.

Tim apparently assumed the kids were now publicly his. He once planned to attend a parent's night at the church. When he heard that I was also going to go, he called and said, "You must not go." I wrote him a letter saying he'd have to understand that our children have two parents and they shouldn't have to choose. Both of us should be present at the events in their lives.

I tried to build a new family, being involved in the kids' activities, creating traditions around holidays. We worked at forming a new circle of friends, some from our past, some new. When Arthur and I married a year or so later, a part of the ceremony included the kids. We told them they had two families and we valued their relationships with both. Tim married shortly after I did, but the anger continued to fester, in both of us.

My son fell victim to that anger. He began to get into real trouble. The stakes became so high that both families finally went to a family therapist. I said to Tim then, "I don't know how we can really help our son when we are all so angry." Tim was surprised. He said, "What do you mean all of us are angry?" I said, "Why do you think we divorced? I have been filled with rage for years because of our relationship."

Tim and I talked about it in front of all of those people in the therapy session and he was finally able to say, "I now understand that Arthur didn't end our marriage. You and I did." I was able to tell him I didn't use good judgment in the way we had split up. Each of us took responsibility. We also said that the anger had been debilitating. It prevented both of us from living our lives. We made a pledge to each other to do what we could to support our kids' relationships with each other.

I never would have picked this way—a crisis—to deal with the unfinished business between Tim and me. I tell my friends to go for separation counseling. However, my kids now say that it is a gift to them that there are not angry feelings between their two parents.

Jim Lawrence, a single parent from New Jersey, says:

. . . *One day Betty came to me and said, "I've got to tell you something I've been telling my other friends. I haven't been straight with you. I don't love you anymore."*

I got married in my twenties. I think I had a stylized vision of marriage and for the most part it was externals—the house, the car, and the kids.

It was a tremendous sense of loss. Like most people, I would have gone to almost any lengths to preserve that image of my family, even if it was only an illusion by any rational assessment of the relationship.

We hope that marriage will be intimate. By that I mean we allow ourselves to be vulnerable. We allow our defenses to be down, to be seen naked physically, psychologically, and emotionally. We put a great deal of trust in that other person who we hope will be protective of our vulnerability. When we find that is not happening, it is very scary. You feel you're not safe and that's hard to get over.

I went through a long period of introspection and it was hell. I missed my wife and my child. I kept hoping my wife would come back and we could work it out. I kept thinking, "If only Betty would listen to me," or "If only Betty would change."

One night I found myself with a mental image of hanging on tightly to a trapeze. I realized that I was keeping myself in the past. I said to myself, "But I don't know what's going to happen if I let go." Then I started to say, "Let go. Let go. Let go." It was exhilarating to give myself permission to let go, to get over the anger and hurt, to move on.

It was helpful to think of anger as a secondary reaction to abandonment and the loss of my fantasy. I had been giving Betty power over me by staying angry. I had been keeping the relationship alive through anger.

For me, one of the essential ingredients is to acknowledge to yourself—and to each other if you can—that you got married for good reasons, you each did the best you could. You celebrate the relationship for what it was and you move on.

Nicole and her ex-husband came together to deal with what she calls the "unfinished business," although it took their son's crisis to do so. Jim did it without his ex-wife by finding other men to talk to; he even formed a group of men to discuss divorce. In addition, he read as much as he could. Nevertheless, they both followed similar routes:

- separating the ex-spouse from the co-parent in their minds
- realizing that anger is as much of a bond as love is
- determining that they were hanging on to the relationship through anger and pain
- seeing that they were giving psychological control of their lives to their ex-spouses by wishing for a different tomorrow
- and finally working on "letting go" of the negative past, acknowledging the good past, and creating a present in which they could co-parent

Both found that by moving beyond the anger, they were more successful as co-parents.

New Relationships

Q *How do you deal with "other" relationships?*

Many single parents hope eventually to form a new, satisfying, and successful relationship. They wonder how to meet people, how to avoid old pitfalls, how to feel strong when the separation is still painful, and finally how and when to include their child in this relationship.

New relationships develop in different patterns. Some divorcing parents form an immediate attachment to what has been called a "transitional" person. In a study of families undergoing divorce, E. Mavis Hetherington and her colleagues found that in 70 percent of the families, at least one spouse was involved with another person who gave him or her the emotional support to make the break. However, fewer than 15 percent of these people eventually married the transitional person. The researchers concluded that "once the initial stress of divorce has passed, the transitional person was viewed less favorably and fulfilled fewer immediate needs and the relationship disintegrated."

It is also common for divorcing parents to engage in a flurry of social relationships. These relationships may serve the purpose of dispelling loneliness or convincing the divorcing parent that they are attractive. By the end of the first year, both men and women tend to become dissatisfied with transitory relationships and seek sustained relationships.

Children's Responses to New Relationships

Susan Richardson, a divorcee with a three-and-a-half-year-old, met a man named Nick two years after her separation. Since he was someone with whom she thought she would have an enduring relationship, they began living together soon after her divorce.

> ... *Tom, my son, showed a lot of anger toward Nick. I felt a lot of manipulation on Tom's part, a lot of trying to get my attention, to get my loyalty—like he was asking himself how much was he going to lose because of this guy.*
>
> *Tom is generally outgoing and cooperative, but at first he would throw all of his toys off the shelf, turn over his dinner plates, knock over plants, and have other accidents like that. He seemed angry at me for not living with his father and being with someone else.*

A parent's relationship with a new person threatens the preschool child's wish to reconstitute the family. Children may react with hostility or fear to the newcomer, who is, in one sense, taking the parent away from the child and disrupting the child's sense of closeness and security with him or her. Competitive feelings emerge. As Susan says, Tom was "asking himself how much he was going to lose because of this guy." Furthermore, there may be issues of divided loyalty with the other parent, especially if that parent criticizes or questions the child about the new relationship.

As Tom and Nick began to get to know each other, Tom warmed up:

> ... *One morning Tom came into the bedroom and wanted to crawl into bed beside me. Nick encouraged him to come between us. Tom looked suspicious, and Nick just patted the bed, very invitingly. So Tom went over and got in the middle. Nick tucked him in. The three of us were packed in like sardines.*

The newcomer enters a complex web of family relationships. There are frequent opportunities for competition, sometimes initiated by the child, sometimes by the parent who yearns for the luxury of time to get to know the new person and who feels self-absorbed in the relationship. Such fantasies, however, remain elusive for most divorced parents. Time must be scheduled; interruptions are frequent and often uncontrollable—such as a sick child or a child-care arrangement falling through. Divorced parents wish they were free of responsibilities (perhaps even childless) and at the same time they know that if this relationship is going to last, the children must be accepted. Nick was able to accept Susan and Tom—mother and son—and established intimacy with both of them.

If the relationships leads to sex, as it did for Susan, complicated issues arise. Should my child (or others) know? Should my child see us in bed together? What messages is this giving? Susan, however, trusted Nick enough to let the relationship move to this stage.

The Ending of a Relationship

After a few months, this relationship ended:

> • • • *Unfortunately Nick and I broke up. I didn't know how to handle that. Tom has questions about Nick from time to time such as "When will we see Nick?" or "Can Nick come to my birthday party?" The questions decrease as time goes on. It's been three months since we split up. I've had a lot of difficulty responding to all this.*

If the new relationship ends, the divorced parent is thrown back into a state of loss.

> • • • *When I got divorced, I felt angry at my ex-husband, but when Nick and I split, I felt sad. Like a bubble had burst.*

Despite his initial reserve, Tom had grown close to Nick, so the ending of this relationship was particularly hard for both Tom and Susan. As with divorce, the preschool child cannot help but think that he or she did something to cause the split.

Robert Weiss contends that there are critical differences between the breakup of a marriage and the breakup of a new relationship. Divorcing parents generally remain connected because of their mutual children, but this is not true with a new relationship. "When a new figure leaves, the parent and the children are together in their feeling of loss." Secondly, such an ending doesn't usually necessitate logistical changes the way a divorce does: a change in status, moving, finding new friends, perhaps returning to work. When Nick and Susan stopped seeing each other, the family's routines did not change.

A Danger: Leaning on the Child

Susan states:

> • • • *My first response was to do what I do with my girl friends—to tell Tom everything that happened. Once I did talk to him about Nick and then I sat there waiting. I began to ask myself, "How come I'm waiting?" Tom was acting muddled. He was sort of checking me out. At that point, I told him, "I want to be alone right now." I went up to my room. I hugged my pillow, and I thought, This is what I want right now. I want*

> *somebody to hug me. I realized that I had wanted Tom to hug*
> *me and take care of me.*
>
>   *Sometimes I've been shocked by what I wanted from Tom.*
> *I have felt myself wanting to unburden all this emotion. But*
> *this is forcing roles and behavior on him that are not appropriate*
> *for an almost-four-year-old.*

At one end of the spectrum of the single-parent/child relationship is the potential for conflict; on the other end is one of closeness. For some parents, closeness means companionship; for others there is a tendency for the parent to lean on the child. Those parents with few other sources of support are more likely to depend on their children. According to Wallerstein and Kelly, "At both younger and older ages, [some children] were pressed into being advisors, practical helpers, buffers against loneliness and despair, replacement for other adults—in other words, parents for their own parents." While closeness is positive for the parent and child, as Susan has clearly realized, the preschool child cannot be responsible for the emotional well-being of the parent. That is a responsibility beyond the child's years.

SOLUTIONS

When to Introduce the Child to a New Relationship

Susan has come to a new conclusion about when to introduce Tom to the men she dates:

> **. . .** *I'm finding that the period of time between when I meet a*
> *man and when I want to introduce him to my child is length-*
> *ening.*
>
>   *I don't want Tom to have a concept that men in relationships*
> *with women just come and go, in and out of your life. I want*
> *Tom to see men as my friends.*

Developing the New Adult/Child Relationship

Once the child is introduced, the parent should remain in charge of the child/new-person relationship. The single parent will do better to set limits, making it clear that the primary relationship is (at least initially) between the parent and new person. If the friend invites the child somewhere (such as the zoo), the parent can say, "She (or he) is doing this because she's *my* friend."

It is better to start a new relationship between the child and the new person without grandiose expectations about what this person can mean to the child. If he or she is seen as compensating for all the shortcomings of the former spouse, disappointment is likely to ensue. By allowing the relationship between the child and the new person to take its own time, it can develop in a more relaxed way. It is also important to spend time alone with your child, knowing that feelings of competition are inevitable.

After time has passed and the relationship has proved to be relatively durable, many parents such as Susan let the child form his or her *own* relationship with the new person. At that time, parents can discuss the implications with the new person, addressing and trying to agree on some issues: "Will you continue to have a relationship with my child even if we break up?" "Could he call you occasionally? Write you?" As with prenuptial agreements, if the boundaries are agreed upon in advance, everyone involved is more likely to share similar expectations.

Q *I'm a new stepparent and it hasn't been easy. What makes it hard? How can it get better?*

Judith Canton had been divorced for ten years when she met Brad. He had custody of his children, Margaret, seven, and Philip, five:

• • • *I knew from the beginning that I liked Brad and maybe could even love him. But his children were not very nice to me. The first time I came to their house, they told me, "Our dad threw our mother out the window and his last girl friend, too. You'd better be careful because he'll probably throw you out." I had no children and most of my friends didn't either, so I really didn't know how to react to what these kids said.*

Soon after that, I went home to visit my family and told my sister, "I've met a wonderful man, but I'll probably stop dating him because he has children." She was horrified and said, "You're one of six children yourself. You love your nieces and nephews. Go back and give it a try."

I was looking for a relationship, but not for children. Brad had made it clear that his children were part of the package.

Without intending to, Judith had chosen a parent to fall in love with. Brad was a full-time parent even on weekends. Margaret and Philip had to be included in plans; what they wanted for dinner or which movie they wanted to see had to be considered. Ideally, courtship is a time to explore each other's goals and values, but when children are omnipresent there is little time for each other. Sometimes Judith longed for "life again as an unattached woman," when everything seemed less complicated.

Remarriage

A year later, however, she and Brad decided to get married. Judith found herself an instant parent and the children had a new adult in their lives. The changes came quickly and no one was quite prepared for them.

According to Brad, he and his children had been a well-functioning single-parent household:

> ▪ ▪ ▪ *I hired a housekeeper to look after the house and be with them after school, but emotionally I was the parent. The kids had their responsibilities. Every afternoon, they called my office and checked in. On weekends, the children and I did errands and planned something fun just for the three of us.*

When Judith and Brad married, household routines were reorganized to accommodate Judith's work schedule. Space was rearranged; part of the family room was turned into her sewing area.

But most important, the remarriage meant dramatic changes for the children. Margaret and Philip were used to being quite self-sufficient. They liked feeling they had a part in the day-to-day running of the house. Like many children whose parents remarry, they felt a loss of status and responsibility with the addition of another adult.

Children endure other losses when a parent remarries. Because the children have to share that parent, they usually experience a loss of intimacy. In addition, they also have to give up the fantasy that their parents might get together again. Although remarriage is a time of excitement and jubilation for adults, it can bring on unhappiness in children and marked behavioral changes even when they like their new stepparent.

Experts in the field remind stepparents that remarriage is a time of transition for children and adults and that a period of disequilibrium is to be expected. Eventually stability can be achieved again.

Defining Roles

Judith told Brad that she was not going to become a suburban housewife just because she had married. She said, "These are your children and your responsibility." She intended to continue her career, and Brad supported her decision.

It was clear to Judith that she did not want to replace the children's own mother. But Judith suspected that Brad harbored other expectations:

> ▪ ▪ ▪ *He's more of a traditionalist than I. Even though he is for my working, I think he really wants me to give to the children what they didn't get from their own mother. She had neglected*

them even when she lived with them. Brad knew how much their mother had hurt them, especially Philip, who was about three when his mother moved out.

Professionals who work with stepfamilies say that stepparents who imagine themselves replacing the nonresident parent are more likely to have problems. There are ex-spouses, but there are never ex-parents. Even a parent who dies or disappears lives on in the child's memory and retains a place in his or her life. There was no doubt that Margaret's and Philip's mother was important to them. They looked forward to seeing her, albeit infrequently; they gave her presents on Mother's Day.

Judith's desire not to assume a parenting role extended to disciplining the children:

▪ ▪ ▪ *From the beginning, I told Brad, "I will be married to you, but I don't want to do any disciplining." He said that was not very practical but that he would try to accommodate me.*

In fact, most professionals recommend that at first the custodial parent take primary responsibility for discipline. If stepparents try to take over too soon, they are perceived as intruders, and the stepchildren become resentful. As in most families, whether intact or not, effective discipline is based on a relationship between a parent and a child.

There are many ways for stepparents and stepchildren to form a bond. For example, they can work on a project together or share a special activity. One stepmother taught her stepchildren how to cook Mexican food. With younger children, participating in their play is one avenue (see the section on play, pages 61–78). A stepfather of a four-year-old had a part in the child's bedtime ritual: he would read what he called the "warm-up" story, but then the child's own mother would read the final story and tuck the child into bed. The goal is not to make the child love you but to let the child get to know you.

But being an adult friend is different than being a peer friend. At times, adults do have to assert their authority; in fact, children expect that adults will guide them and keep them safe.

Gradually, Judith assumed more parental responsibility:

▪ ▪ ▪ *Not too long after we were married, Brad had to go on a business trip for fifteen days. He was traveling abroad where he was out of reach by phone. I was really on my own with the children. He prepared a book for me, listing the names and phone numbers of the childrens' friends, doctors, teachers. He drew maps of how to get to these places. He wrote out all the rules around doing homework, TV, and bedtime. I was so terrified of being left with the children that the only way I could survive was with this book.*

Brad's absence was very hard on all of us. One night Philip was really giving me a hard time, resisting anything I asked. His father had written in the book that he was to empty the dishwasher but Philip refused. His attitude was, "You're not my parent, you can't make me do it." I didn't plan to say this, it just came out: "I'm not your parent, but you still need to do your job." And I reminded him that his father wanted him to do it. That seemed to help, but he was not very cooperative until his father came home again.

In her study of remarried families, sociologist Lucille Duberman found that most problems for the new couple centered on child-rearing. The parent who has grown up with the children has had the time to establish family rules and to work out a discipline style. But after a remarriage, stepparents are plunged into issues around parenting, and immediate decisions must be made. In fact, developing child-rearing strategies takes time, but most stepfamilies aren't prepared for the stage of fumbling and experimentation.

The Stepfamily Association of America sees working out these issues around child-rearing as a central task for remarried families. This process can begin even before the marriage because couples must make decisions about money (how much to spend on each child), household routines (mealtimes, bedtimes), and discipline. The association recommends that rules be established for the household that will apply to all children whether they live there or only visit.

Jerry Harrison, mother of a four-year-old and a seven-year-old, has just begun to live with Jeff, the father of two young adults who live elsewhere. She describes how they discipline:

. . . *I'm still the primary disciplinarian. Jeff watches me and follows my lead. But he isn't afraid to step in if I'm not around. Sometimes I've disagreed with the way he's handled things, so I tell him later in private.*

Even when stepparents share discipline, they still may feel protective of their own children. The Perrys are both stepparents; each has custody of two children from a previous marriage. Madeleine Perry admits:

. . . *When my husband reprimands one of my children, I recoil. I know he reacts like this when I scold his children. Although we*

respect each other's right to discipline, we also respect each
other's right to recoil as the biological parent of the child. But
we try to keep our recoil reactions to ourselves.

Stepfamilies also find it reasssuring to know that families who have never
experienced divorce have problems with discipline, too.

Some experts contend that the quality of the parent-child relationship in
the stepfamily is different than in never-divorced families; others disagree.
Santrock and Sitterle, psychologists at the University of Dallas, compared
parent-child relationships in sixty-nine remarried families and intact families who had children seven to eleven years old living with them. Their
sample was matched on income, age, and educational level of the parents.
The research was carefully designed to obtain multiple measures of the
quality of the relationships. The children and adults were interviewed
and filled out a scale assessing the parents' emotional and physical availability in matters ranging from discipline to celebrating special occasions.
Observations were made in a laboratory of how the children and their
parents (biological and stepparents) interacted around two tasks; teachers
also rated the children's adjustment in school. Here are their major
findings:

- Remarried fathers and intact fathers were alike in their interactions and
  involvement with their children. The children of the remarried fathers
  reported that these men were very sensitive to their emotional needs.
- Stepmothers were less involved than intact mothers; the children's reports
  concurred.
- The adults described different patterns in stepmother and stepfather families: remarried mothers were more involved with their children than
  remarried fathers were; stepmothers were more involved than stepfathers
  were.

Their conclusion is that remarried parents can maintain high levels of
involvement with their children, but that stepparents tend to be less involved with their stepchildren than the biological parents are.

Redefining the Family
Judith says:

· · ·   *A stepfamily is like an arranged marriage. In both cases, you're*
        supposed to act like a family, like you really belong together,
        but in fact you really don't know how to.

Judith is right, but the myth prevails that the stepfamily should be a nuclear family. Members of stepfamilies often hold onto this expectation because the nuclear family is known—it may have been what they grew up in as children; it was what they created in a previous marriage; it is recognized by society. For example, most school forms have only enough space for the names of two parents; children are supposed to make only one card for Mother's or Father's Day. What is the child to do who has two biological parents and two stepparents?

But stepfamilies are different from nuclear families in fundamental ways. Many people think that a stepfamily and a nuclear family are similar because they both contain an adult couple. In *Stepfamilies: A Guide to Working With Stepparents and Stepchildren,* Emily and John Visher, professionals who are also stepparents, describe what makes a stepfamily distinct:

- There is a biological parent elsewhere (unless that parent has died).
- Virtually all members have recently sustained a primary relationship loss.
- The relationship between one adult (the biological parent) and their children predates the new marriage.
- Children are members in more than one household.
- One adult (stepparent) is not legally related to a child (stepchild).

In fact there are more similarities in the family structure between stepfamilies and single-parent families.

The emotional conflicts in a stepfamily often arise from the ties to the ex-spouse, the child's other biological parent. This creates what Lillian Messinger calls "permeable boundaries." There is no cultural norm for defining where the stepfamily begins and ends, and this often causes difficulty for stepfamilies. Does the family include all parents, as well as grandparents, cousins, aunts, and uncles? Does it only refer to the group that lives together, excluding stepchildren who visit periodically?

The boundary issue has been resolved in Judith's stepfamily; the children visit their mother and her relatives during vacation. But in Jerry Harrison's family the issue is still painful. Jerry's former in-laws (her ex-husband's parents) refuse to speak to her. Whenever the children are with her, they have no contact with their paternal grandparents.

In many stepfamilies, the question of boundaries comes up around birthdays, teacher conferences, and other activities that involve children and their parents. Jerry says:

. . . *My ex-husband is still so angry and upset that he didn't want Jeff at my son Peter's birthday party. He said I had to choose between his being there or Jeff's being there. I felt bad, but I thought that Peter would really want his father at his party. So Jeff worked behind the scenes. He made the pirate flag and helped decorate the house. Peter knew and appreciated all that Jeff did. But then Jeff had to leave the house before the guests arrived.*

What seems to work best for most stepfamilies is to see the children as members of two family units. It is better if all members of the stepfamily accept and keep the boundaries open to both old and new family ties. Attempting to shut out these relationships is to deny reality. Research on remarried families shows that if a child has a satisfactory amount of contact with the noncustodial parent, his or her adjustment in the stepfamily is better. Work with children of divorce has also found that the children fare better when they have a stable, loving relationship with both parents.

The message for stepfamilies is clear: children need contact with both biological parents. If the two parents can put aside or attempt to resolve constructively old issues, children are freed from conflicts in loyalty and can adjust to the new arrangements.

The Children's Perspective

Just as stepparents cannot be expected to love their stepchildren instantly, neither can stepchildren be expected to love their new stepparents right away. Some children insulate themselves from the fear of another loss when a new adult enters the scene; they become hostile and rejecting. This reaction was evident in Margaret and Philip's threat to Judith ("you'll get thrown out the window"). At the same time, the children were also protecting their relationship with their father. Other children seem so eager to be loved by an adult that they are overly demanding of the stepparent's attention and affection. In response, some stepparents withdraw, leaving the child with yet another loss. The best strategy for both stepparents and stepchildren is to give the relationship time to evolve.

At the time of remarriage, children's primary concern is, "Where do I belong?" The familiar givens are no longer there. The oldest child may no longer be that; the only child may have stepsiblings; a parent's attention may be divided among more children. Seven-year-old Louisa, Jerry's daughter, questioned her mother:

• • • *"Who do you love more—me or Peter [her younger brother]?" Then the questions escalated. "Who do you love more? Jeffrey or me?" Then the big question—"Who do you love more, Jeffrey or Daddy?" I realized that she was trying to find her place in this tangle of relationships.*

Her brother Peter asked "where do I belong" in another way. He wanted to know what he should call Jeffrey because "he's not my daddy." He decided to call him a friend. Following Peter's lead, Jeffrey began to introduce both children as his friends.

Deciding on a label can be difficult. Sometimes stepparents are called by their first name, or "my other daddy." Older children often go to lengths to avoid calling them anything. Many people dislike the prefix "step," which in Old English means bereaved or orphaned; it came into usage at a time when a parent's death (not a divorce) led to remarriage of the surviving parent. Professionals, too, struggle over terms; "blended," "reconstituted," and "reconstructed" are sometimes used, but stepfamily remains the most common.

The age of the stepchildren is a factor in determining the stepparent/stepchild relationship. Generally, the younger the child, the more forgiving and open. For the preschooler, continuity in the parenting relationships is essential. If there is a sustained relationship, young children can endure the disequilibrium and often accept a new parental figure. Adolescents tend to have the hardest time accepting a stepparent. In their search for identity, they want to break away from the family, not reintegrate. The sexual relationship between the biological parent and stepparent also may add to the teenager's discomfort in the new family.

Stepparents need to keep a long perspective. The relationships with stepchildren, while perhaps difficult at first, can evolve into satisfying friendships in the future.

Stepsiblings

When parents remarry, children may suddenly find a new set of siblings thrust upon them. New bonds must be formed, even if the stepchildren don't like each other very much. Furthermore, children feel pushed aside as their biological parent begins relating to stepchildren. As one five-year-old laments, "Here's my dad playing with these other kids on weekends and I don't have enough time with him."

"Turf" issues often surface between stepsiblings. Who has the bigger bedroom or who gets to choose TV shows? Generally it works best if stepchildren have their own space; even children who visit only on weekends can have a drawer set aside for their belongings. Jealousies arise; usually stepchildren feel their stepparent favors his or her biological children. They may feel envious when stepsiblings go to visit another parent and return home with new possessions or stories of the fun times they had.

The relationship between stepsiblings needs time to develop, but there is the possibility that a close bond will form. Most children enjoy being with other children and having stepsiblings around the same age may mean that a child has more playmates. And all siblings, whether stepsiblings or not, will fight and play one parent against another. As Ray Perry says:

> ■ ■ ■ *My stepchildren and children would argue: "This is my fork," "No, it's not." But once they went outside, they would defend each other to the end. Often, one of my stepchildren and one of my children would pair off and play together; that would cut down on the usual sibling rivalry between the natural brothers and sisters.*

Most stepsiblings relate well to each other. In fact, spending more time together seems to improve the likelihood of their getting along. One study found that when both sets of children lived in the same household, their relations tended to be better than if they lived apart.

SOLUTIONS

Maintaining Strong Relationships

Mental health professionals and parents agree that a cohesive relationship between husband and wife is essential to any healthy family. But that's even more necessary in stepfamilies. As the Vishers say:

> In stepfamilies there are more strains than in most intact families, and as a result, the alliance or coalition between the couple seems particularly important and also more difficult to achieve and maintain.

Stepparents need strength and endurance to work through their problems and build relationships among family members. When the couple is convinced that their own relationship is worthwhile, it is easier for them to sustain their patience and optimism in the face of difficulties.

For stepchildren, several factors seem to facilitate adjustment: the quality of their relationship with the custodial parent and the quality of their relationship with the noncustodial parent. Children need access to both parents and to other sources of support in the extended family. Recent studies show that in spite of the difficulties involved in stepfamilies, most stepchildren adjust well. Two national surveys reported no social or psychological differences in high school students from stepfamilies and intact families.

Changing Expectations

In each family, particular factors may contribute to the children's adjustment. Common among them is revising expectations to be more realistic. Judith says:

• • •   *I see myself as a nurturing, caring adult in the children's lives. I want to teach them to be as good as they can be. From that perspective, I'm able to say, "This is the kind of food you should eat, this is how you should treat your brother or sister." It's ironic that in the beginning I was most afraid of having to teach the children—what would I teach them? Now I realize that my values and standards are worth passing on to them.*

At first I was so reluctant to show disapproval if they did something I didn't like. I was trying hard not to be the wicked stepmother, so I just kept quiet. I developed stomach pains I was so tense. But I felt resentful and I'm sure they could feel it. Now I take a part in disciplining.

My advice to other stepparents is don't be so hard on yourself and don't have unrealistic expectations. I'm lucky that the children are as articulate and as nice as they are and that Brad is as good a father as he is. Sometimes I'm sorry that I'm not the children's mother. I am important to them, but I know it's not the primary relationship for them. But I think I can shape the kind of people they will become.

Madeleine Perry, mother and stepmother, says that the most important task in bringing their family together was redefining her role. She had wanted to be Supermom, raising a large family of young children.

• • •   *At first I treated my stepchildren better than my own. If they wanted a special meal, I made it; if they wanted a separate bedroom, we moved the other children around. I was acting out of guilt, thinking I had to prove I could love them. I was feeling resentful, yet I had brought that on myself. I finally realized that everyone would be better off if I stopped hovering and smothering.*

When Madeleine backed off, the relationship with her stepchildren improved.

• • •   *I had been treating them like guests when they needed to be treated like normal kids. At dinner now, if they say, "I don't like this," I say, "Well, that's what we're having."*

Like many stepparents, Madeleine had to learn that she couldn't force a bond between herself and her stepchildren. It evolved over time, as she showed that she cared about them.

CONCLUSIONS

Seventy to seventy-five percent of divorced people remarry, making more than 25 million stepparents and 15 million children who live with remarried parents. It's estimated that 1,300 new stepfamilies are formed every day, and that by 1990, 25 to 35 percent of all children will be members of a stepfamily. These statistics indicate that family reorganizations are increasingly common for many children.

What do parents and children gain from being members of a stepfamily? Like any potentially stressful situation, this one presents opportunities for growth and learning. Adults can develop a strong bond as a couple and take satisfaction in having solved problems together. Ray Perry, a stepparent for eighteen years, says:

> ▪ ▪ ▪ *There isn't anything that could break up this marriage. It would have already happened. We can survive anything and that's a very secure feeling.*

Stepchildren have the opportunity to learn to be flexible, to be exposed to different ways of doing things, and to have a variety of role models. They learn to negotiate complex human relationships and to find strength in themselves and others. And as children who have suffered the pain of family disruption and loss, stepchildren can have the example of a loving, caring relationship between two adults who are committed to building a family.

SIX

Family Work

Housework

Q *How can my husband and I divide up housekeeping chores so that we both feel it's fair?*

At a corporate work/family seminar, Mary Beth Andrews introduced the issue she had been struggling with:

. . . *My husband and I have a problem figuring out who will be responsible for certain household chores. Every time I figure out a plan, it works for about half a day. I'm not getting too far with this problem.*

Note that she says, "I figure out a plan." I pointed out Mary Beth's use of the word "I," asking the other women participants if they, too, were in charge of the family work. Not surprisingly, they were. Research confirms this fact. Studies in which women and men keep time diaries, noting exactly what they do over several days, reveal that women, whether employed or not, spend more time cleaning, doing the laundry, and shopping than men do. In addition, they administrate—they tend to make the grocery lists, know when laundry detergent is running low, and when the windows need cleaning or repair. Furthermore, they take responsibility for revising the division of labor, and in Mary Beth's case, attempting to correct an inequity.

Why Don't Men Participate More?

Research reveals that couples negotiate the division of family work primarily on the basis of each spouse's relative economic power. The more equal the husband's and wife's earning power, the more likely the husband is to share in the family work. Conversely, the greater the discrepancy, the less likely he is to participate.

Studies have also shown that couples who share household chores before they have children settle into more traditional roles once the first child is born, particularly if the wife leaves her job to care for the child.

The power relationship, however, is also affected by the family's perceptions, beliefs, and value system. If both the husband and wife believe that they should share, then they usually work at doing so. Research indicates that the woman's commitment to a more equitable division usually makes the critical difference in what happens. If she is convinced that a man should clean the bathroom, cook, and vacuum, then chances are he will perform these tasks.

Men's and women's perceptions of the division of labor in their homes do not always reflect reality. Yogev and Brett from Northwestern University asked couples if their spouse did "more than his or her share" and compared the perceptions with the actual time spent on chores. They found that two husbands spending the same number of hours on family chores could be seen as doing "more than" or "less than" their share. Not unexpectedly, the couple's satisfaction with their marriage was strongly linked to a perception that the spouse took on more responsibility.

Like many research findings, this is a chicken-and-egg dilemma. The study does not indicate which comes first, the perception of doing more family work or marital satisfaction. The same dilemma exists for a finding of ours in the Bank Street research: that stress-related health problems are associated with a perception of one's spouse not doing a "fair share." We have found that men who felt their wives were not doing their share of housework were more likely to have more psychosomatic symptoms such as back problems, headaches, racing or pounding hearts. For women, the feeling that their husbands were not helping enough with child care was likewise predictive of more psychosomatic symptoms.

Sexual Stereotyping

Men are quick to argue that women circumscribe their definition of family work. As one man said:

■ ■ ■ *Women don't include balancing the checkbook, raking the leaves, repairing the gutter, or taking the car for repairs. When women think of family work, they think of their jobs—like cleaning up after dinner.*

This comment depicts the stereotypical division of labor: women are responsible for the caretaking roles—feeding, nurturing, cleaning up— while men tend to take on the physical or financial tasks. The women's movement notwithstanding, these traditional roles have been slow to change.

A major difference between "men's" and "women's" work is that women's jobs must be repeated daily; men's work—such as fixing the roof or mowing the lawn—is more sporadic. Using an expanded definition of family work to include tasks usually done by men often surprises couples by decreasing the perceived disparity between time and effort men and women devote to family work—although the women's share still tends to remain larger.

Changing Roles

A favorite topic for work and family life researchers is to trace how the increasing number of mothers in the labor force has affected men's domestic responsibility. Joseph Pleck of Wheaton College has followed this phenomenon for the past decade. He concludes that while in absolute terms, women do more family work, men with working wives are beginning to do more. On average, men spend 2.6 hours a day on family work. The proportional division of labor has shifted more dramatically. Whereas men used to contribute approximately 20 percent of household work, this figure has risen recently to 30 percent, that is, men are doing more and women are doing less. Women, particularly those with jobs, have decreased the amount of time they spend cleaning the house or preparing food, but not the amount of time they spend caring for their children.

Although many women have lowered their housekeeping standards, they often criticize themselves harshly for doing so. At a seminar for employees of a metropolitan hospital, one woman confessed that she had "the dirtiest house in the world." I asked how many of the other one hundred attendees also qualified for the dirtiest house award. A majority raised their hands—to the amazement and delight of the first woman.

Giving up the perfect house generally involves a symbolic rejection of one's mother: "Our house was always clean. I never saw a dustball until I started housekeeping myself. When my house is a mess, I feel I'm degrading all the values that were important to my mother."

Why Do Women Remain in Charge?

Women at our seminars often state that household responsibility has been a traditional source of power and authority for them. Some are loath to give it up when there is still not that much access to comparable sources of authority outside the home.

By and large, women have been raised to take responsibility for family work. Mothers are more likely to tell a daughter than a son, "When you made a sandwich, you left crumbs all over the counter," and then remind her to clean up. Carol Gilligan from Harvard University has also found that girls are raised to be more aware of the interpersonal aspect of life, more cognizant of other's needs than boys are.

Thus many women both want and do not want to share family work, and as a result say to men: "Do it, but do it my way." How many men have been told that the dishes they washed were not done well or that they should have broken the lettuce into smaller pieces for the salad? At one seminar, a group of Texas women asked if men could see as well as women:

> ▪ ▪ ▪ *How come they never notice that the stove is greasy or that there are chocolate smudges on the kitchen cabinets or that the floor under the sink is littered with parsley and breadcrumbs?*

At this point in seminars, men typically speak out:

> ▪ ▪ ▪ *She says she wants me to help but every time I do something, it's wrong. I finally quit. Why should I listen to someone telling me how to chop carrots? What difference does it make how they're cut?*

One woman said:

> ▪ ▪ ▪ *When I finally stopped telling my husband what to do and how to do it, things changed. No longer was he "helping me." We were both in there together, doing what had to get done.*

Family Games

When a disagreement between a couple cannot be resolved directly, both parties may settle into complicated family games (or "wars"). This is what has happened in Mary Beth Andrews' family:

> ▪ ▪ ▪ *When Rob didn't do the dishes, I'd just do them myself while telling him, "You were supposed to do the dishes."*

We asked Mary Beth what Rob was willing to do.

> ▪ ▪ ▪ *Eat, drink, watch television. He does do the laundry because he always did his own laundry before we were married.*
>   *One thing he does that really drives me crazy is to take off his socks and leave them on the floor on my side of the bed. I'd just throw them back on his side of the room. Finally I found a better tactic. I pick up the dirty socks and throw them back in the drawer with his clean socks so he can't figure out which socks are clean or dirty. That way it becomes his problem, not my problem.*

Mary Beth notes that Rob appears to take pleasure in driving her crazy. "Sometimes," she says, "I think he's begging me to yell at him."

This is a common pattern among husbands and wives, particularly when one is unable to express negative feelings directly. If Rob has had a hard day or feels guilty about something he has done, he prods his wife into an outburst. Thus, she both expresses the negative feeling he was harboring and, with her outburst, punishes him for having bad feelings.

When this pattern occurs, the power relationship becomes skewed. Mary Beth is clearly in charge. She says, "When *I* figure out a plan." She has become a mother to Rob: powerful, simultaneously controlling and punishing. Rob leaves the dirty dishes cluttering the sink; his dirty socks on her side of the bedroom floor—messes for the mother (his wife) to clean up.

SOLUTIONS

Deciding What Works

In numerous families, a traditional division of labor works well. The partners have made an agreement, spoken or unspoken. In families like the Andrews, one partner wants to change, the other does not. What is the case in your family? Is the division you now have tolerable or intolerable? If one or both of you want to change, the following solutions have proved successful.

Stop Playing the Family Game

The only way the cycle in the Andrews family can be broken is for Mary Beth or Rob to decide to stop tricking each other and to refuse to get drawn into predictable fights in which Rob provokes and Mary Beth retaliates and punishes.

Making this decision is much easier than living up to it; a family pattern has endured because it has fulfilled each spouse's needs. A successful attempt must be a joint undertaking. Because the impetus will probably come from Mary Beth (she's more dissatisfied), she might say something like, "The way I've been behaving with you is bothering me and I'd like to try to change it, but I'll need your help." In this way, she puts the onus on herself rather than slipping into the familiar pattern of accusing Rob.

Discussing the old scenarios and agreeing upon substitute behaviors is helpful. "What would be a constructive reaction if you don't do the dishes?" or "How can I explain how I feel without making you angry?" During this discussion, listen and, rather than defend or attack, reflect your spouse's feelings back to him or her. "You feel angry when I put the dirty socks in your drawer." Then discuss alternative ways until you find a solution agreeable to both.

Such solutions are initially short-lived. Old patterns take a long time to change. When the new plan does not work the cycle of anger, blaming, protecting and fighting is easily resumed. Particularly at first, the life span of a solution will probably be a day to a few weeks at most. When a plan begins to disintegrate, the couple should talk about what didn't work, why one of them "set the trap," the other "fell in." Afterward, they can begin to devise a new plan.

Making a List of Who Does What

As part of parenting seminars we often conduct informal experiments: Men and women keep track of their chores for a day and they find, to their surprise, that their view of the distribution of family work is distorted. One woman said, "I guessed that my husband did very little, but when we wrote everything down, I saw he was doing much more than I had been giving him credit for." A man said, "I thought I was doing fifty/fifty but I realized it was more like thirty/seventy."

This technique is useful when viewed as a genuine learning experience rather than a vehicle for one spouse to scold the other: "I told you so."

Negotiating a New Trade-Off

One couple made a list of family jobs, rated them on a scale of disagreeable to agreeable, and then paired them. For example, since they both disliked cleaning the bathroom and balancing the checkbook, these tasks were paired. They then alternated having first choice at each of the paired tasks.

Renegotiating the Sexual Division of Labor

Sexual stereotypes are hard to dislodge. The cultural view that liberation contradicts femininity is deep and pervasive. But, as many have found, learning that women can change tires or that men can cook can be exciting. Do not assume that you dislike certain things simply because you have never tried them.

Giving Up Perfection

Many adults have survived the pressure of too much to do and not enough time by relinquishing their standards of perfection. As one mother of two young children said, "In my house you used to be able to eat off the floor, but then I realized, who'd want to? A clean house is less important than spending time with my children or my husband."

The mother of a five-year-old says:

> . . . *I never asked my husband if he wanted the house spic-and-span—I just always thought it was important to him. Finally I asked and it turned out he doesn't care. I was taking my own*

expectation and putting his name on it. He'd rather we spend time together.

Getting Help

If they can afford it, many families get help with housework: "I hired a cleaning person and it's worth every cent in terms of reducing my anxiety." Another parent says, "I don't pay much for help. I use neighborhood teenagers to cut the grass, rake the leaves, and wash the windows."

One mother admitted how hard it was to ask for help:

. . . *I had to prove I could do a good job on my house. If I got someone else to do it, I was a failure. I saw myself as unable to cope on my own. I have now learned to tell my husband I need his help and to let him do it his own way. It's been a reeducation for me.*

Q *How much can children be expected to help around the house?*

> Mother: Please pick up your toys.
>   Child: I'm too tired.
>
> or
>
> Father: It's your turn to set the table.
>   Child: Later. I'm doing something now.
>
> or
>
> Mother: Put all of the cereal boxes away after you take them out.
>   Child: I can't reach the shelf.
>
> or
>
> Father: Help me put away the tools after we worked together.
>   Child: It's too hard.

Why Do These Conflicts Occur?

Children's attention span is shorter than ours. A task that seems manageable to us can seem overwhelming to them. Furthermore, it is usually easier for us to set the table or feed the dog than argue about who should be doing what. In addition, the way children perform their chores may leave something to be desired:

. . . *When Betsy feeds the dog, she leaves a trail of dog food all over the kitchen. It takes me more time to clean up after she's done it than to do it myself.*

We may also harbor an uncertainty about how much to expect of young children:

. . . *When Joey is falling apart before dinner, I feel it's my job to take care of him, so I'll pick up his toys or set the table, even though he can do these things all by himself.*

Sometimes children refuse to help because they really don't want to— they'd rather be doing something else. A "No, I can't" may also express their autonomy, their desire to be a separate, independent person.

Playing One Parent Off against the Other

Parents may have different ideas about children's participation in family work. If one parent thinks that children develop character from helping ("I always worked hard when I was little") while the other feels they are too young to do much, the children can become adept at setting off battles: for example, saying to the father, "Mom is making me feed the dog but the smell of the dog's food makes me sick."

The Effects of Children's Participation

Little is known about the effect of children's participation in household work in our culture; however, cross-cultural studies indicate that when children perform tasks that contribute to the family's welfare, they learn to be responsible and develop a sense of competence.

Different Circumstances

Lois Hoffman from the University of Michigan has found that when mothers enter the labor force, children are, in general, expected to help more around the house. The same has been found for children living in single-parent households. As a new single parent says:

. . . *One thing I've noticed that I'm really happy about: my kids are helping so much now. They never did beans around this place before. Amanda [age four] makes her bed every day. She and Lucy [age six] take turns letting the dog in and taking out the garbage. They'll both sit down and shell peas or husk corn for dinner.*

The difference in these families can be attributed to the parent's visible need for help as well as to the parent's feeling of legitimacy in asking the children to contribute. How parents feel in asking children to participate makes a difference in children's level of cooperation.

SOLUTIONS

Considering the Abilities of the Children

Developmental capacity is the primary consideration when including the children. A two-year-old can help pick up toys but needs adult supervision; a five-year-old can be more responsible.

There are several principles to keep in mind:

Focus the child's attention on the task before it is time to begin. Say, "When we finish dinner, you can carry your plate to the sink."

Give the child a manageable task. A young child confronted with an entire room in shambles (even though she may be responsible for the mess), will feel overwhelmed. Give the child a discrete task: "You pick up the red blocks, I'll pick up the blue ones."

Let children help shape the family division of labor. In a family meeting, a mother in New Jersey draws a floor plan of the house on the kitchen blackboard. The responsibilities are divided up room by room. The person in charge of a particular room writes his or her name in the room on the floor plan. The jobs are shifted every three weeks. The preschool children take smaller jobs such as picking up or running the Dustbuster. A family in Minnesota makes a weekly job chart listing all tasks, divided into adult jobs and children jobs.

There are many jobs that preschoolers can do. For example:

- mate socks
- sort laundry by whites versus colored
- tear up lettuce for salad
- fill the pepper mill
- wipe up spills
- decorate cookies
- add premeasured ingredients to soups and stews
- turn on the toaster
- pick up their toys
- throw the diapers in the diaper pail
- put mail in the mailbox

Avoiding Criticism

If you assume the role of judge you place your children in an inferior and demeaning position. Offering positive suggestions is different from criticizing. If you do not like the way a child has picked up the living room, saying, "What a mess" elicits less cooperation than saying, "I always put the magazines next to the couch, so I can read them. Could you please find them and put them here?" One mother found that it was more effective not to punish her child for not doing his job (setting the table) but to say, "As soon as you've set the table, we can have dinner." The language used does make a critical difference. It is better to say *"As soon as* you do your job, *then* I'll be able to do mine," rather than *"If* you don't do what you're supposed to, *then* I won't help you." "If" implies a threat whereas "as soon as" suggests cooperation.

Developing Consequences

All family systems need ongoing evaluation, updating, and change. Build in realistic, relevant consequences (agreed upon by the family) for not doing one's job. For example, one mother never washed her children's clothing unless it was put in the hamper.

Using Job Boards

Marsha Crow, from Angwin, California, has developed an interesting system to minimize conflict. In her words:

• • • *In our family all children two years or older are expected to work around the home. For a long time this seemed to be a constant source of frustration and conflict between my children and myself. The kids complained about having to work ("I'm too tired," "It's too hard," "I don't like it," etc.) and did everything possible to avoid doing it ("I forgot," "I didn't know I was supposed to do it," "It's her turn," "I'll be late for school," etc.).*

I developed a "job board" (the word "job" seems more positive than "chore"). The success of the board is that it assigns jobs, allows for jobs to be changed or rotated whenever desirable (daily, weekly, monthly), is easy for both parent and child to see and understand, motivates simply by its appearance and method of use, and rewards instantaneously.

Next to each child's name, there is a series of nails. On each nail, I hang a disk with the job written on it (water plants, etc.). As soon as a child completes the job, he removes the disk from the nail, and flips it over. The child and the parent can also see at a glance which jobs are done and which are to be completed. Next to the board, each child has a small sheet of paper with the days of the week on it. Each day that the children complete all their assigned work they put up a happy face sticker for that day. At the end of the week they receive a special star if each day has a happy face. When a specified number of stars is reached the child receives a prize out of a grab bag. This is an excellent long-term motivator for work done consistently.

We rotate our jobs each Sunday morning and I let the children take turns choosing which jobs they would like that week (at first I assigned them according to ability, but now that they both know how to do them all I let them choose).

The kids know exactly what they are responsible for without being told, they know when in the day the jobs must be completed, they feel rewarded both short-term and long-term when they see the stickers, and they seldom gripe and complain. And me? I know who should be doing what and if it is completed and find that I hardly ever need to get after them about their work. We are definitely a happier family!

Q *Should children be paid for their work?*

Younger children are usually satisfied to be involved (running the Dustbuster is fun for them) and have yet to develop a sound concept of money and its use. But as children get to be five or six years old, they may begin to ask for money in return for family chores. Families have very different ideas about whether children should get paid and, if so, for doing what.

If you decide that you do want to pay your children, differentiating between regular and special chores is useful. Regular chores are those you believe the children should do to help the family function, like cleaning up their toys, taking their dishes to the sink, and so forth. Special chores go beyond the children's regular responsibilities and might deserve payment, for example, raking leaves or cleaning windows.

Once you identify the tasks, figure out how much you will pay and on what basis (25¢ to vacuum each room with a maximum of $1.50 for one Saturday, for example). If you are not clear about definitions, your children will ask you for money every time they pick up a sock from the floor.

Note, however, that this system perpetuates the idea that everyday, routine tasks (traditionally women's work) are taken for granted, while nonroutine tasks (traditionally men's work) are deemed worthy of pay. To counteract this, you can ensure that paid, nonroutine tasks are not gender-specific, and include such necessities as washing the sinks, washing the mirrors, or polishing the silver.

Some parents hold that as family members children have certain rights (getting an allowance) coupled with certain responsibilities (their jobs). Others sever the allowance from work—children receive allowances simply for living, and jobs must be done because family life depends on their getting done. When children fail in their obligations, they still receive their allowance, but there are other consequences (e.g., "You can't go out, watch television, etc., until you've done your job").

As the children grow older, they will compare themselves with other children: "Betsy gets 50¢ when she helps wash the dog and you only give me 25¢." "Susan gets a bigger allowance than I do." Being clear about your rationale helps in these discussions. You can say, "That's the way Betsy's family handles money. We have a different way."

Giving preschool children some experience in handling their own money is useful: they learn how much things cost and make decisions to purchase or not. In addition, they learn how to save up for desired toys.

Child Care

Q *How can I get my husband to share in the care of our daughter?*

Andrea Bauer says:

▪ ▪ ▪ *My husband, Steve, works very long hours. When he's at home, he's so uncomfortable about taking care of Amanda [two years] that he pretty much doesn't do it. We were discussing how to change a diaper last week, and he said, "I don't know where the diaper pail is." I think he needs time with her but he's not going to do that until she's older or until his job situation improves.*

Determining who is going to do what is one of the most difficult issues that parents of young children face. When working with parents before and after the birth of a child, I've frequently seen a remarkable change. Before the birth there is the feeling of "we're in this together." After the birth, the differences ripple out so that in a number of cases the prevalent tone in parent groups when discussing sharing child care is bitter and divisive.

Following the birth of a child, couples enter a critical period when they renegotiate their relationship. How to allocate child-care responsibilities is the surface issue, but it can be linked to deeper emotions. Andrea's situation gives us a chance to look at a complex situation.

Traditional and Changing Expectations

Andrea's first response is to blame Steve's lack of involvement on his job. Her husband is tied to his office; his hours are long and irregular. Young mothers in parent groups echo Andrea's feeling: "My husband's job keeps him away from our child." This point of view reflects a traditional definition of roles: in the early years the woman is the child rearer, the man is the economic provider and not as involved until the children are older.

These social definitions, however, are changing. Many women now expect to work *and* be at home, to look out for themselves as well as care for others. Men expect to be economic providers as well as take care of the children. Andrea and Steve are caught in this web of complex expectations for themselves and each other.

The Division of Child Care: Time-Use Studies

Do Steve's long hours away from home explain his lack of involvement in child care? When time diaries are kept, do the number of hours worked determine how much time parents spend with their children? Reviewing the research, Joseph Pleck concludes that fathers on the average spend approximately fifteen to twenty-five minutes a day in direct participation—playing with and caring for their children—and from two to four hours a day indirectly participating in more broadly defined child-care tasks. The number of hours worked makes little difference. Whether or not the mother is employed is not that important either. In studies where women and men work exactly the same number of hours, women are still more involved in child care. Recent studies are showing, however, that many men have slightly increased the time they spend being with their children and taking care of them.

Job Absorption

Research has shown that being absorbed in one's job does make a difference. People who carry their work home in their heads, such as Steve, have a harder time being with their families even though they are physically present.

The Psychological Parent

Reading a story, tucking a child into bed, and doing the laundry is providing care but is only one aspect of raising children. The other aspect is the psychological responsibility. One parent tends to be in charge: overseeing the appointments, knowing when to feed the child, what will comfort the child in distress, and noting changes in behavior. Not surprisingly, women are usually the psychological parents.

Attachment: A Possessive Relationship

In my research on parental growth, I've found that the relationship with a young child involves both push and pull feelings. Fathers and mothers alike are drawn to the child yet also wish to escape. Both, often to their surprise, feel possessive about the child.

The negotiation of these possessive feelings is the substance of the critical period between husband and wife that I believe takes place in the first years of parenthood. Ironically, these normal possessive feelings belie the desire to share. For example, a wife who wanted her husband to be an equal participant was shocked by the intensity of her jealousy and competition with him after their son was born. If her husband touched the baby when she held him, she found herself wanting to push her husband's hand away. At the same time, her fantasy life centered on running away, being by herself. He, likewise, had contradictory feelings—sometimes he didn't want to come home after work; just as often, he'd race with his wife to see who could get to the child first.

In our culture, women tend to act on the pull feeling, men on the push feeling. Men who have withdrawn sometimes describe themselves as feeling left out. A father says:

. . . *I didn't recognize it until later, but I think I was deeply affected by not being with my child much when she was little. I'd come home at the end of the day and my wife would talk about what they did that day. I felt cheated that I didn't see it, didn't participate in it. Very self-centered, I guess, but I was jealous.*

Research on Sharing Care

Two points are essential to the successful division of child care: sharing child care is ultimately a power negotiation, and sharing works best when couples arrive at a consensus on how to share.

Sharing Power. The power relationship between the husband and wife —who has more money, higher status, or more self-assurance—plays an important role in how involved men will be. In general, women have more power over the home and family and determine how actively men are involved in child care. Michael Yogman from Harvard University calls women the "gatekeepers" of men's participation. James Levine of Bank Street College, well-known for his efforts to involve men more in child-rearing (called "New Fatherhood" or "The Fatherhood Movement") has noted that many of the strongest opponents to this movement have been women (both liberal and conservative) who feel that men are taking over women's traditional stronghold—the home.

It is harder than is usually acknowledged for women to bypass their possessive feelings and share the power of child-rearing. On the other hand, it has been equally hard for men to divest themselves of their source of power—being the economic provider. This conclusion is supported by the research showing that men who earn significantly more money than their wives, like Steve Bauer does, participate less.

Arriving at a Consensus. It is a truism that men and women both must believe in sharing child care for this to happen. According to Andrea, she and Steve have quite different views:

■ ■ ■ *Most of the time he doesn't want to take care of Amanda. He wants to be entertained and if she doesn't do that, he gets bored.*

In addition, if they disagree on how to take care of their child, the situation worsens:

■ ■ ■ *I've never hit Amanda. But last week when he asked her to stop doing something and she kept doing it, he threatened to hit her. I didn't feel so good about his child-rearing talents after that. He wasn't really disciplining her—he was just angry because she didn't do what he demanded.*

While Andrea wants to share, she doesn't always approve of Steve's behavior with Amanda. Andrea's response is typical of many mothers struggling with this issue. They leave children with the father and then are critical of what he has done: "He let them wear their good shoes to the playground," or "He didn't pack a snack for the car so my daughter was fussy." One woman asked me: "Are men less competent than women in raising children?"

Men's Competence in Child Care

Parke and Sawin investigated just this question. Observing fathers and mothers in hospitals following the birth of a child, they found that men were as nurturing, as sensitive, as attuned to the infant's behavior and as responsive as women.

The next question is: Do men interact with children differently than women? Evidence here is more divided. Analyzing videotapes of mother-infant pairs and father-infant pairs, pediatrician Berry Brazelton has shown that fathers are more playful and stimulating, whereas mothers calm and nurture their infants.

It therefore seems that in many families the father's competence is the playing card in the renegotiation of complex feelings between mothers and fathers. In the Bauer family, there are competitive feelings. They have less time to spend with each other, less attention to give to each other. Now Andrea's primary focus is on Amanda and she feels that Steve intrudes: "When he shows up, things change." By insisting that he do things as she does, she avoids her own competitive feelings.

Andrea has taken on the role of child-rearing expert, the superparent, yet Andrea, like most new parents, feels unsure deep down: "It's the blind leading the blind." By taking a superior role, she is perhaps attempting to bolster her own sense of uncertainty.

This mix of competitive and anxious feelings is developmentally normal for new parents. Unfortunately, however, the expression of these normal feelings can ultimately block the very goal the parents began with: sharing child care.

The Effect of Father Participation on Children

Numerous studies proclaim the importance of fathers taking care of children. Having two people with different styles stimulates children to adapt to change. If, as Mary Ainsworth from the University of Virginia argues, the child's thinking capacity grows out of responding to the clues and cues in the informal give-and-take that occurs between parent and child, then two caretakers can be better than one. It is further argued by Nancy Chodorow from the University of California that a nurturing father helps both boys and girls retain their feminine and masculine sides—to care about people as well as to achieve.

The long-term validity of these arguments has yet to be proven. One thing, however, is certain: the outcome of father involvement *depends*; it depends on the relationship the father establishes with his child, and it also depends on how much support the mother and father give each other for these new roles.

The Child's Perception of the Father

Andrea's view about Steve does have repercussions. Directly and indirectly, she translates her perceptions to her daughter. Psychiatrist Richard Atkins finds that the mother's representation of the father greatly influences the child's earliest view of him. If women react to their husband's presence with apprehension (implying that Daddy's arrival will spoil what they are doing together), the child can form negative images. If, on the other hand, mothers are enthusiastic ("Won't it be fun when Daddy is here?"), the child will undoubtedly be more positive. Andrea says:

• • • *This realization led my husband and me to stop and take stock. We realized that while we both wanted the best for our own daughter, our attempts to achieve a more equitable sharing were doing the opposite. We decided to try to change.*

SOLUTIONS

As a first step, the father and mother have to have a similar goal: that they will share. One cannot impose this on the other. A Pittsburgh father of two says:

> ■ ■ ■ *If the mother tries to teach the father, she'll lose him. She'll make him into another child, feeling incapable and incompetent. If the father wants to change, he will. How does this happen? I'm not sure, but telling certainly isn't the way.*
>
> *What worked for me is empathizing with my children: Thinking back to how I felt about my own parents when I was growing up, thinking about how I want my children to remember me. Then I could plan ways to make this happen.*

Agreeing on the Important Goals

Parents can then discuss what both want for their children; for example:

- not growing up in an atmosphere of dissension
- an opportunity to know and care about both parents
- feeling good about themselves

Agreeing about overall goals for the children sets the stage. It also changes the focus of the issue from being the mother's concern to being one that both parents share and work on together.

Accepting Differences

Very few parents do things exactly the same way, yet most child-rearing books advise parents to be "consistent," causing guilt when inevitable differences between them emerge. The point is for the mother and father to determine the *few* values most central to each of them (e.g., building a child's self-esteem) and *agree to agree* or to support each other on these values. Then the parents can *agree to disagree* on the differences that are not so important (e.g., eating with fingers). In fact, children benefit from learning to accept the differences between their mothers and fathers. Problems arise not when parents are different but when parents undermine each other. Sharing child care by necessity means accepting differences.

Problem-Solving

When important differences arise over sharing care, it is necessary to talk about them and work toward resolution. Adele Faber and Elaine Mazlish in *How to Talk So Kids Will Listen and Listen So Kids Will Talk* suggest a technique for problem-solving that can be applied to children and adults alike:

1. *Talk about the other person's feelings and needs.* Andrea might say to Steve, "You must have been upset when Amanda didn't listen when you asked her to stop." She can then encourage him to talk about his feelings. Steve could also use this technique with Andrea. They both can use it with Amanda as she becomes more verbal.

2. *Talk about your feelings.* Andrea might then say, "On the other hand, I felt upset when you hit her."

3. *Suggest solutions.* Here, they might talk about what Amanda at age two is capable of; how they can discipline; or how they can share child care more equitably.

4. *Decide upon a mutually acceptable solution.*

5. *Try out your solution.* Test the solution you've agreed on, give it a fair chance. If it doesn't work, it is more constructive not to slip back into criticism but to say, "It isn't working, let's problem-solve again." One of my biggest disagreements with most how-to books for parents is that one solution is given per problem. As a parent, I know that no solution works indefinitely. The art of parenthood is repeated problem-solving.

Changing the Expectation That Sharing Is 50/50

Magazine and newspaper articles have promulgated the concept that responsibilities should be divided equally. In seminars, I meet many mothers and fathers who are discouraged or angry because their own attempts to share fall short of this ideal. In reality, sharing is never 50/50. The ratio changes daily and weekly to reflect the circumstances of the parents' lives. What's important is that, over time, a satisfactory balance is achieved.

Assuming Responsibility for the Child

Charles Sims, the father of a three-year-old, says:

■ ■ ■ *Being a parent is like anything else you do—it's a job and there are skills. It took me a long time to sharpen my skills. I did it by learning, hands-on. I finally said, "This is my son. I love him and I'm going to care for him," and from that day on I did everything that my wife did. I feel any father that doesn't do this is not only missing out but isn't learning. Simply by bathing him, I learned the best times for a bath and the best ways to give him a bath. That gave me confidence.*

Another mother at home full time stresses the importance of keeping her husband informed. They talk on the phone during the day and set aside time in the evening to recount the children's activities. When the father is with the children, time should be saved for him to tell the mother what's happened. Parents can also leave each other notes.

Spending Time with Other Fathers

Fathers (as do mothers) enjoy spending time with other parents. One father plans regular outings to the zoo or park with his neighbor and child. Others join more formal fathers' groups where the fathers talk together and sometimes bring in speakers.

Scheduling Time and Tasks

Many families have developed schedules of how they will share the time and tasks of child care. A father in New Jersey takes care of his two- and five-year-old daughters while his wife jogs in the morning. He gives them breakfast while she showers and dresses for work. A family in Atlanta devotes time at the end of the day for each parent to be alone with a child.

A father summarizes the joy in being involved:

■ ■ ■ *Having kids is a definite cure for tunnel vision. It opens up a whole new world of priorities. Before we had kids, I spent a whole lot more time on the job both physically and mentally. Now I have a lot more in my life.*

Managing Time

Q *How can I get everything done?*

Peggy Church says:

■ ■ ■ *I wake up in the morning and feel like there's no way in the world that I have enough energy to keep going, to do everything I have to do. We have a three-year-old. I worked for ten years before he was born and am now an administrator at a private school. I literally run from six in the morning to midnight.*

Not Enough Time

In our research on work and family life, we looked at the sources of stress and satisfaction for working parents. Most parents in our surveys identify the number of hours they work as having the most negative repercussions on home life. "If the day could be increased by another ten hours, then maybe it would be possible to get everything done," a father wrote. It is not unusual for working parents to load laundry in the washer or balance the checkbook in the middle of the night.

Contrary to the opinion of some people who have never tried to take care of young children full time at home, mothers at home must deal with similar pressures. Husbands and employed friends may be envious of the long stretches of so-called free time without understanding how difficult it is to balance the plea to "watch me" with doing other tasks, to have the children wake up early from their naps just as one is settling down to get something done, or to clean the house with a child glued to one's leg.

Jeannie Fox is a mother at home with two young children:

> • • • *The hardest part for me is the incredible amount of time I spend in the car: carpooling to nursery school, running to the cleaners and the grocery store, then picking up the kids and taking them to their afternoon activities. When I worked, I felt I could stay in one place and get one task done at a time. I could also delegate things to other workers. Now, at the end of the day, there is still so much undone.*

When a mother is employed, there are the same general demands (the children wanting and needing attention, dishes to be washed, photographs —if taken at all—to be pasted into the album, lunches to be made for the next day, income taxes to compute) but with even less time. Several studies indicate that the greater the number of hours worked—by mothers or by fathers—the more likely there is to be family tension.

Scheduling Incompatibility

Our research at Bank Street, however, has found that hours away from home are not the single cause of the kind of tension that Peggy describes. A variety of other circumstances feed into it, such as tension with a boss, problems with co-workers, or the lack of job control. The problem for Peggy, however, is schedule incompatibility.

> • • • *The worst times are when the schedules collide, and there doesn't seem to be any way in the world to make them work. Like when I have to be at a meeting at the same time I need to pick up my son from the babysitter. I get a clenching feeling in my stomach . . . it just makes me want to die. I always find a way to make it work, but it takes a toll.*

According to a large national survey, many women, like Peggy, reported that inconvenient work hours were the problem.

Expectations of Being Superparents

Peggy says:

• • • *I suppose I'm trying to be a superwoman. I'm dean of the
school, and because of my background in education, I feel
pressure to raise my own child as perfectly as I can. Everything
has to be done just right, all clean and organized. No markings
on the walls, no paper on the floor. It takes a lot of energy to
keep trying to be perfect.*

Peggy's ideas are typical of this generation of parents. The work ethic with
its emphasis on using every minute productively, the explosion of advice-
to-parents books, the desire to raise our own children differently than our
parents raised us, and the fact that many of us have been pioneers, creating
new models of parenting, have led to the pervasive desire to be superpar-
ents. However, the current culture alone has not created this phenomenon.
My research on parent development indicates that the desire to be perfect
is part of the normal process of parental change. With each new child comes
a feeling of starting over, a passion to do the best possible job. Ultimately
this is very positive because it means that we care; we try hard; we are
committed to raising our children well. Ironically, however, this positive
desire can also create havoc. One of the tasks of the early years of parenthood is moving away from being perfect to being what Donald Winnicott
calls "good enough," that is, to adjust our ideas of perfection to what is
realistically possible.

It may seem that the superparent phenomenon primarily affects employed mothers, but it does not. Because it is a normal aspect of parental
growth, it affects all mothers and fathers, although to different degrees.
Parents, however, tend to attribute the cause to the specifics of their lives.
Peggy sees her background in education as the cause; because she is a
professional teacher, she must be perfect with her own child. Other employed parents point to their working as the cause; because they are away
from their children, they must be perfect when they are together. On the
other hand, some at-home mothers think that because they are devoting
their full time and energy to child-rearing, they must do it perfectly—better
in fact than other mothers, or else the decision not to work may not really
be worth it. Numerous fathers have a notion of perfection too; they want
to be more available to their children than their fathers were to them.

These normal expectations of perfection can lead to problems in managing time. Although there is never enough time to begin with, expecting
ourselves to run everything without any hitches leads to stress. As Peggy
says, "It takes a lot of energy to keep trying to be perfect."

Personality Style

Peggy's personality also contributes to this situation:

> ▪ ▪ ▪ *I'm a person with a real sense of the work ethic. My mother was a single mother with no child support and I was always such a grown-up kid that I've had to teach myself to let go. Given a choice, I'd always choose work over play. I'm also not that good about talking to other people. I'm always the one that everyone else talks to. That's part of the stress, too.*

   Peggy might be considered what David Elkind calls "a hurried child," someone who grew up too fast. By remaining the person that others depend on and not allowing herself to lean on others, Peggy is cutting off some basic human needs. As parents, we all need to help and to be helped, to support and to be supported. Study after study points to the importance of social support, being able to turn to others for practical or emotional help.

SOLUTIONS

Scaling Down Expectations

Peggy Church has created what she calls a "should test" to help herself change:

> ▪ ▪ ▪ *One day I did everything I thought I "should" do and at three in the morning, I was still up, folding the laundry. That test really put me at ease about not trying to do it all. I could finally say, "Well, to hell with it; there's no way I can do it all." So now I do what I can. The best way of managing is to gain some acceptance and serenity about the fact that it is going to be a mess at times. It's riding with things rather than trying to control them all the time.*

Living in the Present

A father says:

> ▪ ▪ ▪ *I have a problem trying to do too many things in one day. I'll wake up and say, "Well, I'm going to have time for myself, do some of the chores, and spend some time with the kids." Then when I try to do something for myself, I feel guilty because it's taking time from my responsibilities so I don't enjoy the experience. When I'm with the kids, I'm resentful, think-*

ing, "Why am I spending time with them when I have so much to do?" I've tried to learn to give up the idea of doing everything.

This father was never able to enjoy what he was doing fully because he was projecting into the future and thinking about everything else he had to accomplish. Concentrating on the here and now helps reduce stress.

Establishing Priorities

The language we use to refer to time can connote a sense of powerlessness. For example, we usually say, "Time ran out." Many parents have found it helpful to try to shift to a feeling that "I am in charge. I am setting priorities of what's most and least important to me."

I now pick one thing to accomplish (not ten, as I used to do) during the morning or evening, and then when I complete it, I feel successful. Kate Reeves, a bank vice-president with a young child, says:

. . . *One Friday night, I wrote down all the things I wanted to do over the weekend. I prioritized them and estimated how long each would take. The list was way too long, so I had to drop a few things. That weekend was pretty good; I got done what I really wanted to get done—such as doing the wash, going shopping. I left free time when my daughter was awake so I could play with her because I knew it was unrealistic to do something else during that period. But sometimes even when I do plan, it doesn't work. I've learned you have to be able to say, "Okay, it's not going to work today—what's the one thing I most want to do?"*

Alan Lakein, in *How to Get Control of Your Time and Your Life*, stresses the importance of making A (most important), B (important), and C (least important) lists, and in the process, recognizing what criteria you use in making these lists. As others have pointed out, making these decisions involves tradeoffs, giving up some things to emphasize others. Kathleen Tribe, who conducts seminars for parents through the Dellcrest Children's Centre in Toronto, Canada, has found it useful to ask three questions: Do I *have* to? Do I *need* to? Do I *want* to?

Doing Worst Things—or Best Things—First

Betsy Newman, a mother of a two- and a five-year-old, says:

> • • • *First, I do the thing I dislike most. Otherwise it just hangs over my head. When I get that done, I feel such a relief that I can sail through my other chores.*

Other parents do their favorite jobs first, as incentives.

Skipping Unimportant Tasks

The mother of three children has learned to accept her limits and not push herself all the time:

> • • • *You make these demands and assumptions, but sometimes you just say, "Hey, I'm not going to do it." So the dishes pile up in the sink; when you're ready, you do the dishes. It takes only a little bit longer if you have twice as many dishes.*

Paul Williams, says:

> • • • *We have a rule we've developed that is "when in doubt, throw it out." People come in and say, "Gee, what a large apartment you have." What they don't realize is we have very little furniture because simplicity really helps. If you have fewer things to clean, it takes less time.*

Using Time-Saving Recipes and Equipment

Lots of parents have a repertoire of fast recipes: English muffin pizzas made with shredded mozzarella and tomato sauce; pasta and sauces. A commuting mother of two says, "We never eat anything that isn't steamed, boiled, or stir-fried. Everything else takes too long." Another parent prepares spaghetti sauces on the weekend and freezes half for use later in the week.

Another mother, in the insurance industry, says:

> • • • *My big thing when I came home at night was to have time to be with my child without feeling guilty that I didn't have dinner on the table when my husband got home. A microwave has really helped. I also made a decision: if my daughter needs me, I stop and don't cook dinner. My husband can wait, he can play with her—or he can cook. Before I was trying to do everything, but forget that. It didn't work.*

Developing Systems

Systems for keeping track of and managing the household can make the work go more quickly. Here are a few that parents find useful:

- A large calendar on a bulletin board to keep track of invitations, doctors' appointments and other family events, such as upcoming birthdays. Invitations can also be tacked up on the bulletin board.
- An erasable message board near the phone to take messages.
- A mail-sorting system. My daughter constructed a large open box with spaces marked for each member of the family as well as a space for bills and one for junk mail.
- A marketing list on the refrigerator or near by. Whenever you run out of an item, add it to the list immediately.
- A reusable list of information, emergency procedures, and telephone numbers for caregivers who come to your house.
- A pocket calendar to keep track of your life. Mine includes an address book (always written in pencil), a to-do list for each week, a place to keep track of expenses, and blank paper.

Getting Help

The decision to turn to others for help is complicated. For some, it is tantamount to saying, "I failed, I can't manage." For others, cost is a factor. However, getting help is an invaluable way of saving yourself for the really important tasks.

As one parent admits:

. . . *My husband and I used to spend all weekend fighting about who was going to do what. We figured that getting someone to clean was cheaper than marriage counseling.*

A mother of four says:

. . . *I have a neighbor who likes earning a little extra money. She comes once in a while, and we clean together. Just having her there gives me energy. We do just the kitchen or just the living room. I pay her, but I can't afford much—it's more the moral support of having another person there.*

When my daughter was small, I found it useful to invite one or two older children in the neighborhood to play with her occasionally. When I really needed to accomplish something (cook dinner, prepare something for work), they could amuse her. They were too young to care for her alone but loved the opportunity to be with a small child with one or both parents present.

Flexibility

Although planning and prioritizing are important, the unforeseen does occur. Parents who are able to be flexible manage these times best.

The mother of a two-year-old says:

> ▪ ▪ ▪ *It took me about a year before I got to the point of being flexible. The first year was just trying to understand the child, the schedules, and things like that. I didn't have time to plan anything. It was just getting the food on the table, survival. The second year was when I could actually let go and enjoy whatever was going on. I found it took a while to get to know the child, to just accept that "this is how it's going to be" and adjust to whatever happens.*

Finding "Down" Time

Bruce Baldwin, author of *All In Your Head: Life Style Management Strategies for Busy People!*, contrasts traditional time management (increased productivity at all costs) with the humane approach (reasonable productivity with health maintenance). He writes, "It is imperative that you find a leisure activity that is enjoyed just because it is pleasurable to you" as well as taking retreat time every day.

Letting Your Child Set the Schedule: Having Fun

A mother with a high-pressure job notes the importance of taking a day off with no plans and having fun with her daughter:

> ▪ ▪ ▪ *I think it's important to let my daughter set the schedule at times—because most of the time she has to adapt to adult schedules. Sometimes I'll say, "What do you want for breakfast?" And if it's pancakes and a whole big deal, then we'll take two hours for breakfast. Or if she wants to run around in PJ's all day—I let her do it.*

Having fun is not just for the times when there's nothing else to do. Child development specialists and mental health experts all agree that finding time to play is vital to our well-being. We come away relaxed and refreshed, having a better perspective on what is important in life.

Congratulating Yourself

Kate Reeves, the bank vice-president, points to the importance of taking note of your own successes:

• • • *Every day is a time management challenge. Today I laid out my daughter's clothes, and she put them on! And of course it's raining. I left the house with her, her lunch, and the umbrella. I took her to her family day-care home and I even managed to make the train. When I got on and sat down, I was very impressed with myself.*

Time for Self

Q *How can I get time for myself?*

Linda Babbitt says:

• • • *As a parent with young children, I sometimes find it's all too much, and the place that I've really lost energy is in taking care of me. I take a Saturday or an evening and just go off, but it's not hitting where I need it.*

Becoming a parent disrupts our equilibrium; the way we parcel out our time and energies is thrown off balance. That such a small person can take over our lives comes as an incredible realization to parents, particularly those who had declared in advance, "I'm not going to let children change me. I'm going to do just what I did before I had children." Yet in the early years of parenthood, children do change us. Many of us initially respond by trying to do it all, to compress what we were doing before into less time, or to become more efficient. After a while these strategies begin to take their toll. The aspect of our former lives that most parents, particularly women, renounce is time for self. Nevertheless, the need to give to ourselves cannot be suppressed.

At a recent seminar attended primarily by mothers, I asked, "What is the one thing you really wish for?" The answer was a uniform chorus:

> *I need a mother.*
> *She could cook for me.*
> *She could clean up.*
> *She could do all of the things I'm supposed to do.*

One participant, musing on the possibility of her mother moving in, joked, "No, I don't want my mother—just a robot who's programmed to do everything my mother would do."

The more we give to others, the greater the need to take care of ourselves. Mothers and fathers, however, seem to respond differently to this need. Men may feel pangs of guilt when they do things for themselves, but for the most part it doesn't stop them, while guilt seems to block many women. In fact, the questions that men and women ask at seminars for parents are substantially different. Men ask, "How can I stop feeling selfish when I bowl or read a book or jog?" Women, on the other hand, simply ask, "How can I manage to get *any* time for myself?"

Factors besides guilt prevent finding time for oneself:

Time

Linda Babbitt, a mother of four children, feels that her primary problem is the finite number of hours in a day weighed against the seemingly endless number of things to be accomplished—making sure food is on the table, her children have haircuts, clean clothes, and so forth. "It literally takes me until one or two in the morning some days, and this is with a husband who really shares the work."

"It's a trade-off," said another mother. "If I go to a gym, I have to give up time with my children. Before I had children, I never had to make such difficult compromises."

Space

Another mother with two children finds that her problem stems from a lack of space to call her own:

> ∎ ∎ ∎ *I just went back to work, and I need a place that's all mine. The bedroom belongs to my husband as well and all the other rooms are family rooms. I have to go someplace else to be really alone.*

Energy

A third mother, Kate Bridges, said:

> ∎ ∎ ∎ *When I want time for myself, I have to program it in. It can take two hours to get a babysitter, and when I finally organize something, I'm so tired that all I really want to do is go sit in a dark corner.*

Again, it is a trade-off. The energy Kate must expend to carve out some time for herself doesn't seem worth the renewed energy she gains, so she doesn't do it very often.

Money

For most parents, leisure activities are expensive—child care, the health club fee, the admission to a movie. On a limited budget, parents ask, "Is such an expenditure worthwhile?"

What Is the Stress?

Both mothers and fathers find that without some breathing room, without some peaceful place, without an activity that is "just for me," tension increases:

· · · *If I keep trudging along doing things for everybody but myself, I get resentful. I have a physical reaction—noises bother me more and I don't want to be touched. The smallest thing can set me off.*

Another said:

· · · *When I don't take care of my body and my spirit, I suffer an energy drain, depression, even illness.*

The stress described is more than the compilation of the things that must be accomplished. Parents at seminars readily agree that the tension resides in the omnipresent responsibility of parenthood.

A father with two young sons said: "It's not what you do with your hands—it's what's on your mind." A mother added, "The mental weight of having everything depend on me—that's ninety percent of the stress I feel."

Who Stops You?

"Who stops you from taking time for yourself?" I asked this group of parents at the seminar.

Harriet Burns said:

· · · *My husband. This weekend, I asked my husband to cook supper so I could have some time off. He went out in the kitchen and every five mintues he was back, asking "Where's this? Where's that?" When he finished, I looked around at the mess everywhere, and I thought, I should have done it myself.*

Jack Sussman said:

· · · *My wife stops me. I wanted to take a course in the continuing education department one night a week. My wife was so criti-*

cal about my spending time away from the family that I dropped it, but I really resent having to give it up.

A complex drama obviously takes place between men and women; a game, if you will, that causes certain resentments but that continues because it is rooted in deeply held assumptions. Here are the most frequent assumptions:

"*I should be productive all the time.*" Because this generation has been raised on the work ethic, parents feel guilty if they are not accomplishing something. Taking care of yourself can seem frivolous and indulgent. The exception seems to be exercise; sports are considered worthwhile in our society because they involve staying healthy.

"*I should be giving to others.*" Many women have been taught to be nurturers, but the nurturing is to benefit others first, oneself last. A mother says:

• • • *The hardest part of being a full-time mother is remembering that you as a mother have real needs that, though they may be lowest on everybody's priority list, somehow must get filled. I'm really good at telling myself that my needs don't matter.*

"*I should be able to do it all.*" Many of today's parents have high expectations of what they can accomplish. The more they take on, the more they demand of themselves. In my view, the wish to be as perfect as possible is a normal and healthy aspect of new parenthood but as the demands of everyday life escalate, parents need to readjust their expectations and figure out what is possible and what is important.

"*Work time (or family time) is my time for myself.*" Some parents equate time at work with time for themselves. Numerous women feel that their job is all the time off they deserve. Other parents consider family activities time for self. Parents must evaluate what works for them.

"*I am selfish if I do something just for me.*" Even when the topic of a seminar is time for self, parents have difficulty talking about what they really want to do with their time off. The assumption that doing something "just for me" is selfish and wrong is so ingrained that when parents do finally describe a favorite activity, it often includes unconscious self-punishment.

• • • *We did go away for the weekend without the kids but I was sure the plane would crash. Then every time the phone rang, I was convinced one of the kids was seriously ill.*

"*I want my spouse to realize I want some time off and organize it for me.*" "Do you ask or tell your spouse when you need some time off?" I frequently ask at seminars. No is the usual answer from women. "He sees how hard I'm working and *should* offer to give me a break." The more one feels that time for oneself is undeserved, the more difficult it becomes to demand or ask for it. Thus, parents often have the fantasy that their spouse will read their minds and give them what they need. This same desire leads the participants in the seminar to wish for a mother, someone who seems to know their thoughts, who understands, who takes care of them.

The problem is that when the spouse does not fulfill this fantasy tension mounts—and explosions and accusations fly. Time for self can become a battleground for the couple, a prize to be withheld from one another.

Who Really Stops Us?

Ultimately it is not our husbands or wives who stop us from taking time for ourselves, but we ourselves. Even when we do take time for ourselves, we may emit ambivalent or guilty signals that invite blame or punishment. Before leaving to visit a friend, a wife may pick a quarrel with her husband ("Whenever I leave the kids with you, they fight"). Parents must decide that time off is unequivocally right for them and then simply leave.

What Do I Really Want?

Linda Babbitt is struggling with a different issue, she's not sure what she really needs:

■ ■ ■ *I have this aimless longing, this gut feeling that there is something that I want. I go to the movies, I swim, but there's something that's more central to my own growth. It sounds corny, but I want something for me that I'm not catching onto or doing and I'm the only one who holds me back.*

SOLUTIONS

Self-Esteem: Recognizing that You Deserve Time for Yourself

A mother of two said:

■ ■ ■ *The long view about parenthood is that you have your children for about sixteen to eighteen years and then they begin to drift away, and if you don't start building the pattern of carving time to write, to think, to listen to music, you're stuck. If you've invested nothing in yourself to be somebody when they go, you'll be messed up. Parents must realize that their needs and rights are as legitimate as their children's—no more, no less.*

Recognizing the legitimacy of your own needs grows out of a sense of self-esteem. Self-esteem is not based on the ideal of perfection but, rather, acknowledges your strengths and recognizes that no human can give constantly and without measure. We must also receive in return simply to keep going. We deserve time off, just as others do.

Furthermore, as a practical matter, most parents find they take better care of their families when they also take care of themselves.

Scheduling Time for Oneself

Once you feel that having time to do what you want is legitimate, it becomes more possible to make this part of your routine. Waking up on a Saturday morning, a mother with young children will fantasize about the day—taking a walk in the newly fallen snow, reading a magazine that arrived yesterday. Then the children tumble in, starved for breakfast—and somehow the day slips by with the walk and the reading distant memories.

One mother counters the tendency to renounce her own time:

• • • *I program time for myself. I write it in on the calendar, and I do it. The third Tuesday of every month I have dinner with a friend. We sit in the back of a restaurant and act disgracefully but have a wonderful time.*

When scheduling this time, try to ensure that it does not become one more complication (and thus a source of stress) in an already busy schedule. Setting aside time for self should refresh, not exhaust you.

How frequently parents schedule this time varies from person to person. One father plays basketball every Saturday morning. A mother plays tennis. Still another plans a weekend away with a good friend every few months.

It's healthy to have something special to look forward to. On the day when pandemonium breaks loose and the bills need paying but the bank account is low, the children are housebound with the flu and the crack in the ceiling is getting larger, it is sustaining to know that on the calendar there's something coming up that will give you pleasure and renew you.

Curbing Punishment

If you set up punishments for yourself, try to be aware of this and curb this tendency. If your spouse makes it difficult for you, assert your right to have some time off, as this mother did:

*... The first time I left my husband with the two kids, it was
merely to go to the store to buy something, but I needed to get
out.*

*When I came back, I couldn't open the front door, there
were so many toys and things on the floor.*

*He was standing by the door. I said, "Did the kids eat?" He
said, "They had peanut butter and jelly for dinner because
that's what they asked for."*

*I said to myself, "Let it ride." I said to him, "Wonderful.
They love peanut butter and jelly." I could have said, "What
happened to the vegetables and fruit that I had fixed?"*

*He was clever. He figured that if I saw the chaos at the
front door, I'd never go out again. But I planned to go out the
very next Saturday.*

If you are being punished for taking time for yourself, explore why and
discuss it. Perhaps your spouse feels jealous of your interest in an activity
or of the friend you spend time with. Perhaps your spouse feels anxious
about being at home alone with the children.

If punishing has become a pattern, couples can devise ways of avoiding
this. One wife would call her husband from a pay phone near home and
say, "Before I come home, let's talk. If you're angry at me for going out, let's
deal with it on the phone and not make a scene in front of our daughter."

Making Equitable Arrangements for Time for Self

Investigating how the issue of time off affects the marital relationship,
Skinner and McCubben found that when husbands have much more time
for themselves than their wives do, the family suffers a great deal of tension.

To arrive at an equitable division, both spouses must state what they
need and want. It's important not to be judgmental about what one's
spouse wants to do with the time by making such comments as, "You want
to do what—go shopping?" or "I can't stand that gym you go to."

Using Found Time

A mother described how she takes advantage of everyday moments to
provide time for herself:

*... I've made comfy places around the house. My bathroom has
inspirational literature. I go in there and refuse to let anyone
bother me. I have a place in my bedroom where I can read.
When I put the kids down for a nap, I do my own thing even
though I know they're not always napping. I go into the living
room and teach myself to play the recorder.*

One father said:

> ▪ ▪ ▪ *I sometimes take my kids places that I want to go. I take them to movies, to museums, to the store.*

Taking the Long and Short View

> ▪ ▪ ▪ *When I'm too busy or don't have enough breathing space I say to myself: "This is a stage. Then there will be another stage and another."*

This mother is managing the present by putting a time frame on it, by noting that the more disagreeable aspects of her life will change. Other parents plan for the future: "When things aren't going well, I sit down and make a list of my fantasies for myself and then decide which are possible and how I'm going to make them come true."

The negative side of this coping strategy is that it focuses on the future, not the present. Numerous parents find that when they are always thinking of what is to come, they have a harder time enjoying what is happening right now. Parents can cope with this tendency by concentrating on whatever is enjoyable about the present moment:

> ▪ ▪ ▪ *If I'm at the sandbox with my kids, rather than wishing I were somewhere, anywhere else, I concentrate on watching the children move and talk and play, thinking about what the experience of the sandbox must be like for them.*

Figuring out How to Spend Time for Self

Linda Babbitt, the mother of four young children said, "I have this aimless longing, this gut feeling that there is something that I want."

Here are some things that satisfy the need for time for self.

"*I need a break.*" Many parents determine that what they need is a change of routine, a break from their everyday life. Sports are a popular choice. One mother commented that sports work for her because:

> ▪ ▪ ▪ *When I dance or swim, I can only pay attention to that and I lose myself. That makes it possible for me to go back to my job and my child feeling refreshed.*

"*I need to be taken care of.*" Linda Babbitt describes a fantasy of getting sick—not too sick—and having to check into the hospital. Other parents imagine lying in the sun on tropical islands.

The fantasy of being cared for can be realized. Parents can (money and time permitting) eat out. One woman schedules a massage which, to her, means that she's being taken care of and that she is going to feel and look her best afterward.

Another woman, whose husband is in divinity school, describes how the church acknowledges that succor of spouses is a necessary and worthwhile activity:

■ ■ ■ *There are scheduled weekend retreats for the spouses at a monastery. They are wonderful. I have a room alone and can do whatever I want to all day.*

"*I need something that will be fulfilling.*" Linda Babbitt's need was greater than simply getting a break. She wanted to build something meaningful into her life, "central to my own growth." The other participants at the seminar nodded. One said, "It's like the feeling that I'm not sure what I want to do when I grow up even though I'm supposedly grown-up already."

The search is not easy, but as the group prodded Linda a little, asking her, "What do you like to do the most?" and "When do you feel best about yourself?" Linda revealed a hidden fantasy:

■ ■ ■ *I grew up poor and in a single-parent home. I'd like to change my work so I could give something back to the kind of men and women that I grew up with.*

To carve out something for ourselves in the midst of children, jobs, homes, bills to be paid, and our other responsibilities is a struggle, but a struggle worth embarking on. At the least, it can give us renewed energy to reinvest in our families and, at most, it can give us new insight and direction for our lives.

SEVEN

Work and Family Life

Effects of Employment

Q *How are children affected when their mothers are employed?*

Newspapers and magazines are filled with contradictory statements from experts on this subject. One expert is quoted saying that if mothers are employed* before their children are three, the children are "at risk." Another expert asserts the opposite: maternal employment can be good for children. Parent's questions parallel these divergent points of view. They ask:

- What will this generation of children be like? Will they be group-oriented and care less about their mothers and fathers because they have to be away from their parents at such a young age?
- Will they be followers because they have had to conform to the often-hectic schedules of their parents or the long hours of group care?
- Because of child care will they be more competent and comfortable in social situations? Will they be more verbal and more knowledgeable?
- Will the children of employed parents become adults who have had to grow up too fast, "hurried," without the classic carefree childhoods we imagine other generations of children had?
- Will these children feel pushed aside, in the deepest sense, because their employed parents put their own needs first? Will they be self-centered and self-serving, the result of their parents' guilty attempts to make up for time away from them?
- Will these children be strong, sure of themselves, recipients of positive role models?

A thorough review of the research convinces me that neither extreme position is correct. Children are not necessarily harmed or helped by the

* I use the term "employed" mothers rather than "working" mothers. Mothers at home are working at this job, too.

fact that their mothers are employed and they are cared for by others. The impact of a mother's employment depends; it depends upon the children's experiences in their families and in their child-care situations.

Mother/Child Attachment

When large numbers of mothers began to join the work force in the 1960s and 1970s, social scientists responded by asking: Does maternal employment hurt the child's attachment to the mother? Studies focused on the child's emotional relationship to the mother because this relationship was considered the cornerstone of the child's subsequent development. Notice, however, that mothers (not fathers) were the subjects of these studies and notice also the emphasis on the idea of harm. Interestingly enough, during this same period, the father's *lack* of employment was examined as potentially harmful for the child.

I will describe the research on mother/child attachment in detail because so many contradictory descriptions of it have appeared in other books and magazines. There are essentially two kinds of attachment studies. One asks if beyond-the-family child care can shift infants' or young childrens' primary attachment from their parents to their caregivers. The data clearly indicate that this does not occur. As Thomas Gamble and Edward Zigler from Yale University say, the chance that child care can "prevent the formation of primary attachments to parents, or cause them to be directed elsewhere, seems small indeed." Studies show that young children are capable of becoming attached to many people—their brothers, sisters, caregivers, and grandparents—but the primary attachment is to their mothers and fathers.

The second kind of study has focused on children whose mothers returned to their jobs in their first year (there is virtually no evidence that there are problems when mothers return to their jobs later). In general, these studies compare the quality of the mother/child attachment of very young children with mothers at home and that of employed mothers. Researchers have assessed the quality of attachment by using the "strange situation" procedure developed by Mary Ainsworth and her colleagues: Typically, laboratory researchers stage separations and reunions of twelve- to eighteen-month-olds and their mothers in the presence and absence of strangers. There are seven three-minute sequences: (1) the mother arrives in the experimental laboratory playroom with the baby and puts the child on the floor, (2) an unfamiliar adult (a stranger) comes in and attempts to interact with the baby, (3) the mother leaves the room, (4) the mother returns and the stranger leaves, (5) the mother leaves again and the baby is alone, (6) the stranger returns, and (7) the mother returns and greets the baby. This sequence is intended to increase stress on the baby, thus eliciting behavior that reveals the quality of the attachment to the mother.

Researchers have begun to differentiate between three styles of attachment: secure, insecure/avoidant, and insecure/resistant:

- Secure babies approach and greet their mothers after the separation and, if distressed, respond positively to their mothers and are comforted by them.
- Insecure/avoidant babies ignore or avoid their mothers after the separation or continue to play.
- Insecure/resistant babies take an even more active stance in resisting contact with their mothers after the separation by pushing the mothers away or by crying angrily. Their mothers' presence does not comfort these babies in distress.

Two new studies have made headlines around the country because they found that a small but statistically significant number of the infants who were away from their mothers for more than twenty hours a week in their first year were more likely to have insecure attachments to them. This finding was of concern to these researchers, who speculate that insecure attachments might lead to greater aggression in later years. They reason that if the mother is not present for much of the time the child is developing the attachment relationship, the child might begin to doubt her availability and love. This insecurity might then be expressed as anger or aggression toward others (the mother, father, teachers, and other children) or withdrawal in the preschool years.

These assumptions are based on another set of studies that have examined the long-term outcomes of the early relationship between mother and child. These studies have in fact shown that infants with secure attachment relationships were more likely to be able to solve problems, to explore, and to be independent in the toddler years. Preschoolers who were securely attached as infants tended to be more constructively involved at school and in play with their friends. They were more compliant and cooperative with adults, showed less negative behavior, and were more resilient to stress.

Theoretically, all of these positive outcomes could be linked to a secure mother/child attachment. Furthermore, several other studies have found that children with child-care experiences were more aggressive. It is not surprising, then, that if a small group of children displays an insecure relationship even in a few studies, it will be of concern to researchers and the public at large. However, the argument that maternal employment during the first year causes a disrupted attachment relationship and subsequent aggression is flawed for several reasons:

1. The strange situation procedure is intended to put the child under stress by separating the child and mother. This measure may not be effective in measuring the attachment of children who experience daily separations.

Child-care authorities Alison Clarke-Stewart and Greta Fein suggest that perhaps children who are used to leaving their mothers "have simply become more experienced in the type of situation used to assess attachment, so they find it less stressful and therefore exhibit less overt and intense attachment behavior." Continuing to play with a toy upon the mother's return can be coded as an insecure attachment, but might also indicate persistence and adaptiveness rather than avoidance for the child who is used to daily separation. Clearly, this measure should not be the only indicator of the attachment relationship in future research.

2. The numbers of children coded as insecure are small. Clarke-Stewart has examined sixteen studies comparing children with full-time child care in their first year and those with no child-care experiences. Across these studies, 29 percent of the children with no child care have insecure attachments, while 38 percent with full-time extra-familial care are insecure. Although statistically significant to researchers (that is, a percentage higher than accounted for simply by chance), the difference in the actual number of children is small.

3. When children with early child care exhibit more aggression, the causes may not be an insecure attachment but the way aggressive acts are handled by the child-care provider. For example, one longitudinal study of children in an intervention program at the University of North Carolina did find that the children who attended their program from infancy on were more aggressive with other children upon entering public kindergarten. The researchers decided to develop a curriculum specifically to teach social skills, rather than the current "haphazard process of randomly praising appropriate and punishing inappropriate behavior." With this systematic approach, they were able to reduce the amount of aggressive acts by 90 percent. Subsequent assessments of the children who experienced this curriculum found them no more aggressive than the children with no child care. Researcher Neal Finkelstein concludes that aggression is not necessarily the result of child care per se, but of "a failure to provide systematic opportunities to encourage the development of prosocial behaviors."

4. A few studies have shown that employed mothers tend to compensate for their time away from their children by showing them excessive attention and keeping the father at a distance from the child. According to Jay Belsky, a leading figure in the child-care debate: "By trying, possibly, to make up for lost time, working mothers may inadvertently exceed the information-processing capacities of their infants, causing them to avoid interactions and contact." This overload may lead to an ambivalent response, as assessed by the strange situation procedure. Thus future research efforts must assess the quality of the mother/child and father/child relationship when the child and parents are together.

5. Since not all studies find that infants with full-time employed mothers

are likely to have avoidant attachments, it is obvious that other factors are at work. Employment per se cannot be the single cause. Some families in the studies whose infants demonstrated insecure/avoidant attachments faced other stresses as well (divorce, marital discord, frequently changing child-care providers and job problems). Our own research at Bank Street College indicates that job stress spills over into family relationships. In future research, it will be important to investigate how family and job stress influence the child.

What Do We Know from the Attachment Research to Date?

In 1987, a group of sixteen experts was convened by the National Center for Clinical Infant Programs and Edward Zigler from Yale to discuss this question. It was felt that the continued media attention to this issue might, in fact, be making employed parents more anxious, perhaps even to the point of affecting their relationships with their young children in negative ways. I was present at this "summit meeting," so-called because it brought together most of the experts who have researched and studied this issue, including people who disagreed strongly on whether or not early maternal employment was potentially harmful to very young children. After much discussion, we agreed to the following statement:

> *When parents have choices about selection and utilization of supplementary care for their infants and toddlers and have access to stable child-care arrangements featuring skilled, sensitive, and motivated caregivers, there is every reason to believe that both children and families can thrive.*

We agreed that the quality of the child's care, whether in the child's own home, in someone else's home, or a center, made a big difference in how the child fares (see Chapter 8 for how to evaluate high-quality child care).

This meeting made it clear that in our field we can no longer assess the impact of maternal employment as simply the absence of the mother and ignore what happens to the child during the hours apart from his or her mother and father as well as the hours they spend together as a family.

The research on how children's intellectual and social development are affected when their mothers are employed has not been fraught with as much controversy as the attachment research but is equally complex. Rather than focusing solely on maternal employment (and subsequently children who are in all kinds of child care), many of these studies have looked at children in center care.

Social Development and Child Care

Parents who select group child care sometimes worry: "Will my child be more likely to fight because he is with other children so much?" As said earlier, studies both confirm and refute this parental fear. Children who attend child-care centers can be more sociable, more willing to play with unfamiliar children, more cooperative, and more empathic. They can also be more assertive and aggressive with their friends and less cooperative with adults.

Besides the way that child-care providers handle aggression, the size of the group makes a difference. If the group is very large, there is a greater likelihood of fighting among the children.

IQ and Day Care for Younger Children

Many parents who use day care say that their children are more intelligent because of all of their learning experiences. When IQ is used as a measure (keeping in mind that IQ is a rather narrow measure of a child's intelligence), the research findings do not support this observation. Belsky's review of the literature indicates that children in child care make gains on IQ tests, but most of these gains disappear after the child leaves the program. It is possible, based on other studies of IQ, that these IQ gains might be sustained if the children were to enter high-quality elementary school programs and if the parents remain involved in their children's schooling.

Studies have found that results differ for children who are more "at-risk" than the average middle-class child (for example, children who are very poor or have congenital problems). Early childhood enrichment programs for at-risk infant populations seem to prevent the IQ decline that these children typically show at about eighteen months.

Language Development and Child Care

Child-care experiences can affect the development of language. In Bermuda, 90 percent of the children are in day care by their second year and thus provide a population where differences in family background, income and education can be accounted for. A large-scale study there found that children in the highest quality programs were more advanced in language development and usage than those in lower quality programs regardless of their family background. The quality of the child care, specifically, being in a language-rich environment, had more impact than the sociological characteristics of the family. This finding is particularly important because numerous studies have shown that children with better language skills are viewed by their teachers as more intelligent—thus potentially influencing the way the children feel about themselves and the way they subsequently perform in school.

Academic Achievement and Older Children

The research on the effect of mothers' employment on the academic achievement of older children (in a variety of different kinds of child-care arrangements) shows that "the children of working mothers do not differ from the children of nonworking mothers." The one exception is the somewhat puzzling, highly controversial finding in several (though not all) studies that the sons of middle-class employed mothers do not do as well in the early years of elementary school as the sons of nonemployed mothers. In working-class families the reverse has been true—the sons of employed mothers are generally higher achievers than their counterparts with at-home mothers. One explanation for this finding is that the advantages of employment in working-class families may outweigh the disadvantages; that is, having more money and more social stimulation for all family members might more than compensate for any potential problems.

Effects of Mother's Employment on Boys Versus Girls

In addition to the finding that middle-class boys may not do as well in school when their mothers are employed, there are other indications that the boys in mother-employed families may fare differently than girls. The most compelling evidence comes from a study by Urie Bronfenbrenner and his colleagues at Cornell University. They asked parents from different social classes to describe their three-year-olds. In contrast to other studies where parents of preschoolers consistently describe their sons more positively than their daughters, Bronfenbrenner found that the least attractive portraits were given by full-time employed mothers of sons.

In general, girls with employed mothers seem to prosper. In her review of this research, Lois Hoffman concludes that daughters of employed mothers "generally appear to be more independent, outgoing, higher achievers, to admire their mothers more, to have more respect for women's competence." For a variety of reasons, employed mothers seem to be effective role models for their daughters.

There are a number of possible explanations of why boys may be more at risk than girls:

1. Studies of sex differences find that boys are more active than girls. Perhaps the combination of tired parents and active boys spells trouble.

2. A few studies are beginning to investigate how various aspects of parents' jobs affect children. Chaya Piotrkowski from St. John's University found that tension at work can be carried home. In addition, she found that stressed mothers and fathers react differently to their sons and daughters. Sons are more likely to be treated with hostility; girls with indifference or withdrawal.

3. When there is family stress, boys tend to be more vulnerable, particularly in the early years. This is a consistent finding in the divorce research.

4. Studies have found that older children with employed mothers are expected to be more independent than those with at-home mothers. Lois Hoffman hypothesizes that independence may have a different effect on boys and girls: "previous research has shown that American parents en-

courage their sons' independence more than their daughters'. If maternal employment increases the independence training for both sons and daughters, as indeed the data indicate, it might have a positive effect on daughters, but may involve a push toward independence in sons that is too early or too much."

5. Perhaps boys express stress earlier or in different ways. For example, the early years of school are less geared to the activity level of boys than girls, and this may trigger already present problems. Some life-span studies indicate that girls are not immune to stress—they express it in less obvious ways or later on in their growing-up years.

My Conclusions

Does this mean that the employed parents of sons should panic, worrying that they have harmed their children? Not so. The contradictory findings again reveal that other forces are at work. As Adele Gottfried and her colleagues concluded after six years of studying the children of employed mothers: "It is the experiences to which children are exposed that are important to their development regardless of maternal employment status." Likewise Judith Rubenstein and Carollee Howes state: "For later emotional development, individual differences in the actual experiences and behavior of toddlers in day care are more important than is attendance in day care per se."

What experiences make the greatest difference? After reviewing the research, I have identified four.

The Mother's and/or Family's Attitude toward Employment. If the mother does not believe she should be employed, or if the father is opposed to his wife's employment, then family stress can result, which, in turn, can affect the child. Conversely, if the mother and father feel that the mother's work is integral to the family's stability or to her own well-being, then children can pick up a sense of pride and the feeling that "we're in this together."

The Mother's and/or Father's Job. Tension with co-workers and the boss, lack of job control, and other severe employment stresses can be carried home and affect the child.

Other Stressful Events within the Family. The impact of stress is, in part, additive: the more problems, the more likely they will affect the child. The way parents perceive the problems (as situations to be remedied rather than as devastating), the way they cope (particularly by taking steps to solve the problems), and the kind of social support they have can greatly reduce, maybe even block, the negative effects of stress.

The Quality of the Child Care. Children's development is clearly affected by the quality of child care they receive. The responsiveness of the caregiver to the child's needs and the consistency of the care make an important difference. Group size makes a difference, as does the discipline style of the caregiver and the verbal interaction between the caregiver and child. Also important is a positive, supportive relationship between the caregiver and the parents that serves the best interests of the child.

VIEWPOINT: QUALITY TIME VERSUS QUANTITY TIME

For the past several years, I have heard the argument: "It's not the quantity of time that parents and children spend together that matters; it's the quality of time." This statement is intended to reduce the guilt of employed mothers.

In my opinion, there are some problems with this point of view. On an absolute level, we certainly do not know how much time together is enough, but there should be enough time so that every moment together is not too compact and compressed. Children need "hang-around time" with their parents, relaxed time as well as intensely involved time.

Secondly, many parents become distressed when their quality time is not perfect. We have long since given up the notion that marriage means walking off into the sunset together. Although the desire for perfection is normal in parents, it's important to understand that the time parents spend with their children will have its ups and downs. To me, quality time includes dealing constructively with the stress of such situations as being burned out at the end of the day; it involves solving the family problems that inevitably arise in the course of living together. Children learn a great deal more when they help deal with problems than when their parents are tied up in knots because their quality time has gone to pieces.

Q *I can't believe that when mothers work, it doesn't automatically hurt their children. Think of the long hours away from the mothers, think of how upset the children are when their mothers leave every morning.*

Barbara Mason, an air traffic controller, made her point at a seminar I was conducting for the employees at a metropolitan airport:

. . . *I have a five-year-old, and every morning when it's time to go to work, she grabs me and won't let go. I tell her how much fun she'll have with the kids in her child-care group. I show her the things in our house, especially her toys, and tell her we wouldn't be able to have them if I didn't work. She says she doesn't care. She'd rather give up all of her toys to have me stay home and play with her.*

"I think I'd say the same thing as your daughter," responded another attendee. "Is that the choice you're really making: working to buy her toys versus being with her?"

"No," said Barbara. "I'm a single parent and I have to work, but I thought I'd put it in terms she'd understand. That's not the issue, anyway. I just can't believe that the research doesn't show that kids are more insecure, more unhappy when their mothers work."

"The research," I answered, "shows that whether the mother is employed or not doesn't necessarily tell us anything about her child. There are all kinds of homes, all kinds of child care, all kinds of jobs—and these seem to make more of a difference than just whether or not the mother is employed."

"Is your daughter putting up a fuss because she doesn't like the sitter she has?" asked a clerical worker.

"No. She's been with the same woman since she was two and a half and they love each other. That's not the problem. I know that my being away from her is doing damage."

"How do you know that?" I asked.

"Because my mother worked when my older brother and sister were little and they blame her for getting rid of them. She stopped working when I was born, and they resent me. They say she favors me more. It's true. She wanted me to be with her. My mother is much closer to me than she is to my sister or brother."

"You must have felt terrible when you had to go to work," I said.

"I did," Barbara answered. "All of my life I'd looked forward to having a baby and being with her. Then when I got divorced, it was as if all my dreams were dumped in the garbage. I'm so afraid my daughter will resent me. She's going to blame me for getting rid of her. We're not going to be as close as we might have been if I could be at home with her."

"She's already beginning to do that," I said, "when she reproaches you for leaving to go to work. Remember what I said about the parent's attitudes? A study conducted over twenty years ago by Marion Yarrow and her colleagues assessed whether mothers who were employed had more discipline problems with their preschool-aged children than mothers who stayed at home. They found that the mother's employment was not the critical factor—it was the mother's attitude. If she was doing what she thought was more or less right, whether it was taking a job or being at home, she was more likely to have a better relationship with her child.

"Another study found that when there was incongruence between what the mother thought she should be doing—being employed or staying home

—and what she was doing, her children were more likely to be insecurely attached."

"Do you think a self-fulfilling prophecy could be at work?" another air traffic controller asked Barbara. "Because you don't want to work, you assume that your daughter will have trouble. Maybe she'll start picking up those messages and then act them out."

"It's always hard to pinpoint the exact cause of a problem in any child's development. You've also been through a divorce, and that might have been hard for you and your daughter. Let's do an experiment. How many of you had mothers who were employed when you were three, four, and five?"

Ten people raised their hands.

"How many of you resented your mothers for leaving you?" I asked.

"I did resent her because she never had time for me when she came home. She was always too exhausted," said one participant.

"My mother didn't have a job," said another attendee. "She was on committees in the neighborhood, and they always met at night so she was gone all of the time. When she was home, she was too busy for me."

"So the critical issue for each of you was how involved your mothers were in your lives, how much they seemed to care about you and what you were doing. Is that true?" I asked.

"Yes," the participants of the seminar agreed.

"One recent study bears this out," I said. "Earl Grollman and Gerri Sweder interviewed over a thousand children whose parents were employed to understand how the children's daily life was affected. They found that the parents played a pivotal role in developing their children's self-esteem. These authors advise parents 'that a simple show of interest' can tell your child that he or she is worthwhile in your eyes. In the interviews conducted for this study, the children agreed that is the measure that counts most."

"Parents can also go overboard on this score," one participant stated. "My mother worked but she was always on top of me, running my life."

"Of course," I said. "It's a matter of balance. That's the point Jay Belsky from Penn State is making about mothers of infants. When mothers feel guilty and deprived, they may overwhelm their children. That problem can be remedied. If you pay attention to your child's behavior and notice that the child is pulling away, you may be overstimulating him or her. Then you can try a more low-keyed approach. The other issue, not paying enough attention, requires that you find some way to put your work problems aside and spend time with your child: listening, hanging out, doing the things your child likes to do.

"But what about the rest of you who had employed mothers? How did you feel?"

"I knew my mother loved her work, and we were proud of that. Sure, I have complaints. When I was older, I wished I didn't have to take care of my brothers, but that wasn't so bad, either. I knew how to take care of a house and children when I had my own."

"What do I do?" said Barbara. "I have to work and I don't want to."

"I'd suggest trying to find some way to deal with this problem as an adult without letting it spill over on your daughter," I answered. "If you can change the amount of time you work, do that. If you can't, find some way to resolve the anger and resentment. I would recommend counseling and/or meeting with other single parents who are in your situation."

"You know, just saying how I feel makes me feel better, but as a single parent I've got so much to do at night I don't have time to call up my friends. They'd probably be too busy to talk anyway."

"Then maybe you could have lunch together," said another attendee.

"It's complicated," I added. "You're most fearful about harming your relationship with your child, yet because you're angry about having a job, that anger can be transmitted to her, and you may end up creating the situation you most fear. That's why you have to try to come to terms with these feelings."

"We could have a single-parent group that meets together at lunch every few weeks," said Barbara.

"She has to work," said another employee, "but what about me? I made a decision to work and it's not so cut-and-dried. I wish at times that I had no choice, that I had to work in order to bring home food. Then I wouldn't feel so guilty."

The concomitant of choice is anxiety. Most people in today's world question what they are doing. Mothers who are employed wonder about the cost of this decision for their children. Mothers at home wonder about the cost to themselves. Will they be able to reenter the labor market? Will they only get low-level jobs? Do others look down on them because they are not employed? Resolving your feelings doesn't mean that lingering questions will be dispelled, but resolution is different from the out-and-out anger that Barbara has about being employed. Try to come to terms with the fact that there are trade-offs however you live, and do what you think is "more or less" right. Aim for what is "good enough" rather than what is perfect and then try to enjoy and appreciate the everyday moments with your child.

Q *How do I handle my guilt?*

A mother of a four-year-old:

. . . *As a working mother I feel guilty over so many things—but mostly because I'm always pushing my four-year-old to fit into* *my schedule, which is something I don't believe is supposed to happen. Other mothers I talk to feel the same way. We wonder what we're doing to our children.*

A father of a five-year-old:

. . . *I've just had a vacation. Now that I've gone back to work, my daughter has started to whine more—you know, that kind of high-pitched sound that can totally destroy you. It upsets me a lot.*

A mother of a four-year-old:

. . . *Everything comes to a head if my child asks me to take a day off from work. I usually turn right around and start a fight with my husband.*

Guilt results from the dissonance between the way we believe we should behave and the way we actually do behave. It is our internal monitor telling us that we have transgressed, stepped beyond the "shoulds" we have erected for ourselves. Because societal attitudes remain ambivalent about how mothers and fathers should act, we cannot help but be caught up in that uncertainty.

As the well-known pediatrician Berry Brazelton puts it in his book *Working and Caring,* today's employed families are "families without a culture." They are given very mixed messages about what they are doing and have few, if any, role models to look to. In addition, many of today's parents had mothers who stayed at home. They have memories of being read to, being helped with homework, and offered—as the syndicated columnist Ellen Goodman says—"something lovin' from the oven" when they came home after school. Thus their internal models of mother differ from the way they are living. But is this reality or fantasy? I once assigned a graduate class an interview with their own mothers about their early years of parenthood. Contrary to their expectations, many of their own mothers had not lived the picture-book life their sons and daughters imagined. As new parents thirty to forty years ago, many had been as uncertain and as ambivalent as their grown children are today.

In my own studies of parenthood, I have found that the time of being a new parent is a time of insecurity. Parents worry about the decisions they make—what to feed their child, how to discipline, and so forth. Thus, the uncertainty concerning being employed or not is also part of a normal developmental process.

Triggers for Guilt

In addition to trangressing societal or personal expectation, guilt arises from other sources:

- missing your child
- worrying that your child is missing you
- concern about the immediate implications of what you are doing (e.g., have you found good child care?)
- concern over the long-term implications (e.g., how can you be sure that you are not jeopardizing your child's future development?)

Guilt can be intensified by a conflict, minor or major, between parent and child. Laura Bendel, mother of four-year-old Vicky, describes such an incident:

■ ■ ■ *Our greatest problems occur when I'm trying to get Vicky off to school on time. She's a late riser. We keep her up until nine so my husband can see her when he gets home. As a result, she's often tired in the mornings.*

My impatience in the mornings has been a source of conflict for us most of her life. I hate spending my morning saying, "Come on, let's go. If you don't have that shirt on by the time I get out of the bedroom, I'm going to have to put it on for you." I'll come back, and the shirt's not on. It escalates into a conflict: I try to dress her and, of course, that threatens her independence and she cries.

It upsets me a lot because it's our first encounter of the day and we have only this one hour together before we go our separate ways. I feel tremendous guilt about the fact that day after day what she hears me say is, "Hurry up. Let's go. Hurry up."

As any parent can attest, hassles in the morning, whether the mother is employed or at home, are a normal feature of life with a preschool child. But if the employed parent is employed for an organization with strict time policies, pressure is added.

In Laura Bendel's case these morning encounters violate her image of the way she is supposed to behave and set off her own uncertainty about the repercussions of employment. In her mind, she has forged a trade-off. In return for having a job, she will devote almost all of the remainder of her time to Vicky. She expects her hours with her daughter to be quality time, that is, conflict free. When things fall apart, Laura blames herself:

● ● ● *When I pick Vicky up at school, she doesn't want to come with me. That has really become chronic. I know she's probably angry that I left her at school. One day she said, right out loud in front of everybody, "I don't want to go home with you." And I said, "Let's put your jacket on and go." I'd been dealing with this for so long with such patience and then for her to say that!*

When I got in the car, I said, "Don't you dare feel that way about coming home." I know it was the wrong thing to say, because I was trying to tell her what to feel, but at that moment I didn't care. I also told her if she ever did it again, I would think of a "wonderful" punishment for her because I was really angry.

I was still angry when I walked in the house. I wasn't able to do anything except just sit there. Vicky came in very quietly, eyeing me. I looked right back at her. She began playing with a toy on the table in front of me. We never let go of our eye contact.

Finally she said, "Mommy." I said, "Yes." She said, "Aren't you ever going to talk to me again?" Children have this wonderful way of defusing all your feelings. I just reached out and hugged her. She really held on tight.

I felt that I had scared her to the point of having her take care of me. I said, "I want you to understand the reason I was so hurt was because when I come to pick you up, I'm full of good feelings for you. I want to see you after having been gone all that time. And if you say to me out loud, in front of everybody, 'I don't want to go home with you,' it hurts me. It makes me feel sad. It embarrasses me in front of all your teachers."

Again, a conflict with her daughter had triggered the hidden expectations Laura has. She understands that Vicky's resistance at departure may be caused by her involvement in the play at school or that refusing to leave gives Vicky the control she must surrender by complying with her mother's schedule in the morning. Nevertheless, Vicky's rejection counters Laura's hope that Vicky will be happy to see her at the end of the day, that their time together (as in the mornings) will be devoid of problems. An even more subtle fear is that Vicky's rejection reveals publicly the unspeakable possibility that Laura is one of those neglectful, self-absorbed employed mothers.

Another mother, Lynn Russell, feels guilty when she turns down her child's invitation to spend a day at home:

> ▪ ▪ ▪ *One morning when I was getting ready to walk out the door,*
> *Amanda said, "I don't want to go to the babysitter's today. I*
> *want to stay at home and play with you."*
>
> *I answered that I'd like to stay home with her, too—to have*
> *lunch together, to be together, but I could not do it that day.*
> *"We've only got four more days till the weekend and then we*
> *can have a day together."*
>
> *Amanda finally bought what I said, and she went to the*
> *babysitter, but I'm not so sure I really buy it. I felt miserable*
> *all day. What would be so awful about taking a day and*
> *playing hooky together?*

Assuaging the Guilt

As children, many of us learned a simple formula for assuaging guilt: We
did something wrong, we felt bad, and we then acted bad until we were
punished. The bad deed was absolved; our conscience was clean.

As adults, we may follow a similar pattern. The blowups between Laura
and her daughter are Laura's "deserved" punishment; her daughter is then,
in her words, "paying me back." As soon as parents become aware that
they are feeding the conflict by setting up their own punishments, they can
try to put a stop to it.

Another way to appease guilt is to offer compensation. On the day that
Amanda asked her to stay home from her job, Lynn Russell found herself
in a store near her office:

> ▪ ▪ ▪ *I bought a little box of cookies and put them on Amanda's seat*
> *in the car. When I picked her up from the babysitter, I said,*
> *"There's a surprise for you." I guess it was my way of handling*
> *the guilt! I was thinking, "I might not be with you but I'll get*
> *you a little present to let you know I was thinking about you."*

Guilty parents commonly try to reduce their discomfort by giving their
children presents. This friendly gesture does not solve the problem. When
used as a regular tactic, children sense their parents' uncertainty and will
probably feel uncertain themselves. The result is that children often begin
to demand presents, perhaps to quell their own anxiety. As one parent
remarked, "It eventually made me mad that my daughter insisted that I
bring her something every day."

The Happiness Trap

In her book, *Loving Your Child Isn't Enough,* Nancy Samalin describes a
phenomenon called the Happiness Trap: If we don't cater to our children's
happiness, we are bad parents. As she puts it, the child, "like the judge in a

black robe," picks up on the guilt and "pronounces the verdict": unfit mother or father.

In sum, all parents feel guilt (the "everyday garden variety guilt," I call it) at one time or another. Problems ensue when the guilt causes us to tip the scale so that we are trying to compensate for our absences or indirectly asking our child to judge or punish us. Then we have stepped too far out of the role of parent to be a source of support and guidance for children as they themselves grapple with these issues.

SOLUTIONS

Reducing the Immediate Guilt

Guilt, at least in its initial manifestations, is not harmful. It can be seen as a signal of an unmet expectation, giving the parent an opportunity to uncover the expectation and ask if it is realistic or not. There are several typically unrealistic expectations:

Family life should be 100 percent child-centered or 100 percent adult-centered.   In conducting workshops for employed parents at corporations, I find that many parents, like Laura, compensate by devoting themselves 100 percent to the young child when they are together. This can give the child a frightening sense of his or her own omnipotence, and the child, in turn, often pushes or is more hostile, almost as a way of asking the parents to set some boundaries. The parent begins to resist the demands of the child and pulls back, insisting that the child suddenly be independent. Or the parent comes down too hard and sets limits that threaten the child's autonomy.

Clearly the child needs a great deal of time and attention from the parent, but not 100 percent of the time. Neither is it realistic to expect family life to center around the needs of the adult. The art of parenthood is the tightrope task of trying to strike a balance between ensuring that the child's needs are met but not totally at the expense of the adult's needs.

I have found in these seminars that parents have difficulty giving to others, including their children, if they don't feel given to. Parents say they are better parents when their own needs are met—whether it's time for themselves, for rest, or for pursuing a stimulating interest.

Quality time should be conflict free.   Growth for children (and adults too) stems from the resolution of problems. It is constructive for parents to change their view of quality time—from an illusion in which parent and child are happy, relaxed, and enjoying each other every minute to a realization that quality time also involves family problem-solving.

No is a rejection.   One principle of effective parenting is that both parent and child are allowed to express feelings without an implied judgment about the other's moral worth. When Vicky refuses to leave her child-care center, she should not be judged as bad or disobedient but rather as a child expressing a legitimate feeling: "I don't want to leave." When Laura feels bad about her daughter's response, she is not an unfit mother who needs to explain or justify her employment.

The fact that Vicky does not want to go home is not necessarily a consequence of her mother's employment. Children often store up their negative feelings until day's end when they can release them against the person with whom they feel most safe—the parent. Furthermore, children reject parents whether they are with them every minute of the day or not. This is a normal expression of the child's need to be more independent. What is important, therefore, is not the child's rejection of the parent but *how* it is handled. For example, telling a child who is fussing at the end of child care to be happy to see the parent denies or undermines the child's own feeling. Instead, the parent can accept the child's own point of view with such statements as, "I know that you don't want to leave."

Likewise, saying no to a child need not be a rejection. When parents cannot take a day off, they can do as Lynn did and tell their children that they would really like to even if they cannot.

Long-Term Guilt

Coming to terms with the deeper and more profound anxiety of whether your job will in fact "harm" your child is more difficult. Because this is also part of the developmental uncertainty of settling into a new role as a parent, the questioning never entirely goes away.

To Reduce Guilt, It Must Be Acknowledged

Berry Brazelton finds that parents respond to guilt either by admitting it and working it through or by denying it and rationalizing it away. This latter tendency is worrisome. Denied guilt is more dangerous because it pops up in unexpected, unintended ways. Some parents become detached or resentful, going through the motions of care while avoiding eye contact or conversation with their child, showing no open affection. In fact, some care so deeply that they turn off their feelings because they fear their inadequacies as a parent. If your resentment is very high, it is useful to talk to friends or your spouse or seek professional help.

Guilt Is Reduced by Paying Attention to How Your Child Is Doing

Judith Rubenstein at Boston University Medical School has conducted numerous studies on the effects of mothers' employment on young children. She has devised a list of warning signs for parents:

- excessive anxiety, such as fears, nervous habits, nightmares
- excessive avoidance of the mother

- excessive crying
- excessive clinging
- excessive aggressiveness

If your child exhibits these signs, consider the following factors:

Temporary Separation Distress. When children first begin child care, they are likely to be upset. Contrary to usual opinion, a child does not separate once and for all; separation is a gradual process of venturing out and returning for reassurance. Children may also show increased separation distress just before making a big move toward independence, such as becoming toilet trained. If this is the case, give your child more than the usual comfort and positive attention during this time and the distress will usually abate. It is also helpful to look at the process of separation as an opportunity for growth, for enlarging the child's world.

Problem in the Child-Care Program. Emily Berger, the mother of a preschool-aged son, explains this approach:

■ ■ ■ *When Tom seems tense or moody, the first thing I do is check with other parents. Is this something he's going through because of his age? Is something wrong at school?*

Once I found there really was a problem at school. All the parents said their kids were acting funny. So we checked further, and there was a new teacher who was putting the kids down.

Other aspects of child care can cause children distress. The first thing that parents fear is abuse; because of its importance, this subject is covered in separate sections (see the section on sexual abuse, pages 428–429). A conflict or lack of "goodness of fit" between the child-care provider and the child or between the provider and parent can also cause problems. For example, the provider may want the child to sit still and listen to a story while the child is happiest exploring a mud puddle. The values of parent and provider may differ: the provider may emphasize the need for a balanced diet, whereas the parent allows the child to eat whatever he pleases in hopes of avoiding future eating problems. Rubenstein also notes that tension between the children in the child-care program (for example, the sedate child in a group of active runners) can be another source of stress to a child.

Preoccupation by Parents with Work or Other Family Stress. Emily Berger also finds that on occasion she is so absorbed in her own problems that she becomes distant and withdrawn with Tom. She says:

■ ■ ■ *I realized I had been wrapped up with some problems in my marriage. Even though I was with Tom, I was drifting off and not paying attention to him. Once he put his hand on my chin and turned my face toward his, saying, "Listen to me." I then realized that I had to separate out my own concerns and not let them prevent me from enjoying him. When I did that I found that the fun we were having even helped me.*

In addition, a change on the job, such as longer hours or greater job pressure, can carry over to the child. So can family changes: a move, the birth of a new child, and so forth.

Improving the Fit Between Parent and Child

This is one source of Laura Bendel's problems with Vicky—Vicky is slow, Laura moves quickly:

. . . *One of the things that turns out to be a real asset for me as a working mother is that I'm fast. I eat fast, I walk fast. I'm probably a typical Type A personality. These are not excellent characteristics for raising children. When you raise children you really have to accommodate yourself to their pace a lot of the time. So we come naturally into conflict here.*

Research has shown that children are born with and retain what has been called a constitution or temperament (see the section on temperament, pages 170–181). One of the most enduring traits is activity level. In general, when there is what Thomas and Chess call "goodness of fit" between the tempos of parent and child, the relationship is less subject to strain. Laura has been trying new approaches to help reduce the tension caused by their differences. To handle the morning hassles, she gave her daughter an alarm clock. This gave Vicky the responsibility for getting dressed just at the point when she wanted more independence:

. . . *The very first day I overslept. When I woke up, I thought, "Oh, my God, today is going to be terrible." I got up and went out into the hall, and there was Vicky. She said, "Mommy, look. The alarm went off, and I got up. I'm all dressed."*

At going-home time, Laura could work with Vicky to set up a routine. When Laura arrives at the child-care center, Vicky could set a timer (or use a clock) for five more minutes of play before time to leave. Or they could establish a routine around a shared activity, for example, reading one story together every day before leaving. Finally, if the teacher is willing, Vicky could use this transitional time to borrow something from school to take home overnight and return the next day. The toy becomes a physical connection to the good experiences from the day at school. It also becomes a promise that Vicky will return to school soon.

Sometimes no suggestions work. One of you is tired or has had a difficult day. No matter what you do, things fall apart. You may end up carrying a crying child home from child care or rushing in the morning and then feeling guilty. Parents suggest:

- - - *I just try to avoid a war with my child, maybe we'll have a minor skirmish, but not a war.*

- - - *If I can, I keep a sense of humor and remember that tomorrow's a new day.*

- - - *I try not to let guilt get me down. I remember that my kids and I are doing the best we can, and you can't ask for more than that.*

VIEWPOINT: MOTHERS AT HOME VERSUS MOTHERS WHO ARE EMPLOYED

I see signs of an increasing conflict in many community forums.

- At a superintendents' conference, a suggestion by an educator was made that public schools needed to rethink their mission—perhaps some schools should become all-day schools for employed parents. This remark caused outrage among the mothers who were not employed. They were tired, they said, of catering to the children of mothers with jobs—picking them up from school if they were sick because their own parents couldn't come, having the children to their houses for playdates that were seldom reciprocated.
- At a corporate seminar, the parents lambasted the mothers at home—"for always trying to see problems and deficits in my children." They wondered if the children whose mothers were at home were not suffering from "mother smother."
- A television show actually pitted the two groups against each other and ended in a screaming match.

The causes for the conflict, I believe, grow out of the normal insecurity we all feel as new parents. We wonder if we are doing the right thing for our children—from the food we give them to our employment status. As Carol Austen, the mother of a three-year-old, said:

> *. . . After surviving motherhood for three years and talking to many other parents, I've come to realize that whatever you do, you feel you're doing it wrong. If you work part time, full time, or stay at home, you think you should have made a different choice. I still feel guilty (I work full time, from necessity), but I now also know that guilt comes with the territory.*

The doubts we feel often give rise to the need to be right, to protect our choice: "If what I am doing is okay, then another parent who takes a different path must be wrong." Therein lies the roots of the conflict.

Yes, of course, there can be real grievances: a parent who takes advantage of your accommodating nature; someone who is so all-sufferingly perfect that everyone else pales by comparison. These are people we do better to avoid. Nevertheless, the generic conflict between mothers at home and mothers who are employed disturbs me. To disapprove of other parents diminishes and undermines us all. We have more to gain by banding together—to promote the value our society puts on parenting in general.

Q *How does my job affect me and my family?*

At 7:00 P.M. on a weeknight in Seattle, a department store at a suburban mall was offering a special program for their customers—not the customary fashion show, but a seminar on work and family life. This would not have happened even five years ago. The fact that work and family life seminars are scheduled at department stores and corporations represents a change comparable to the magazine and television ads that picture a father doing (not praising his wife for doing) the family wash, or a mother in a business suit (not a housedress) fixing breakfast cereal for the children. One of the momentous changes in American life is the movement of mothers into the workplace, bringing with it a whole new set of questions:

A mother of a three-year-old says:

> *. . . I work as a word processor. I wonder how you can discipline and yet maintain a loving relationship with a three-year-old in just three hours a day.*

A father of a five-year-old says:

- - - *I have to punch a time clock at the plant where I work. If I don't come in on time, I get in trouble and could even get fired. My problem is that I wait with my five-year-old until the school bus comes. When it's late, I'm late. I don't want Aviva to wait alone. You can't win—you're having to choose against taking care of your child or taking care of your family by keeping your job.*

A mother with a ten- and a five-year old says:

- - - *I'm a first-grade teacher. I have a demanding job. Because of the increased pressure from parents for their children to succeed, my school system is putting younger children in the first grade, and often they aren't ready. What's more, the school is understaffed and underequipped. I care about my job, but I wonder sometimes if it's all worth it. I wonder how this is affecting me and my family?*

A mother with a four-year-old says:

- - - *I feel positive about my job—in fact, I think it helps me be a better parent, but then I have a great deal of freedom to decide when and how I do things.*

A father with a two-year-old says:

- - - *I feel the same way, but it's because of my boss. As far as I'm concerned, he could walk on water. He always makes me feel like I'm doing a wonderful job.*

A mother with a two-year-old says:

- - - *I am at home with my two-year-old, but my husband's job is hard on me. If he's had a bad day, I can tell from the way he turns the handle on the front door, slams the door, throws his coffee cup in the sink, and slams the bedroom door to change. He doesn't have to say anything. You can see it on his face.*

I have conducted numerous seminars for employed parents and no matter what the auspices, no matter the part of the country, parents tend to blame themselves whenever there are problems. If they run out of milk at dinnertime or end up doing the laundry at midnight, they feel "It's my fault. I don't manage time well enough."

According to one father at a seminar:

> ▪ ▪ ▪ *I never feel I've done everything I need to at work and at home. It goes from bad to terrible. I was convinced there was something wrong with me and everyone else was keeping their heads above water—I was the only one who was sinking.*

This viewpoint reflects the cultural attitude of "rugged individualism"—if there is a problem, the individual is solely to blame. It also reflects the belief that work and family life do not affect each other, that they are, in the words of Rosabeth Moss Kanter from Yale University, "separate, non-overlapping worlds."

With the influx of mothers into the labor force, these attitudes are being called into question. Perhaps problems result not only from the lack of such skills as time management. Perhaps certain aspects of employment are likely to have an effect on workers.

In the past ten years a new field of research on work and family life has emerged to investigate these questions. With increasing sophistication, researchers have begun to disentangle the complex chain of cause and effect and to identify those aspects of jobs that have the greatest potential impact, for good or for ill, on employees. They have found the most salient factors to be these:

- the number of hours worked
- job insecurity
- job demands
- job autonomy
- relationships at work

Time

When I asked the participants at the Seattle seminar to name their biggest problem, the majority replied time. "There's never enough to do what I need to do," said Anita Smith, a word processor with a three-year-old.

It is assumed that most workers work a forty-hour week. In a nationally representative survey of two-parent-employed families with children twelve or under that Diane Hughes and I conducted for *Fortune* magazine, we found that most parents work longer hours. In fact, only 4 percent of the men and 23 percent of the women were employed fewer than forty hours. Thirty-seven percent of the men and 13 percent of the women were employed more than fifty hours per week.

In our various research projects, we have examined the question "Is the number of hours employed predictive of more problems?" The answer has almost always been yes. For example, in the *Fortune* study, we found that the more hours on the job, the more likely the workers were to have experienced stress and a greater sense that their job interferes with their family life. Other studies, however, indicate that excessive work hours lead to stress only in conjunction with other problems such as tension on the job.

Schedule Conflicts

Marvin King, the father waiting for the school bus, has a problem aligning his family schedule with his work schedule. So does the employed mother whose boss asks her to stay late at the last minute but who must pick up her child from a child-care center promptly at 5:30. So do the employed parents invited to attend a nursery school open house on a weekday afternoon.

According to the Quality of Employment Survey—a nationally representative study—schedule conflicts are a primary source of stress for employed parents, particularly mothers. This problem results largely from the unevenness of social change. Family life, particularly the increase in the number of employed mothers, is changing faster than insititutional response. Such practices as strict adherence to the time clock or the agrarian model of schooling, with short days and long vacations, are predicated on having one parent (i.e., the mother) at home.

Job Insecurity

The problem for Marvin King, however, was not just one of schedules. If he is late more than two or three times, his job would be jeopardized. Sometimes he fabricates excuses to his boss: "There was a horrible traffic jam," or "The battery was dead." The tension of job insecurity is carried home. He often finds himself withdrawing and worrying.

Our research at Bank Street College has found that feeling insecure about one's job is predictive of greater stress for both employed mothers and fathers. Today, with corporate cutbacks, mergers and acquisitions, and competition from foreign manufacturing, employers are less likely to promise "a job for life." The relationship between employer and employee is shifting, and job insecurity is on the rise.

Job Demands

Jackie Fuller, the teacher, was concerned about the way her job dominated her time and thoughts at home. There was so much pressure and so little help, that she often had to bring her work home:

■ ■ ■ *If I am going to do a good job, I have to spend every evening grading papers and preparing assignments. After dinner, I feel as if I'm going into a war—demands from my children, de-*

mands from my husband, and the pressure to prepare for school the next day.

In every study we have conducted, we have found that the more demanding and hectic the job, the more likely the workers are to have higher levels of stress and to experience greater conflict between work and family life. These workers also are more likely to have more tension-related health problems: pounding and racing heart, backaches, headaches, shortness of breath, trouble sleeping, etc. Other research, most notably studies conducted by Karasek, have had similar findings: employees with very demanding jobs are in the high-risk category for health problems.

Job Autonomy

Karasek also found that when a demanding job is coupled with little freedom or decision-making power, workers are even worse off. Indeed, he found this combination predictive of heart problems.

On the other hand, when workers have "job autonomy," they are much more likely to be satisfied with their jobs as well as with life in general. Job autonomy means that workers have some control over the tasks and timing of their jobs; they are not governed by rigid, inflexible policies issued from above.

Relationships at Work

It goes without saying that the degree of job autonomy depends largely on the boss. In our research on stress in work and family life, we have found that the relationship with the boss is pivotal in how satisfied workers are in their jobs, how stressed they are, and even how physically healthy.

The relationship with the boss involves support for on-the-job tasks. Does he or she respect your abilities? Do you consider your boss competent? Does your boss help you get your work done, and can you turn to him or her if there is a problem? Does your boss make you feel like you are doing a good job? A study by Rena Repetti from the University of Pennsylvania found that a nonsupportive boss is the strongest predictor of anxiety and depression.

In our research at Bank Street College, we are looking at yet another component of the supervisory relationship: How supportive is the supervisor of the worker's family life? Is he or she flexible when there is a family emergency or when the employee has everyday family matters to attend to? How comfortable is the employee in speaking about family issues with the supervisor and how understanding is she or he in response? We have found that having a boss who is supportive during a work/family problem is a link to better psychological and physical health. As Nancy Inglis, mother of a three-year-old and a seven-year-old, puts it:

. . . *I have been able to work full time and not lose my mind only because I have had understanding supervisors. They've stood by me through chicken pox and innumerable ear infections, the shifting sands of child-care arrangements, and all the other important but unpredictable demands kids can make on your time.*

In all of our studies we ask about top management: How concerned is top management about employees' welfare? How flexible are they if workers have a family problem? We have found that the perception of a lack of support from the top is predictive of more stress, more tension-related health problems, and a more pervasive conflict between job and family responsibilities.

Sometimes a good relationship with co-workers can counterbalance difficulties with management. Chaya Piotrkowski found that conflict with co-workers can affect the workers' children. She measured conflict by surveying all members of various work groups and assessing each group's problems with co-workers. Those in hostile and conflict-ridden groups were much more likely to have children who were depressed and suffered more colds and other illnesses.

In one of our studies we interviewed a number of the employees' school-aged and teenaged children. At the end of the interview, we asked what they would like to see done to improve their family lives. The children's suggestion was to stop the infighting among the workers—so their parents would not come home so "wired."

Work/Family Spillover

When we reported the children's idea to their parents, they were surprised. Although they were fully aware of the tension at work, they did not suspect their children felt its repercussions. Although most people consider work and family separate spheres, studies indicate that employment conditions distinctly affect home life. Lisa Joseph knows all too well how her husband's moods reflect his day at work:

. . . *When Arthur has had a bad day, he comes home and wants nothing to do with our daughter, Julia. He sits in his chair, puts on the TV, and yells if we make noise.*

If he talks, he wants to talk about his problems: "Mark (his boss) showed me this, didn't show me that."

If I have a problem with the bills, he says, "Well, you do the bills. You take care of it." He doesn't want to hear about my day with Julia.

Other times when he comes home, all he cares about is seeing Julia. I love that.

Lisa is describing what has been defined by work/family researchers as spillover. Ann Crouter of Pennsylvania State University interviewed employed parents at the end of the work day, and then two hours later at home; she found that run-ins with the boss led to quarrels within the family. Diane Hughes and others identify three types of spillover—of mood, energy, and irritability. Employment can be exhausting or stimulating, and that depletion or enhancement of energy carries over into family responsibilities. In addition, a good or bad day at work affects one's mood and irritability.

How Prevalent Is Work/Family Interference?

In our research, we assessed the overall degree to which work and family life responsibilities conflict with each other for the general population (parents and nonparents). At one corporation, 43 percent of all women and 42 percent of all men experienced a high degree of interference. However, for parents of young children (under six years old), the numbers were even higher: 51 percent of the men and 68 percent of the women.

This response makes clear that problems do not result only from "bad time-management skills." Jobs can and do affect families.

Coping

Whether stressful situations at work and at home result in actual stress or not has to do with how the individual perceives the situation and then copes with it. Two social scientists who have studied stress, Lazarus and Launier, conclude that "the ways people cope with stress may be even more important to overall morale, social functioning, and health/illness than the frequency and severity of episodes of stress themselves." Researchers on work/family stress concur that taking action to cope with work/family problems is indisputably associated with good mental and physical health.

The following section describes techniques that employed parents have used successfully to master the work/family problems in their lives.

SOLUTIONS

Making a List of the Problems

The first step in handling work/family spillover is to understand it. Making a list of all sources of stress is helpful because they become less of a confusing morass or, as Jackie Fuller, the teacher, put it, "pressures pulling every which way."

Jackie's list might include the following:

School Problems:
- administration—lack of understanding
- budget—not enough money
- demands from parents
- needs of children
- lack of classroom help

Problems at Home:
- finding time for everything
- finding time for myself
- handling tension

Understanding Expectations and Seeing if They Are Realistic

Once the list is completed, the second step is to understand the role that expectations play in each situation—what are the "shoulds" and are they realistic or not?

Some of Jackie's stress resulted from her anger that things were not as they *should* be: A school administrator *should* manage the budget and resources better so that Jackie could have an easier time teaching; her pupils *should* be better prepared for first grade; her husband and children *should* know to help her; her home *should* be clean and neat all the time; and she *should* be able to do it all. Once she became aware of these expectations, she was able to figure out that she wanted her pupils to do well—a realistic expectation—but she could not expect her principal to manage things more efficiently or provide help. At home, she decided that she could not take care of everything for everyone all the time—she needed others to help, and this was not an admission of her own inferiority or failure.

By talking about these issues, Jackie and the other participants in the seminar could understand their hidden expectations and begin the process of making sense of them.

Solving One Problem at a Time

The third step is to select one area to resolve. Tackling everything at once can be overwhelming; selecting one issue provides an opportunity for success. As the research on work and family life indicates, taking action or making a plan to deal with a problem can lead to diminution of stress.

Whose problem is it? Deciding whose problem it is is a technique developed by Thomas Gordon. This was a useful tool for Lisa, who realized that it wasn't just Arthur's problem—if his moods affected her, then she, too, had a problem.

Give "I" messages.   It was important for Lisa not to hold her feelings in:

▪ ▪ ▪ *Finally this past weekend, I talked to Arthur. He never realized I was miserable.*

Once it is clear whose problem it is, it is more productive to express it by giving "I" messages. Because Lisa said, "It bothers me when you come home so angry," she enlisted a more cooperative attitude from Arthur than if she had accused, blamed, or confronted him.

Keep the problem out in front, separate from the individuals involved, and problem-solve.   Expressing the problem with an "I" message makes it clear that the problem is of one's own making. When a father was bothered about the chaos at dinnertime every night, he found that if he wrote this problem down on paper, listing possible suggestions with their pros and cons, he was less likely to blame others. When he, his wife, and children did this together, it became cooperative problem-solving.

Compartmentalizing

Some work problems can be brought home; others are best dealt with at work. Jackie Fuller decided that complaining at home all the time upset her family. Neither her children nor her husband could do anything to help her; they did not fully understand the situation. Their advice sounded accusatory and would set off a family argument.

Instead, Jackie decided to try to secure a teaching assistant provided for by the school budget. She could also let the children in her class help grade papers. Finally, she could have the parents read with their children one night a week. This would give her the night off.

At another work/family seminar, several airline employees came to a similar conclusion: deal with certain work problems at work. Their jobs were aggravating. All day long they took reservations on the telephone, handled complicated fares and travel schedules, and dealt with complaints under severe time pressures, frequently with "rude, impatient, and abusive" customers. They went home "like snakes ready to bite."

These employees found that while they really wanted sympathy, their spouses responded with lectures, advice, or accusations. Because they were employed in the same office, they could help each other by talking about their problems. If and when they did turn to their families, they could state what they wanted: "I just want you to listen to me and give me sympathy. I don't want you to tell me what to do."

Keeping a Sense of Humor

One way that the airline reservation clerks handled their work stress was to joke about it. At the end of the day, they would nominate the "worst" and "best" customer of the day, and turn the aggravations into funny stories. Other employed parents agree that a sense of humor is an antidote to stress. In the desire to do it all, to be perfect, they had been taking everything too seriously.

Escaping

Another suggestion to relieve work stress is to escape. For one employed parent, it was reading mystery novels for half an hour, even when the dishes were waiting to be done. For another, it was watching television while pedaling on an exercise bike. For still another, it was a regular dinner with college friends.

Exercising

Exercise releases stress. Problems, however, arise when exercise becomes one more requirement to fit into a busy schedule. After spending several hundred dollars to join a health club, Jackie Fuller found it a burden, something she "should" do but never got to. Exercise is more effective if it fits comfortably into your schedule. Numerous parents get up early and jog before breakfast; others jog during their lunch hour. Some join team sports such as soccer or volleyball so that exercise becomes a social activity. At one workplace, a group of employees arranged for an aerobics class at the end of the day.

Meditating

Meditating is another natural release for tension. A computer programmer turns off her machine at the end of the day and meditates for several minutes before going home to her three-year-old.

Finding Social Support

Turning to others for help runs against some entrenched notions in American culture:

- Dependence is weakness.
- Your spouse should meet all of your needs, therefore you should not have to go beyond the family.
- Problems on the job (or in parenthood) are self-caused, an indication that you have not achieved the perfection that is so desired.

Social support has a very different underlying philosophy:

- At different times in their lives all people face problems.
- Growth comes from facing problems when they emerge.

The most supportive and constructive relationships are interdependent, consisting of give-and-take, sometimes leaning on others, sometimes helping them.

In general, employed parents need a variety of people to form networks of support: friends at work with whom one can talk honestly without regard for office politics, as well as friends for talking through concerns about the children or other home issues. The litmus test of a supportive relationship is feeling good after spending time together, more empowered, better able to face problems, even to laugh at them. This doesn't mean that relationships "just happen" this way. We must work to create mutually beneficial relationships.

For example, one employed mother with three children (eight, six, and three) decided that she needed to be given "strokes" for managing a job and a family so well. And so she told her husband that's what she needed. She, in turn, began complimenting him.

Being a supportive person ultimately begins with treating oneself well. After a stressful day at the job, one man would tell himself what a good job he had done that day.

"These are new patterns we are creating," a seminar participant said. "And it's not always easy."

Practical Aspects of Employment

Q *I've just gone back to my job and I've had trouble handling this with my son.*

Isabelle Savin is the mother of a three-and-a-half-year-old, Philip. When she first returned to her job, things were, in her words, "terrible":

• • • *I'd made up my mind that the easiest way to manage was to do everything myself. The first morning I got Philip up and dressed him. When I picked him up to take him downstairs, he began to resist. He tried to crawl back into bed, curling into the fetal position, just trying to get safe. In retrospect, I think he was trying to get some kind of control over what was happening to him.*

When I finally got him downstairs, I gave him breakfast. It was very regimented. I walked to the car, commanding, "You have to walk faster, you're not walking fast enough." I felt he was dillydallying along the way. He wasn't really dillydallying, he was walking like a normal three-and-a-half-year-old, but I perceived it differently that morning.

The next morning, I decided I hadn't felt good about hassling Philip to get to the car. So I picked him up at the front door and carried him. He was limp in my arms, like a baby.

I felt this rising level of anxiety that hadn't ever been there before. That certainly affected my perception of Philip. My tolerance for what a three-and-a-half-year-old could do went way off scale. I ranged from treating him like a baby, actually carrying him, to expecting very grown-up behavior. I wanted him to understand what I needed, what I wanted, and what I had to do.

That first week, everything was a burden—from finding a pencil at work to getting my son up in the morning.

Work and Family

Major changes such as taking a new job disrupt the previous order and systems that people have established and make the simplest task seem complex. Little research has been conducted on the return to employment, but it is clear that like any other life transition, such as the birth of a child or divorce, there are both short-term and long-term effects.

Separation

One issue in this transition for Isabelle is the increase in time away from Philip. Parents deal with this separation in many ways. Some feel a sense of loss. Parents carry pictures of their child; are lonely, feel guilty, worry that they are harming their child by being away, or have flashes of fear in which they imagine disasters occurring while they are apart. Seeing another parent with a child during the workday can trigger feelings of mourning. Other parents block out ambivalence, rigidly defending what they are doing, and shielding themselves from the loss. For still other parents, these two ways of coping commingle: parents feel the pain, then defend against it. Clearly, the parental response to separation depends on the age and temperament of the child, the child's reaction to the new situation, and prior experiences with separations.

Isabelle is one of those parents who initially focused on herself and her own needs. When parents behave this way, others sometimes assume they do not care about the child. It is, however, important to understand that this initial reaction is normal, much like the focus on the self following divorce. The fact that Isabelle saw Philip as more grown-up and more capable is similar to mothers who, following the birth of a second child, suddenly begin to pressure their firstborns for more adult behavior. Like birth or divorce, returning to employment is a life-changing event, involving a transformation in one's sense of self. Warding off the immediate impact is not uncommon—and is only problematic if it persists, blinding the parent to the needs of the child.

Expectations about Going Back to Work

Consciously or not, parents have expectations about the mother's employment, including whether or not the mother should be employed and, if so, when, for how many hours, and in what kind of job. There are also expectations about the children's response—both in terms of child care and psychological adaptation. If an expectation is not realized, parents can feel disappointed, upset, or angry. If the mother and father have divergent expectations, family stress is likely to result.

Isabelle is a single parent, divorced for over a year. She must be employed for economic reasons and is comfortable with this situation. She is a secretary; although her job does not correspond to the career expectations she had in college, she is content:

. . . *I've got my hands full just getting back into full-time work. I'd like to have a career someday, but I need to learn more about full-time work and being a single parent before I take on a career.*

One expectation has not come true. Isabelle expected Philip to respond more positively to her own needs. While he did not rebel or fight back as another child might have, he did retreat, pushing her away. His behavior clashed with her vision of herself as a mother. She remembers:

. . . *I went to work those first few days with this feeling of not being a good mother. I was full of anxiety, of tension, of not liking the way things had gone.*

That conflict became the impetus for Isabelle to change.

Child's Loss of the Known Mother

In some ways, Philip had been well prepared for his mother's return to full-time employment. The transition was gradual. Isabelle had been employed free lance and had already found child care (see the sections on evaluating early childhood programs, pages 407–423, and on entering a program, pages 429–437). Philip was thus familiar with his child-care center, already attached to the teachers, and involved with his friends.

In other ways, however, the entry was abrupt. The regimen of getting up and getting out of the house in record time was new to him. Isabelle explains:

... Looking back, I was just doing things to Philip, without explaining anything. Not only were there new routines, but I think he was seeing a whole new mother and he resisted that. He showed a lot of fear—not wanting to move. In a sense, I was hauling him, pulling him, even carrying him without even asking or talking to him. At first, it never occurred to me to involve him.

Isabelle makes an important point. Philip was faced with a combination of new experiences: changes in the morning routine and in his mother who was behaving in different ways. Philip underwent a double loss: the loss of time with his mother and the loss of his "known" mother. This double loss clearly eroded Philip's emerging sense of control over his environment and he retreated to babyish behavior. A sense of control is still fragile for most preschool children—witness the amount of blustering that preschool children use to convince themselves they are in charge.

In the development of a relationship between parent and child, the ability to predict each other's actions is essential, especially to the child's feeling of security and sense of self. This does not mean that the parent must never change; young children are, in fact, attracted to novel stimulation. Jerome Kagan, however, notes that the young child's emotional state is affected by his ability or inability to assimilate discrepant events. "An event that can be assimilated after some effort produces excitement, but one that cannot be assimilated produces uncertainty." This principle describes Philip's response to his mother's return to employment: it was too discrepant and he became anxious.

Losses for the Parents

Returning to a job also involves losses for the mother. Gone is the freedom to linger in the mornings, gone, at least so it feels at first, are the moments to savor with the children.

The father also experiences disruption. Routines change and so does the division of labor. Dinner may now consist of fast food. A father who was ambivalent about his wife's return told her, "You're shirking your responsibility. You told me that things wouldn't change."

Life of necessity changes and the change encompasses all family members. The less understanding the couple is of each other's needs and losses, the more problematic this transition. As one father said:

... When I complained to my wife about how hard it was for me, she listened without striking back. She told me how she was suffering, too. I didn't realize that and it helped.

SOLUTIONS

Establishing Priorities

Families have to establish new priorities and new schemes to make them happen. Isabelle did not want to give up her leisurely moments with Philip or be rushed all the time—those were her priorities. She talked with friends who had gone back to their jobs and together they came up with suggestions.

Getting up Earlier

Isabelle now sets her alarm thirty minutes earlier to have time for herself before waking Philip up. She says, "This was a real struggle. I don't like to get up early but I've done it because it was so important to me to feel better about the morning." This extra time also allows for a playtime with Philip.

Creating Morning Rituals

The next change Isabelle made was to establish a routine in the morning:

• • • *Philip likes to wake up slowly. There's a lot of touching and rocking and patting and soft talking until it's time to wake up. Then he wants to play.*

   We play for a little while on his bed, although he could continue for a long time. We've never come to the point where he has stopped playing on his own—it's always me saying, "All right, now it's time to start getting dressed. Now it's time to have breakfast." After enjoying the morning ritual, Philip is usually fairly agreeable about getting up.

Explaining the Parents' Needs/Giving the Child Responsibility

It also occurred to Isabelle that by carrying Philip to the car, she was infantilizing him. Instead, his cooperation could be enlisted:

• • • *I thought, why not expect Philip to get to the car on his own? That's when I started talking to him, saying that it was important for me to be at work on time. I also reminded him how important it was to him to be at day care on time for the morning circle time. I felt a real genuine response from him. "That makes sense. Yes. That's good. I'll do this for Mommy and for myself."*

   It was not enough to just say this to him. I needed to provide him with some techniques of how to do it. So we began to play about getting to the car. We'd march together. One time he left the house and got to the car first. When I came out the door he yelled, "Mommy, I'm here!" I knew at that point he'd gotten it. Now it's a routine.

Creating Bedtime Rituals

Bedtime routines can also contribute to the ease with which a child handles the morning. Isabelle changed these:

. . . *At first I had wanted him to get into bed, get covered up, and go to sleep in three seconds. I realized that my expectation was wrong, that there are some things I do to prepare myself for sleep. Philip said he'd like to have a song or a story before bedtime. We've also included some kind of closure: "How did your day go? You got a scratch from Tommy at school? How is it now?" Then we plan tomorrow—what he's going to wear, what the morning's going to be like, what's going to happen at school. Our bedtime ritual includes an ending for today and a projection of tomorrow.*

In this way, Isabelle is setting the stage for a cooperative morning as she gets ready for her job and her son gets ready for school. The routines are known, her behavior familiar. She has helped her son adapt to her return to employment.

Q *I travel for my job and I have young children. How can I make it work for them and for me?*

You pull your suitcase down with foreboding: "Do I really have to go? Is the plane safe? Do I have enough time to make the connection? Why did I book such an early flight?"

Before you finish packing, you realize you've left something you needed at work. Your clothes need ironing, and there is only one good tube of toothpaste and your family needs it, so you leave it at home. The shampoo bottle leaks. The final blow is when your four-year-old puts his arms around your legs and pleads, "Don't go."

Eventually you say goodbye to your children. As the plane lifts off, or the car pulls out, you feel relief. You've made it.

There are a number of techniques parents can use to get from that moment of foreboding to the arrival back home.

Planning in Advance

If you travel frequently, you can save time by photocopying master lists: the essentials to be packed, household instructions, and emergency backup numbers. For each trip, add the phone numbers where you can be reached. Prepack a case of things like a sewing kit, safety pins, Band-Aids, and items for travel emergencies. If you need child care, arrange it as far in advance as possible, and have a backup plan in place. Nothing is more upsetting than, suitcase in hand, receiving a call saying your child-care provider is sick.

Preparing the Children

Young children can manage your travel much better if they are prepared for it. Here are some techniques that help:

- A map with stick-on dots showing where you are going. Even though your children may not understand all of this, it is comforting for them to compare where you live with where you are going.
- A calendar on the wall or refrigerator with pictures of the major activities for your children while you're away and a pencil nearby to X out each day until you return.
- A packet of something special (a book of stickers or Livesavers) that contains the same number of items as days that you will be gone. Your children can take one a day and see or count how many are left until you return.
- A series of notes with a message for each day to be read to the children in the mornings. Again the number of notes remaining will serve as a reminder of how soon you will come home.
- A photograph of you for your child to keep in his room or take to school. Let your children know that you also carry photographs of them with you wherever you go.
- A "surprise package" for you made by your children. You can encourage them to put together a collection of drawings or messages, one for each day you will be gone.

Saying Goodbye

Even if difficult, it is important to tell your children that you are going and to say goodbye. If you are leaving before the children are awake, you can say goodbye the night before and leave a note.

Not saying goodbye can cost you the trust of the child. A mother of a four- and a two-year-old in Phoenix who resorted to this describes her experience:

- - - *It was the most terrible two weeks before I left for my business trip. First both kids got sick. I asked my parents to come and they got sick. Then my husband got a job offer, and he had to decide about that. I was going back to graduate school on top of working. Plus we were getting ready to move, so our apartment was upside down. Normally I would sit down and prepare the kids for my going away (I don't travel much), but I was at the end of my rope and couldn't face a scene.*

I just took them to school and left. When I called that night, the children were devastated. The older one had said to my husband, "Mommy wouldn't do that."

Particularly at this time of so much turmoil and change in the children's lives, it was all the more necessary to prepare the children so that they could muster their resources to cope with the separation.

Keeping in Touch

How you keep in touch with your children while away depends on their ages and individual styles. Most parents telephone; although hearing your voice may be a painful reminder that you are gone, it lets the children know that they can be in touch even though you are traveling.

The timing of calls can make a difference. Just before bedtime may be more difficult than late in the afternoon or right after dinner.

One mother whose telephone calls upset her children sends them a postcard for every day that she is away. A father tells his five-year-old to call early in the morning if she feels like it.

Bringing Home Presents

Families develop different practices concerning presents. The main thing to avoid, however, is assuaging your guilt by bringing home expensive presents on a regular basis. Such a pattern can lead to the children's demanding gifts and your resenting their insistence. Keep in mind that the purpose of bringing gifts home is to share something from your trip and to say, "I was thinking of you."

If you are a frequent traveler, you may want to start some sort of collection for your child—a pretty rock, an airport T-shirt with the name of the city, postcards, or travel activity books. If your child has a strong interest, for example, in Lego blocks, you may want to buy some special pieces and give one to your child each time you return. Drawing a simple book for your child about your trip can be particularly meaningful.

Preparing to Be Rejected

Just because you have missed your family and they have missed you does not in any way guarantee that the homecoming will be pleasant. Typically, young children shun their parent upon return, perhaps to assert control after being left behind. A mother describes such a scene:

• • • *I left my daughter with my mother. It hadn't been a great trip anyway, and it didn't help that my boss seemed completely unaware of how difficult it was for me to make this trip. I walked into the house to get my daughter and my mother was holding her. She reached out for me, then turned back to my mother and clasped her tightly. My mother said, "It serves you right for leaving her."*

A woman whose husband travels says:

• • • *When my husband comes back from being out of town, he's all geared up from his business deals. The kids and I are in our own routine and he walks in and tries to take over. We're happy to see him, but he has to learn to move in more gradually.*

You are home once again. You unpack what seems like a mountain of dirty clothes. Your four-year-old has refused to look at the book you so carefully drew on the plane. The suit you need for tomorrow is at the dry cleaners and the washing machine broke while you were away. Then your four-year-old comes and puts his arms around your legs and it is truly wonderful to be back.

EIGHT

Schools and Child Care

Choosing a Program

Q *How do I know what kind of child care is best for my child?*

Child care* is categorized primarily by *where* it is provided. There are three major forms: (1) in-home care by relatives or child-care providers (2) family day care; that is, care provided in a neighbor's or relative's home for a small group of children; and (3) center care; that is, care in a child-care center, or preschool extended-day program. Each kind of care has advantages and disadvantages.

IN HOME

Advantages	Disadvantages
1. more familiar to the child	1. possible lack of other children to play with
2. possibly more individual attention	2. parents are not necessarily sure what the child does all day
3. no need for transportation and other complicated arrangements	3. child-care provider can get sick, be late, or need to go away, leaving parents without child care
4. can be more flexible (some child-care providers can be there early, stay later, get dinner started, etc.)	4. sometimes more expensive depending on the going rate in the community and whether or not this is live-in care

* We define child care as all forms of nonparental care.

FAMILY DAY CARE

1. homelike and possibly more flexible, though family day providers do have their own personal and family needs
2. companionship with other children of different ages who usually live close by

3. can be less expensive—though if good adult/child ratio and small group size are adhered to (in most states the legal requirement is fewer than six children), and the caregiver is decently paid, family day care is not cheap

1. sometimes less structured but not necessarily less educational than center care
2. unless there is a backup system, parents are without child care if family day-care provider becomes sick or your child is sick
3. much family day care in this country is not licensed or registered, so parents are less sure about how to judge its quality

CENTER CARE

1. usually an emphasis on education
2. reliable programs don't close when a teacher or provider is sick

3. center care is usually regulated and inspected so programs have minimum standards to meet

1. can have too much of a group emphasis, too much structure
2. less flexible; centers generally open and close at fixed times and find it difficult to accommodate parent's individual work schedules
3. more costly, though again cost is directly related to quality issues such as group size and staff/child ratio and teachers' salaries

As you can see from the preceding list, almost every statement is qualified, with such words as "generally" or "usually." In-home, family day care, and center care can vary enormously. For example, family day care is usually more homelike, but I have known center programs that were modeled on family life, with mixed-age groups, a man and woman as head teachers, and furnishings that resembled homes.

The most important element of child care is the actual teacher-caregiver*
who cares for your child. It is therefore essential to look until you find a
person as well as a form of child care that you feel comfortable with.

When parents discuss child care they are often adamantly in favor of the
kind of care they have chosen and vehemently opposed to the other kinds.
Such comments may lead other parents to suspect that one kind of care is
best. In fact, this is untrue. According to research, no one kind of care is
better than another for *all* children; however, there certainly can be a form
of care and a particular provider who is best for your child.

To make the decision about your child's and your family's child-care
needs, consider the following:

Location.   Do you want your child to be in your home, close to home
or near you at work?

Cost.   What percentage of your *family* budget can you afford to spend
on child care? I say family budget because child care is considered by most
to be a woman's expenditure. It is thought that the cost of care should be
less than the mother's salary minus her working expenses. Recent studies,
however, continue to reveal that child-care workers are in the lowest paid
category of all workers in the United States, earning less than zookeepers
or bartenders despite the fact that many family day-care providers and
center teacher-caregivers have college or graduate degrees. The low pay and
lack of respect for this work is contributing to an exodus from the field.
Thus, to the extent you can afford it, it is important to pay your child-care
provider as well as you can.

Hours of Coverage.   What hours do you need covered? Do you need
flexibility about arrival and departure times?

Parents' Values.   Do you want an informal or more formal situation?
What style of teaching do you prefer? What do you want your child to
learn?

Child's Needs.   Does your child function best alone with an adult or
with a group of children? Is he or she better with children of the same age
or different ages? Under what kind of circumstances does your child do
best now? What do you estimate your child will need in three months? In
six months?

---

* I use the term teacher-caregiver to connote the dual functions of this job. I never
use the word babysitter (except when quoting parents). People do not sit on babies.
This is a critically important job and its name *must* indicate respect.

Q *What's the difference between schools and child care?*

If a large opinion survey were conducted on the difference between schools and child care for preschool children, I am quite sure a clear distinction would emerge. School-based programs (nursery schools and kindergartens) would be described as more educationally focused, while child-care programs would be seen as more custodial. This perception arose at a time when working mothers were more atypical and there was a fairly widespread disapproval of child care. Now that over half of the mothers of all preschoolers are in the labor force, the distinction has blurred. Nursery schools and kindergartens have extended hours, day-care centers have educational programs. However, the stereotypes remain strongly etched in popular opinion.

In fact, the only way to differentiate programs is by the *location* (in a home or institution), by the *length of the program* (ranging from two hours to all day), and by the *auspices of the program* (public school, nonprofit-private, and for-profit organization). The elements of a quality program remain the same, no matter where or what it is. For this reason when describing the ingredients of high-quality preschool programs in the following section, I do not differentiate between types of program. Instead, I focus on what has been learned about the best early childhood programs.

Q *What aspects of early childhood programs are the most important in promoting positive growth for children?*

- A mother and father have the names of two different nursery school programs, and they feel overwhelmed. Each place tells them that its program is the best for their child, and they do so in words that seem foreign: "cognitive growth," "the whole child," "peer interaction," "socioemotional gains." How do they evaluate? Do they select on the basis of cost, of location, or on curriculum goals, and how can they tell the difference between one program and another?
- A mother has interviewed two women to care for her two-year-old and five-year-old. One is too strict, the other too lenient, although she's the one who had more fun with the children. The strict woman was prompt and neat. The second says that she never misses work, but sometimes she's a little late because it's hard for her to get going in the mornings. "How do I decide?" the mother asks, "And how do I know my children will be safe and well cared for?"

Whether selecting in-home or out-of-home care the questions that I hear from parents are similar and so are the feelings: a desire to get this over as quickly as possible in order to escape the confusion and uncertainty, a sense of competition with all the other parents who may be making different choices, and a nervousness about how their choice will affect their child.

This is an auspicious time for parents to be expressing these feelings and asking these questions. Today, more than ever before, there are answers. The answers come from two sources:

1. an increasing number of studies are investigating how variations in child-care or preschool arrangements affect children, and

2. professionally agreed-upon standards and industrywide statements of the determinants of high-quality programs.

- *Accreditation Criteria Procedures of the National Academy of Early Childhood Programs.* Over a three-year-period these criteria were developed by the National Association for the Education of Young Children (NAEYC) by reviewing approximately fifty evaluation documents and the research literature; tested by submitting them to two hundred and fifty early childhood specialists; published in NAEYC's journal, and then field tested in thirty-two early childhood programs.
- *Early Childhood Environment Rating Scale.* Developed by Thelma Harms and Richard M. Clifford from the Frank Porter Graham Child Development Center at the University of North Carolina, this scale is now broadly used as a measure of high quality for group programs.

My review of the ingredients of quality will use the NAEYC criteria as a framework, within which I will incorporate findings from current research. Overall, three aspects of early childhood arrangements make a difference:

- the personal interaction between the teacher-caregiver and child and what they do together
- the features of the arrangement that are generally subject to state regulation—numbers of children, group size, the training of the teacher-caregiver, health and safety considerations, and so forth
- the linkage between the program and the family

THE PERSONAL INTERACTION

It is the everyday relationship between the teacher-caregiver and the child —the greeting in the morning, the comments made when the child has drawn a picture, the affection and respect demonstrated—that is the single most important determinant of quality. It is through this relationship that children learn about themselves and develop a healthy self-concept. It is also through this relationship that children learn about their world—facts, figures, and concepts that enable them to understand more about how their world works. Finally, it is through this relationship that children learn about the processes of learning: how to tackle something new, how to organize their thinking, and how to solve problems.

The relationship between adult and child has several aspects.

The Interpersonal Relationship

- In high quality early childhood programs there is frequent contact between the teacher-caregiver and the children—one to one, in small groups, and occasionally in large groups.
- Children are treated with affection.
- Children are treated with respect.
- Children are not discriminated against because of their race, religion, or ethnic background.
- Boys and girls are offered the same opportunities to use materials or take part in activities and are encouraged to do so.

The Teaching Relationship

Teaching, whether formal or informal, takes place primarily through the use of language. One large study, conducted in Bermuda where almost all children are in group child care and where the quality varies widely, found that a high degree of verbal interchange between the child and the teacher-caregiver not only promoted the child's acquisition of language but also influenced the child's positive emotional development.

- In high quality programs, the teacher-caregiver frequently speaks to the individual child as opposed to the whole group.
- The teacher-caregiver serves as a model for language development, speaking to the children clearly and well. This provides children with opportunities to understand words and ideas; in other words, "receptive language development."
- Children also have a chance to talk frequently, in informal conversations as well as in teaching situations.
- Adults listen to what the children say.
- Children use "expressive language," language that describes their experiences and conveys their emotions.
- Children have opportunities to reason, and to respond to "what," "how," and "what if" questions.

The Activities

Assessing the activities provided for the child by a teacher or caregiver may be one of the more difficult tasks that parents face. One study of child-care centers conducted in Pennsylvania by Susan Kontos and Richard Fiene found that parents were often drawn to the splashy elements of a center: "the carpeting, piped in music, overly neat and austere surroundings." In fact, these bear little, if any, relationship to the quality of the program.

Parents in general forget how they learned when they were very young. Their memories of learning come primarily from their later school years when knowledge is more likely to be equated with the acquisition and memorization of facts and figures in quiet, solitary pursuit and in teacher-directed activities. The preschooler, in contrast, learns through direct experience, by doing and acting upon his environment. In touching, tasting, seeking, hearing, experimenting, and playing, the child builds ideas and concepts. An important aspect of learning is also the opportunity for children to play together, share ideas, and cooperate on tasks.

One study shows that a key determinant of high quality (as measured by the Harms and Clifford scale) is the opportunity for children to play. The play of children is not seen as a "break" from important work but as the essence of the work itself. In play, children use replicas of the objects of their everyday environment (toy cars, kitchen equipment, dress-up clothes, and blocks) to reproduce and thus make sense of the experiences in their lives. (See the section on play, pages 61–71.)

High quality early childhood care arrangements are characterized by the following elements:

- The teacher-caregiver has a well-thought-out plan for the activities.
- Children engage in constructive play and have the opportunities to select what they do from a sufficient, though not overwhelming, number of choices.
- The teacher-caregiver is flexible about changing activities when the child seems to need to do so.
- The activities include indoor and outdoor times, noisy and quiet times that are both child-initiated and adult-initiated.
- The activities also include the chance for children to develop fine motor skills (scissors, puzzles, etc.) as well as gross motor skills (games such as follow the leader).
- There are creative activities—art, music, blocks, sand, and water play. Projects in which all children copy an adult model (all making the same Halloween pumpkin or Thanksgiving turkey) are rare.
- There are opportunities for children to look at books, to be read to, and to dictate their own stories.
- Transitions from one activity to another and routines are seen as learning activities.
- Children are free not to participate. The children, however, do not wan-

der around aimlessly. Several studies have revealed that children in low-quality programs are more likely to be unoccupied and that such behavior seems to lead to later problems in learning.

The Disciplinary Relationship

A considerable number of studies have been conducted on how different methods of parental discipline affect children and these findings can be applied to preschool programs. Studies have found that children develop self-control, are more compliant, cooperative, and considerate of the feelings of others if the following approaches are used:

- Adults focus children's attention on the problem or task to be accomplished before asking children to comply: "In a few minutes, it will be time to clean up."
- Reasoning is used as a technique. Not do it "because I say so" but because there is a logical reason: "The toys have to be put away so we can find them tomorrow."
- Other-oriented discipline is used. Teachers or caregivers explain how a child's behavior affects others: "John is upset because Emily pulled his hair."
- Problem-solving is encourged: "Both of you want the same toy. What ideas do you have to solve this problem?"
- Cooperation among children is fostered rather than competition.
- Positive reinforcement is given rather than criticism. Vandell and Powers found that in the highest quality programs, children had many more positive interactions with staff than in the low-quality ones.
- The rules are clear and consistent.
- The space and toys are set up so that few nos are necessary.

Stability

Research on child development has uniformly found that when the child is exposed to one caregiver after another after another, the child becomes at-risk for social and emotional problems. Studies have determined that young children who have to adjust to a large number of different child-care providers (whether in home-based or center-based care) are more likely to have anxious attachments to their mothers as measured by the strange situation procedure. Carollee Howes from UCLA has found that when young children change caregivers frequently, they look less competent in their interactions with other children, and materials in later years. This could be a chicken-and-egg situation—a parent who has to change the caregivers frequently may be more upset and anxious and this could influence the parent/child relationship.

A recent study by Mark Cummings from West Virginia University found that children had a much easier time separating from their mothers when they were being cared for by well-known caregivers and when they were in small groups.

It's also been found that children who have spent time together in child care are a source of support and comfort to each other when leaving their parents or in times of distress.

Parents usually think of stability in terms of their moving their child from one arrangement to another, but the high rate of staff turnover in family day care and center care has added a new dimension to this problem. As far as possible, try to select teachers or caregivers who have a commitment to working with young children and plan to stay in this profession.

THE FEATURES

As previously stated, the relationship between the child and the person who cares for him or her is the most important determinant of the quality. "In order to achieve that," says Sue Bredekamp, who directs the accreditation project at NAEYC, "other aspects come into play—that the adults have training, for example, or that there are enough adults per number of children. These don't absolutely determine that the programs will be of good quality but they make it much more likely."

Training

In the mid-1970s, the federal government launched a study to investigate how various features of day-care centers affected the quality of care received by children. This study, the National Day Care Study, concluded that one of the most important ingredients of quality was the ongoing relevant training of the teacher-caregiver. In programs in which the teachers-caregivers had early childhood training, the children behaved more positively and were more cooperative as well as more involved in the program. These children also made gains on standardized tests of learning.

Child-care directors agree that training is important. In a survey conducted by the leading magazine for directors, *Child Care Information Exchange,* two hundred and fifty directors rated twenty indices of quality. Close to the top of the list were teacher personality and teacher knowledge.

It stands to reason that training ranges in quality—some good, some not so good. Alison Clarke-Stewart found in her research that when teachers were trained, the children did better in academics but not as well in social relationships. "It's important," she says, "to stress the well-roundedness of training; that is, it includes how to promote social as well as academic skills."

Applying these center-based findings to all kinds of early childhood arrangements, here's what to look for:

- Teachers-caregivers who are open to acquiring new skills and knowledge in relation to the important job of caring for and teaching children.
- Teachers-caregivers who participate in training when it is available (training sessions, conferences, courses, etc.) and seek out opportunities to learn (reading books and articles).

Leadership/Management

Leadership qualities and management skills are important in the individual teacher-caregiver and in the administrators of the child-care program.

Likewise, the 250 directors who responded to the *Child Care Information Exchange* survey also felt that leadership was the number one determinant of good child care. Here's what to look for:

- The leader has a strong commitment to the importance of providing good child care and to the value of this job.
- The leader is familiar with community resources and uses them for the children and parents.
- In group care programs, the leader hires thoughtfully and well and forms a cooperative, supportive relationship with the staff.
- In group programs, there are written procedures, personnel policies, insurance coverage, child progress and health records, and long-range budgeting.
- In family day-care homes, centers, and preschools, the program meets the local licensing regulations. Research has found that though these standards vary widely, state by state, compliance with regulations is, at least, a minimum assurance of quality.

Staffing: Group Size and Adult/Child Ratio

The National Day Care Study concluded that besides relevant training for teachers-caregivers, the quality of care was closely related to the number of children in a group. They found that in smaller groups, as opposed to larger ones, the adults spent more time being with the children and less time simply watching them. The children were more verbal and more involved in activities. They were also less aggressive with each other. Finally, the children in smaller groups made the greatest gains on standardized tests of learning and vocabulary.

In family day-care homes, young children also seem to fare much better when not in very large groups. In larger groups, children may become more disruptive and the caregiver may spend more time on discipline than on learning activities.

The number of teachers to children, that is the adult/child ratio, is also important, but perhaps less important in the preschool years than the overall number of children, according to the National Day Care Study. If you are deciding between a large group—even one with a high adult/child ratio —versus a smaller one, the smaller one would be a better choice, all other factors being equal. If you are thinking of a group program, the following standards proposed by the National Association for the Education of Young Children can be used as an indication of what educators consider the very best.

STAFF-CHILD RATIOS WITHIN GROUP SIZE

Age of Children*	6	8	10	12	14	16	18	20	22	24
Infants (birth–12 mos.)	1:3	1:4								
Toddlers (12–24 mos.)	1:3	1:4	1:5	1:4						
Two-year-olds (24–36 mos.)		1:4	1:5	1:6**						
Two- and three-year-olds			1:5	1:6	1:7**					
Three-year-olds					1:7	1:8	1:9	1:10**		
Four-year-olds						1:8	1:9	1:10**		
Four-and five-year-olds						1:8	1:9	1:10**		
Five-year-olds						1:8	1:9	1:10		
Six- to eight-year-olds (school age)								1:10	1:11	1:12

*Multi-age grouping is both permissible and desirable. When no infants are included, the staff-child ratio and group size requirements shall be based on the age of the majority of the children in the group. When infants are included, ratios and group size for infants must be maintained.

**Smaller group sizes and lower staff-child ratios are optimal. Larger group sizes and higher staff-child ratios are acceptable only in cases where staff are highly qualified.

Accreditation Criteria and Procedures, National Association for the Education of Young Children, 1987.

The Physical Layout

Footage. A study by Rohe and Patterson found that as the number of children per square foot in group programs increased, so did the children's aggressiveness, destructiveness, and aimless behavior.

- NAEYC recommends that in group programs there be thirty-five square feet of indoor play space per child and seventy-five square feet of usable play space outside.
- In home-based programs, there should be enough space for children to run around and be active.

Room Arrangement. Parents with children in child-care centers often worry about the effect of leaving young children for long days in group care, particularly in school-like groups. They worry about too much "institutionalization" too soon. The best early childhood programs offer an antidote to this potential problem by dividing the space into interest centers so that children can be alone or in small groups. The institutional feeling is also countered by the provision of soft and cozy spaces. Look for the following:

- There are spaces with rugs, sofas, rocking chairs or cushions.
- The space is arranged so that equipment is clustered together into areas —for blocks, dramatic play, science, woodwork, water play, etc.
- There are private areas for children to look at books or to play by themselves.
- In group programs, the total space is planned so that children do not interrupt each other moving across the room and so that the noisiest activities (music, for example) are not next to the quietest ones (the book corner).

Equipment. A study by Vandell and Powers defined a quality program as one in which there were carefully selected toys and materials appropriate to the children's level of development. Here's what to look for:

- The toys and materials can be manipulated, experimented with, used in imaginative and constructive ways.
- The equipment is durable, safe, and attractive.
- The equipment is arranged so that it is available and accessible to children for independent use.
- Children's own work is treated with respect, displayed and stored with care.

Health and Safety

Health. A great deal of media attention has recently been paid to the health risks in child care. Some headlines suggested that disease spreads at alarming rates in group day-care programs. Susan Aronson, a pediatrician from the Medical College of Pennsylvania, has been studying the health risks in group programs for the past decade. She has observed a clear demarcation between those early childhood programs in which children become ill often and those in which they do not: when adults wash their hands frequently, children are healthier.

- Adults in high quality child-care programs have regular medical exams.
- Children also have their required checkups, and medical records are kept.
- In group programs, the sick policy is clearly written or explained. It states

when sick adults can work and when sick children can participate in the program (e.g., children should not be with other children until their temperature has been normal for twenty-four hours).

- Emergency health care is planned for, including an arrangement for hospital emergency room care, easily accessible telephone numbers where parents can be reached throughout the day, and posters or books that explain routine first aid. In group programs, one adult should be trained on a regular basis in first aid.
- A first-aid kit is fully stocked.
- Staff washes hands frequently, particularly before meals or snacks and after changing the diapers of younger children.
- Toys (particularly those likely to have been chewed on or put into children's mouths) are washed regularly.
- Bathrooms and sinks are accessible to children and are kept clean.

Safety.   Parents often worry about safety: "How do I know my child will be safe, won't be left unattended, won't be placed in dangerous circumstances and won't be abused?" The media have elevated the issue of sexual abuse out of proportion to the frequency with which abuse has occurred in group programs. The media portrayal, in my view, was not just sensational press. It reflects the ever-present and normal fears that parents have whenever they leave their children in the care of others. The following safeguards promoting health and safety have been established in high quality programs:

- There is constant adult supervision.
- Children are not released to adults unless written consent is given by the parents.
- The teachers-caregivers are well screened.
- In group programs, there is a written procedure for dealing with cases of suspected abuse and for reporting this to parents.
- Parents are welcome to drop in unannounced at any time.

Nutrition and Food

Whenever I conduct question-answer sessions with parents on the topic of early childhood programs, the subject of food is always raised: "How do we know our children are being fed well when we are not there to see what's being served?" "How can we deal with the nutrition of our children when we can't control the food they are given?"

- NAEYC accreditation standards specify that meals and snacks meet the child's needs as recommended by the Child Care Food Program of the United States Department of Agriculture.

- Children are fed on a regular basis.
- Parents are given information about the food served.
- Family or cultural food requirements are honored. The child's allergies and food preferences are also respected.
- Food brought from home is stored safely.
- The scheduling of meals is relaxed, eating groups are small, and the conversation is educationally focused. The study by Kontos and Fiene found this kind of atmosphere was an important indicator of quality.

Evaluation

In order to maintain the quality of any early childhood arrangement, there needs to be a continual process of stock-taking.

- The children's growth is assessed and planning for each child is done on that basis.
- Teachers-caregivers evaluate themselves and, in group programs, are evaluated by administrators using agreed-upon criteria.
- The program is evaluated and changes made accordingly.

As William Hooks and I discovered in researching *The New Extended Family*, good programs are in a constant state of evolution. The adults are open to new ideas as they stay in touch with and respond to their own needs as well as the needs of the children and families they serve.

THE LINKAGES

"One of the most important elements of good quality and one that is not usually discussed," says Urie Bronfenbrenner from Cornell University, "is the importance of linkages between the family, the day care, and the world of work." One of the most important aspects of out-of-home arrangements is their effect on the family. "If the child care enhances the power of family, there are excellent results for the child. If the family is undermined, then the outcome is not beneficial for the child."

Numerous studies have been conducted on the long-term effects of preschool programs, particularly the government-funded Head Start programs. One of the most noteworthy findings is that when preschool programs are effective, they do much more than teach the child. The parents are affected and, through this experience, become better teachers, motivators, and advocates for their children. As Schweinhart and Weikart state in summarizing their analysis of high quality preschool programs: "The parent-teacher relationship should be built on mutual respect and a pooling of knowledge about individual children and child development principles."

Teacher-Parent Interaction

In the research that we conducted on child care, we found that teachers and caregivers in exemplary family day care programs and centers clearly understood that parents are the major influence in their children's lives. Teacher-caregivers never considered themselves "substitutes" for the parents but rather "supplements," helping and supporting the family, serving, in effect, as a "new extended family."

- In high quality programs, the teacher-caregiver explains her or his approach and program to parents. In group programs, the procedures for orientation, for payment, and for care of sick children is conveyed in writing.
- There are frequent and supportive conversations between the parent and teacher-caregiver about the child's activities and development. In group programs, there are also parent/teacher conferences.
- Problems with a parent or child are solved constructively.
- Parents have a regular opportunity to give feedback, and where appropriate, the teacher-caregiver makes changes.
- In sum, competitive tendencies are rechanneled into cooperative relationships between the parent and teacher-caregiver.

Bronfenbrenner notes that there are ways to assess how strong the linkage is between the child care or teacher and the family. "Find out," he says, "if the child-care provider knows the names of the child's family. Do the parents know the parents of their child's friends?"

Arthur Emlen from Portland State University expands this notion of linkages to include the ease with which these programs help families manage their other responsibilities. Is the program affordable and accessible? How do its hours fit with the schedules of family members? Does the program help parents find resources in the community (parent interest groups, social services, etc.)?

In the public mind there is a clear dividing line between child care and school. Children, however, cannot be divided. As Docia Zavitkowsky, the past president of NAEYC, wisely states, "In order for children to learn, they must be well cared for. In order for them to be nurtured, they must also be taught." Bettye Caldwell from the University of Arkansas proposes we use new words to connote this—"educare" and "educarer."

The public mind also holds that those whom we entrust with our children should be unstintingly loving and giving despite our unwillingness to pay or respect teacher-caregivers accordingly. Teacher-caregivers have their own needs (for stimulation, training, cooperation, and adequate pay and working conditions) that must be met in order for them to function effectively.

Finally, in the public mind there is a conflict between child care and the family—child care is often portrayed as breaking up or lessening the influence of the family. As we have seen, high quality early childhood programs, whether nursery schools, centers, or family day-care homes, extend and enhance the power of the family to provide for and raise children.

Q *How can I evaluate a preschool program? How do I know if it is good?*

The following questions, developed from the preceding section, will help you judge the quality of early childhood programs.

The Relationship Between the Teacher-Caregiver and the Child

- Ask the teacher-caregiver to describe another child she or he has cared for. Is the description warm and enthusiastic or judgmental and punitive?
- If possible, watch the teacher-caregiver discipline a child. Is the child made to feel bad or are alternatives to the unacceptable behavior offered?
- Ask the teacher-caregiver "what if" questions: "What would you do if my child was fussy all day?" or "Refused to cooperate?" or "Seemed to be getting sick?" See if the answers match the way you think these situations should be handled.
- Listen to the tone of the room. Is it pleasant, filled with the sound of happy, busy voices?
- If this is an individual teacher-caregiver, ask about her or his goals for the future and how long she or he wants to stay in this job. Ask what would happen if the provider were ill.
- If it is a child-care center, ask about staff turnover. How many teachers left last year and had to be replaced? The national turnover rate is nearly 40 percent—so the lower the rate of the program you are considering, the more able your child will be to form consistent and caring relationships with the teachers-caregivers.

The Activities

- If there are other children present, are they busily involved when you come in or do they have so little to do that they all rush right up to you when you walk in?
- If there are other children, are different children pursuing different activities or is everyone doing the same thing all the time?
- Watch the teacher-caregiver with your child. Does she or he provide interesting things to do?

Teacher-Caregiver Development

- Ask the caregiver what interests him or her most about her job. See if he or she ever listens to the radio about children, reads about them, attends meetings on education or child development.
- If the program is more formal, is staff training provided?

Staffing/Group Size

- Ask yourself if there are enough adults to have time to talk to and care for each child.
- Are there enough adults to remove the children quickly in the case of an emergency?
- Do the adults spend most of the time with the children rather than with the other adults?

Physical Environment

- Ask yourself if you'd like to spend time there.

Health, Safety, and Nutrition

- Ask "what if" questions: "What would you do if a child got hurt?" "Got sick?" "Refused to eat?"
- Ask to have the emergency procedures described.
- Visit when a meal is being served.
- See if the space is childproof, that is, safety plugs in electrical outlets and breakable materials out of reach.

Parent/Teacher-Caregiver Relationship

- Ask the teacher-caregiver about other parents she or he has worked with. Are parents described positively or negatively?
- Ask "what if" questions: "What would you do if I got upset because my child's sweater got lost?" "My child seemed especially tired?" "My child had trouble with what you were teaching?" See how you feel about the answers.
- Ask for the names of other parents this teacher-caregiver has worked with. Call them as references, asking what was best and what was most difficult. Try to get as complete a picture as possible so you have a realistic understanding about the teacher-caregiver's strengths and weaknesses.
- Is the teacher-caregiver supportive or competitive with you and other parents?

All in all, you want a program that is good, day in and day out.

- Drop in for an unannounced visit. See if the program looks the same as when you first visited. See how welcome you are for this unannounced visit.

VIEWPOINT: THE CRISIS IN EARLY EDUCATION

There is a crisis in early education today that has been caused by the convergence of a number of demographic factors.

There are more young children. We are in "the echo of the baby boom." As the baby boomers have children, the population of children under six is increasing for the first time in several decades —from 19.6 million in 1980 to 21.7 million in 1986.

There are more employed mothers needing child care. In 1987, 57 percent of the mothers of preschool children were employed, up from 39 percent in 1975. The fastest-growing segment of the labor force is mothers of children under three—up to 53 percent in 1987 from 35 percent in 1976.

There are more parents wanting early childhood programs for their children. The number of three- and four-year-olds attending nursery school has nearly tripled in fifteen years—from 14.1 percent in 1970 to 38.9 percent in 1985. In 1985, 96.1 percent of all five-year-olds attended kindergarten, up from 66.9 percent in 1970.

There are fewer potential teachers. The baby bust generation has come of age. The number of eighteen- to twenty-four-year-olds will drop from 30.4 million in 1980 to a projected 25.8 million in 1990, causing shortages in all fields, including early education.

There is high turnover in this field. The lower the salary level in this field, the higher the turnover. Elementary school teachers earn an average of $422 a week—their turnover rate per year is 9.2 percent. Prekindergarten and kindergarten teachers earn $274; their turnover rate is 14.9 percent. Finally, child-care workers make $182 and, not surprisingly, nearly 40 percent leave the field every year.

The National Committee on Pay Equity finds that child-care workers are the second most underpaid profession in this country (after clergy). Most earn wages that keep them below the poverty level.

This is clearly a crisis. The extent to which it affects parents is becoming known. In a survey that we designed for *Fortune* magazine, we found that 27 percent of the men and 24 percent of the women in a nationally representative sample reported that their child-care arrangement had broken down two to five times in the past three months. We also found that the more often parents had to make special arrangements because their usual arrangements fell through, the more likely they were to have stress-related health problems.

What can we do about this crisis?

- We can pay teachers and child-care workers as well as we can and stop trying to think of getting a "bargain."
- Since many of us deplore the low salaries in the field, we can work toward local, state, and national efforts to increase the status and compensation of early childhood teachers.
- We can remember to acknowledge the very hard and important work that teacher-caregivers do. It takes incredible skill to be a good early childhood professional.

Q *How can I locate preschool programs?*

More and more communities are providing R&R—child-care resource and referral agencies. These organizations offer in-person or over-the-telephone information about local child-care and school programs. After learning of the parent's needs (hours of coverage, age of child or children, location preferred, cost requirements, educational goals, etc.) R&R staff provide a parent with a list of referrals as well as counseling on how to make a selection. Some R&R programs follow up later to see if the parent has made a satisfactory arrangement. Because they are in touch with so many parents and receive constant feedback about programs from them as well as from licensing authorities, they are able to refer parents to better quality programs and providers.

Close to one thousand companies are now providing R&R to their employees. Ask your personnel officer if your company offers this service. For an updated list of R&R services nationwide, call the National Association of Child Care Resource and Referral Agencies, in Rochester, Minnesota, (507) 287-2020. You can also check the yellow pages in your phone book (usually under preschool, day care, or child care) for a listing under "Information and Referral" or "Resource and Referral."

If no agency exists in your community, use word of mouth. Ask professionals who work in related fields (for example, your pediatrician) and all of your friends, particularly those who have just gone through the process of finding child care. Check the yellow pages and call programs that are listed. Find out which agency is responsible for licensing (often the health or welfare department) and call to see if they have lists. You can put ads in newspapers. Follow every lead until you find what you want.

VIEWPOINT: MISEDUCATION

David Elkind, the noted educator from Tufts University, has entitled a book on early education *Miseducation*, reflecting the increasing tendency of many programs to ignore the way young children learn best and to impose adult ways of knowing and adult pressures on young children. For example, a curriculum for five-year-olds covers "our community" in one week using workbooks, an approach that is confusing and abstract. Young children learn about how communities work by taking trips out into the neighborhood over the year, by having opportunities to re-create and thus synthesize their experiences through building with blocks, dictating stories, and having group discussions about their observations.

I've used a mild example. Some early childhood programs do not even provide a curriculum that centers on the child's understanding his or her world. They may expect little children to have a unit on China or Egypt when the children hardly know their own neighborhood. Worse yet, they may expect four- and five-year-olds to sit at desks all day, memorizing facts, numbers, and letters.

Young children learn through their hands, their eyes, their experiences. In order to learn pre-reading skills, what better way than for teachers to write down the children's own stories? Then they see that reading and writing have a purpose—that of human communication. Then they can begin to learn to sound out and write what they want to say. After all, the purpose of early education is not only to impart knowledge, it is to engender in children the sense that they can and want to become learners. Instead, they are often made to feel like failures at a very young age.

A mother told this frightening story:

> ▪ ▪ ▪ *On the first day of kindergarten they were teaching the children to write their names. Robert has trouble with handwriting and he came home with a paper all full of corrections. The teacher had graded it—a low grade—and drawn a sad face on the page. Robert had failed writing his name on the very first day of school!*

Another parent assessed what happens when children are inappropriately pushed:

> ▪ ▪ ▪ *It's like asking them to walk across a tightrope. Maybe they manage to do it but what they learn is to be scared to death. The actual result is not at all what the school really intended.*

The early push for inappropriate learning comes from many sources—from parents who want the best for their children, that is, to succeed in an increasingly technological society. It comes from teachers who have had to conform to school systems emphasizing skills and to deal with cutbacks in funding for the so-called frills (art, music, library, etc.). It comes from a society that devalues children and misunderstands their development.

Whenever I hear a parent say, "You can't change the schools," or "Your child will be jeopardized if you make any waves," I feel discouraged. Be aware that there are thousands of educators across the country who want education to be developmentally appropriate.

Recently, the National Association for the Education of Young Children, representing over 62,000 teachers of young children, and the National Association of Elementary School Principals held a joint news conference condemning inappropriate early academics as damaging to children's future as learners. They noted that teaching three-, four-, and five-year-old children as if they were six or seven with workbooks, desks, and chairs, and teacher-directed activities creates the real possibility of burnout in grade school. According to Samuel Sava, the executive director of the National Association of Elementary School Principals, we can thus "waste the promise of early childhood education."

David Elkind gives parents guidelines for evaluating their children's experiences.

> Parents can know whether their child is being inappropriately taught by answering a few simple questions. When your four-year-old goes to school, does she bring home dittoed worksheets? Her own artwork? Is she being taught lessons? Or is she engaged in learning through projects such as making soup or building a puppet theater? Is her learning limited to memorizing the alphabet and reciting the numbers? Is her thinking challenged by being read stories, taking field trips, or planting a garden? Does she come home quiet and withdrawn? Or is she joyful and talking a mile a minute about her school? If you answer "yes" to the first half of each of these questions, your child is probably being taught inappropriately.

VIEWPOINT: PARENTS AND PROFESSIONALS DEFINE QUALITY

A study by Caroline Zinsser reveals that when parents select pre-school programs, the most important considerations are the way the teacher or caregiver treats children and the physical appearance of the program. When professionals assess quality, other aspects come into play. Is the program licensed? What is the adult/child ratio? What is the group size, etc.?

I urge you to think of all the ingredients of quality when you select. If there ever is a problem, you'll see how important all these aspects are. An example: a parent enrolled her two-year-old in a program because of its remarkable teachers. She didn't pay much attention to the director. A year or so later, the director failed to pay the teachers. This parent then discovered that funds had been misappropriated, but little could be done because the board of the center consisted entirely of the director's family. The center ultimately closed down, owing everyone money, including the parents. As this parent concluded, "The next time I select a program I am going to ask about the administrative procedures and the degree of parent involvement."

Obviously, choices are limited in many communities and there will be tradeoffs in the decisions you make but, nonetheless, find out as much as you can about the program so you have a sense of its strengths and weaknesses. Find a program whose problems you can live with and whose strengths will enhance your child's life.

Q *How do I know my child will be safe, that there is no abuse going on?*

The media response to the incidents of child sexual abuse has raised this as an important issue for parents to investigate. In fact, the amount of sexual abuse in child care is quite small (1 to 1.5 percent of all reported cases, according to the American Humane Association). Nevertheless, parents should follow these guidelines:

- Make sure you can visit the program at any time. Do so whenever you can.
- Check with your state licensing authority to see if fingerprinting and criminal checks of staff have been conducted at your program. Make sure there are procedures to report any suspected abuse to the parents immediately.
- If your child's behavior changes (the child doesn't want to go, is clinging

or unusually quiet, depressed or secretive) and nothing at home seems to have caused this change, speak to the teacher-caregiver about it. Also speak to other parents. If other children are also exhibiting similar behavior, try to find out why.

Children often exhibit this kind of behavior as a normal part of growing up and becoming more independent from their parents. It is important to investigate changes in the child's behavior, to differentiate those caused by normal development from those caused by problems in the child care.

Entering a Program

Q *How can I help my child get off to a good start in a new program?*

As with all new experiences, parents' expectations exert a powerful influence. Despite the significant developmental differences between a two-year-old entering a toddler group and a five-year-old enrolling in kindergarten, we tend to make assumptions that can prove problematic.

Assumption: Enrolling in a New Program Is an Experience That Only Affects Children

We find that the repercussions of this new beginning spread out to affect the whole family, especially the parents. Children respond in many different ways—at different times of the day. In the morning, one child is fearful, another champing at the bit to leave. In the evening, the fearful child may be relaxed, the enthusiastic child exhausted. Children can become more irritable and demanding, taxing your patience. Some regress, wetting their beds or refusing to let you out of their sight. Dependence is expressed in other ways: children want to be waited on, dressed, carried. They go back to sleeping with mounds of stuffed animals. Fingers are sucked and "blankies" are carried about. Parents may feel desperate, wanting their children to be more independent. Another common reaction is the child who resists you at pick-up time. As Nancy Balaban observes in her excellent book *Learning to Say Goodbye,* these behaviors represent the child's way of saying:

> *"You left me here this morning. Now it's my chance to leave you by staying here. Now I can give you a dose of what you gave me this morning."*

Some children become cocky, imbued with their new status. The father of a kindergartner says:

. . . *Rochelle has been testing us constantly. It's like "I'm the big person" and "I know all the answers."*

Because we may not have expected ourselves to react, we can be surprised by the velocity of our emotions, especially if our children disrupt our expected timetable and separate too soon or too late:

. . . *I anticipated problems with Elizabeth because I'm working on the same days she's going to nursery school. The preschool recommended that I stay for a short period of time. So I arranged to be forty-five minutes late to work. I got to preschool, and none of this happened the way I had expected. Elizabeth shouted a few things to me while we were standing there and sort of marched off into the sunset with this teacher she and I had never seen before, without even a backward glance. And I stood there feeling, "You ingrate." I drove to work feeling very glum, not so much because Elizabeth hadn't gotten upset, but because I had expected at least a little time for me to separate. I had this strange feeling of not having enough time to get used to the idea that I was leaving her care and welfare up to other people.*

The best early childhood programs understand that children *and* their parents are undergoing a separation; their routine includes the parents staying a while for the first few days. In fact, one program invited several parents from the previous year to address the new parents. The veterans described their own feelings—sorrow and pride, elation and depression, anger and relief—thus helping the new parents know what to expect.

Assumption: When Children Enter an Early Childhood Program, Parents Give Up the Last Full-Blown Chance to Impart Their Own Values

This is a common expectation. As the mother of the two teenage children, I can confidently report that the era in which to impart parental values is only just beginning in the preschool years. Starting school is a separation, but with all endings comes new beginnings especially in forming new kinds of connections with our children. Among the changes in the relationship with our children we experience are the following:

New Routines. For some children, getting up, dressing, and eating breakfast to a carefully clocked schedule is a new experience. For others, it may be catching a school bus, riding in a car pool, or going to an extended-day program that is new. All of these routines affect family life as well as the relationship between parent and child.

Less Time Together.   The children who have been home with their mothers (or fathers) have fewer hours together. The quality of time can change too—from more leisurely to more structured.

Less Awareness of the Details of the Child's Day.   The older children get, unfortunately, the less likely some programs are to inform parents of their children's experiences. A mother bemoans this loss:

> ● ● ●   *In day care, I saw Pam's teachers both morning and night so if she had a bad day or didn't eat or didn't sleep, I knew about it. In kindergarten, I never see the teacher and have no feedback whatsoever.*

Furthermore, when we ask our children about their day, the reports may be meager: "It was okay," or "I had fun." In high-quality programs, teachers make every effort to keep parents informed.

Perceiving Our Child as One of Many.   A father reports:

> ● ● ●   *In my mind my daughter has always been the best in the world and all of a sudden I realize that others don't necessarily see her that way.*

Feeling Judged as Parents.   As James Comer, the educator from Yale, notes, we are showing our "handiwork" in public and we feel confirmed or condemned by our child's adaption.

In high quality early childhood programs, teachers and caregivers know that children's and parents' self-esteem is closely related to their openness to learning. These professionals work hard to preserve the feeling that every child and every parent is special.

Having More Interests in Common.   Children come home with new insight, new abilities, and new knowledge. The baby that you cared for seemingly yesterday is now using metaphors: the rain is like "teardrops," the moon has been "pasted on" the black sky, the wind "tickles" their ears. With every loss in parenthood comes the potential for incredible gain.

Assumption: Children's Earlier Experiences Will Determine Their Response to the New Situation

This experience can take two forms: "If children have had prior group experience, they will react positively," or "If children have had no prior group experience, they will react negatively."

While I know of no research that specifically addresses these assumptions (for example, does nursery school experience make the adjustment to kindergarten easier?), a number of parents have found these assumptions do not hold. There are simply too many other factors that affect the child's adjustment to school.

The Child's Developmental Readiness.   Children mature at different rates. A child who was not ready for a group experience at three years may welcome it at four. Thus children's response to a program at the interview or visit several months earlier does not necessarily predict how they'll act on the first day, as this mother of a three-and-a-half-year-old notes:

. . . *When we had observed this program last spring, Brad sat on my lap like glue. I anticipated that he would be clingy, but that was not at all the case. I guess over the summer he started to want to be with other children.*

The Child's Customary Way of Approaching New Experiences.   Children's temperaments play a part in their response to a new program. Some children stand back and observe before joining a group while others plunge in.

Children's Expectations.   The mother of a five-year-old says:

. . . *Matthew visited his kindergarten classroom last spring, and they pointed out the reading and math areas. Over the summer he got increasingly upset. Finally he said, "I don't know how to read and I don't know math." He was sure that he had to know all these things before he went to kindergarten.*

Unfortunately some schools are misguided enough to expect this knowledge from children before they walk in the door, but high quality early childhood programs are the place to learn new skills. When children have stringent and unrealistic expectations of themselves, the first day looms as very forbidding.

Other Fears.   Children have other worries: "Where is the bathroom?" "What will happen if I have an accident?" "Will I have to take naps there?" "What if I don't go to sleep?" "How will I make friends?"

Familiar Aspects of the New Program.   Going to school with a friend, feeling comfortable with the routines and materials of early childhood programs, and having mastered other separations from parents seem to promote an easier entry.

The Parents' Way of Approaching Separation.   The research of Ellen Hock indicates that the parents' attitudes influence the child's adjustment. Using a scale to measure maternal separation anxiety ("an unpleasant emotional state reflecting a mother's apprehension about leaving her child"), Martin-Huff found that the greater the mother's separation anxiety prior to the first day, the more likely the child was to have a more difficult adjustment to kindergarten, as assessed by the child's teachers. Of course, a study like this does not show cause and effect. It is possible, for example, that the more anxious mothers knew from past experience that their children, by nature of their temperamental differences, were slower to adjust and this anxiety represented a legitimate parental concern.

The way the mother tells the child about an impending separation is also critical. Weintraub and Lewis found three characteristic ways of leave-taking. One group of mothers left without telling their children. A second group told the children that they were going and would come back. The third group did what the second group did but also told the children what to do during their time apart. Children whose mothers informed them of their departure coped with the absence most successfully.

Another study experimented with different styles of departure. Adams and Passman had mothers of two-year-olds make brief (ten seconds) and more extended departure statements (forty seconds). Both groups gave the same information: that they were leaving, would return soon, and that the child should play. The brief statement worked better. Those children were more busily occupied during the mother's absence. Perhaps the longer message signaled to the child greater uncertainty and anxiety on the part of the mother.

These are the messages in this research:

- It is normal for both parents and children to feel some anxiety at leaving each other.
- Providing succinct and reassuring information to the children is helpful.
- Indicating to the children that they will be okay is important.

The Programs' Strategies for Handling Separation.   The following strategies, developed by educators around the country, can facilitate a smoother beginning for children:

- A prior visit or orientation to the program.
- A home visit by the teacher.
- A written or verbal account of what the first day will be like, including such specifics as where the bathrooms are and how food is served.
- A gradual entry procedure arranged so that younger children come in small groups for short sessions for the first few days. Thus teachers get to know the children as individuals before the program begins full swing. Some children need their parents for a short time, others for longer, so the best gradual entry programs allow for this diversity.

I have also seen this strategy carried to excess—such as a mandatory procedure spread out over several weeks. Such a program can disrupt parents' work schedules and seem anticlimatic to some children who want the full program to start. Some educators take the opposite approach. They say that children should separate from their parents "cold turkey," saying goodbye on the first day at the entrance to the classroom or the school itself. I disapprove of this procedure, particularly for children under five. It makes separation a frightening hurdle to overcome rather than a constructive opportunity to learn how to leave one's parents feeling safe and confident, excited about a new experience.

- A teacher who gets to know the children quickly and addresses them by name. The mother of a two-year-old says:

■ ■ ■ *Jonathan's separation went smoothly and I'm sure it had a lot to do with his teacher. She was very affectionate, asked him lots of questions about himself, and was not at all pushy about him separating from me.*

Contrast Jonathan's experience to that of Glenn's. Over the summer, five-year-old Glenn had collected art materials for school as a letter to the new pupils suggested. When he presented this gift to his new teacher on the first day, she took it without a word, without even glancing at him. He came home in tears, saying "I don't want to go back."

- A classroom organized so that each child has a place for his or her own belongings. Many children need to bring a "transitional object" (something from home to help them feel safe); this should be permitted, although it is appropriate to set limits on its use for older preschoolers: "You can keep your toy car in your cubby during school."
- A program that is developmentally appropriate and does not push children far beyond their capacity. The mother of a five-year-old describes a kindergarten program that was inappropriate:

■ ■ ■ *Tricia came home from kindergarten very wired because she had spent hours at her desk memorizing an autumn poem. She was distraught because she couldn't seem to remember stanza three. How they could expect her to do this is beyond me.*

The National Association for the Education of Young Children publishes a booklet, *Developmentally Appropriate Practice,** which describes standards for age-appropriate practices for young children.

---

* Copies of *Developmentally Appropriate Practice* may be obtained for a small fee by writing NAEYC, 1834 Connecticut Avenue N.W., Washington, DC 20009-5786.

- A group that is not too large and overwhelming. A mother of a three-year-old says:

■ ■ ■ *Up until now Allissa had not had a hard time leaving me, but she has not wanted to go to nursery school. I think part of the problem is that there are twenty-four children in the class with two full-time teachers. That's a lot of children to adjust to all at once.*

(See page 417 for the chart of NAEYC's recommended staffing patterns.)

SOLUTIONS

Preparing Your Child

Providing Specific Information Before the Program Begins.   Exactly what you say and when you say it depends on your knowledge of your child. Some children adjust better if they have a great deal of advance warning; others function better with less notice.

The parent of two preschoolers observes:

■ ■ ■ *I definitely think you can overtalk. Birthday parties are a good example of this. It's almost impossible not to talk about birthday parties, but by the time the day arrives the kids are off the wall in anticipation. The same can be true for starting school.*

- Be matter-of-fact: "When summer vacation is over, you'll go to your new center."
- Give specific information about what the day will be like (including eating, napping, and bathroom procedures). Children like to know if any friends are going to this program. If you refer to time, use references the child can understand: "Your preschool begins when the morning TV news is over and lasts until after lunch."
- Avoid setting up unrealistic expectations: "You'll love your first day of school." You can be positive without dictating the child's feelings.
- Be open to opportunities for the child to bring up any concern or questions.

Arranging a Visit in Advance.   It is very helpful for children to see their new program beforehand, preferably not too far in advance. It is usually easier to imagine mastering the known than the unknown.

Setting Up New Routines.   If you try out and establish the family routines before the first day of the program, they function more smoothly. Above all, however, avoid threatening children and making them anxious: "If you're as slow as that on a school day you'll miss your car pool." Instead of criticizing, keep adjusting the routine until it works.

Guiding Children through the Transition

If a child has a hard time with a separation, think of how to teach him or her the skills needed to master it.

As Nancy Balaban states:

> Here at school entry lies a wonderful opportunity for parents to enhance their [children's] self-confidence through separations that are well achieved. Children who are supported by their teachers and parents as they separate from home have the opportunity to move fearlessly into new realms of learning and growth.

Supporting the Child.

- If you or a familiar adult accompany the child to the program on the first days and stay until the child feels safe, the child will usually move in more comfortably. If kindergarten programs don't permit this and your child seems to need help, insist on changing the school rules or find a transitional object (a reminder of you) that the child can take: a photograph of you, a handkerchief or scarf, a note from you, etc.
- Develop set ways of saying goodby and do not leave without telling the child.

Supporting Yourself. Some parents find they need special pampering during this period. For some, it is reassuring to talk to a friend who has gone through this before and understands the range of children's reactions and parents' emotions.

Providing Opportunities for Children to Express Their Feelings. Some children articulate their emotions in no uncertain terms: "I hate it," "I love it." Others, as one mother put it, "lump all their apprehensions together in one ball and are not specific about any one thing they're worried about." Books about beginning school offer an opportunity for children to focus on someone else (the protagonist) and verbalize their emotions in a safe context.

Realizing That Children Manage This Transition in Different Ways. There is nothing intrinsically better about a child who happily bounces off to school the first day and a child who is wary, watchful, and takes a longer time to separate from his parents and join the group. Neither one nor the other is smarter, better adjusted, or destined for a better life. Above all, don't judge yourself or allow others to judge you or your child harshly if your child takes time in beginning a program. Protests of "I don't want to go" are not, in and of themselves, meaningful if the child eventually leaves and comes back relatively happy.

Give it time. Think back to the last time you had to go off to a totally new place in order to understand what your child is accomplishing.

Separation distress over the preschool years comes in waves. The child who marches off the first day may cling four weeks later. The child who took a while to say goodby may regress after a long weekend or a holiday. It can take a long time to learn how to let go of the ones you love and move into a new experience.

If a program is not working for your child, it will become obvious. Your child will turn more and more resistant, holding onto you for dear life. He or she may become very depressed and apathetic. If that happens, talk to the teacher, observe, seek help if needed, or make a change. If you do need to make a change, do not let others make you feel that your child is manipulating you or is a quitter. The most responsible parents, after all, are those who do what they must to ensure the best experiences for their children.

Q *What's the best way to say goodby?*

Saying goodby can be as heartrending for the parent as for the child. If the child protests or cries, the parent often begins to think "what if":

"What if this is really a traumatic experience?"

"What if my child gets hurt while I'm gone?"

"What if my child is really sick and that's why the big protest?"

Assuming that you are leaving your child with a caring and safety-conscious person at home or away from home, some guidelines can make leave-taking easier:

Setting Up a Routine

A familiar ritual will make saying goodby much easier. One parent has her child wave goodby from the window or walk her to the door; another reads her child a story.

Avoiding Sneak Out

The temptation to disappear without telling your child can be strong if your child gets fussy or if you are leaving after your child is asleep. That one moment of peace, however, is costly because you will be creating a situation of nontrust and doubt as well as depriving your child of learning how to deal positively with this everyday occurrence.

A mother describes such a situation:

• • • *We left after Sarah was in bed, so we didn't tell her and of course she woke up and cried. When I came home, she was so upset that she said, "I don't want a babysitter again." And for a while after that she was watching us all the time and was particularly clingy.*

Explaining That You'll Return

The mother of a two-and-a-half-year-old says:

• • • *I tell him that he can have some fun with somebody else and that "you can tell me how you spent your day when I come home and I tell you how I spent my day. We'll have supper together."*

Other parents leave a physical reminder of themselves with a child—a photograph, an old set of keys, a picture that they have drawn for the child, even a tape-recorded message or a cassette of themselves reading a favorite story.

Checking Up On the Child Later

If your child has an especially difficult time you can call to make sure everything is all right. Some parents get out of sight and wait until the fussing has subsided. A New Jersey father explains:

• • • *The first couple of times you feel sad and guilty about leaving. But every sitter told us uniformly that the crying stopped within thirty seconds. In fact, we could wait in the garage until the screaming stopped. So by the time we were ready to leave, it was a collective sigh of "thank God that's over."*

Thinking of Separation as a Learning Experience

Saying goodby can be regarded as a negative or positive experience. Goodby also implies hello—to a new experience, to a new person or people. It is at this point in life that children begin to learn about developing initiative, venturing out, trying new things, and you can help them learn to do this.

Q *How do I handle a conflict with my child-care provider?*

Bill Robinson says:

• • • *My babysitter lets Brian watch a lot of television when we're not home. I don't like that. How big of a deal should I make it?*

Jo Ann Norton says:

• • • *My family day-care provider equates caring for Anita with feeding her well. She's always trying to stuff her with food and making her finish everything on her plate. That's not important to me, plus I don't want Anita to get hung up about food. What do I do?*

Robin Cohen says:

• • • *Ivy, my babysitter, was wonderful with Jack when he was little, but now that he's two and a half, she still treats him like a baby. She tries to get him to stay still most of the day.*

When there is a conflict with a child-care provider, ask yourself several questions:

How Is This Problem Affecting Your Child?

Thinking about the total care, how pervasive is this problem? Is the overall relationship good and this just one minor problem, or is it beginning to affect your child? How does your child behave after spending time with the provider?

Bill Robinson says:

• • • *Brian loves Mrs. R. and is very happy with her. I just don't like the TV.*

Robin Cohen says:

• • • *When I come home from work, Ivy has Jack dressed up in some nice outfit his grandmother sent. His curly hair is so combed that not a strand is out of place. As soon as Ivy leaves, Jack roars around the dining room table like one of those toy airplanes with its motor on fast forward.*

In thinking about how his child was affected, Bill concluded, "Not much," while Robin felt that Jack was being constrained and this resulted in "pretty frenetic behavior." Robin began to think about finding someone else while Bill offered alternatives to television. He said:

> • • • We now leave pretty precise instructions: Brian can take a walk, visit the next-door neighbors, go to the playground. But if he does watch TV, it won't kill him because she's good with him otherwise.

To What Degree Does This Problem Represent a Competition Between you and the Child-Care Provider?

Jo Ann Norton says:

> • • • I think my babysitter is competitive with me. The other day Anita was covered with mosquito bites and she insisted that Anita got the bites at my house, not hers. Another time Anita had heat rash, and again it was my fault for dressing Anita too warmly.

Just as parents can feel possessive about children, so can child-care providers. When I ran a child-care center, I found that these possessive feelings followed a predictable pattern. After a few weeks in the program, the teachers would begin to complain about the parents, saying that one parent was too permissive, another was too strict, and still another did not seem to care. These comments reflected the fact that the teachers had become attached to the children, a positive development, but at the same time they were feeling jealous. My job was to channel these strong possessive feelings into an alliance rather than a rivalry with the parents.

Parents also feel a tug-of-war emotion. Katie Farkas, Ashley's mother, says:

> • • • I suffered terribly when my daughter got hurt and she would run clear across the house to find comfort from our house-keeper. I would look so devastated that my daughter would come up, caress my face and say, "Tomorrow you, Mommy."

The parent's possessive feelings often begin as the normal fear that the child will care more about the child-care provider than the parent and become intensified when the child shows any allegiance.

As Katie now sees it:

. . . *I was getting into some role reversal. I was expecting Ashley to take care of me. In order to change, I tried to let go of the anxiety and competition and realize that I was the mother.*

When I did that, the rapport between the three of us improved. Just the knowledge that I was in charge was a relief and gave me strength. One positive feeling seems to build other positive feelings.

Child-care providers frequently feel put down by parents, often as a result of competition. Furthermore, society offers few accolades for the work they do, and that work is demanding and tiring. In addition, because they are child-oriented, providers tend to divert any negative feelings away from the child and direct them instead to the adult.

Jo Ann Norton says:

. . . *When my babysitter began to blame me for everything, I really got mad and my instinct was to blame her right back. I told her that Anita didn't have any mosquito bites when I dressed her in the morning. I also told her that if Anita was dressed too warmly, she could take off some of her clothes.*

Reacting in this way only fans the competition. If Jo Ann compliments her child-care provider (when appropriate), telling her specifically how much she and Anita value her, she is more likely to build a cooperative rather than a conflicted relationship.

What Are Your Alternatives?

The decision to use another child-care provider is difficult. Parents wonder how the change will affect their child. Some dread the process of looking, of meeting with strangers, figuring out what they are like, and starting over. It is often easier to say; "There are no other choices."

In my experience, there is almost always an alternative. Parents must weigh the emotional cost to themselves of looking for someone new versus the cost to their child of not doing so.

Robin Cohen says:

. . . *Ivy, the babysitter, had been so wonderful with Jack when he was little. I didn't want to face the fact that she wasn't working out now. I ignored his wild behavior, telling myself, "It's just a stage." One day Jack said to me, "No Ivy." He was determined. I then found a child-care center—he was actually ready to be with other kids.*

When you do find a good situation, all the problems will not disappear. In any intense relationship there are moments of conflict as well as moments of pleasure. All teachers-caregivers and all parents have strengths and weaknesses, so it is a matter of finding a person or a situation with strengths you appreciate and weaknesses you can live with.

Parents are the first and primary teachers and nurturers of their children. Good child-care providers believe and support this. Keeping this perspective may help you deal with a potential flare-up or rivalry between you and your provider.

PARENTS SPEAK: CONFLICT WITH A TEACHER

Suzanne Morris, the mother of Peter, age five, says:

• • • *If seems much harder to make a fuss about a teacher than someone you have hired to take care of your child—it's more of a structured, bureaucratic system and you wonder if you are right or not. You also wonder if you will be labeled "difficult" and whether that will affect the kind of treatment your child gets.*

I first realized that something was wrong when Peter started coming home from kindergarten all wound up. So one day I dropped in on his class a little before pick-up time. Peter was running around the classroom. He does that kind of thing infrequently and usually when he's really hungry.

My first impulse was to send him to school with lots of snacks. I also spoke to the teacher, explaining that Peter could be wild if he didn't eat. I asked her to make sure that Peter ate frequently.

Mrs. Wood, the teacher, was pretty negative about Peter. That upset me because I know how schools are and how teachers talk. I did not want Peter to get a reputation that he would have to live with throughout his school years.

My husband and I asked Mrs. Wood for a conference. We were primed to discuss Peter's strengths as well as to figure out what to do about this problem. I began by saying, "Before we talk about Peter's disruptiveness, I'd love to hear about what he does well." It was one of the most incredible experiences I've ever had. Mrs. Wood could not come up with one positive thing about Peter. She sat there, pulling out one beautiful collage after another that Peter had made, showing us these great stories Peter had dictated, all the while saying negative things about my son.

I was almost in shock. Finally it occurred to me that Mrs. Wood simply didn't like Peter. She's a very controlled person, very orderly, and having this active, creative, disruptive child must have bothered her. I finally got up my nerve and asked, "Do you like Peter?"

Mrs. Wood looked surprised. She said, "Of course, I like all the children." She still didn't say anything that was even remotely positive about Peter.

After the conference, I talked to some of my friends. One told me about her four-year-old son's teacher, who valued playing and creative nursery school stuff, but her child was into numbers and letters and could already read. The teacher was always saying that Ben should learn to play, implying that my friend was one of those pushy mothers who was deliberately taking away his toys and insisting that he work all the time. She said, "This teacher upsets me, but at least it's not really bothering Ben. He can still take motors apart and put them back together in the classroom. He can still read his books. So I guess I can live with it and hope that next year he'll have a teacher who appreciates him."

I talked with another friend about her daughter's kindergarten teacher. The teacher was always insisting that her daughter color in workbook pages and put this child down for not staying within the lines. My friend thought that was ridiculous but could explain it to her daughter. She told her, "We like you to do your own drawings. It's not important at all to us that you stay within the lines—it's important that you have a good time drawing. I also said that in school, everyone has to do some things they don't like to do, and that teachers don't always do the best things for all kids."

In comparing my friends' situation and mine, there was one important difference. Peter was definitely being affected. He was more and more tense at home. He even lined up all of his superhero toys in rigid formations in his closet and told everyone not to touch them. He didn't want anything in his room moved. I figured that he was trying to put some order into his life at home, to control—I guess to overcontrol—his home life when he must have felt out of control at school.

The crowning blow came one day when Peter took a small toy to school. Mrs. Wood took it away. Peter was just trying to have something to give him comfort but it seemed to me that Mrs. Wood was fighting him on everything. It had become a battle of wills and Peter was losing.

I pulled myself together and asked the principal to switch Peter to another classroom. It was December and this school never moved kids this late in the year. I was determined. If I had to take Peter out of the school and send him elsewhere, I was going to do it.

I told the principal that Mrs. Wood was a gifted teacher—that's true—but there was a clash of personalities with my son. I think because I was so sure of myself and because I didn't blame the school, the principal eventually agreed to move Peter.

Peter was placed with a teacher who appreciated his creativity. The first day, she commented on his wonderful drawings. She also helped monitor his food and suggested we take him to an allergist. It turned out he was allergic to eggs (the food he ate most often). This was a wonderful classroom for him.

In retrospect, I'm very happy that I insisted that Peter change classes. It was a real loss of innocence for me. I had assumed that I was turning my child over to professionals who knew best. Well, they often do know a lot more than I do but they don't know my child as well as I do. The realization came one night when I was looking at Peter sleep. I understood that he would be with this teacher for a short period of time but he would be my son for the rest of my life. I realized that I would not be able to face myself if I didn't assume full responsibility for my own son and make whatever changes were in my power to make.

EPILOGUE

In the preschool years, your child will double in height and weight, will change from tottering baby to a surefooted child, and will go from repeating your phrases to having opinions on everything, including you as a parent. During these very few years, change is rapid and with change comes wonderful memories:

> *The first night your child spends in a big bed.*
>
> *Saying "hangaburger" for hamburger.*
>
> *An act of daring, followed by your child cuddling close.*
>
> *The several-sizes-too-big pants to grow into that won't stay up.*
>
> *The shirt that is a collage of your child's day: emblazoned with paint, peanut butter, dirt, and apple juice.*
>
> *The first time your child writes his or her name.*
>
> *Middle-of-the-night visits because "there's a dragon in my closet."*
>
> *Packing up the bottles and the diaper equipment for storage, to keep for another baby—yours or someone else's.*
>
> *Realizing that your child has not carried his or her "blankie" everywhere for several days.*
>
> *Seeing your child in shoes that "I put on all by myself."*
>
> *Walking away, still feeling their touch on your skin, after saying goodbye on the first day of preschool.*

It is a time in which parents also change. Our children's displays of temper, the no-win contests, force us to lay bare any illusions we might have about ourselves. It is as if we have stepped into a dressing room in a department store with three-sided mirrors: we see new aspects to ourselves. We see strengths and vulnerabilities we did not know we had. We see our past linked to our future. We bring attitudes and knowledge from our forebears; we transpose and then transfer this heritage to our children and the coming generations.

From the vantage point of having children who are almost grown, it is clear that parenthood has been the most profound experience of my life— it is the most draining, the most enriching, the most infuriating, the most serene. The lows are the lowest, the highs the most exhilarating.

As I look at my children now, I am in awe of the richness of understanding and love that they have brought to me.

NOTES

....

INTRODUCTION

p. xii *my book:* Ellen Galinsky, *The Six Stages of Parenthood* (Reading, Mass.: Addison-Wesley, 1987); originally issued, *Between Generations: The Six Stages of Parenthood* (New York: Times Books, 1981).

p. xiii *micro- and macroenvironments:* Urie Bronfenbrenner, personal communication.

ONE: DISCIPLINE

p. 7 *"compliance" and "self-control":* Alice Sterling Honig, "Compliance, Control, and Discipline," *Young Children* (January 1985), p. 50.

p. 7 *paradox in parental goals:* Lawrence Balter with Anita Shreve, *Dr. Balter's Child Sense* (New York: Poseidon Press, 1985), p. 14.

p. 7 *"The struggle for autonomy":* Karen L. Haswell, Ellen Hock, and Charles Wenar, "Oppositional Behavior of Preschool Children: Theory and Intervention," *Family Relations,* vol. 30 (1981), pp. 440–446.

p. 8 *overall percentage of children's compliance:* Cheryl Minton, Jerome Kagan, and Janet A. Levine, "Maternal Control and Obedience in the Two-Year-Old," *Child Development,* vol. 42 (1971), pp. 1873–1894; Hugh Lytton, "Disciplinary Encounters Between Young Boys and Their Mothers and Fathers: Is There a Contingency System?" *Developmental Psychology,* vol. 15, no. 3 (1979), pp.

256–268; H. Rudolph Schaffer and Charles K. Crook, "Child Compliance and Maternal Control Techniques," *Developmental Psychology,* vol. 16, no. 1 (1980), pp. 54–61.

p. 8 *"in the main end up complying":* Martin L. Hoffman, "Moral Internalization: Current Theory and Research," *Advances in Experimental Social Psychology,* ed. L. Berkowitz (New York: Academic Press, 1977), p. 88.

p. 8 *three disciplinary styles:* Diana Baumrind, "Current Patterns of Parental Authority," *Developmental Psychology Monographs,* vol. 4, no. 1, part 2 (1971), pp. 1–103.

p. 8n *effects last through adolescence:* Sanford M. Dornbusch, Philip L. Ritter, P. Herbert Leiderman, Donald F. Roberts, and Michael J. Fraleigh, "The Relation of Parenting Style to Adolescent School Performance," *Child Development,* vol. 58, no. 5 (October 1987), pp. 1244–1257.

p. 9 *sensitive, responsible, cooperative mothers:* D. J. Stayton, R. Hogan, and Mary D. Salter Ainsworth, "Infant Obedience and Maternal Behavior: The Origins of Socialization Reconsidered," *Child Development,* vol. 42, no. 4 (1971), pp. 1057–1069.

p. 9 *"power assertion techniques":* Hugh Lytton and Walter Zwirner, "Compliance and Its Controlling Stimuli Observed in a Natural Setting," *Developmental Psychology,* vol. 11, no. 6 (1975), pp. 769–779.

p. 10 *cooperative relationship with hard-to-manage children:* Susan Crockenberg, "Infant Irritability, Mother Responsiveness, and Social Support Influences on the Security of Infant-Mother Attachment," *Child Development,* vol. 52 (1981), pp. 857–865.

p. 10 *warmth in parenting made a difference:* Lois Barclay Murphy, "Coping, Vulnerability, and Resilience in Childhood," *Coping and Adaptation,* eds. G. V. Coelho, D. A. Hamburg, J. E. Adams (New York: Basic Books, 1974).

p. 10 *customarily irritable parents have disruptive children:* Gerald Patterson, quoted in *New York Times,* July 29, 1986, pp. C1, C3.

p. 11 *supermarket as a triple threat:* George Holden, "Avoiding Conflict: Mothers as Tacticians in the Supermarket," *Child Development,* vol. 54 (1983), p. 234.

p. 11 *arrange shopping with child's rhythms:* Ibid.

p. 12 *direct child's attention to the next task:* Schaffer and Crook, "Child Compliance."

p. 12 *suggestions elicited more cooperation than commands:* Hugh Lytton, "Three Approaches to the Study of Parent-Child Interaction: Ethological, Interview and Experimental," *Journal of Child Psychology and Psychiatry,* vol. 14 (1973), pp. 1–17; Lytton and Zwirner, "Compliance and Its Controlling Stimuli."

p. 12 *"I" messages:* Thomas Gordon with Judith Gordon Sands, *P.E.T. in Action* (New York: Wyden, 1976).

p. 12 *neutral language:* Haim G. Ginott, *Between Parent and Child* (New York: Macmillan, 1965).

p. 13 *"ultimate threat of abandonment or separation":* Hoffman, "Moral Internalization."

p. 13 *"notion that your parent does not love you is terrifying":* Martin L. Hoffman, quoted in *New York Times,* July 29, 1986, p. C3.

p. 13 *inductive approach:* Hoffman, "Moral Internalization."

p. 13 *independent thinking rather than fear:* Ibid.

p. 15 *"other-oriented discipline"*: Martin L. Hoffman, "Parent Discipline and the Child's Consideration for Others," *Child Development*, vol. 34 (1963), pp. 573–588.

p. 16 *discipline based on logical consequences:* Rudolf Dreikurs and Vicki Soltz, *Children: The Challenge* (New York: Hawthorn Books, 1964).

p. 16 *effective parenting:* Michael K. Meyerhoff and Burton L. White, "Making the Grade as Parents," *Psychology Today*, vol. 20, no. 9 (September 1986), pp. 38–45.

p. 16 *"The Three Cs":* Pat Libbey, personal communication.

p. 18 *problem-solving approach:* Myrna B. Shure and George Spivack, "Interpersonal Problem Solving as a Mediator of Behavioral Adjustment in Preschool and Kindergarten Children," *Journal of Applied Developmental Psychology*, vol. 1 (1980), pp. 29–44; "The Problem-Solving Approach to Adjustment: A Competency-Building Model of Primary Prevention," *Prevention in Human Services*, vol. 1 (½) (Fall/Winter 1981), pp. 87–103; "Interpersonal Problem-Solving in Young Children: A Cognitive Approach to Prevention," *American Journal of Community Psychology*, vol. 10, no. 3 (1982), pp. 341–356.

p. 19 *those who can problem-solve are "better adjusted than those who cannot":* Shure and Spivack, "The Problem-Solving Approach to Adjustment," p. 88.

p. 19 *"These thinking skills helped impulsive children":* Ibid., p. 93.

p. 22 *"When I think back":* Shana Lowitz, personal communication.

p. 28 *think of a color:* Stanley Turecki, M.D., personal communication.

p. 45 *"In beating their children":* Alice Miller, *For Your Own Good: Hidden Cruelty in Child-Rearing and the Roots of Violence,* trans. Hildegarde Hannum and Hunter Hannum (New York: Farrar, Straus & Giroux, 1983), p. 16.

p. 45 *physical force creates more resistance and less cooperation:* Lytton and Zwirner, "Compliance and Its Controlling Stimuli."

p. 46 *five types of psychological maltreatment:* James Garbarino, Edna Guttman, Janice Wilson Seeley, *The Psychologically Battered Child* (San Francisco: Jossey-Bass, 1986).

p. 47 *"ability to react appropriately later in life":* Miller, *For Your Own Good,* p. 65.

p. 50 *parents can encourage inhibited children to be more outgoing:* Jerome Kagan, *The Nature of the Child* (New York: Basic Books, 1984).

p. 50 *teaching problem-solving to inhibited children:* Shure and Spivack, "Interpersonal Problem-Solving in Young Children," p. 354.

TWO: THE LEARNING, GROWING CHILD

p. 57 *autonomy and initiative:* Erik H. Erikson, "Eight Ages of Man," *Childhood and Society*, 2nd ed. (New York: W. W. Norton, 1963), pp. 251–258.

p. 58 *four stages of intellectual development:* Jean Piaget, *The Origins of Intelligence in Children* (New York: International Universities Press, 1952).

p. 59 *meaningful, understandable problems:* Margaret Donaldson, *Children's Minds* (New York: W. W. Norton, 1979).

p. 59 *toddlers display empathy:* National Institute of Mental Health, *Emo-

tions in the Lives of Children, prepared by Marian Radke-Yarrow (Washington, D.C.: U.S. Government Printing Office, 1977).

p. 60 *to grow and learn, children need problems to solve:* Jean Piaget, *To Understand Is to Invent* (New York: Penguin, 1973); E. Duckworth, "The Having of Wonderful Ideas," *Harvard Educational Review,* vol. 42, no. 2 (May 1972), pp. 217–231; Constance Kamii and Rheta DeVries, *Physical Knowledge in Preschool Education: Implications of Piaget's Theory* (Englewood Cliffs, N.J.: Prentice-Hall, 1978).

p. 62 *children who enjoy playing more seem to be happier:* Jerome and Dorothy Singer, "The Values of the Imagination," *Play and Learning,* ed. Brian Sutton-Smith (New York: Gardner Press, 1979), pp. 195–218.

p. 62 *peek-a-boo:* Jerome S. Bruner and V. Sherwood, "Peekaboo and the Learning of Rule Structures," *Play: Its Role in Development and Evolution,* eds. Jerome S. Bruner, Alison Jolly, and Kathy Sylva (New York: Basic Books, 1976), pp. 268–276.

p. 62 *use language to connect actions:* Jacqueline Sachs, "The Role of Adult-Child Play in Language Development," *Children's Play,* ed. Kenneth H. Rubin (San Francisco: Jossey-Bass, 1980), pp. 33–48, no. 9, New Directions for Child Development Series, series ed. William Damon.

p. 62 *more adjectives and adverbs:* Corinne Hutt, quoted in Paul Chance, M.D., *Learning Through Play,* Johnson & Johnson Baby Products Company Pediatric Round Table 3 (New York: Gardner Press, 1979), p. 23.

p. 62 *"We're selling juice":* Bank Street film strip, *Why Dramatic Play?,* Ellen Galinsky, 1977.

p. 63 *"collective symbolization":* Greta G. Fein, "Pretend Play: New Perspectives," *Young Children* (July 1979), pp. 61–66.

p. 63 *positive attitudes toward problem-solving:* Kathy Sylva, Jerome Bruner, and Paul Genova, "The Role of Play in the the Problem-Solving of Children 3–5 Years Old," *Play: Its Role in Development and Evolution,* eds. Jerome Bruner, Alison Jolly, and Kathy Sylva (New York: Basic Books, 1976), pp. 244–257.

p. 64 *"learning about the world by playing about it":* Barbara Biber, "Dramatic Play: Interpretation, Reorganization, and Synthesis," *Early Education and Psychological Development* (New Haven: Yale University Press, 1984), pp. 187–207.

p. 64 *play expresses psychological conflict:* Jan Drucker, "Toddler Play: Some Comments on Its Functions in the Developmental Process," *Psychoanalysis and Contemporary Science,* vol. 4., ed. Donald P. Spence (Madison, Conn.: International Universities Press, 1976).

p. 65 *"variation-seeking":* Brian Sutton-Smith, "Novel Responses to Toys," *Merrill-Palmer Quarterly,* vol. 14 (1968), pp. 151–158.

p. 65 *new uses for objects:* J. L. Dansky and I. W. Silverman, "Effects of Play on Associative Fluency in Preschool Aged Children," *Developmental Psychology,* vol. 9 (1973), pp. 44–54.

p. 65 *play helps society evolve:* Brian Sutton-Smith, quoted in Paul Chance, M.D., *Learning Through Play,* Johnson & Johnson Baby Products Company Pediatric Round Table 3 (New York: Gardner Press, 1979), p. 35.

p. 65 *creative children:* D. W. Bishop and C. E. Chace, "Parental Conceptual Systems, Home Play Environment, and Potential Creativity in Children," *Journal of Experimental Child Psychology,* vol. 12 (1971), pp. 318–338.

p. 66 *"Are you sure you wanna work?":* Zick Rubin, *Children's Friendships,* The Developing Child Series, eds. Jerome Bruner, Michael Cole, Barbara Lloyd (Cambridge, Mass.: Harvard University Press, 1980), p. 75.

p. 66 *fantasy helps preschoolers take the perspective of others:* P. K. Smith and Susan Syddall, "Play and Non-Play Tutoring in Pre-School Children: Is it Play or Tutoring Which Matters?" *British Journal of Educational Psychology,* vol. 48 (1978), pp. 315–325.

p. 67 *ideas:* Fred Rogers and Barry Head, *Mister Rogers' Playbook* (New York: Berkley Books, 1986).

p. 68 *reminisce, dream log, daydreams:* Dorothy G. Singer and Jerome L. Singer, *Partners in Play* (New York: Harper & Row, 1977), pp. 17–23.

p. 69 *your participation depends on your child's individual style:* Jennifer M. Shotwell, Dennie Wolf, and Howard Gardner, "Exploring Early Symbolization: Styles of Achievement," *Play and Learning,* ed. Brian Sutton-Smith (New York: Gardner Press, 1979).

p. 69 *differences in mother's and father's play:* Michael E. Lamb, "The Changing Roles of Fathers," *The Father's Role: Applied Perspectives,* ed. Michael E. Lamb (New York: John Wiley, 1986), pp. 11–12.

p. 69 *rough and tumble teaches difference between playful and hurtful physical contact:* N. Blurton-Jones, "Rough-and-Tumble Play among Nursery School Children," *Play: Its Role in Development and Evolution,* ed. Jerome S. Bruner, Alison Jolly, and Kathy Sylva (New York: Basic Books, 1976), pp. 352–363.

p. 70 *playing fireman:* Marilyn Segal and Don Adock, *Just Pretending: Ways to Help Children Grow Through Imaginative Play* (Englewood Cliffs, N.J.: Prentice-Hall, 1981), p. 102.

p. 71 *safety guidelines:* Consumer Product Safety Commission, Office of Public Affairs, 5401 West Bard Avenue, Bethesda, Maryland 20207.

p. 72 *under threes need concrete reminders of the real thing:* M. A. Pulaski, "Toys and Imaginative Play," *The Child's World of Make-Believe,* ed. Jerome Singer (New York: Academic Press, 1973), pp. 74–103.

p. 73 *help children move beyond a violent focus:* Nancy Carlsson-Paige and Diane Levin, *The War Play Dilemma: Children's Needs and Society's Future,* Early Childhood Education Series (New York: Teachers College Press, 1987).

p. 74 *"certain types of play may well be more effective":* Dina Feitelson, paper presented at Child Advocacy Conference, Yale University, Summer 1979.

p. 75 *"[Play] teaches [the child]":* Bruno Bettelheim, *A Good Enough Parent* (New York: Alfred A. Knopf, 1987), p. 171.

p. 76 *drilling did not promote reading skill:* M. M. Clark, *Young Fluent Readers: What Can They Teach Us?* (Portsmouth, N.H.: Heinemann, 1976); Dolores Durkin, *Children Who Read Early* (New York: Teachers College Press, 1966).

p. 76 *pushing your child:* David Elkind, *The Hurried Child: Growing Up Too Fast Too Soon* (Reading, Mass.: Addison-Wesley, 1981); David Elkind, *Miseducation: Preschoolers at Risk* (New York: Alfred A. Knopf, 1987); Jeanette McCarthy Gallagher and Judith Coché, "Hothousing: The Clinical and Educational Concerns Over Pressuring Young Children," *Early Childhood Research Quarterly,* vol. 1, no. 3 (1987).

p. 77 *famous artists:* Benjamin S. Bloom, ed., *Developing Talent in Young People* (New York: Ballantine Books, 1985).

p. 77 *multiple intelligences:* Howard Gardner, *Frames of Mind: The Multiple Theories of Intelligences* (New York: Basic Books, 1983).

p. 77 *"Later lessons acquired in school":* Maria W. Piers and Genevieve Millet Landau, *The Gift of Play: And Why Young Children Cannot Thrive Without It* (New York: Walker & Co., 1980), p. 28.

p. 80 *preschoolers watch over three hours of TV a day:* Nielsen Television Index, *National Audience Demographics Report, 1982* (Northbrook, Ill.: A. C. Nielsen Co., 1982).

p. 80 *prosocial film vs. antisocial or neutral films:* L. K. Friedrich and A. H. Stein, "Aggressive and Prosocial Television Programs and the Natural Behavior of Preschool Children," *Monographs of the Society for Research in Child Development,* serial no. 151, 38, no. 4 (1973).

pp. 80–81 *watching educational TV increases social contacts:* Brian Coates, H. Ellison Pusser, and Irene Goodman, "The Influence of 'Sesame Street' and 'Mister Rogers' Neighborhood' on Children's Social Behavior in the Preschool," *Child Development,* vol. 47, no. 1 (March 1976), pp. 138–144.

p. 81 *sitcoms stimulate more imaginative play than action-adventure:* Jerome L. Singer and Dorothy G. Singer, *Television, Imagination, and Aggression: A Study of Preschoolers* (Hillsdale, N.J.: Lawrence Erlbaum, 1981).

p. 81 *when an adult discusses the fantasy parts of an educational show:* Jerome L. Singer and Dorothy G. Singer, "Can TV Stimulate Imaginative Play?" *Journal of Communication,* vol. 26 (1976), pp. 74–80.

p. 81 *children gain in letter and number recognition:* S. Ball and G. Bogatz, "A Summative Research of 'Sesame Street': Implications for the Study of Preschool Children," *Minnesota Symposia on Child Development,* vol. 6, ed. A. Pick (Minneapolis: University of Minnesota Press, 1972).

p. 82 *frequency of violence:* George Gerbner, Violence Profile Databank, Annenberg School of Communications, University of Pennsylvania.

p. 82 *after TV violence, children more aggressive and hurtful:* R. M. Liebert and R. A. Barron, "Some Immediate Effects of Televised Violence on Children's Behavior," *Developmental Psychology,* vol. 6 (1972), pp. 469–475.

p. 82 *TV logs:* Singer and Singer, *Television, Imagination, and Aggression.*

p. 82 *violent TV in childhood causally related to aggression at older age:* Leonard D. Eron, L. Rowell Huesmann, Monroe H. Lefkowitz, and Leopold O. Walder, "Does Television Violence Cause Aggression?" *American Psychologist,* vol. 27 (1972), pp. 253–262.

p. 82 *watching televised violence led to increased aggression:* National Institute of Mental Health, *Television and Behavior: Ten Years of Scientific Progress and Implications for the Eighties,* vol. I: *Summary Report* (Washington, D.C.: U.S. Department of Health and Human Services, 1982).

p. 83 *aggressive children more susceptible to TV aggression:* Friedrich and Stein, "Aggressive and Prosocial Television Programs."

p. 83 *less achievement-oriented:* Leonard D. Eron, "Parent-Child Interaction, Television Violence, and Aggression of Children," *American Psychologist,* vol. 37 (1982), pp. 197–211.

p. 83 *even when children are disposed toward aggression:* Singer and Singer, *Television, Imagination, and Aggression.*

p. 83 *Canadian Study:* Helen Featherstone, *The Harvard Education Letter,* vol. 1, no. 2 (April 1985).

p. 83 *brighter children watched less TV:* Hilda T. Himmelweit, A. N. Oppenheim, and P. Vince, *Television and the Child: An Empirical Study of the Effect of Television on the Young* (London: Oxford University Press, 1958).

p. 83 *once TV was introduced:* Featherstone, *The Harvard Education Letter.*

p. 84 *TV helps some low-income, lower IQ children:* Jerome L. Singer and Dorothy G. Singer, "Psychologists Look at Television," *American Psychologist,* vol. 38, no. 7 (1983), pp. 826–834; M. Morgan and L. Gross, "Television Viewing, IQ, and Academic Achievement," *Journal of Broadcasting,* vol. 24 (1980), pp. 117–133.

p. 84 *favoring of right brain:* Marie Winn, *The Plug-In Drug* (New York: Viking, 1977).

p. 84 *"The active child learns to be unnaturally passive":* Dorothy H. Cohen, "Television and the Child Under Six," *Television Awareness Training: The Viewer's Guide for Family and Community,* eds. Ben Logan and Kate Moody (New York: Media Action Research Center, 1979), p. 4.

p. 84 *males outnumber females three to one:* National Institute of Mental Health, *Television and Behavior.*

p. 84 *TV promotes impulsiveness:* Patricia Marks Greenfield, *Mind and Media: The Effects of Television, Video Games, and Computers,* The Developing Child Series, eds. Jerome Bruner, Michael Cole, and Barbara Lloyd (Cambridge, Mass.: Harvard University Press, 1984); Singer and Singer, "Psychologists Look at Television."

pp. 84–85 *preschoolers wanted advertised product:* Z. Stoneman and G. H. Brody, "The Indirect Impact of Child-Oriented Advertisements on Mother-Child Interactions," *Journal of Applied Developmental Psychology,* vol. 2 (1981), pp. 369–376.

p. 85 *cranky and irritable:* Winn, *Plug-In Drug.*

p. 85 *TV inhibits imaginative play:* Singer and Singer, *Television, Imagination, and Aggression.*

p. 85 *scary scenes stimulate fears and night terrors:* Ibid.

p. 85 *"Why didn't you answer me?":* Dorothy H. Cohen, "Structure and Program in the Early Years," unpublished paper, p. 11.

p. 85 *cannot distinguish purpose of commercial and program:* Stephen R. Levin, Thomas V. Petros, and Florence W. Petrella, "Preschoolers' Awareness of Television Advertising," *Child Development,* vol. 53 (1982), pp. 933–937.

p. 85 *some TV literacy:* Greenfield, *Mind and Media.*

p. 85 *compares media of print and TV:* Ibid.

p. 86 *TV presents simpler vocabulary:* Michael Liberman, cited in *The Harvard Education Letter,* vol. 1, no. 2 (April 1985).

p. 86 *first exposed to TV:* Singer and Singer, *Partners in Play.*

p. 87 *no child would watch TV:* Singer and Singer, *Make Believe: Games and Activities to Foster Imaginative Play in Young Children;* (Glenview, Ill.: Scott, Foresman, 1985).

p. 88 *one to two hours of quality programming per day:* Dr. William Dietz, Chairman, American Academy of Pediatrics Subcommittee on Children and TV, personal communication, 1988.

p. 89 *help child become a critical viewer:* Action for Children's Television, 20 University Road; Cambridge, Mass. 02138.

p. 90 *children like computers:* Betty D. Boegehold, *Getting Ready to Read* (New York: Ballantine Books, 1984), p. 126.

p. 91 *computers promoted skill development:* Sandra Anselmo and R. Ann Zinck, "Computers for Young Children? Perhaps," *Young Children* (March 1987), pp. 22–27.

p. 92 *Lego before LOGO:* B. J. Barnes and Shirley Hill, "Should Young Children Work with Microcomputers—Logo before Lego?" *The Computing Teacher,* May 1983, pp. 11–14.

p. 92 *"the experience is reduced":* Harriet K. Cuffaro, "Microcomputers in Education: Why Is Earlier Better?" *Teachers College Record,* vol. 85, no. 4 (Summer 1984), p. 563.

p. 93 *computer violence promotes aggression:* Steven Silvern and P. Williamson, "Computer Games Increase Aggression," *Report on Preschool Education* (Arlington, Va.: Capitol Publications, 1982).

p. 95 *a favorite of innumerable twos and threes:* Margaret Wise Brown, *The Runaway Bunny* (New York: Harper & Row, 1942).

p. 97 *children in orphanages and hospitals:* John Bowlby, *Attachment and Loss:* vol. 1, *Attachment* (New York: Basic Books, 1969).

p. 97 *when children are securely attached in infancy:* L. Alan Sroufe, "The Coherence of Individual Development," *American Psychologist,* vol. 34 (1979), pp. 834–841.

p. 98 *importance of mother's sensitivity to baby's signals:* Mary D. Salter Ainsworth, "The Development of Infant-Mother Attachment," *Review of Child Development Research,* vol. 3, eds. Bettye M. Caldwell and Henry N. Ricciuti (Chicago: University of Chicago Press, 1973).

p. 98 *"one in which the child's emotional needs are met effectively":* L. Alan Sroufe, Nancy E. Fox, and Van R. Pancake, "Attachment and Dependency in Developmental Perspective," *Child Development,* vol. 54 (1983), p. 1617.

p. 98 *mother can adjust to temperamental traits:* Sroufe, "The Coherence of Individual Development."

p. 98 *some children biologically disposed to inhibition:* Jerome Kagan, J. Steven Reznick, Charlotte Clarke, Nancy Snidman, and Cynthia Garcia-Coll, "Behavioral Inhibition to the Unfamiliar," *Child Development,* vol. 55 (1984), pp. 2212–2225; J. Steven Reznick, Jerome Kagan, Nancy Snidman, Michelle Gersten, Katherine Baak, and Allison Rosenberg, "Inhibited and Uninhibited Children: A Follow-up Study," *Child Development,* vol. 57 (1986), pp. 660–680.

p. 98 *at birth infant has no sense of separateness of self:* Margaret S. Mahler, *Of Human Symbiosis and the Vicissitudes of Individuation,* vol. 1, *Infantile Psychosis* (New York: International Universities Press, 1968).

p. 99 *"First comes the formulation of self and other":* Daniel N. Stern, *The Interpersonal World of the Infant: A View from Psychoanalysis and Developmental Psychology* (New York: Basic Books, 1985), p. 70.

p. 99 *"a decisive encounter with his environment":* Erikson, *Childhood and Society,* p. 271

p. 99 *new experiences challenge children to explore:* Piaget, *Origins of Intelligence.*

p. 100 *"separation/connection":* Ellen Galinsky, *The Six Stages of Parenthood* (Reading, Mass.: Addison-Wesley, 1987); originally issued, *Between Generations: The Six Stages of Parenthood* (New York: Times Books, 1981).

p. 100 *focus shifts from parents to age-mates and other adults:* Willard H. Hartup and E. Duwayne Keller, "Nurturance in Preschool Children and Its Relation to Dependency," *Child Development,* vol. 31 (1960), pp. 681–689; Marjorie Stith and Ruth Connor, "Dependency and Helpfulness in Young Children," *Child Development,* vol. 33 (1962), pp. 15–20; Karl E. Wilson and Carolyn Uhlinger Shantz, "Perceptual Role-Taking Ability and Dependency Behavior in Preschool Children," *Merrill-Palmer Quarterly,* vol. 23, no. 3 (1977), p. 207–211; Sroufe, Fox, and Pancake, "Attachment and Dependency."

p. 100 *child's way of functioning is being reorganized:* Piaget, *Origins of Intelligence.*

p. 102 *bonding research:* Marshall H. Klaus and John H. Kennell, *Maternal-Infant Bonding* (St. Louis: C. V. Mosby, 1976); "Mothers Separated from Their Newborn Infants," *Pediatric Clinics of North America,* vol. 17 (November 1970), pp. 1015–1037; "Parent-to-Infant Attachment," *Mother/Child, Father/Child Relationships,* eds. Joseph H. Stevens, Jr. and Marilyn Mathews (Washington, D.C.: National Association for the Education of Young Children, 1978).

p. 104 *children must find their own solutions to anxiety:* Selma H. Fraiberg, *The Magic Years: Understanding and Handling the Problems of Early Childhood* (New York: Charles Scribner's Sons, 1959).

p. 104 *classic fairy tales:* Bruno Bettelheim, *The Uses of Enchantment: The Meaning and Importance of Fairy Tales* (New York: Alfred A. Knopf, 1976).

p. 106 *"aggressive skills" and "aggressive controls":* Marjorie J. Kostelnik, Alice P. Whiren, and Laura C. Stein, "Living with He-Man: Managing Superhero Fantasy Play," *Reducing Stress in Young Children's Lives,* ed. Janet Brown Mc-Cracken (Washington, D.C.: National Association for the Education of Young Children, 1986–87), pp. 6–12.

p. 107 *"object permanence":* Piaget, *Origins of Intelligence.*

p. 108 *children's fears:* Marion Carey Hyson, "Lobster on the Sidewalk: Understanding and Helping Children with Fears," *Reducing Stress in Young Children's Lives,* ed. Janet Brown McCracken (Washington, D.C.: National Association for the Education of Young Children, 1986–87), pp. 2–5.

p. 109 *"visual cliff" experiment:* Robert N. Emde and J. E. Sorce, "The Rewards of Infancy: Emotional Availability and Maternal Referencing," *Frontiers of Infant Psychiatry,* vol. 2, eds. J. D. Call, E. Galenson, and R. Tyson (New York: Basic Books, 1983).

p. 112 *"the point is . . . to help children think of many solutions":* Hyson, "Lobster on the Sidewalk," p. 5.

p. 113 *half of all middle-class American children use an attachment object:* Mary Renck Jalongo, "Do Security Blankets Belong in Preschool?" *Young Children,* (March 1987), pp. 3–8.

p. 113 *"transitional objects":* Donald W. Winnicott, *Playing and Reality* (New York: Basic Books, 1971).

p. 113 *twos and threes accompanied by their blanket:* Richard H. Passman, "Providing Attachment Objects to Facilitate Learning and Reduce Distress: Effects of Mothers and Security Blankets," *Developmental Psychology,* vol. 13, no. 1 (1977), pp. 25–28.

p. 113 *first possession and creation:* Winnicott, *Playing and Reality.*

p. 114 *creative artists more likely to have had transitional objects or imaginary companions:* Ibid.

pp. 115–116 *consider duration, intensity, emotional distress:* Jalongo, "Security Blankets," p. 5.

p. 116 *symbolic treatment of independence and dependence:* Maurice Sendak, *Where the Wild Things Are* (New York: Harper & Row, 1963).

p. 117 *early interactions:* C. C. Eckerman, J. L. Whatley, and S. L. Kutz, "Growth of Social Play with Peers During the Second Year of Life," *Developmental Psychology,* vol. 11 (1975), pp. 42–49.

p. 117 *toys and objects vital to toddlers' interaction:* Ibid.

p. 117 *secure relationship with an adult lays groundwork for social competence:* Everett Waters, Judith Wippman, and L. Alan Sroufe, "Attachment, Positive Affect, and Competence in the Peer Group: Two Studies in Construct Validation," *Child Development,* vol. 50 (1979), pp. 821–829; Alicia F. Lieberman, "Preschoolers' Competence with a Peer: Relations with Attachment and Peer Experience," *Child Development,* vol. 48 (1977), pp. 1277–1287; Donald I. Pastor, "The Quality of Mother-Infant Attachment and Its Relationship to Toddlers' Initial Sociability with Peers," *Developmental Psychology,* vol. 17, no. 3 (1981), pp. 326–335; M. Ann Easterbrooks and Michael E. Lamb, "The Relationship between Quality of Infant-Mother Attachment and Infant Competence in Initial Encounters with Peers," *Child Development,* vol. 50 (1979), pp. 380–387.

p. 117 *distinctive styles of interaction:* Lee C. Lee, "Social Encounters of Infants: The Beginnings of Popularity," paper presented at the International Society for Behavioral Development, Ann Arbor, 1973.

p. 118 *71 percent of infants had at least one friend:* Carollee Howes, "Patterns of Friendship," *Child Development,* vol. 54, no. 4 (August 1983), pp. 1041–1053.

p. 118 *young children more imaginative when together:* Judith L. Rubenstein and Carollee Howes, "The Effect of Peers on Toddler Interaction with Mother and Toys," *Child Development,* vol. 47 (1976), pp. 597–605.

p. 118 *tight group forms around favorite playmates and activities:* F. Strayer, "Child Ethology and the Study of Preschool Social Relations," *Friendship and Social Relations in Children,* eds. H. Foot, A. Chapman, and J. Smith (New York: John Wiley, 1980); Don Adcock and Marilyn Segal, *Making Friends: Ways of Encouraging Social Development in Young Children* (Englewood Cliffs, N.J.: Prentice-Hall, 1983).

p. 118 *boys tend to like boy activities:* K. H. Rubin, T. L. Maioni, and S. M. Hornung, "Free Play Behaviors in Middle and Lower Class Preschoolers: Parten and Piaget Revisited," *Child Development,* vol. 47 (1976), pp. 414–419.

p. 119 *valued qualities of a good playmate:* Willard W. Hartup, "Peer Interaction and Social Organization," *Carmichael's Manual of Child Psychology,* 3rd ed., vol. 2, ed. P.H. Mussen (New York: John Wiley, 1970).

p. 119 *some conflict and disagreement is growth enhancing:* Rubin, *Children's Friendships;* Adcock and Segal, *Making Friends.*

p. 119 *nature of friendship changes:* J. Gottman and J. Parkhurst, "A Developmental Theory of Friendship," *The Minnesota Symposia on Child Psychology,* vol. 13 (Hillside, N.J.: Lawrence Erlbaum, 1978).

p. 119 *momentary and chance encounters:* Robert L. Selman, *The Growth of Interpersonal Understanding: Developmental and Clinical Analysis* (New York: Academic Press, 1980).

p. 121 *being possessive as first step in social interaction:* Laura E. Levine,

"*Mine:* Self-Definition in Two-Year-Old Boys," *Developmental Psychology,* vol. 19, no. 4 (1983), pp. 544–549.

p. 121 *spontaneous cooperation and sharing:* Edward C. Mueller and Deborah Vandell, "Infant-Infant Interaction," *Handbook of Infant Development,* ed. Joy D. Osofsky (New York: John Wiley, 1979), pp. 591–622.

p. 126 *child bullies grew up to be adult bullies:* L. Rowell Huesmann, Leonard D. Eron, Monroe M. Lefkowitz, and Leopold O. Walder, "Stability of Aggression over Time and Generations," *Developmental Psychology,* vol. 20, no. 6 (1984), pp. 1120–1134.

pp. 128–129 *training in friendship skills:* Melinda L. Combs and Diana Arezzo Slaby, "Social-Skills Training with Children," *Advances in Clinical Child Psychology,* vol. 1, eds. B. B. Lahey and Alan E. Kazdin (New York: Plenum Press, 1977); Phillip G. Zimbardo, *Shyness: What It Is, What to Do About It* (Reading, Mass: Addison-Wesley, 1977).

p. 129 *temperamentally slow-to-warm-up baby:* Alexander Thomas, Stella Chess, and H. G. Birch, *Temperament and Behavior Disorders in Children* (New York: New York University Press, 1968).

p. 129 *heightened wariness towards strangers:* K. Tennes, K. Downey, and A. Vernadakis, "Urinary Control, Excretion Rates, and Anxiety in Normal One-Year-Old Infants," *Psychosomatic Medicine,* vol. 39, no. 3 (1977), pp. 178–187.

p. 129 *physiological measures:* Cynthia Garcia-Coll, Jerome Kagan, and J. Steven Reznick, "Behavioral Inhibition in Young Children," *Child Development,* vol. 55 (1984), pp. 1005–1019; Reznick, Kagan, Snidman, et al., "Inhibited and Uninhibited Children."

p. 129 *nearly one-fourth of shy toddlers became less inhibited:* Kagan, Reznick, Clarke, et al., "Behavioral Inhibition to the Unfamiliar."

p. 129 *80 percent described themselves as shy:* Phillip G. Zimbardo and S. L. Radl, *The Shy Child: A Parent's Guide to Preventing and Overcoming Shyness from Infancy to Adulthood* (New York: McGraw-Hill, 1981).

p. 130 *tend to erect barriers:* Zimbardo, *Shyness.*

p. 130 *pair shy children with younger playmates:* Wyndol Furman, Donald F. Rahe, and Willard W. Hartup, "Rehabilitation of Socially Withdrawn Preschool Children through Mixed-Age and Same-Age Socialization," *Child Development,* vol. 50 (1979), pp. 915–922.

p. 130 *the floppy game:* E. P. Sarafino, *The Fears of Childhood: A Guide to Recognizing and Reducing Fearful States in Children* (New York: Human Sciences Press, 1986), p. 112.

p. 131 *cautious, observant style associated with intellectual pursuits:* Jerome Kagan and Howard Moss, *Birth to Maturity* (New Haven: Yale University Press, 1983).

p. 132 *children have imaginary friends:* Martin Manosevitz, Norman M. Prentice, and Frances Wilson, "Individual and Family Correlates of Imaginary Companions in Pre-School Children," *Developmental Psychology,* vol. 8, no. 1 (January 1973), pp. 72–79; Singer and Singer, *Television, Imagination, and Aggression.*

p. 132 *firstborns more likely to invent playmates:* Manosevitz, Prentice, and Wilson, "Individual and Family Correlates."

p. 132 *preschoolers who invent companions:* Jerome L. Singer, *The Child's World of Make Believe: Experimental Studies of Imaginative Play* (New York: Academic Press, 1973).

p. 132 *scored high on standardized measures of fantasy:* Singer and Singer, "The Values of the Imagination."

p. 132 *"literary creativity":* C. E. Schaeffer, "Imaginary Play Companions and Creative Adolescents," *Developmental Psychology,* vol. 1 (October 1969), pp. 747–749.

p. 133 *hard-of-hearing child:* L. Joseph Stone and Joseph Church, *Childhood and Adolescence: A Psychology of the Growing Person,* 3rd ed. (New York: Random House, 1973).

p. 133 *"splitting" into "good people" and "bad people":* Otto Kernberg, *Object Relations Theory and Clinical Psychoanalysis* (New York: Jason Aronson, Inc., 1976).

p. 134 *child who employs his imagination:* Fraiberg, *Magic Years,* p. 23.

p. 138 *children reared in institutions:* Bowlby, *Attachment and Loss;* René Spitz, "Hospitalism: An Inquiry into the Genesis of Psychiatric Conditions in Early Childhood," *Psychoanalytic Study of the Child,* vol. 1 (New York: International Universities Press, 1945), pp. 53–74.

p. 138 *giving reasons and explanations:* Martin L. Hoffman, "Affect and Moral Development," *Emotional Development,* eds. Dante Cicchetti and Petra Hesse (San Francisco: Jossey-Bass, 1982), no. 16, New Directions for Child Development Series, series ed. William Damon.

p. 140 *six-stage sequence of moral reasoning:* Lawrence Kohlberg, "Stage and Sequence," *Handbook of Socialization Theory and Research,* ed. D. A. Goslin (Chicago: Rand McNally, 1969); Lawrence Kohlberg, *The Philosophy of Moral Development* (San Francisco: Harper & Row, 1981).

p. 141 *rules not yet inner convictions:* Jean Piaget, *The Moral Judgment of the Child* (New York, The Free Press, 1965 [originally published in 1932]).

p. 142 *judge by its consequences:* Ibid.

p. 142 *girls' morality emphasizes interpersonal:* Carol Gilligan, *In a Different Voice: Psychological Theory and Women's Development* (Cambridge, Mass.: Harvard University Press, 1982).

p. 143 *born with capacity to empathize:* Hoffman, "Affect and Moral Development."

p. 143 *twos empathy is egocentric:* Marian Radke-Yarrow and Carolyn Zahn-Waxler, "The Emergence and Functions of Prosocial Behaviors in Young Children," *Readings in Child Development and Relationships,* 2nd ed., eds. R. C. Smart and M. S. Smart (New York: Macmillan, 1977).

p. 143 *preschoolers asked which is worse:* Larry P. Nucci and Elliot Turiel, "Social Interactions and the Development of Social Concepts in Preschool Children," *Child Development,* vol. 49 (1978), pp. 400–407; Judith G. Smetana, "Preschool Children's Conceptions of Moral and Social Rules," *Child Development,* vol. 52 (1981), pp. 1333–1336.

p. 143 *mothers who were responsive:* D. J. Stayton, R. Hogan, and Mary D. Salter Ainsworth, "Infant Obedience and Maternal Behavior: The Origins of Socialization Reconsidered," *Child Development,* vol. 42, no. 4 (1971), pp. 1057–1069.

p. 144 *"Religious faith":* Thomas Lickona, *Raising Good Children: From Birth through the Teenage Years* (New York: Bantam Books, 1985), p. 329.

p. 147 *"This is a chance to obey":* Ibid., p. 124.

p. 147 *certain child-rearing practices foster empathy:* Hoffman, "Affect and Moral Development."

p. 147 *mothers who talked to their firstborns:* Judy Dunn and Carol Kendrick, *Siblings: Love, Envy, and Understanding* (Cambridge, Mass.: Harvard University Press, 1982).

pp. 147–148 *"go with the flow" or "challenge":* Kohlberg, "Stage and Sequence"; Lickona, *Raising Good Children,* p. 99.

p. 148 *experiences with other children lay the groundwork for cooperation, equality, fairness:* Willard W. Hartup, "Peer Interaction and the Processes of Socialization," *Early Intervention and the Integration of Handicapped and Nonhandicapped Children,* ed. M. J. Guralnick (Baltimore: University Park Press, 1977).

p. 149 *"Toys left out make parents mad":* Lickona, *Raising Good Children.*

p. 150 *three aspects of sex role development:* Alice Sterling Honig, "Sex role Socialization in Young Children," *Young Children,* September 1983, pp. 57–70.

p. 151 *threes and fours know sex stereotypes:* Eleanor E. Maccoby and Carol Nagy Jacklin, *The Psychology of Sex Differences* (Stanford: Stanford University Press, 1974).

p. 151 *psychodynamic theories:* Sigmund Freud, *Some Physical Consequences of the Anatomical Distinction between the Sexes,* vol. 19, ed. and trans. James Strachey, The Standard Edition of the Complete Psychological Works of Sigmund Freud (London: Hogarth Press, 1953–1966).

p. 151 *"girls and boys differ from each other":* Corinne Hutt, "Neuroendocrinological, Behavioral, and Intellectual Aspects of Sexual Differentiation in Human Development," *Gender Differences: Their Ontogeny and Significance,* eds. C. Ounstead and D. C. Taylor (London: Churchill Livingstone, 1972), p. 73.

p. 151 *more areas in which no sex differences found:* Maccoby and Jacklin, *The Pyschology of Sex Differences.*

pp. 151–152 *after surveying sex differences:* Jeanne H. Block, "Differential Premises Arising from Differential Socialization of the Sexes: Some Conjectures," *Child Development,* vol. 54 (1983), pp. 1335–1354.

p. 152 *differences in hemispheres of brain:* Aletha C. Huston, "Sex-Typing," *Socialization, Personality, and Social Development,* ed. E. Mavis Hetherington, vol. IV: *Handbook of Child Psychology,* ed. Paul H. Mussen (New York: John Wiley, 1983), pp. 387–467.

p. 152 *manipulates "gender labels":* H. L. Frisch, "Sex Stereotypes in Adult-Infant Play," *Child Development,* vol. 48 (1977), pp. 1671–1675.

p. 153 *more pleasure and fewer fears:* J. Condry and S. Condry, "Sex differences: A Study of the Eye of the Beholder," *Child Development,* vol. 47 (1976), pp. 812–819.

p. 153 *sons receive more physical stimulation:* Maccoby and Jacklin, *The Psychology of Sex Differences.*

p. 153 *inconclusive if daughters receive more verbal stimulation:* Ibid.

p. 153 *no differences in social interaction:* Michael E. Lamb, "The Development of Parental Preferences in the First Two Years of Life," *Sex Roles,* vol. 3 (1977), pp. 495–497.

p. 153 *parents praise and criticize boys:* Cheryl Minton, Jerome Kagan, and Janet A. Levine, "Maternal Control and Obedience in the Two-Year-Old," *Child Development,* vol. 42 (1971), pp. 1873–1894; Judith H. Langlois and A. Chris

Downs, "Mothers, Fathers, and Peers as Socialization Agents of Sex-Typed Play Behaviors in Young Children," *Child Development*, vol. 51 (1980), pp. 1217–1247.

p. 153 *parents respond favorably to sex-stereotypes:* B. I. Fagot, "The Influence of Sex of Child on Parental Reactions to Toddler Children," *Child Development*, vol. 49 (1978), pp. 459–465.

p. 153 *parents pressed sons but not daughters:* Jeanne H. Block, "Conceptions of Sex Role: Some Cross-Cultural and Longitudinal Perspectives," *American Psychologist*, vol. 28 (1973), pp. 512–526.

p. 153 *daughters fulfill high expectations:* A. H. Stein and M. M. Bailey, "The Socialization of Achievement Orientation in Females," *Psychological Bulletin*, vol. 80 (1973), pp. 345–366.

p. 153 *survey of independent tasks:* Lois Wladis Hoffman, "Early Childhood Experiences and Women's Achievement Motive," *Journal of Social Issues*, vol. 28 (1972), pp. 129–155.

p. 153 *differences in ego and cognitive development:* Block, "Differential Premises."

p. 154 *fathers enforce traditional sex-typing:* Huston, "Sex-Typing."

p. 154 *parents more accepting of daughters' cross-sex play:* Langlois and Downs, "Mothers, Fathers, and Peers."

p. 154 *teachers give boys both positive and negative attention:* C. Etaugh, G. Collins, and A. Gerson, "Reinforcement of Sex-Typed Behaviors of Two-Year-Old Children in a Nursery School Setting," *Developmental Psychology*, vol. 11 (1975); L. E. Berk, "Effects of Variation in the Nursery School Setting on Environmental Constraints and Children's Modes of Adaptation," *Child Development*, vol. 42 (1971), pp. 839–869.

p. 154 *teachers reward boys for high complexity:* B. I. Fagot, "Sex-Determined Consequences of Different Play Styles in Early Childhood," paper presented at the Annual Meeting of the American Psychological Association, Toronto, August 1978.

p. 154 *toys for sons encourage physical activity:* H. L. Rheingold and K. U. Cook, "The Content of Boys' and Girls' Rooms as an Index of Parents' Behavior," *Child Development*, vol. 46 (1975), pp. 459–463.

p. 154 *TV perpetuates sex-role stereotypes:* J. Lemon, "Women and Blacks on Prime-Time Television," *Journal of Communication*, vol. 27, no. 4 (1977), pp. 70–79.

p. 155 *males independent, females deferential:* L. Z. McArthur and S. V. Elsen, "Television and Sex-Role Stereotyping," *Journal of Applied Social Psychology*, vol. 6 (1976), pp. 329–351.

p. 155 *20 percent of TV's married women are employed:* H. F. Waters, "Life According to TV," *Newsweek*, December 6, 1982, p. 136.

p. 155 *heavy TV viewers have stereotyped views of sex roles:* B. S. Greenberg, "Television and Role Socialization: An Overview," *Television and Behavior: Ten Years of Scientific Progress and Implications for the Eighties*, eds. D. Pearl, L. Bouthilet, and J. Lazar, Vol. 2, *Technical Reviews* (Rockville, Md.: National Institute of Mental Health, 1982).

p. 155 *commercials promote sexual stereotypes:* R. P. Ross, T. Campbell, J. C. Wright, A. C. Huston, M. L. Rice, and P. Turk, "When Celebrities Talk, Children Listen: An Experimental Analysis of Children's Responses to TV Ads with

Celebrity Endorsement," unpublished paper, Center for Research on the Influence of Television on Children, University of Kansas.

p. 155 *employed mother broadens children's ideas of sex roles:* Huston, "Sex-Typing."

p. 156 *loosening of stereotyped concepts:* Grace K. Baruch and Rosalind C. Barnett, "Competence-Related Behaviors of Preschool Girls," *Genetic Psychology Monographs,* vol. 103 (1981), pp. 80–103.

p. 156 *androgynous parents make little difference:* Diana Baumrind, "Are Androgynous Individuals More Effective Persons and Parents?" *Child Development,* vol. 53 (1982), pp. 44–75.

p. 156 *adolescents with androgynous parents scored higher:* Janet T. Spence, "Comments on Baumrind's 'Are Androgynous Individuals More Effective Persons and Parents?' " *Child Development,* vol. 53 (1982), pp. 76–80.

p. 156 *androgynous parents pass on their values:* Jack Block, A. Von der Lippe, and Jeanne H. Block, "Sex-Role and Socialization Patterns: Some Personality Concomitants and Environmental Antecedents," *Journal of Consulting and Clinical Psychology,* vol. 41 (1973), pp. 321–341.

p. 158 *children attracted to concrete gender symbols:* Lawrence Kohlberg and Dora Ullian, "Stages in the Development of Psychosexual Concepts and Attitudes," *Sex Differences in Behavior,* eds. R. C. Friedman, R. M. Richart, and R. L. Vande Wierle (New York: John Wiley, 1974), pp. 209–222.

p. 164 *"The sperm goes into the mommy":* Anne C. Bernstein and Phillip A. Cowan, "Children's Conceptions of How People Get Babies," *Child Development,* vol. 46 (1975), pp. 77–91.

p. 164 *not until eleven or twelve years:* Ibid.

p. 164 *adult explanations strain credulity:* Frailberg, *Magic Years,* p. 200.

p. 168 *born before adopted:* Sandra Panetta, personal communication, 1988.

p. 170 *child masturbating in public:* Lawrence Balter with Anita Shreve, *Dr. Balter's Child Sense* (New York: Poseidon Press, 1985).

p. 171 *temperament defined as "inborn behavioral style":* Thomas, Chess, and Birch, *Temperament and Behavior Disorders in Children.*

p. 172 *"difficult" temperament:* J. E. Bates, "The Concept of Difficult Temperament," *Merrill-Palmer Quarterly,* vol. 26 (1980), pp. 299–319.

p. 172 *longitudinal studies report:* Jerome Kagan and Howard A. Moss, *Birth to Maturity* (New York, John Wiley, 1962); reissued 1983: New Haven, Yale University Press; Alexander Thomas and Stella Chess, "Temperament and Follow-Up to Adulthood," *Temperamental Differences in Infants and Young Children,* Ciba Foundation Symposium 89, eds. R. Porter and G. M. Collins (London: Pitman, 1982).

p. 173 *children tend to grow away from extreme behavior:* J. E. Ledingham and A. E. Schwartzman, "A Longitudinal Investigation of Aggressive and Withdrawn Children," paper presented to the Society for Research in Child Development, Detroit, April 1983.

p. 173 *middle-class American parents tend to value boldness and extroversion:* Jerome Kagan, *The Nature of the Child* (New York: Basic Books, 1984).

p. 173 *92 percent said discipline style was ineffective:* Stanley Turecki, M.D., and Leslie Tonner, *The Difficult Child* (New York: Bantam, 1985), pp. 242–243.

p. 173 *intense relationship with primary caretaker:* Ibid.

p. 174 *"goodness of fit"*: Alexander Thomas and Stella Chess, *Temperament and Development* (New York: Brunner/Mazel, 1977).

p. 174 *parents' attitudes toward sleeping and waking patterns:* Judith Dunn, "Individual Differences in Temperament," *Scientific Foundations of Developmental Psychiatry,* ed. Michael Rutter (Baltimore: University Park Press, 1981), pp. 101–109.

p. 174 *goodness of fit as parents' readiness to accept child's style:* Stella Chess, personal communication, 1987.

p. 175 *difficult children need socialization pressures:* Eleanor E. Maccoby, M. E. Snow, and Carol Nagy Jacklin, "Children's Dispositions and Mother-Child Interaction at 12 and 18 Months: A Short-Term Longitudinal Study," *Developmental Psychology,* vol. 20 (1984), pp. 459–472; D. Olweus, "Familial and Temperamental Determinants of Aggressive Behavior in Adolescent Boys: A Causal Analysis," *Developmental Psychology,* vol. 16 (1980), pp. 644–666.

p. 176 *temperament an important factor in coping with family stress:* Alexis P. Barron and Felton Earls, "The Relation of Temperament and Social Factors to Behavior Problems in Three-Year-Old Children," *Journal of Child Psychology and Psychiatry,* vol. 25, no. 1 (1984), pp. 23–33.

p. 176 *if "a behavior stems from temperament":* Turecki and Tonner, *Difficult Child,* p. 106.

p. 176 *assessing if behavior has temperamental base:* Richard R. Abidin, *The Parenting Stress Index (PSI)* (Charlottesville, Va.: Pediatric Psychiatric Press, 1983); Turecki and Tonner, *Difficult Child.*

p. 177 *difficult behavior linked to food allergies:* Ben F. Feingold, *Why Your Child is Hyperactive* (New York: Random House, 1975); Lendon H. Smith, M.D., *Improving Your Child's Behavior Chemistry: A New Way to Raise Happier Children into Healthier Adults* (Englewood Cliffs, N.J.: Prentice-Hall, 1976).

pp. 178–179 *crises most difficult for the slow-to-adapt child:* Turecki and Tonner, *Difficult Child.*

p. 179 *temperamental tantrum vs. manipulative tantrum:* Ibid., p. 139.

p. 186 *magical thinking about death:* Gerald P. Koocher, "Children's Conceptions of Death," *Children's Conceptions of Health, Illness, and Bodily Functions,* eds. Roger Bibace and Mary E. Walsh, (San Francisco: Jossey-Bass, 1981), pp. 85–99, no. 14, New Directions for Child Development Series, series ed. William Damon.

p. 186 *kindergarteners reenacted a fatal accident:* Nancy S. Brown, Nancy E. Curry, and Ethel Tittnich, "How Groups of Children Deal with Common Stress Through Play," *Play: The Child Strives Toward Self-Realization,* eds. Nancy E. Curry and Sara Arnaud (Washington, D.C.: National Association for the Education of Young Children, 1971).

p. 187 *"good grief":* Sandra Sutherland Fox, *Good Grief: Helping Groups of Children When a Friend Dies* (Boston: New England Association for the Education of Young Children, 1985).

p. 187 *Boy had trouble falling asleep after a newborn died of respiratory disease:* Rose Zeligs, *Children's Experience with Death* (Springfield, Ill.: Charles C. Thomas, 1974).

p. 188 *prepared each child:* Judith S. Rubenstein, "Preparing a Child for a

Good-bye Visit to a Dying Loved One," *Journal of the American Medical Association,* vol. 247, no. 18 (May 14, 1982), pp. 2561–2570.

p. 189 *children asked about dying grandfather:* Ibid.

THREE: AT-HOME AND AWAY-FROM-HOME ROUTINES

p. 198 *between 10 and 30 percent of parents of preschoolers say their children are picky eaters:* Judith Dunn, "Feeding and Sleeping," *Scientific Foundations of Developmental Psychiatry,* ed. Michael Rutter (Baltimore: University Park Press, 1981), pp. 119–128.

p. 199 *cleaning one's plate obscures the child's own hunger:* Jane Hirschmann and Lela Zaphiropolous, *Are You Hungry? A Completely New Approach to Raising Children Free of Weight and Food Problems* (New York: Random House, 1985).

p. 200 *longitudinal study:* Lois Barclay Murphy and Alice E. Moriarity, *Vulnerability, Coping, and Growth: From Infancy to Adolescence* (New Haven: Yale University Press, 1976), pp. 348–349.

p. 201 *"You'll spoil your appetite":* Hirschmann and Zaphiropolous, *Are You Hungry?,* p. 8.

p. 202 *"Are you hungry?":* Ibid., p. 34.

p. 207 *forewarns parents of external pressure to toilet train:* T. Berry Brazelton, M.D., personal communication, 1986.

p. 207 *signs of readiness:* Vicki Lansky, *Toilet Training,* rev. ed. (New York: Bantam, 1986).

p. 213 *"To hold can become":* Erik Erikson, *Childhood and Society,* 2nd ed. (New York: W. W. Norton, 1963), p. 251.

p. 213 *"From a sense of self-control":* Ibid., p. 254.

p. 214 *"children differ in their ability to sleep":* Richard Ferber, M.D., *Solve Your Child's Sleep Problems* (New York: Fireside; Simon & Schuster, 1985), p. 17.

p. 216 *analogy of adult with pillow:* Ibid., pp. 58–59.

p. 218 *child who talked to herself:* Daniel N. Stern, *The Interpersonal World of the Infant: A View from Psychoanalysis and Developmental Psychology* (New York: Basic Books, 1985), p. 173.

p. 219 *self-hypnosis:* T. Berry Brazelton. M.D., personal communication, 1987.

p. 219 *protector character:* Stanley Turecki, M.D., personal communication, 1987.

p. 220 *lengthen time between visits:* Ferber, *Solve Sleep Problems,* p. 78.

p. 224 *demand items once a minute:* George Holden, "Avoiding Conflict: Mothers as Tacticians in the Supermarket," *Child Development,* vol. 54 (1983), pp. 233–240.

p. 231 *four rules:* Sherryll Kerns Kraizer, *The Safe Child Book* (New York: Dell, 1985).

p. 231 *"what if" game:* Ibid., pp. 21ff.

p. 235 *"sex maniacs":* Sally Koblinsky and Nory Behana, "Child Sexual Abuse: The Educator's Role in Prevention, Detection, and Intervention," *Young Children* (September 1984), pp. 3–15.

p. 235 *teach children basic skills for all situations:* Jacqueline Ellis, "Sexual Abuse Prevention: Teaching the Broader Skills," *Beginnings* (Fall 1985).

p. 235 *recommendations for preventing sexual abuse:* Cornelia Spelman, *Talking About Child Sexual Abuse* (Chicago: National Committee for Prevention of Child Abuse, 1985).

FOUR: HAPPY AND SAD TIMES

p. 245 *"shopping" week: The Pleasure of Their Company: How to Have More Fun with Your Children,* ed. William H. Hooks, Betty D. Boegehold, and Seymour V. Reit (Radnor, Pa.: Chilton Book Co., 1981).

p. 247 *Thanksgiving story can lead to others:* Patricia Ramsey, "Beyond 'Ten Little Indians' and Turkeys: Alternative Approaches to Thanksgiving," *Young Children,* (September 1979), pp. 28–32, 49–52.

p. 250 *car games:* Frances M. Lappé, *What to Do after You Turn off the TV: Fresh Ideas for Enjoying Family Life* (New York: Ballantine, 1985).

p. 253 *feeling loss of control results in stress:* Michael Rutter, "Stress, Coping and Development: Some Issues and Some Answers." *Journal of Child Psychology and Psychiatry and Allied Disciplines,* vol. 22, no. 4 (October 1981), pp. 323–356.

p. 254 *average transition time for adults is sixteen months:* Employee Relocation Council, *The Effect of Job Transfer on Employees and Their Families* (Washington, D.C.: Employee Relocation Council, 1983).

p. 254 *moving more stressful than birth of a sibling:* N. Galen and J. L. Johns, "Children in Conflict," *School Library Journal,* vol. 26, no. 3 (1979), pp. 25–28.

p. 255 *"where my real mommy lives":* Erika Keller, "Moving with Children," *Boston Parents' Paper* (April 1986), p. 11.

p. 257 *work as a team:* Patricia C. Nida, *Families on the Move: Human Factors in Relocation* (Dubuque, Iowa: Kendal-Hunt, 1983).

p. 263 *prelogical, egocentric, "magical":* Roger Bibace and Mary E. Walsh, "Children's Conceptions of Illness," *Children's Conceptions of Health, Illness, and Bodily Functions,* eds. Roger Bibace and Mary E. Walsh (San Francisco: Jossey-Bass, 1981), pp. 31–48, no. 14, New Directions for Child Development Series, series ed. William Damon.

p. 263 *stethoscope:* Margaret S. Steward and David S. Steward, "Children's Conceptions of Medical Procedures," *Children's Conceptions of Health, Illness, and Bodily Functions,* eds. Roger Bibace and Mary E. Walsh (San Francisco: Jossey-Bass, 1981), pp. 67–84, no. 14, New Directions for Child Development Series, series ed. William Damon.

FIVE: FAMILY RELATIONSHIPS

p. 267 *for 83 percent, birth of the child precipitated a crisis:* E. E. LeMasters, "Parenthood as Crisis," *Sourcebook in Marriage and the Family,* 2nd ed., ed. Marvin B. Sussman (Boston: Houghton Mifflin, 1963).

p. 267 *transition to parenthood:* Everett D. Dyer, "Parenthood as Crisis: A

Re-Study," *Marriage and Family Living,* vol. 25 (May 1963), p. 196–201; Daniel F. Hobbs, Jr., "Parenthood as Crisis: A Third Study," *Journal of Marriage and the Family,* vol. 27 (August 1965), pp. 367–372; Daniel F. Hobbs, Jr., and Sue Peck Cole, "Transition to Parenthood: A Decade Replication," *Journal of Marriage and the Family,* vol. 38 (November 1976), pp. 723–731.

p. 268 *"Parents and nonparents alike reduced":* Susan M. McHale and Ted L. Huston, "The Effect of the Transition to Parenthood on the Marriage Relationship: A Longitudinal Study," *Journal of Family Issues,* vol. 6, no. 4 (December 1985), p. 430.

p. 268 *having children increases family work:* Ibid.

p. 268 *move to traditional sex-stereotyped roles:* Carolyn Pape Cowan, Philip A. Cowan, Gertrude Heming, Ellen Garrett, William S. Coysh, Harriet Curtis-Boles, and Abner J. Boles III, "Transitions to Parenthood: His, Hers, and Theirs," *Journal of Family Issues,* vol. 6, no. 4 (December 1985), pp. 451–482.

p. 268 *men become more involved when second child is born:* Robert B. Stewart, Susan S. Van Tuyl, Linda A. Mobley, Myrna A. Salvador, and Deborah S. Walls, "The Transition at the Birth of a Second Child: Sources of Parental Stress and Support," paper presented to the Conference on Human Development, Nashville, Tenn., April 1986.

p. 268 *pie exercise:* Cowan et al., "Transitions to Parenthood."

p. 268 *men become authoritarian, women child-centered:* Cowan et al., "Transitions to Parenthood."

p. 268 *females raised to pay attention to emotional and interpersonal issues:* Carol Gilligan, *In a Different Voice: Psychological Theory and Women's Development* (Cambridge, Mass.: Harvard University Press, 1982); Lillian B. Rubin, *Intimate Strangers* (New York: Harper & Row, 1983); Nancy Chodorow, *The Reproduction of Mothering: Psychoanalysis and the Sociology of Gender* (Berkeley: University of California Press, 1978).

p. 268 *"men 'stonewall' to avoid stress":* Cowan, et al., "Transitions to Parenthood," p. 475

p. 269 *"ghosts in the nursery":* Selma H. Fraiberg, E. Adelson, and V. Shapiro, "Ghosts in the Nursery: A Psychoanalytic Approach to the Problem of Impaired Infant-Mother Relationships," *Journal of the American Academy of Child Psychiatry,* vol. 14 (1975), pp. 387–422.

p. 269 *"how you deal with incompatibility":* George Levinger, in Daniel Goleman, *New York Times,* April 16, 1985, pp. C1, C4.

p. 271 *children before and after birth of a sibling:* Lorraine Nadelman and Audrey Begun, "The Effect of the Newborn on the Older Sibling: Mothers' Questionnaires," *Sibling Relationships: Their Nature and Significance Across the Lifespan,* eds. Michael E. Lamb and Brian Sutton-Smith (Hillsdale, N.J.: Lawrence Erlbaum, 1982), pp. 13–38.

p. 271 *mild depression after childbirth is common:* Judy Dunn and Carol Kendrick, *Siblings: Love, Envy, and Understanding* (Cambridge, Mass.: Harvard University Press, 1982).

p. 271 *possessiveness within parents toward new baby:* Ellen Galinsky, *The Six Stages of Parenthood* (Reading, Mass.: Addison-Wesley, 1987); originally issued, *Between Generations: The Six Stages of Parenthood* (New York: Times Books, 1981).

p. 272 *primary source of stress:* Stewart, et al., "Transition at Birth."

p. 272 *study of birth of the second child:* Dunn and Kendrick, *Siblings.*

p. 273 *93 percent of older siblings negative:* Ibid.

p. 273 *children regressed:* Ibid.

p. 273 *under twos cling, threes and fours demand:* Judy Dunn, *Sisters and Brothers,* The Developing Child Series (Cambridge, Mass.: Harvard University Press, 1985).

p. 273 *boys withdraw, girls regress:* Nadelman and Begun, "Effect of Newborn"; Dunn and Kendrick, *Siblings.*

p. 273 *children eager to help with baby:* Dunn and Kendrick, *Siblings.*

p. 273 *first meeting not predictive of future feelings:* Ibid.

p. 274 *Anna Freud's advice:* Ibid., p. 49.

p. 275 *give reminder of yourself to child:* Vicki Lansky, *Welcoming Your Second Baby,* rev. ed. (New York: Bantam, 1987).

p. 276 *child's playing with or imitating newborn is positive:* Dunn and Kendrick, *Siblings.*

p. 276 *"more likely to enter the child's pretend games":* Ibid., p. 74.

p. 276 *fathers get more involved with firstborns:* Stewart, et al., "Transition at Birth."

p. 277 *mothers who encouraged children to help:* Dunn and Kendrick, *Siblings,* p. 75.

p. 278 *referred to baby's wants and needs:* Ibid.

p. 280 *confining definitions can last a lifetime:* Stephen P. Bank and Michael D. Kahn, *The Sibling Bond* (New York: Basic Books, 1982).

p. 281 *battles are "normal and natural":* Seymour Reit, *Sibling Rivalry* (New York: Ballantine, 1985), p. 1.

p. 281 *fighting is commonplace:* Rona Abramovitch, Debra J. Pepler, and Carl Corter, "Patterns of Sibling Interaction among Preschool-Age Children," *Sibling Relationships: Their Nature and Significance Across the Lifespan,* eds. Michael E. Lamb and Brian Sutton-Smith (Hillsdale, N.J.: Lawrence Erlbaum, 1982), pp. 61–86.

p. 282 *"siblings are important individuals in each other's lives":* Rona Abramovitch, Carl Corter, Debra J. Pepler, and Linda Stanhope, "Sibling and Peer Interaction: A Final Follow-up and a Comparison," *Child Development,* vol. 57 (1986), p. 229.

p. 282 *well before age three:* Dunn and Kendrick, *Siblings.*

p. 282 *older siblings function as teachers:* Robert B. Stewart, Jr., "Sibling Interaction: The Role of the Older Child as Teacher for the Younger," *Merrill-Palmer Quarterly,* vol. 29, no. 1 (January 1983), pp. 47–68; Gene H. Brody, Zolinda Stoneman, and Carol E. MacKinnon, "Role Asymmetries in Interactions among School-aged Children, Their Younger Siblings, and Their Friends," *Child Development,* vol. 53 (1982), pp. 1364–1370.

p. 282 *"equal is less":* Adele Faber and Elaine Mazlish, *Siblings Without Rivalry* (New York: W. W. Norton, 1987).

p. 282 *as if they lived in different homes:* Denise Daniels, Judy Dunn, Frank F. Furstenberg, Jr., and Robert Plomin, "Environmental Differences within the Family and Adjustment Differences within Pairs of Adolescent Siblings," *Child Development,* vol. 56 (June 1985), pp. 764–774.

p. 283 *children less than three years apart:* Burton L. White, *The First Three Years of Life* (Englewood Cliffs, N.J.: Prentice-Hall, Inc., 1975), p. 233.

p. 283 *very short interval or long:* Jeannie Kidwell, in Daniel Goleman, *New York Times,* May 28, 1985, pp. C1, C4.

p. 283 *spacing made no difference:* Abramovitch et al., "Patterns of Sibling Interaction," "Sibling and Peer Interaction."

p. 283 *similar results:* Dunn and Kendrick, *Siblings.*

p. 283 *competition more intense:* Helen Koch, "The Relation of Certain Formal Attributes of Siblings to Attitudes Held Toward Each Other and Toward Their Parents," *Monographs for the Society for Research in Child Development,* vol. 25 (4, serial no. 78), 1960.

pp. 283–284 *sex makes difference earlier but not later:* Abramovitch et al., "Patterns of Sibling Interaction."

p. 284 *sex makes difference when younger:* Dunn and Kendrick, *Siblings.*

p. 284 *"relatively little power in accounting for psychological outcomes":* Brian Sutton-Smith, "Birth Order and Sibling Status Effects," *Sibling Relationships: Their Nature and Significance Across the Lifespan,* eds. Michael E. Lamb and Brian Sutton-Smith (Hillsdale, N.J.: Lawrence Erlbaum, 1982), p. 153.

p. 284 *"closeness, intimacy, support":* Dunn, *Sisters and Brothers,* p. 74.

p. 284 *"goodness of fit":* Alexander Thomas and Stella Chess, *Temperament and Development* (New York: Brunner/Mazel, 1977).

p. 284 *when parents are negative, children band together:* Bank and Kahn, *Sibling Bond;* Dunn and Kendrick, *Siblings.*

p. 285 *older children interested in interactions between mother and younger sibling:* Judy Dunn and Carol Kendrick, "Siblings and Their Mothers: Developing Relationships within the Family," *Sibling Relationships: Their Nature and Significance Across the Lifespan,* eds. Michael E. Lamb and Brian Sutton-Smith (Hillsdale, N.J.: Lawrence Erlbaum, 1982).

p. 285 *when mother present, children interacted less:* Carl Corter, Rona Abramovitch, and Debra J. Pepler, "The Role of the Mother in Sibling Interaction," *Child Development,* vol. 54 (1983), pp. 1599–1605.

p. 285 *families taught not to intervene in sibling fights:* cited in Dunn, *Sisters and Brothers.*

p. 285 *"special time" reduced fighting:* Ibid., pp. 122–123.

p. 285 *employing both strategies also successful:* Ibid.

p. 286 *parents identify with one or another of the children:* Frances Fuchs Schacter, "Sibling Deidentification and Split-Parent Identification: A Family Tetrad," *Sibling Relationships: Their Nature and Significance Across the Lifespan,* eds. Michael E. Lamb and Brian Sutton-Smith (Hillsdale, N.J.: Lawrence Erlbaum, 1982), pp. 123–152.

p. 286 *second wife (or husband):* Penelope Leach, *Your Baby and Child: From Birth to Age Five* (New York: Alfred A. Knopf, 1984), p. 398.

p. 287 *allowing for bad feelings:* Faber and Mazlish, *Siblings Without Rivalry,* p. 69.

p. 288 *negative stereotypes of only child:* Toni Falbo, "Only Children in America," *Sibling Relationships: Their Nature and Significance Across the Lifespan,* eds. Michael E. Lamb and Brian Sutton-Smith (Hillsdale, N.J.: Lawrence Erlbaum, 1982), pp. 285–304.

p. 288 *1.7 percent said ideal family has one child:* J. A. Davis, *General Social Surveys, 1972–1983: Cumulative Codebook* (Chicago: National Opinion Research Center, 1983), cited in Norval D. Glenn and Sue Keir Hoppe, "Only Children as

Adults: Psychological Well-Being," *Journal of Family Issues,* vol. 3, no. 5 (September 1984), pp. 363–382.

p. 290 *stereotype of maladjusted only child is false:* Glenn and Hoppe, "Only Children as Adults."

p. 291 *only children IQs:* J. G. Claudy, W. S. Ferrell, and C. W. Dayton, "The Consequences of Being an Only Child: An Analysis of Project Talent Data." Final Report (No. NOI-HD-82854), Center for Population Research, National Institutes of Health, December 1979.

p. 291 *only children get more attention:* Falbo, "Only Children in America."

p. 291 *only children seek out others:* Ibid.

p. 291 *only children more likely to be cooperative:* Ibid.

p. 293 *"Four-fifths . . . were not provided":* Judith S. Wallerstein and Joan Berlin Kelly, *Surviving the Breakup: How Children and Parents Cope with Divorce* (New York: Basic Books, 1908), p. 39.

p. 293 *sons of divorce more aggressive, more easily upset:* Jeanne H. Block, Jack Block, and Per F. Gjerde, "The Personality of Children Prior to Divorce: A Prospective Study," *Child Development,* vol. 57 (1986), pp. 827–840.

p. 293 *"divorce was a bolt of lightning":* Wallerstein and Kelly, *Surviving,* p. 11.

p. 294 *little correlation between children's preseparation relationships:* Ibid.

p. 294 *egocentric logic:* John H. Neal, "Children's Understanding of Their Parents' Divorce," *Children and Divorce,* ed. Lawrence A. Kurdek (San Francisco: Jossey-Bass, 1983), no. 19, New Directions for Child Development, series ed. William Damon; E. Mavis Hetherington, "Divorce: A Child's Perspective," *American Psychologist,* vol. 34, no. 10 (October 1979), pp. 851-858; Kathleen A. Camara, "Family Adaptation to Divorce," *In Support of Families,* eds. Michael Yogman and T. Berry Brazelton, M.D. (Cambridge, Mass.: Harvard University Press, 1986), pp. 175–192.

p. 295 *nightmares and regression:* Wallerstein and Kelly, *Surviving,* p. 57; Camara, "Family Adaptation"; Hetherington, "Divorce: A Child's Perspective."

p. 295 *most children react with hostility and anger:* Wallerstein and Kelly, *Surviving,* pp. 74–75.

p. 295 *adults took one to two years to recover:* E. Mavis Hetherington, Martha Cox, and Roger Cox, "The Aftermath of Divorce," *Mother/Child, Father/Child Relationships,* ed. Joseph H. Stevens, Jr., and Marilyn Mathews (Washington, D.C.: National Association for the Education of Young Children, 1978).

p. 295 *parent's interpretation influenced by who instigated split:* Wallerstein and Kelly, *Surviving,* pp. 17, 100.

p. 295 *diminishment of ability to parent:* Hetherington, "Divorce: A Child's Perspective"; Kathleen A. Camara, Octave Baker, and Charles Dayton, "Impact of Separation and Divorce on Youths and Families," *Environment Variables and the Prevention of Mental Illness,* ed. P. M. Insel (Lexington, Mass.: Lexington Books, D. C. Heath, 1980); Wallerstein and Kelly, *Surviving,* pp. 36–38.

p. 296 *"mothers were more responsive to their daughters":* Wallerstein and Kelly, *Surviving,* p. 101.

p. 296 *children slip into role of parenting:* Neal, "Children's Understanding."

p. 298 *"sequence of experiences":* Hetherington, "Divorce: A Child's Perspective," p. 85.

p. 298 *men's income increases while women's declines:* Lenore J. Weitzman, *The Divorce Revolution: The Unexpected Social and Economic Consequences for Women and Children in America* (New York: Free Press, 1985).

p. 298 *multiple moves:* Wallerstein and Kelly, *Surviving,* pp. 182–183.

p. 299 *"task overload":* Hetherington, "Divorce: A Child's Perspective."

p. 299 *"sense of bonding to the spouse":* Robert S. Weiss, "The Emotional Impact of Marital Separation," *Journal of Social Issues,* vol. 32, no. 1 (1976), p. 138.

p. 300 *new relationship of co-parenting:* Camara, Baker, and Dayton, "Impact of Separation."

p. 300 *less affection, more erratic discipline:* Hetherington, Cox, and Cox, "Aftermath of Divorce."

p. 301 *preseparation relationships not predictive of postseparation:* Wallerstein and Kelly, *Surviving,* p. 122; Hetherington, "Divorce: A Child's Perspective."

p. 301 *sensitive period:* Wallerstein and Kelly, *Surviving,* pp. 120–131.

p. 301 *noncustodials who established best relationship:* Ibid., p. 130.

p. 304 *"immature grasp . . . rendered them especially vulnerable":* Wallerstein and Kelly, p. 57.

p. 304 *youngest children seemed better adjusted:* Judith Wallerstein, "Children of Divorce: Preliminary Report of a Ten-Year Follow-Up of Older Children and Adolescents," *Journal of the American Academy of Child Psychiatry,* vol. 24 (1985), pp. 545–553.

p. 304 *young children chief beneficiaries of mother's concern:* Wallerstein and Kelly, *Surviving,* p. 109.

p. 304 *girls recovered most easily:* Wallerstein and Kelly, *Surviving,* p. 166; Hetherington, Cox, and Cox, "Aftermath of Divorce."

p. 304 *boys exposed to more fighting:* Wallerstein and Kelly, *Surviving,* p. 109.

p. 304 *boys respond more aggressively:* Hetherington, Cox, and Cox, "Aftermath of Divorce."

p. 304 *boys more likely to be disciplined:* Wallerstein and Kelly, *Surviving,* p. 166.

p. 304 *boys long for absent fathers:* Ibid., p. 165.

p. 304 *boys remind mothers of ex-husbands:* Ibid., p. 166.

p. 304 *boys buffeted by more conflicted loyalties*: Block, Block, and Gjerde, "Personality of Children."

p. 305 *"The difficult child":* Hetherington, "Divorce: A Child's Perspective," p. 852.

p. 305 *level of conflict or harmony more influential:* Robert D. Hess and Kathleen A. Camara, "Post-Divorce Family Relationships as Mediating Factors in the Consequences of Divorce for Children," *Journal of Social Issues,* vol. 35, no. 4 (1979).

p. 306 *children should see parents together:* Florence Kaslow, in Lawrence Kutner, *New York Times,* June 30, 1988, p. C8.

p. 306 *conflict between parents or between parents and child:* Hess and Camara, "Post-Divorce Family Relationships."

p. 306 *"Young children have more difficulty":* Hetherington, "Divorce: A Child's Perspective," p. 856.

p. 307 *tenacity of anger:* Wallerstein and Kelly, *Surviving,* p. 190.

p. 310 *"transitional" person:* Hetherington, Cox, and Cox, "Aftermath of Divorce."

p. 310 *"transitional . . . relationship disintegrated":* Ibid., p. 283.

p. 310 *flurry of social relationships:* Hetherington, Cox, and Cox, "Aftermath of Divorce"; Wallerstein and Kelly, *Surviving,* p. 32.

p. 312 *"When a new figure leaves":* Robert S. Weiss, *Going It Alone: The Family Life and Social Situation of the Single Parent* (New York: Basic Books, 1979), p. 255.

p. 313 *single-parent/child relationship means companionship:* Doris B. Wallace, Edna K. Shapiro, and Karen S. Blum, "Leaning to Care: Sibling Relationships and Family Structure," unpublished paper, Bank Street College, New York City, 1983.

p. 313 *tendency for parent to lean on child:* Weiss, *Going It Alone.*

p. 313 *"parents for their own parents":* Wallerstein and Kelly, *Surviving,* p. 103.

p. 315 *children endure other losses:* Emily B. Visher, Ph.D. and John V. Visher, M.D., *Stepfamilies: A Guide to Working with Stepparents and Stepchildren* (New York: Brunner/Mazel, 1979).

p. 315 *period of disequilibrium:* John W. Santrock and Karen A. Sitterle, "Parent-Child Relationships in Stepmother Families," *Remarriage and Stepfamilies Today,* eds. K. Pasley and M. Ihinger-Tallman (New York: Guildford Press, in press).

p. 317 *most problems center on child-rearing:* Lucille Duberman, *The Reconstituted Family: A Study of Remarried Couples and Their Children* (Chicago: Nelson-Hall, 1975).

p. 318 *parent-child relationships:* Santrock and Sitterle, "Parent-Child Relationships."

p. 319 *what makes a stepfamily distinct:* Visher and Visher, *Stepfamilies,* p. 19.

p. 319 *more similarities between stepfamilies and single-parent families:* Ibid.

p. 319 *"permeable boundaries":* Lillian Messinger, "Remarriage Between Divorced People with Children from Previous Marriages: A Proposal for Preparation for Remarriage," *Journal of Marriage and Family Counseling,* vol. 2 (April 1976), pp. 193–200.

p. 320 *contact with noncustodial parent:* Santrock and Sitterle, "Parent-Child Relationships."

p. 320 *stable, loving relationships with both parents:* Wallerstein and Kelly, *Surviving,* p. 215.

p. 322 *better relationships if children live in same household:* Lucille Duberman, "Step-Kin Relationships," *Journal of Marriage and the Family,* vol. 35 (1973), pp. 283–292.

p. 322 *"In stepfamilies . . . more strains than in most intact families":* Visher and Visher, *Stepfamilies,* p. 123.

p. 322 *quality of relationship with custodial parent:* F. F. Furstenberg and J. A. Seltzer, "Divorce and Child Development," paper presented to the Orthopsychiatric Association, Boston, April 1983.

p. 322 *quality of relationship with noncustodial parent:* Wallerstein and Kelly, *Surviving;* Santrock and Sitterle, "Parent-Child Relationships."

p. 322 *most stepchildren adjust well:* Duberman, "Step-Kin Relationships."

p. 322 *no social or psychological differences:* K. L. Wilson, L. A. Zurcher, D. C. McAdams, and R. L. Curtis, "Stepfathers and Stepchildren: An Exploratory Analysis from Two National Surveys," *Journal of Marriage and the Family,* vol. 37 (1975), pp. 526–536.

p. 324 *25 million stepparents:* Elizabeth Einstein, *The Stepfamily: Living, Loving, and Learning* (Boston: Shambhala, 1985).

p. 324 *1,300 new stepfamilies:* Mark Bruce Rosin, "Stepfathers and Step-kids: Can They Get Along?" *Parents Magazine,* vol. 62, no. 4 (April 1987), pp. 221–227.

p. 324 *25–35 percent of all children:* Paul C. Glick, "Prospective Changes in Marriage, Divorce, and Living Arrangements," *Journal of Family Issues,* vol. 5 (1984), pp. 7–26.

SIX: FAMILY WORK

p. 327 *time diary studies:* Joseph H. Pleck, "How Work and Family Issues Involve Men," paper prepared for conference on Work and Family: Seeking a New Balance, April 1986.

p. 327 *division of family work based on each spouse's relative economic power:* Graeme Russell, "Shared Caregiving Families: An Australian Study," *Non-traditional Families: Parenting and Child Development,* ed. M. E. Lamb (Hillsdale, N.J.: Lawrence Erlbaum, 1982), pp. 139–171; Chaya S. Piotrkowski, Robert Rapoport, and Rhona Rapoport, "Families and Work: An Evolving Field" (in press).

p. 328 *more traditional roles once first child is born:* Carolyn Pape Cowan, Philip A. Cowan, L. Coie, and J. Coie, "Becoming a Family: The Impact of the First Child's Birth on the Couple's Relationship," *The First Child and Family Formation,* eds. W. Miller and L. Newman (Chapel Hill, N.C.: Carolina Population Center, 1978), pp. 296–324.

p. 328 *woman's commitment to more equitable division is critical:* Diane Ehrensaft, "Man, Woman, and Child: The New Shared Parenting Family," paper delivered at Conference of the American Orthopsychiatric Association, New York City, April 22, 1985.

p. 328 *perceptions of division of labor are unrealistic:* Sara Yogev and Jeanne M. Brett, *Patterns of Work and Family Involvement among Single and Dual Earner Couples: Two Competing Analytical Approaches* (Washington, D.C.: Office of Naval Research, 1983).

p. 328 *stress-related health problems associated with spouse not doing "fair share":* Diane Hughes and Ellen Galinsky, "Balancing Work and Family Life: Research and Corporate Application," *Maternal Employment and Children's Development,* eds. Adele Eskeles Gottfried and Allen W. Gottfried (New York: Plenum Press, 1988).

p. 329 *men with working wives are beginning to do more family work:* Pleck, "How Work and Family Issues Involve Men."

p. 329 *girls raised to be more aware of interpersonal aspects:* Carol Gilligan, *In a Different Voice: Psychological Theory and Women's Development* (Cambridge, Mass.: Harvard University Press, 1982).

p. 334 *cross-cultural studies:* Beatrice B. Whiting and John W. M. Whiting, *Children of Six Cultures: A Psycho-Cultural Analysis* (Cambridge, Mass.: Harvard University Press, 1975).

p. 334 *when mothers enter the labor force, children are expected to help more:* Lois Wladis Hoffman, "Maternal Employment and the Young Child," *Parent-Child Interaction and Parent-Child Relations in Child Development,* ed. M. Perlmutter (Hillsdale, N.J.: Lawrence Erlbaum, 1984), pp. 101–128, vol. 17, Minnesota Symposia on Child Psychology.

p. 334 *single-parent households:* Robert S. Weiss, "The Emotional Impact of Martial Separation," *Journal of Social Issues,* vol. 32 (1976), pp. 135–145.

p. 339 *number of hours worked makes little difference to father's participation in child care:* Joseph H. Pleck, "Husbands' Paid Work and Family Roles: Current Research Issues," *Research on the Interweave of Social Roles* eds. Helena Z. Lopata and Joseph H. Pleck, (Greenwich, Conn.: JAI Press, 1983).

p. 339 *many men have slightly increased time with children:* Ibid.

p. 339 *being absorbed in one's job:* D. B. Heath, "Some Possible Effects of Occupation on the Maturing of Professional Men," *Journal of Vocational Behavior,* vol. 11, (1977), pp. 263–281.

p. 339 *psychological responsibility:* Jean Curtis, *Working Mothers* (New York: Doubleday, 1976).

p. 339 *women are the psychological parents:* Rosalind C. Barnett and Grace K. Baruch, "Women's Involvement in Multiple Roles, Role Strain, and Psychological Stress," Working Paper 107 (Wellesley, Mass.: Wellesley College Center for Research on Women, 1983).

p. 340 *"gatekeepers" of men's participation:* Michael W. Yogman, "New Stresses and Support for Fathers: The Role of Hospitals and School in Supporting Father Involvement," paper presented at Stresses and Supports for Families in the 1980s, Harvard Medical School Conference, Boston, May 1984.

p. 340 *strongest opponents to "New Fatherhood":* James Levine, personal communication, 1986.

p. 341 *men who earn more participate less*: Russell, "Shared Caregiving Families."

p. 341 *men as nurturing:* Ross D. Parke and Douglas B. Sawin, "Fathering: Its Major Role," *Psychology Today* (November 1977), pp. 109, 111–112.

p. 341 *fathers are more playful*: T. Berry Brazelton, M.D., "Families in the 80s: Support for Parents," paper presented at Stresses and Supports for Families in the 1980s, Harvard Medical School Conference, Boston, May 1984.

p. 342 *importance of fathers:* Ross D. Parke, "Fathers: An Intrafamiliar Perspective," *In Support of Families,* eds. Michael Yogman and T. Berry Brazelton, M.D. (Cambridge, Mass.: Harvard University Press, 1986), pp. 59-68.

p. 342 *child's thinking capacity:* Mary D. Salter Ainsworth, "Object Relations, Dependency, and Attachment: A Theoretical Review of the Infant-Mother Relationship," *Child Development,* vol. 40, no. 4 (December 1969), pp. 969–1025.

p. 342 *nurturing fathers:* Nancy Chodorow, *The Reproduction of Mothering: Psychoanalysis and the Sociology of Gender* (Berkeley: University of California Press, 1978).

p. 342 *mother's representation of the father:* Richard Atkins, "Finding One's Father: The Mother's Contribution to Early Father Representations," *Journal of the American Academy of Psychoanalysis,* vol. 9, no. 4 (1981), pp. 539–559.

p. 343 *technique for problem-solving:* Adele Faber and Elaine Mazlish, *How to Talk So Kids Will Listen and Listen So Kids Will Talk* (New York: Avon Books, 1980), p. 102.

p. 345 *sources of stress and satisfaction for working parents:* Ellen Galinsky, Diane Hughes, and Marybeth Shinn, "The Corporate Work and Family Life Study," unpublished paper, Bank Street College, New York, 1986.

p. 346 *the more hours worked, the more likely is family tension:* P. M. Keith and R. B. Schafer, "Role Strain and Depression in Two-Job Families," *Family Relations,* vol. 29 (1980), pp. 483–488; Joseph H. Pleck, Graham L. Staines, and L. Lang, "Conflict Between Work and Family Life," *Monthly Labor Review,* March 1980, pp. 29–32; Halcey H. Bohen and Anamaria Viveros-Long, *Balancing Job and Family Life: Do Flexible Work Schedules Help?,* (Philadelphia: Temple University Press, 1981).

p. 346 *hours away from home not the single cause of tension:* Ellen Galinsky, "Family Life and Corporate Policies," *In Support of Families,* eds. Michael Yogman and T. Berry Brazelton (Cambridge, Mass: Harvard University Press, 1986); Chaya S. Piotrkowski and Paul Crits-Christoph, "Women's Jobs and Family Adjustment," *Two Paychecks: Life in Dual-Earner Families,* ed. J. Aldous (Beverly Hills: Sage Publications, 1982).

p. 346 *inconvenient work hours:* Graham L. Staines and Joseph H. Pleck, *The Impact of Work Schedules on the Family* (Ann Arbor: Institute for Social Research, 1983).

p. 347 *"good enough":* Donald W. Winnicott, "Transitional Objects and Transitional Phenomena," *Collected Papers* (London: Tavistock, 1958).

p. 348 *"a hurried child":* David Elkind, *The Hurried Child: Growing Up Too Fast Too Soon* (Reading, Mass.: Addison-Wesley, 1981).

p. 348 *importance of social support:* Donald Unger and Douglas R. Powell, "Supporting Families under Stress: The Role of Social Networks," *Family Relations,* vol. 29 (1980), pp. 566–574; Deborah Belle, "Social Ties and Social Support," *Social Support, Lives in Stress: Women in Depression,* ed. Deborah Belle, (Beverly Hills: Sage Publications, 1982), pp. 133–144.

p. 349 *making A, B, and C lists:* Alan Lakein, *How to Get Control of Your Time and Your Life* (New York: New American Library, 1974).

p. 349 *decisions involve trade-offs:* Barry S. Greiff and Preston K. Munter, *Trade-offs: Executive, Family and Organizational Life* (New York: New American Library, 1980).

p. 349 *three questions:* Kathleen Tribe, personal communication.

p. 352 *"imperative that you find a leisure activity":* Bruce A. Baldwin, *All In Your Head: Life Style Management Strategies for Busy People*! (Wilmington, N.C.: Direction Dynamics, 1985).

p. 359 *when husbands have more time for themselves than wives:* Denise A. Skinner and Hamilton I. McCubbin, "Coping in Dual-Employed Families: Spousal Differences," mimeographed paper, Department of Family Resources and Consumer Services, University of Minnesota, 1983.

SEVEN: WORK AND FAMILY LIFE

p. 365 *children are "at risk"*: Burton L. White, *The First Three Years of Life* (Englewood Cliffs, N.J.: Prentice-Hall, Inc., 1975).

p. 365 *maternal employment benefits children:* Sandra Scarr, *Mother Care/ Other Care* (New York: Basic Books, 1984).

p. 366 *maternal employment and attachment:* Lois Wladis Hoffman, "Maternal Employment and the Young Child," *Parent-Child Interaction and Parent-Child Relations in Child Development,* ed. M. Perlmutter (Hillsdale, N.J.: Lawrence Erlbaum, 1984), pp. 101–128. vol. 17, Minnesota Symposia on Child Psychology.

p. 366 *father's* lack *of employment:* Urie Bronfenbrenner and Ann Crouter, "Work and Family Through Time and Space," *Families That Work: Children in a Changing World,* eds. Sheila B. Kamerman and C. D. Hayes (Washington, D.C.: National Academy Press, 1982).

p. 366 *that child care can "prevent the formation of primary attachments":* Thomas J. Gamble and Edward Zigler, "Effects of Infant Day Care: Another Look at the Evidence," *American Journal of Orthopsychiatry,* vol. 56, no. 1 (January 1986), p. 29.

p. 366 *focus on children whose mothers returned to their jobs in child's first year:* Ibid.; Jay Belsky, "Two Waves of Day Care Research: Developmental Effects and Conditions of Quality," *The Child and the Day Care Setting: Qualitative Variations and Development,* ed. Ricardo C. Ainslie (New York: Praeger, 1984), pp. 1–34.

p. 366 *secure or insecure attachment in "strange situation":* Mary D. Salter Ainsworth and B. Wittig, "Attachment and Exploratory Behavior of One-Year-Olds in a Strange Situation," *Determinants of Infant Behavior,* vol. 4, ed. B. Foss (London: Methuen, 1969), pp. 111–136; Jay Belsky, Laurence D. Steinberg and Ann Walker, "The Ecology of Day Care," *Nontraditional Families: Parenting and Child Development,* ed. Michael E. Lamb (Hillsdale, N.J.: Lawrence Erlbaum, 1982), pp. 71–116; Brian E. Vaughn, Frederick L. Gove and Byron Egeland, "The Relationship between Out-of-Home Care and the Quality of Infant-Mother Attachment in an Economically Disadvantaged Population," *Child Development,* vol. 51 (1980), pp. 1203–1214; Gamble and Zigler, "Effects of Infant Day Care."

p. 367 *mother's presence does not comfort:* Belsky, "Two Waves of Day Care Research"; Vaughn, Gove and Egeland, "The Relationship between Out-of-Home Care."

p. 367 *infants away from mothers more than twenty hours in first year:* Jay Belsky and Michael Rovine, "Temperament and Attachment Security in the Strange Situation: An Empirical Rapprochement," *Child Development,* vol. 58, no. 3 (June 1987), pp. 787–795; Peter Barglow, Brian E. Vaughn, and Nancy Molitor, "Effects of Maternal Absence Due to Employment on the Quality of Infant-Mother Attachment in a Low-Risk Sample," *Child Development,* vol. 58, no. 4 (August 1987), pp. 945–954.

p. 367 *characteristics of securely attached infants:* Richard A. Arend, Frederick L. Gove, and L. Alan Sroufe, "Continuity of Individual Adaptation from Infancy to Kindergarten: A Predictive Study of Ego-Resiliency and Curiosity in Preschoolers," *Child Development,* vol. 50 (1979), pp. 950–959; Ellen A. Farber and Byron Egeland, "Developmental Consequences of Out-of-Home Care for Infants in a Low-Income Population," *Day Care: Scientific and Social Policy Issues,* eds. Edward F. Zigler and Edmund W. Gordon (Boston: Auburn House, 1982), pp. 102–125; Susan Londerville and Mary Main, "Security of Attachment, Compliance, and Maternal Training Methods in the Second Year of Life," *Developmental Psychology,* vol. 17, no. 3 (1981), pp. 289–299.

p. 367 *children with child-care experiences were more aggressive:* Judith Rubenstein and Carollee Howes, "Adaptation to Infant Day Care," *Advances in Early Education and Day Care,* ed. Sally Kilmer (Greenwich, Conn.: JAI Press, 1983).

p. 368 *"more experienced in the type of situation used to assess attachment":* Alison Clarke-Stewart and Greta Fein, "Early Childhood Programs," *Handbook of Child Psychology,* vol. 2: *Infancy and Developmental Psychobiology,* eds. M. M. Haith and J. J. Campos; series ed. P. H. Mussen (New York: John Wiley, 1983), p. 956.

p. 368 *sixteen studies comparing children with full-time child care:* Alison Clarke-Stewart, " 'The "Effects" of Infant Day Care Reconsidered' Reconsidered: Risks for Parents, Children, and Researchers," *Early Childhood Research Quarterly,* vol. 3, no. 3 (September 1988).

p. 368 *curriculum to teach social skills:* Neal W. Finkelstein, "Aggression: Is It Stimulated by Day Care?," *Young Children,* vol. 37, no. 6 (September 1982), p. 8.

p. 368 *"a failure to provide systematic opportunities":* Ibid., p. 8.

p. 368 *employed mothers show excessive attention:* F. A. Pedersen, R. Cain, M. Zaslow and B. Anderson, "Variation in Infant Experience Associated with Alternative Family Role Organization," *Families as Learning Environment for Children,* eds. L. Laesa and I. Sigel (New York: Plenum, 1983); Hoffman, "Maternal Employment and the Young Child."

p. 368 *"working mothers may . . . exceed the information-processing capacities":* Jay Belsky, "The 'Effects' of Infant Day Care Reconsidered," *Early Childhood Research Quarterly,* vol. 3, no. 3 (September 1988, in press).

p. 369 *other stresses:* Brian Vaughn, Byron Egeland, L. Alan Sroufe, and Everett Waters, "Individual Differences in Infant-Mother Attachment at Twelve and Eighteen Months: Stability and Change in Families under Stress," *Child Development,* vol. 50, no. 4 (December 1979), pp. 971–975.

p. 369 *"When parents have choices":* National Center for Clinical Infant Programs, press release (733 Fifteenth Street NW, Suite 912, Washington, D.C. 10005: November 25, 1987), p. 1.

p. 370 *children who attend child-care centers are more sociable, assertive and aggressive:* Rubenstein and Howes, "Adaptation to Infant Day Care"; Belsky, Steinberg, and Walker, "The Ecology of Day Care."

p. 370 *if group is very large, more fighting among children:* Abt Associates, *Children at the Center: Final Report of the National Day Care Study* (Cambridge, Mass.: Abt Associates, 1979).

p. 370 *IQ gains disappear after child leaves program:* Belsky, Steinberg, and Walker, "The Ecology of Day Care."

p. 370 *enrichment programs for "at-risk" infants prevent IQ decline:* Belsky, "Two Waves of Day Care Research," p. 6.

p. 370 *Bermuda study:* Kathleen McCartney, Sandra Scarr, Deborah Phillips, Susan Grajek, and J. Conrad Schwarz, "Environmental Differences among Day Care Centers and Their Effects on Children's Development," *Day Care: Scientific and Social Policy Issues,* eds. Edward F. Zigler and Edmund W. Gordon (Boston: Auburn House, 1982), pp. 126–151.

p. 370 *children with better language skills:* Ibid.

p. 371 *"children of working mothers do not differ":* B. Heyns, "The Influence of Parents' Work on Children's School Achievement," *Families That Work: Children in a Changing World,* eds. Sheila B. Kamerman and C. Hayes (Washington, D.C.: National Academy Press, 1982).

p. 371 *sons of middle-class employed mothers do not do as well:* Hoffman, "Maternal Employment and the Young Child."

p. 371 *least attractive portraits given by mothers of sons:* Bronfenbrenner and Crouter, "Work and Family."

p. 371 *daughters "generally appear to be more independent":* Hoffman, "Maternal Employment and the Young Child."

p. 371 *boys more active than girls:* Jeanne H. Block, "Differential Premises Arising from Differential Socialization of the Sexes: Some Conjectures," *Child Development,* vol. 54 (1983), pp. 1335–1354.

p. 371 *tension at work; parents react differently to sons and daughters:* Chaya S. Piotrkowski, paper presented at Research Interest Group, Bank Street College, New York, May 1985.

p. 371 *boys more vulnerable:* Judith S. Wallerstein and Joan Berlin Kelly, *Surviving the Breakup: How Children and Parents Cope with Divorce* (New York, Basic Books, 1980).

p. 372 *"American parents encourage their sons' independence":* Hoffman, "Maternal Employment and the Young Child," p. 26.

p. 372 *boys and girls express stress differently:* Emmy Werner and Ruth Smith, *Vulnerable But Invincible* (New York: McGraw-Hill, 1982).

p. 372 *"It is the experiences to which children are exposed":* Adele Eskeles Gottfried, Allen W. Gottfried, and K. Bathurst, "Maternal Employment and Young Children's Development: A Longitudinal Investigation," paper presented at the annual meeting of the American Psychological Association, Los Angeles, 1985.

p. 372 *"the actual experiences and behavior of toddlers":* Rubenstein and Howes, "Adaptation to Infant Day Care," p. 41

p. 372 *mother's attitude was the critical factor:* Marion R. Yarrow, P. Scott, L. DeLeeuw, and C. Heinig, "Childrearing in Families of Working and Non-Working Mothers," *Sociometry,* vol. 25 (1962), pp. 122–140.

p. 374 *incongruence between mother's should and is leads to insecure attachment:* Ellen Hock, "Working and Nonworking Mothers and Their Infants: A Comparative Study of Maternal Care-Giving Characteristics and Infant Social Behavior," *Merrill-Palmer Quarterly,* vol. 25 (1980), pp. 79–101.

p. 375 *interviewed over a thousand children:* Earl A. Grollman and Gerri L. Sweder, *The Working Parent Dilemma: How to Balance the Responsibilities of Children and Careers* (Boston: Beacon Press, 1986), p. 27.

p. 375 *when mothers feel guilty and deprived:* Belsky, "The 'Effects' of Infant Day Care Reconsidered."

p. 377 *"families without a culture":* T. Berry Brazelton, M.D., *Working and Caring* (Reading, Mass.: Addison-Wesley, 1985), p. xv.

p. 377 _"something lovin' from the oven":_ Ellen Goodman, "Changing Families," speech delivered at "Changing Families/Changing Responses," conference of the Family Resource Coalition, Chicago, September 12, 1986.

p. 380 _Happiness Trap:_ Nancy Samalin with Martha Moraghan Jablow, _Loving Your Child Is Not Enough: Positive Discipline That Works_ (New York: Viking, 1987).

p. 382 _parents respond to guilt by working through or denying:_ T. Berry Brazelton, M.D., personal communication, 1987.

p. 382 _warning signs for effects of mothers' employment:_ Judith Rubenstein, hand-out distributed at "Ain't Misbehavin'," Harvard Medical School Conference, May 12–16, 1986.

p. 383 _tension between children in child care can be source of stress:_ Ibid.

p. 384 _"goodness of fit":_ Alexander Thomas and Stella Chess, _Temperament and Development_ (New York: Brunner/Mazel, 1977).

p. 388 _"separate, nonoverlapping worlds":_ Rosabeth Moss Kanter, _Work and Family in the United States: A Critical Review and Agenda for Research and Policy_ (New York: Russell Sage Foundation, 1977).

p. 388 _most parents work longer hours:_ Ellen Galinsky and Diane Hughes, "The _Fortune_ Magazine Child Care Study," paper presented at the annual convention of the American Psychological Association, New York City, August 1987.

p. 388 _excessive work hours lead to stress in conjunction with tension on the job:_ Chaya S. Piotrkowski and Paul Crits-Christoph, "Women's Jobs and Family Adjustment," _Two Paychecks: Life in Dual-Earner Families,_ ed. J. Aldous (Beverly Hills: Sage Publications, 1982).

p. 389 _schedule conflicts are a primary source of stress:_ Robert P. Quinn and Graham L. Staines, _The 1977 Quality of Employment Survey: Descriptive Statistics with Comparison Data from the 1969–70 and 1972–73 Surveys_ (Ann Arbor: Institute for Social Research, 1979).

p. 389 _job insecurity predictive of stress:_ Ellen Galinsky, Diane Hughes, and Marybeth Shinn, "The Corporate Work and Family Life Study," unpublished paper, Bank Street College, New York City, 1986.

p. 389 _demanding, hectic jobs predictive of stress:_ Ellen Galinsky, Penelope H. Bragonier, Diane Hughes, and Marsha Love, "The Family Study," report to the A. L. Mailman Family Foundation, June 1987.

p. 390 _employees with very demanding jobs:_ R.A. Karasek, "Job Demands, Job Decision Latitude, and Mental Strain: Implications for Job Redesign," _Administrative Science Quarterly,_ vol. 24 (1979), pp. 285–308.

p. 390 _"job autonomy":_ Piotrkowski and Crits-Christoph, "Women's Jobs and Family Adjustment."

p. 390 _relationship with the boss:_ Galinsky, Hughes, and Shinn, "The Corporate Work and Family Life Study."

p. 390 _nonsupportive boss is strongest predictor of anxiety:_ Rena L. Repetti, "Individual and Common Components of the Social Environment at Work and Psychological Well-Being," _Journal of Personality and Social Psychology,_ vol. 52, no. 4 (1987), pp. 710–720.

p. 390 _boss who is supportive:_ Diane Hughes and Ellen Galinsky, "Balancing Work and Family Life: Research and Corporate Application," _Maternal Employment and Children's Development: Longitudinal Research,_ eds. Adele Eskeles Gottfried and Allen W. Gottfried (New York: Plenum Press, 1988).

p. 391 *conflict with co-workers affect children:* Piotrkowski, paper presented at Research Interest Group, Bank Street College, New York City, May 1985.

p. 391 *interviewed children:* Galinsky, Bragonier, Hughes, and Love, "The Family Study."

p. 392 *run-ins with the boss:* Ann Crouter, "Spillover from Family to Work: The Neglected Side of Work-Family Interface," *Human Relations,* vol. 37, no. 6 (1984), pp. 425–442.

p. 392 *spillover of mood, energy, and irritability:* Diane Hughes, "Work-Family Interference," unpublished manuscript, Bank Street College, New York City, 1985.

p. 392 *work and family life responsibilities conflict with each other:* Hughes and Galinsky, "Balancing Work and Family Life"; Galinsky and Hughes, "The *Fortune* Magazine Child Care Study"; Galinsky, Hughes, and Shinn, "The Corporate Work and Family Life Study."

p. 392 *"the ways people cope with stress":* R. S. Lazarus and R. Launier, "Stress-Related Transactions between Person and Environment," *Perspectives in International Psychology,* eds. L. A. Pervin and M. Lewis (New York: Plenum Press, 1978), p. 308.

p. 392 *taking action to cope with work/family problems:* Marybeth Shinn, Nora Wong, Patricia Simko, and Blanca Ortiz-Torres, "Promoting the Health and Well-Being of Working Parents: Coping, Social Support, and Organizational Strategies," unpublished paper, New York University.

p. 393 *deciding "whose problem it is":* Thomas Gordon, with Judith Gordon Sands, *P.E.T. in Action* (New York: Wyden, 1976).

p. 397 *focus on self during life transitions such as divorce:* E. Mavis Hetherington, "Divorce: A Child's Perspective," *American Psychologist,* vol. 34, no. 10 (October 1979), pp. 851–858; Wallerstein and Kelly, *Surviving the Breakup.*

p. 397 *after birth of second child, mothers pressure their firstborns for more adult behavior;* Muriel K. Taylor and Kate L. Kogan, "Effects of Birth of a Sibling on Mother-Child Interactions," *Child Psychiatry and Human Development,* vol. 4, (1973), pp. 53–58.

p. 398 *unrealized expectations result in disappointment, upset, anger:* Ellen Galinsky, *The Six Stages of Parenthood* (Reading, Mass.: Addison-Wesley, 1987); originally issued, *Between Generations: The Six Stages of Parenthood* (New York: Times Books, 1981); Chaya S. Piotrkowski, *Work and the Family System: A Naturalistic Study of Working-Class and Lower-Middle-Class Families* (New York: Free Press, 1979).

p. 398 *spouses with divergent expectations lead to family stress:* T. Mason and R. Espinoza, "Executive Summary of the Final Report: Working Parents Project," (Washington, D.C.: National Institute of Education, 1983).

p. 399 *parent/child ability to predict each other's actions is essential:* Dorothy Huntington, "Attachment, Loss, and Divorce," *The Family Therapy Collection,* vol. 2, ed. Lillian Messinger (Rockville, Md.: Aspen Systems Corp., 1982).

p. 399 *"An event that can be assimilated . . . produces excitement":* Jerome Kagan, *The Nature of the Child* (New York: Basic Books, 1984), p. 38.

EIGHT: SCHOOLS AND CHILD CARE

p. 409 *no one kind of care is better for all children:* Deborah A. Phillips, "Quality in Child Care: Definitions and Dilemmas," paper delivered at "Dimensions of Quality in Programs for Children and Families," a symposium of the A. L. Mailman Family Foundation, White Plains, N.Y., June 27, 1988.

p. 409 *child-care workers earn less than zookeepers:* National Association for the Education of Young Children, "In Whose Hands?", Demographic Fact Sheet (Washington, D.C.: National Association for the Education of Young Children, 1986), see also U.S. Department of Commerce, Bureau of the Census, *Earnings by Occupation and Education,* vol. 2 (Washington, D.C.: U.S. Government Printing Office, 1980); Barbara A. Willer, "The Growing Crisis in Child Care: Quality, Compensation, and Affordability in Early Childhood Programs," publication #751 (Washington, D.C.: National Association for the Education of Young Children, June 1987).

p. 411 *professionally agreed-upon standards:* National Association for the Education of Young Children, *Accreditation Criteria and Procedures of the National Academy of Early Childhood Programs* (Washington, D.C.: National Association for the Education of Young Children, 1984).

p. 411 *measure of high quality for group programs:* Thelma Harms and Richard M. Clifford, *Early Childhood Environment Rating Scale* (New York: Teachers College Press, 1980).

p. 412 *Bermuda study:* Kathleen McCartney, Sandra Scarr, Deborah Phillips, Susan Grajek and J. Conrad Schwartz, "Environmental Differences among Day Care Centers and Their Effects on Children's Development," *Day Care: Scientific and Social Policy Issues,* eds. Edward F. Zigler and Edmund W. Gordon (Boston: Auburn House, 1982), pp. 126–151.

p. 412 *teacher-caregiver as model for language development:* Susan Kontos and Richard Fiene, "Predictors of Quality and Children's Development in Day Care," unpublished paper, Pennsylvania State University.

p. 413 *parents often drawn to splashy elements:* Ibid.

p. 413 *opportunity for children to play:* Ibid.

p. 414 *children in low-quality programs wander unoccupied:* Vandell and Powers, "Day Care Quality."

p. 414 *later problems in learning:* Kenneth H. Ruben, Greta G. Fein, and Brian Vandenberg, "Play," *Socialization, Personality, and Social Development,* ed. E. Mavis Hetherington, (New York: John Wiley, 1983), pp. 694–774, vol. 4, *Handbook of Child Psychology,* ed. Paul H. Mussen.

p. 414 *discipline approaches lead to self-control, compliance, etc.:* Martin L. Hoffman, "Moral Development," *Carmichael's Manual of Child Psychology,* 3rd ed., ed. Paul H. Mussen (New York: John Wiley, 1970); Diana Baumrind, "Current Patterns of Parental Authority," *Developmental Psychology Monographs,* vol. 4, no. 1, part 2 (1971), pp. 1–103; Alice Sterling Honig, "Compliance, Control, and Discipline," *Young Children* (January 1985), pp. 47–52; Karen L. Haswell, Ellen Hock, and Charles Wenar, "Techniques for Dealing with Oppositional Behavior in Preschool Children," *Young Children* (March 1982), pp. 13–18.

p. 414 *positive reinforcement rather than criticism:* Deborah Lowe Vandell and Carol P. Powers, "Day Care Quality and Children's Free Play Activities," *American Journal of Orthopsychiatry,* vol. 53 (1983), pp. 493–500.

p. 414 *children who have to adjust to many different caregivers:* Ellen A. Farber and Byron Egeland, "Developmental Consequences of Out-of-Home Care for Infants in a Low-Income Population," *Day Care: Scientific and Social Policy Issues,* eds. Edward F. Zigler and Edmund W. Gordon (Boston: Auburn House, 1982), pp. 102–125.

p. 414 *more likely to have difficulties with children their own age:* Kontos and Fiene, "Predictors of Quality."

p. 414 *look less competent with other children:* Carollee Howes, "Can Age of Entry and Quality of Infant Day Care Predict Behaviors in Kindergarten?", paper delivered at International Conference on Infant Studies, Washington, D.C., April 1988.

p. 414 *separation easier when caregivers are well known:* E. Mark Cummings, "Caregiver Stability in Day Care: Continuity vs. Daily Association," paper presented at the International Conference on Infant Studies, Los Angeles, April 1986.

p. 415 *children support each other in times of distress:* Judith L. Rubenstein and Carollee Howes, "Adaptation to Infant Day Care," *Advances in Early Education and Day Care,* ed. Sally Kilmer (Greenwich, Conn.: JAI Press, 1983).

p. 415 *"others aspects come into play":* Sue Bredekamp, personal communication, 1986.

p. 415 *need for ongoing relevant training:* Abt Associates, *Children at the Center: Final Report of the National Day Care Study* (Cambridge, Mass.: Abt Associates, 1979).

p. 415 *teacher personality and teacher knowledge: Child Care Information Exchange* (CCIE) 1984 survey, cited by Roger Neugebauer, address to National Association for the Education of Young Children, New Orleans, November 1985.

p. 415 *"promote social as well as academic skills":* Alison Clarke-Stewart, personal communication, 1986.

p. 416 *leadership qualities and management skills:* Ellen Galinsky and William H. Hooks, *The New Extended Family: Day Care That Works* (Boston: Houghton Mifflin, 1977).

p. 416 *leadership the number one determinant:* CCIE 1984 survey.

p. 416 *compliance with regulations . . . a minimum assurance of quality:* Abt Associates, *Children at the Center;* Patricia Divine Hawkins, *National Day Care Home Study: Family Day Care in the United States* (Washington, D.C.: U.S. Government Printing Office, 1981).

p. 416 *children in small groups show more gains:* Abt Associates, *Children at the Center.*

p. 416 *more time on discipline than on learning:* J. Stallings and A. Porter, "National Day Care Home Study: Observation Component," Draft Final Report to the Day Care Division, Administration for Children, Youth, and Families (Washington, D.C.: Department of Health, Education and Welfare, April 1980).

p. 416 *overall number of children:* Abt Associates, *Children at the Center.*

p. 417 *standards:* NAEYC, *Accreditation Criteria.*

p. 417 *number of children per square foot:* W. Rohe and A. Patterson, "The Effects of Varied Levels of Resources and Density on Behavior in a Day Care Center," *Man-Environment Interactions,* ed. D. H. Carson (Washington, D.C.: Environmental Design Research Association, 1974).

p. 418 *dividing space into interest centers:* Kontos and Fiene, "Predictors of Quality."

p. 418 *soft and cozy spaces:* E. Prescott, "Relations Between Physical Setting and Adult-Child Behavior in Day Care," *Advances in Early Education and Day Care,* ed. Sally Kilmer (Greenwich, Conn.: JAI Press, 1979).

p. 418 *carefully selected toys and materials:* Vandell and Powers, "Day Care Quality."

p. 418 *when adults wash their hands frequently, children are healthier:* Susan Aronson, personal communication, 1986.

p. 420 *relaxed scheduling of meals:* Kontos and Fiene, "Predictors of Quality."

p. 420 *good programs in constant state of evolution:* Galinsky and Hooks, *New Extended Family.*

p. 420 *"importance of linkages":* Urie Bronfenbrenner, personal communication, 1986.

p. 420 *effective preschool programs also teach the parents: Lasting Effects After Preschool,* a report of the Consortium for Longitudinal Studies under the supervision of Irving Lazar and Richard B. Darlington, DHEW Publication No. [OHDS] 79-30178 (Washington, D.C.: Department of Health, Education and Welfare, 1978).

p. 420 *parent-teacher relationship built on mutual respect:* Lawrence J. Schweinhart and David P. Weikart, "Early Childhood Development Programs: A Public Investment Opportunity," *Educational Leadership,* vol. 44, no. 3 (November 19, 1986), p. 11.

p. 421 *teachers-caregivers not "substitutes" but "supplements":* Galinsky and Hooks, *New Extended Family.*

p. 421 *"knows the names of the child's family":* Urie Bronfenbrenner, personal communication, 1986.

p. 421 *help families with other responsibilities:* Arthur C. Emlen, personal communication, 1986.

p. 421 *"In order for children to learn":* Docia Zavitkowsky, personal communication, 1986.

p. 421 *"educare" and "educarer":* Bettye Caldwell, personal communication, 1986.

p. 422 *child care turnover rate nearly 40 percent:* Robert C. Granger and Elisabeth Marx, "Who Is Teaching?" unpublished report, Bank Street College, New York City, 1988.

p. 424 *"echo of the baby boom":* U.S. Department of Commerce, Bureau of the Census, *Estimates of the Population of the United States by Age, Sex, and Race: 1980 to 1986,* Current Population Reports, Series P-25, No. 1000 (Washington, D.C.: U.S. Government Printing Office, 1987).

p. 424 *more employed mothers needing child care:* U.S. Department of Labor, Bureau of Labor Statistics, *USDL News Release,* USDL 86-345, August 20, 1986 (Washington, D.C.: U.S. Government Printing Office, 1986).

p. 424 *more parents wanting early childhood programs:* U.S. Department of Education, Center for Education Statistics, *Digest of Education Statistics,* 1987 ed. (Washington, D.C.: U.S. Government Printing Office, 1987).

p. 424 *eighteen- to twenty-four-year-olds in 1980 and 1990:* U.S. Department of Commerce, Bureau of the Census, *Estimates of the Population of the United States by Age, Sex, and Race: 1980 to 1986;* U.S. Department of Commerce, Bureau of the Census, *Projections of the Population of the United States by Age, Sex, and Race: 1982–2050* (advance report), Current Population Reports, series P-25, no. 922, October 1982 (Washington, D.C.: U.S. Government Printing Office, 1982).

p. 424 *teacher wages and turnover rate:* U.S. Department of Labor, Bureau of Labor Statistics, "Weekly Earnings in 1986: A Look at More Than 200 Occupations," *Monthly Labor Review,* vol. 110, no. 6 (Washington, D.C.: U.S. Government Printing Office, 1987); U.S. Department of Labor, Bureau of Labor Statistics, *Occupation Projections and Training Data,* 1986 ed., BLS Bulletin 2251, April 1986 (Washington, D.C.: U.S. Government Printing Office, 1986).

p. 424 *child-care workers second most underpaid profession:* Barbara A. Willer, "Pay Equity: An Issue of Race, Ethnicity, and Sex," (Washington, D.C.: National Committee on Pay Equity, 1987).

p. 424 *breakdown of child-care arrangements:* Ellen Galinsky and Diane Hughes, "The *Fortune* Magazine Child Care Study," paper presented at the annual convention of the American Psychological Association, New York City, August 1987.

p. 425 *deplore low salaries:* Ellen Galinsky with Dana E. Friedman, *Investing in Quality Child Care: A Report for AT&T* (Basking Ridge, N.J.: AT&T, 1986).

p. 425 *programs ignore how young children learn best:* David Elkind, *Miseducation: Preschoolers at Risk* (New York: Alfred A. Knopf, 1987).

p. 427 *"waste the promise":* Samuel G. Sava, "Development, Not Academics," *Young Children* (March 1987), p. 15.

p. 427 *guidelines for inappropriate education:* David Elkind, "Superbaby Syndrome Can Lead to Elementary School Burnout," *Young Children* (March 1987), p. 14.

p. 428 *parents and professionals assess differently:* Caroline Zinsser, *Over a Barrel: Working Mothers Talk about Child Care* (New York: Center for Public Advocacy Research, 1987).

p. 428 *amount of sexual abuse in child care is small:* American Humane Association, "National Study of Child Neglect and Abuse Reporting," unpublished data, Washington, D.C., 1985.

p. 429 *"You left me here this morning":* Nancy Balaban, *Learning to Say Goodbye* (New York: Plume/NAL, 1987), p. 68.

p. 431 *showing off our "handiwork":* James Comer, "Child Care: The Other National Defense," speech delivered at "Excellence: You Make the Difference," A Seminar for Child Care Directors, Baylor University Medical Center, Dallas, September 19, 1987.

p. 432 *parents' attitudes influence child's adjustment:* Ellen Hock, "The Transition to Day Care: Effects of Maternal Separation Anxiety on Infant Adjustment," *The Child and the Day Care Setting: Qualitative Variations and Development,* ed. Ricardo C. Ainslie (New York: Praeger, 1984), p. 194.

p. 433 *the greater the mother's anxiety, the more likely the child had difficult adjustment:* E. Martin-Huff, "Parental and Contextual Influences on Children's Early Adjustment to Kindergarten," Ph.D. dissertation, Ohio State University, Columbus, Ohio, 1982.

p. 433 *three styles of leave-taking:* M. Weintraub and M. Lewis, "The Determinants of Children's Response to Separation," *Monographs of the Society for Research in Child Development,* vol. 42 (4, serial no. 172), 1977.

p. 433 *brief statement worked better:* R. E. Adams and R. H. Passman, "The Effects of Preparing Two-Year-Olds for Brief Separations from Their Mothers," *Child Development,* vol. 52 (1981), pp. 1068–1070.

p. 436 *"self-confidence through separations that are well achieved":* Balaban, *Learning to Say Goodbye.*

INDEX
....

NOTES

. . . .

NOTES
. . . .

NOTES

....

NOTES

....

NOTES

· · · ·

NOTES

....

NOTES
....

NOTES

....

About the Authors

ELLEN GALINSKY is the co-president of the Families and Work Institute in New York City where she conducts research on work and family life. She has served as president of the National Association for the Education of Young Children, the largest professional group of early childhood educators. She has worked with numerous governors and companies in crafting policies that affect family life and children's development. A graduate of Vassar, with a master's degree from the Bank Street College, she has lectured and written for a national audience, and has long served as a child development expert on national television and radio. Recently *Ladies' Home Journal* selected her as one of the 100 outstanding women in America.

JUDY DAVID is on the Graduate Faculty at Bank Street College of Education in New York City where she teaches child development and supervises student teachers. She has also taught at Wheelock College in Boston. She has worked on a variety of research projects in early childhood education, consulted with school systems, written for parents, and made a film of cross-cultural child rearing practices. She received her Ed.D. from Harvard School of Education.